REPUBLIC OF WOMEN

Rethinking the Republic of Letters in the Seventeenth Century

Republic of Women recaptures a lost chapter in the narrative of intellectual history. It tells the story of a transnational network of female scholars who were active members of the seventeenth-century republic of letters, and demonstrates that this intellectual commonwealth was a much more eclectic and diverse assemblage than has been assumed. These seven scholars – Anna Maria van Schurman, Princess Elisabeth of Bohemia, Marie de Gournay, Marie du Moulin, Dorothy Moore, Bathsua Makin, and Katherine Jones, Lady Ranelagh – were philosophers, schoolteachers, reformers, and mathematicians. They hailed from England, Ireland, Germany, France, and the Netherlands. And together with their male colleagues   men like Descartes, Huygens, Hartlib, and Montaigne – they represented the spectrum of contemporary approaches to science, faith, politics, and the advancement of learning. Carol Pal uses their collective biography to reconfigure the intellectual biography of early modern Europe, offering a new, expanded analysis of the seventeenth-century community of ideas.

CAROL PAL is an Assistant Professor of History at Bennington College. She received her Ph.D. in 2007 from Stanford University, where her dissertation won the Elizabeth Spilman Rosenfield Dissertation Prize. She has held a number of library fellowships, including a Francis Bacon Foundation fellowship from the Huntington Library, and an Ahmanson-Getty Postdoctoral Fellowship at the Clark Library, UCLA; she has also won research fellowships from the Mellon Foundation, Woodrow Wilson Foundation, American Association of University Women, and Jacob K. Javits program. The focus of her current research is a reconsideration of the History of the Book, using case studies highlighting the phenomenon of corporate scribal publication.

IDEAS IN CONTEXT

Edited by David Armitage, Jennifer Pitts, Quentin Skinner and James Tully

The books in this series will discuss the emergence of intellectual traditions and of related new disciplines. The procedures, aims and vocabularies that were generated will be set in the context of the alternatives available within the contemporary frameworks of ideas and institutions. Through detailed studies of the evolution of such traditions, and their modification by different audiences, it is hoped that a new picture will form of the development of ideas in their concrete contexts. By this means, artificial distinctions between the history of philosophy, of the various sciences, of society and politics, and of literature may be seen to dissolve.

The series is published with the support of the Exxon Foundation.

A list of books in the series will be found at the end of the volume.

REPUBLIC OF WOMEN

RETHINKING THE REPUBLIC OF LETTERS IN THE SEVENTEENTH CENTURY

CAROL PAL

Bennington College

CAMBRIDGE
UNIVERSITY PRESS

CAMBRIDGE UNIVERSITY PRESS
Cambridge, New York, Melbourne, Madrid, Cape Town,
Singapore, São Paulo, Delhi, Mexico City

Cambridge University Press
The Edinburgh Building, Cambridge CB2 8RU, UK

Published in the United States of America by Cambridge University Press, New York

www.cambridge.org
Information on this title: www.cambridge.org/9781107018211

First published 2012

Printed in the United Kingdom at the University Press, Cambridge

A catalogue record for this publication is available from the British Library

Library of Congress Cataloging-in-Publication Data
Pal, Carol.
Republic of women : rethinking the republic of letters in the
seventeenth century / by Carol Pal.
p.   cm. – (Ideas in context ; 99)
ISBN 978-1-107-01821-1 (Hardback)
1. Literature–Women authors–History and criticism.   2. Women–Intellectual life–17th century.
3. Women scholars–History.   4. Literature and society–History–17th century.
I. Title.
PN471.P35 2012
809′.89287–dc23
2011043660

ISBN 978-1-107-01821-1 Hardback

This book is dedicated to my son, Noah.
I am so proud of you.

Contents

Acknowledgments

The process of researching and writing this book has been a long and wonderful journey, as what began with my senior thesis on one female scholar became a full-fledged obsession with early modern cultures of learning. I found that in uncovering a seventeenth-century intellectual community, I had also entered its present-day equivalent, a modern republic of letters whose citizens were as remarkable for their generosity as they were for their intellect. The process has therefore been a great joy to me – and among those joys is the fact that I can now thank those who have supported and sustained me as I stumbled through.

First and foremost on this list is my graduate mentor, Paul Seaver. Paul has not only shown me how he does history, but also how he inhabits the persona of historian. His kind encouragement continues to sustain me; and, throughout my career, I know I will always be attempting to live up to his example of integrity, intelligence, and insight. But even before working with Paul, I had the amazing good fortune to work with an undergraduate mentor who literally changed my life. Kathleen Noonan saw the historian in me long before I knew that person was there, and gently guided me toward my vocation. She is a wonderful historian, a dear friend, and the teacher I hope to be.

Since this book focuses on female scholars of the early modern era, I am also particularly fortunate in having been mentored and befriended by so many female scholars in the here and now. At Stanford, I had two powerful models of female scholarship in the field: Paula Findlen, a Renaissance woman in every possible way, read multiple versions of each chapter, crucially insisting throughout that I keep refining the questions that I brought to my evidence; and Carolyn Lougee Chappell, scholar of early modern France, kept pushing me to look beyond the obvious. Outside the traditional academic setting, I found fellowship and guidance in two other models of female scholarship: Susan Groag Bell, whose pathbreaking work in women's history helped forge the field in which

I now work and study; and the historian Kirsten Seaver, a keen judge of the difference between fact and fiction. I cannot thank these scholars enough for their kindness, their critiques, and the ways in which they have inspired me.

As the research progressed, I entered further into this republic of letters, benefitting from conversation and correspondence with a community of generous minds. Joyce Irwin was willing to share her work on Anna Maria van Schurman with me while I was still an undergraduate – how lovely is that? It's a story I will tell to my students as long as I live. Lynette Hunter was also extremely generous in agreeing to let me rave at her about Dorothy Moore when we met at the British Library; she then very kindly granted me access to her work on Moore's biography and correspondence during the early stages of my research. Betsey Taylor shared her calendar of Lady Ranelagh's correspondence with an entire gang of scholars working on that "incomparable" woman – a group that happily included me – while Michael Hunter generously shared his expertise on Ranelagh's little brother, Robert Boyle. Mirjam de Baar took an afternoon to show me the places where Anna Maria van Schurman had lived and worked in Utrecht, while Deborah Harkness wisely insisted that I leave the British Library's manuscript room at lunchtime to experience the joys of Pizza Express. And Anne Goldgar was just as generous with her insider knowledge of Amsterdam as she was with her deep knowledge of the republic of letters.

When it came time to turn my mass of files, photocopies, and transcriptions into something readable and coherent, I was again lucky to be surrounded by generous friends and colleagues. At Stanford, my time was graced by the camaraderie of Matthew Booker, Rachel Jean-Baptiste, Shelley Lee, and Lise Sedrez; I will treasure them forever. The same is true of Stacy Clarke and Jackie Fitzpatrick, my fellow travellers from Kathleen Noonan's history seminar at Mills College. Kristin Rebien, Claire Sufrin, and Karen Gover kindly provided me with help in translating documents in German, Hebrew, and Greek; any errors in the final product are entirely my own. Lisa Shapiro, in true republic of letters fashion, shared her translations of the correspondence between Princess Elisabeth and René Descartes in advance of their publication. Then, at Bennington, I was amazingly lucky to make two friends on my very first day as a new faculty member. Barbara Alfano and Valerie Imbruce, I don't know what I would have done without you!

At various points in this process, I was fortunate in being able to present chapters at seminars and conferences, where my ideas evolved in response to the comments and critiques of fellow scholars in the field. I have especially benefitted from the feedback provided by Ann Blair, Julie Campbell, Ruth Connolly, Mordechai Feingold, Anthony Grafton, Mark Greengrass, Brad Gregory, Felicity Henderson, Anne Larsen, Elaine Leong, Tara Nummedal, Alisha Rankin, Diana Robin, Sarah Gwyneth Ross, and various members of the audience at the following meetings, among others: the American Historical Association, the Renaissance Society of America, the Sixteenth Century Studies Conference, the North American Conference on British Studies, the "Spaces of the Self in Early Modern Culture" conference at the William Andrews Clark Memorial Library, the Folger Shakespeare Library Seminar "Women on the Verge of Science", the Republic of Letters workshop at the Stanford University Humanities Center, the "Symposium on The Making of Early Modern Scientific Knowledge" at the University of Warwick, the Society for Renaissance Studies, and the Social Networks in Early Modern England Conference, New College, Oxford University.

Writing a book still requires that one deal with practicalities first – a situation that has changed very little since Virginia Woolf first pointed out that one needs a room of one's own and 500 pounds a year. In San Francisco, that room was provided by Corie Tripoli, who went from being my next-door neighbour to being my refuge, roommate, and friend; in London, that room became a second home, as I joined the household presided over by the fabulous Ingrid Brodie. The requisite 500 pounds a year has, of course, mushroomed considerably; thus it would not have been possible to complete this journey without generous institutional funding and support. I would like to thank the History Department and the program in the History and Philosophy of Science at Stanford University, the American Association of University Women, the Mellon Foundation, the Jacob Javits Scholarship Foundation, the Oakfords, the Woodrow Wilson Foundation, and the Stanford Institute for Research on Women and Gender. Completing the manuscript was made possible by an Ahmanson-Getty fellowship at the Clark Library, UCLA, and a Francis Bacon fellowship at the Huntington Library.

And in order to write a book of history, of course, one needs more than just space and money – one needs libraries and archives first, or there will be no book to write. I therefore wish to thank the librarians, archivists, and staff of the following for their time and their deeply informed assistance: In England, the British Library; the Bodleian Library, Oxford University; Cambridge University Library; the archives of the Duke of Devonshire at Chatsworth House; the University of Sheffield; the London

Metropolitan Archives; Petworth House, Sussex; the Royal College of Physicians; the Royal Society; the Huguenot Library; and the National Art Library at the Victoria and Albert Museum. In the Netherlands, the Koninklijke Bibliotheek, The Hague; the University of Amsterdam; the University of Leiden; and the University of Utrecht. In the United States, the Huntington Library; the Folger Shakespeare Library; the Whitney Medical Library at Yale University; and the Clark Library at the University of California, Los Angeles. Most recently, great thanks are due to Oceana Wilson and Kathy Williams, the goddesses of Crossett Library at Bennington College.

Finally, when it came time to turn my behemoth of a manuscript into a real book, I benefitted enormously from the knowledgeable guidance of Richard Fisher, my editor at Cambridge University Press. It was Richard's insistence on clarity, through many drafts, that enabled me to eventually tame the monster. I am also grateful for the valuable comments and suggestions I received from the anonymous readers of the Press.

There are also many others to thank, and I desperately hope I am leaving no one out. Elinda Hardy, friend, photographer, and fellow traveller from our days on the trading desk to infinity and beyond; Julie Robbins, wise woman extraordinaire, who listened to me blathering on for nearly twenty years; Dr. Robert Carlson, Dr. Denise Johnson, Larry Zaroff, and Netty, Holly, Joyce, and Ashley – they know exactly why; Mirka Prazak, for her friendship and guidance; Annabel Davis-Goff, for wisdom, wit, and walks; Peter Mellini and Peter Stansky, gentleman scholars; Chuck Gruye, the Best Boss Ever; Walter Willliamson, the Mayor of Cloverdale, for being the soul of my time in Los Angeles; The Bun, for being . . . The Bun; Mr. Monty Pal; Maisie and Molly Tripoli; and the gang from 11F – David Basskin, Richard Bingham, Jock Clark, Shiona Finlayson, and Kerry McKinney Cunningham.

Some very important people in my life shared the beginning of this journey, but did not live to see its end. Gertrud Pacheco, Netty Alegria, and my beloved Rosie were an enormous part of my life. I miss them every day, and I remember them here.

Definitions and conventions

TRANSLATIONS

All translations from Latin, French, and Dutch sources, unless otherwise indicated, are my own. For translations from German, Greek, and Hebrew sources, I am grateful to Kristin Rebien, Karen Gover, and Claire Sufrin.

TRANSCRIPTIONS

Sources in English are cited in their original, unmodernized spelling. Exception is made in substituting "j" for "I," "v" for "u," and "the" for "ye." I have also expanded early modern contractions; for instance, "w^{ch}" and "y^r Ma^{ty}" are expanded to "which" and "Your Majesty."

SOURCES IN PRINT

Unless otherwise indicated, I cite from manuscript sources. However, some of this correspondence is now available in English translation. Joyce Irwin has published an excellent translation of a selection of Anna Maria van Schurman's letters, along with her *Dissertatio* and some excerpts from *Eukleria*, in Anna Maria van Schurman, *Whether a Christian Woman Should Be Educated: and other writings from her intellectual circle* (Chicago, 1998); and much of Dorothy Moore's correspondence has been published by Lynette Hunter in *The Letters of Dorothy Moore, 1612–64: The Friendships, Marriage, and Intellectual Life of a Seventeenth-Century Woman* (Aldershot, 2004). In those instances where printed English translations or transcriptions are available, this fact will be mentioned in the footnotes.

ABBREVIATIONS

BL	British Library (London)
CSPD	Calendar of State Papers, Domestic
CSPV	Calendar of State Papers, Venetian

CSPI	Calendar of State Papers for Ireland
HDC	George Turnbull, *Hartlib, Dury, and Comenius*
HMC	Historical Manuscripts Commission
KB	Koninklijke Bibliotheek (The Hague)
ODNB	Oxford Dictionary of National Biography

Prologue

Around 1742, Lady Mary Wortley Montagu received a letter from Anna Maria van Schurman. Montagu was a well-known writer and scholar manqué, while van Schurman was a celebrated Dutch intellectual. Thus their correspondence could be considered a fairly unremarkable exchange between two learned women – but there was just one problem. Van Schurman, by this date, had been dead for over sixty years.

During her lifetime, van Schurman had been a scholarly celebrity – an intellectual prodigy, and the center of an international network of female scholars. Now, however, it seemed she had triumphed even over death. And the apparently indestructible van Schurman, pausing amid the joys of her Elysian intellectual circle, was still managing to find the time to correspond with other female scholars.

Montagu then returned the empyrean favor. She wrote back to say that she was flattered van Schurman would find her worthy of her time and attention, and she applauded the improvement in her correspondent's posthumous literary style. Montagu also thought the departed scholar would like to know that there were now modern, politicized arguments to support women's access to higher learning and participation in the republic of letters. Montagu was proud of her new century. But there were tradeoffs; and perhaps the seventeenth century had given female scholars something that Montagu could only dream of.

The dream was one of belonging to a female scholarly community. Thus Montagu concluded her letter to Heaven with a plaintive postscript:

I am so charmed by your coterie that if you promise to admit me immediately I shall throw myself into the Rhône to seek you, half through desire of seeing you, and half from boredom with all those whom I do see.[1]

---

[1] The letter is undated, but the location of Avignon places it sometime between 1742 and 1746. Lady Mary Wortley Montagu, *Essays and Poems, and 'Simplicity, a Comedy'*, ed. Robert Halsband and Isobel Grundy (Oxford, 1993), 165–7, 392–3. I am indebted to Paula Findlen for this reference.

Van Schurman's "coterie" had not been a coterie at all, but rather an international network of learned women; and, like van Schurman herself, it had ceased to exist. But Montagu clearly wanted more than what her century could offer her. The eighteenth century could offer her a level of inclusion in the abstract intellectual community known as the republic of letters. But what Montagu wanted as well was to be included in a community of female scholars – a Republic of Women.

Republic of Women tells the story of a multinational network of female scholars in the seventeenth century, and reinserts their forgotten history into the narrative of early modern intellectual culture. Together with their male colleagues, these women worked to help further the advancement of learning. Thus in documenting a vital, yet previously unexplored identity – that of the collegial female scholar – the book also documents a surprisingly inclusive, heterogeneous, and dually gendered republic of letters in the middle of the seventeenth century. It is there that this story begins.

Introduction: The Republic of Women and the republic of letters

Between 1630 and 1680, an international network of female scholars flourished within the republic of letters. That network, which I refer to as the Republic of Women, was an intellectual commonwealth whose citizens were all female scholars.[1] However, their community was not isolated by their sex, and this network was in fact an integral component of a much larger intellectual commonwealth, known as the republic of letters. The republic of letters, a transnational, multi-confessional commonwealth of the learned, was an important component of early modern European intellectual culture. It was an epistolary community that literally embodied the world of ideas in the seventeenth century. Yet much of the scholarship on the republic of letters has tended to reify this idealized community, identifying it too narrowly with an elite cadre of erudite men; moreover, it has been assumed that female scholars were excluded from that larger communal enterprise.

Republic of Women takes issue with this assumption. It is a case study, based on an analysis of this network of female scholars; however, this case study in turn argues for a larger reassessment of early modern cultures of learning. It demonstrates that the republic of letters was not a small, heroic cadre of brilliant minds, but rather a much more eclectic, diverse, and conflicted assemblage than we have hitherto believed; and our tidy assumption of an elite, secular, all-male intellectual world is completely undone once we pay attention to the networks of female scholars who were well known and highly respected actors within it. In this analysis, the seventeenth-century intellectual enterprise emerges as a complex structure of smaller interlaced networks, sharing knowledge while pursuing

---

[1] Laura Cereta (1469–99) characterized learned women through the ages as a "*muliebris respublica*," distinguished for both virtue and letters. Laura Cereta, *Collected Letters of a Renaissance Feminist*, ed. and trans. Diana Robin (Chicago, 1997), 76–80.

different goals. Thus the story of the Republic of Women serves to introduce a new, expanded concept of the seventeenth-century community of ideas.

In essence, *Republic of Women* uses the collective biography of seven female scholars to construct the biography of a moment. It was a singularly rich and significant moment in intellectual history, when the birth of modern science meshed with other areas of knowledge – philosophical, natural, religious, and political – to accelerate the gradual demise of scholasticism. It was a moment that ushered in a secular, rational, and empirical approach to learning that still shapes humanistic and scientific enquiry today. And it was a moment populated with a surprisingly diverse array of actors – including zealots, autodidacts, and women – whose names are not generally mentioned along with those of Montaigne, Huygens, Boyle, Mersenne, Descartes, and the other scholars who considered them colleagues in the republic of letters.

I define collegial early modern female scholars as those women who delighted in their studies, who desired to lead lives of active scholarship, and who saw themselves as part of a larger community of like-minded men and women who were interested in ideas. Yet this new concept of the collegial female scholar must first contend with the tradition of the early modern "learned lady."

Learned ladies have usually been seen as exemplary phenomena. They were exceptions so exceptional that, as Bathsua Makin said: "A Learned Woman is thought to be a Comet, that bodes Mischief, when ever it appears."[2] From Boccaccio onward, learned women were celebrated in terms that emphasized their strangeness.[3] Since women were excluded from the academy and unable to practice learned professions, their pursuit of intellectual achievement was considered puzzling, trivial, and ultimately pointless. There were many who admired the erudition of learned women, yet would have agreed with the view expressed by Jean de la Bruyère:

One looks at a learned woman as one does a beautiful gun. It is beautifully crafted, admirably polished, and wonderfully well made; it is a collector's item which one shows to the curious, which has no function, which is useful neither

---

[2] [Bathsua Makin], *An Essay to Revive the Antient Education of Gentlewomen, in Religion, Manners, Arts & Tongues. With an Answer to the Objections against this Way of Education* (London, 1673), 1.
[3] Giovanni Boccaccio, *De mulieribus claris*. Written between 1360 and 1362, the book was immensely popular, and was translated into French, German, Spanish, English, and Italian.

for war nor for hunting, no more than a carousel horse, albeit the best instructed one in all the world.[4]

Thus one finds that even in the literature extolling their virtues, learned women were assigned attributes partaking equally of the utmost goddess-like perfection and the merely freakish. For instance, the scholar Anna Maria van Schurman was continually lauded as "The Star of Utrecht," and "The Tenth Muse." Yet at the same time, her eulogists reported that she was partial to eating spiders.[5] She was also, according to one of them, "a miracle or monster of nature."[6] Thus the intellectual woman is usually pictured as a solitary scholar, and a person with no peers – an admirable anomaly locking herself into her "book-lined cell."[7]

This picture, however, is a distortion, and only one side of the story. Recent scholarship has begun to uncover the presence of a surprising number of Latinate women in early modern Europe, thus this vision of solitary strangeness must now be complicated with another vision: that of a well-known, well-respected, and fully functional community of early modern female scholars.[8] For more than four decades, a very real and supportive intellectual women's network centered around the erudite Anna Maria van Schurman of Utrecht (1607–78). The other core members of the group were the English educator Bathsua Makin (*c.*1600–80), the Anglo-Irish religious reformer Dorothy Moore (*c.*1612–64), the "incomparable" Katherine Jones, Lady Ranelagh (1615–91), the French scholars Marie de Gournay (1565–1645) and Marie du Moulin (*c.*1613–99), and the learned Palatine Princess Elisabeth (1618–80), daughter of Bohemia's "Winter King." Mirroring the male republic of letters, the citizens of this women's intellectual commonwealth represented nations at war, religions in conflict, and epistemologies in contention.

---

[4] Jean de la Bruyère, *Les Caractères de Théophraste. Traduits du Grec avec Les Caractères ou Les Moeurs de ce siècle* [Paris, 1687], ed. Louis van Delft (Paris, 1998): no. 49, "Des Femmes," 83–4.

[5] Jean-Pierre Nicéron, *Mémoires pour servir à l'histoire des hommes illustres dans la République des Lettres*, 43 vols. (Paris, 1729–45), XXXIII, 22.

[6] Louis Jacob, "Elogium eruditissimae virginis Annae Mariae a Schurman, Batavae" in *Question celebre. S'il est necessaire, ou non, que les Filles soient sçavantes* (Paris, 1646), 83–4.

[7] Margaret King, "Book-Lined Cells: Women and Humanism in the Early Italian Renaissance," in Patricia H. Labalme, ed., *Beyond Their Sex: Learned Women of the European Past* (New York, 1980), 66–90.

[8] A point of entry for the wide range of women's writing is the online database of the Orlando Project at Cambridge University Press. *Orlando: Women's Writing in the British Isles from the Beginnings to the Present* [http://orlando.cambridge.org]. For a survey of Latinate women, see Laurie J. Churchill *et al.*, *Women Writing Latin: From Roman Antiquity to Early Modern Europe*, 3 vols. (New York and London, 2002).

Apart from their scholarship, then, the women in this community were characterized primarily by a remarkable heterogeneity. In the middle of the seventeenth century, amid civil war, religious strife, and epistemological revolutions, their epistolary network cut across barriers of religion, nation, class, intellectual allegiance, and family formation. These women were Catholics, Calvinists, and mystical millenarians; they were English, Irish, German, French, and Dutch; they were Aristotelian, Cartesian, and biblicist. On the social scale, they ran the gamut from aristocrats to schoolteachers, and from princesses to would-be preachers.

Some of these women have been noticed before. Some garnered attention as the wives, sisters, daughters, mothers, and protégées of famous men, while others were noticed for their singularity. Margaret Cavendish, the Duchess of Newcastle, for example, is possibly the most well-known and well-studied female natural philosopher of the seventeenth century, and would seem to be an obvious candidate for inclusion in this study. She read widely in experimental philosophy and science, and published in an impressive range of genres. Moreover, she herself reported that she was sometimes present when scholars like Descartes, Gassendi, and Hobbes met in her home while she and her husband were in exile on the Continent. However, she will not be included here because this is a study of *collegial* female scholarship in the early modern era – an analysis of the intellectual women who did their scholarly work in dialogue with other men and women in the republic of letters. And Cavendish, despite her exposure to some of the foremost minds in early modern philosophy, was extremely clear about seeing herself as singular.[9]

The female scholars in this study, on the other hand, made interpersonal contact a vital part of their scholarship. In earlier studies, they have also been spotted lurking in the margins of seventeenth-century male intellectual networks, such as the Royal Society, and the reforming group associated with Samuel Hartlib, John Dury, and Jan Amos Comenius.[10] However, these women were not merely the recipients of intellectual mentoring by their male colleagues and kin. The information, advice,

[9] There is a large body of scholarship on Margaret Cavendish. See, for instance: Lisa Sarasohn, "A Science Turned Upside Down: Feminism and the Natural Philosophy of Margaret Cavendish," *Huntington Library Quarterly* 47 (1984): 289–307; Sarah Hutton, "Anne Conway, Margaret Cavendish and Seventeenth-Century Scientific Thought," in *Women, Science and Medicine 1500–1700*, ed. Lynette Hunter and Sarah Hutton (Phoenix Mill, 1997); Anna Battigelli, *Margaret Cavendish and the Exiles of the Mind* (Lexington, KY, 1998); and Jacqueline Broad, *Women Philosophers of the Seventeenth Century* (Cambridge, 2002).

[10] Lynette Hunter, "Sisters of the Royal Society: The Circle of Katherine Jones, Lady Ranelagh," in Hunter and Hutton, *Women, Science and Medicine*, 178–97.

and correspondence flowed in both directions – thus the position of these women with regard to their respective networks was not marginal at all. In fact, female scholars occupied vital and central positions in a variety of scholarly, religious, and political networks during the seventeenth century.

The problem, then, appears to lie in our concept of the margins themselves, in our defining intellectual networks according to categories that are both too disparate and too small. While the gendered membership of van Schurman's circle made theirs a distinct group within the republic of letters, the evidence also demonstrates that this distinction did not result in their being isolated or segregated within that intellectual community. Thus an analysis of these women as a group – in both their gendered alterity and their membership in the republic of letters as a whole – has important implications for understanding larger issues of gender and knowledge in early modern Britain and Europe. The existence of their correspondence community demonstrates that female scholars were neither anomalous nor invisible. They were, in fact, an important and integral part of the seventeenth-century intellectual revolution. As one follows the evidence, it becomes clear that these women were a collegial presence in the republic of letters, and they were expected to contribute their voices to the intellectual and theological conversation.

Female scholars corresponded with male colleagues to discuss philosophy, theology, and language study, and to offer friendship, advice, and support. At the same time, however, the women inevitably differed from their male counterparts in being limited by their gender; they could never practice learned professions, nor could they participate in the life of the academies. And they had an additional agenda in their correspondence with each other. The members of this intellectual women's network were searching for solutions to the issue they could never quite resolve: how a virtuous Christian woman might reconcile a life of blameless piety with vigorous intellectual pursuits. Thus they functioned simultaneously in multiple networks, participating concurrently in the larger republic of letters, as well as in a gendered subset of that republic.

Although scholars have begun to discuss several of the women involved in this network, no one as yet has analyzed them as a group, a distinct yet integral component of the republic of letters.[11] The present study is a step

---

[11] Several scholars, however, have argued that such a study should be attempted. See, for instance: Pieta van Beek, "Een Vrouwenrepubliek der Letteren? Anna Maria van Schurman (1607–1678) en haar netwerk van geleerde vrouwen," *Tydskrif vir Nederlands en Afrikaans* 3, no. 1 (1996): 36–49; David Norbrook, "Women, the Republic of Letters, and the Public Sphere in the Mid-Seventeenth

toward filling this analytical gap. My aim here is to analyze the circulation of ideas as *embodied* phenomena. By concentrating on the ways in which ideas were developed through the interaction of persons – representing two sexes and an expanded range of social rank – who in turn belonged to various intersecting networks, this study in many ways takes a sociological and anthropological approach to intellectual history. In so doing, it argues that between 1630 and 1680, the work of moral, scientific, and intellectual reform networks in Europe was in fact a dually gendered enterprise.[12]

This, of course, brings up two immediate questions. First, given that the inclusion of learned women contradicts so much of what is known about the intersection of gender and knowledge in the early modern era, how was it that their counterintuitive community could come into existence? Contained in this query are what the late David Underdown called the historian's *first* questions: why this? why here? and, why now?[13] Second, if these women were such a vital part of the seventeenth-century intellectual enterprise, then why is it that we are surprised to learn that this was so? How and why did historical knowledge of their contribution become so obscured in the following centuries?

The answer to the first question flows from the realization that this seemingly sudden outbreak of public female activity was inextricably allied with its background of religious and political crisis; and, seen in this light, the phenomenon was neither isolated nor unique. The middle of the seventeenth century was a period of world-changing instability. The Thirty Years' War devastated the Continent from 1618 to 1648, while England was being torn apart in two civil wars. At the same time, the empirical New Learning of Bacon and the rationalism of Descartes were ushering in an intellectual revolution. Although the process was complex and contingent, observation and experiment eventually displaced scholasticism and humanism.[14] It was a non-stop storm of religious, political, and intellectual ferment that filtered into almost every sphere of existence, causing many to expect the literal end of the world. And, in

---

Century," *Criticism* 46, no. 2 (Spring 2004): 223–40; and Jane Stevenson, "Still Kissing the Rod? Whither Next?", *Women's Writing* 14, no. 2 (2007): 290–305.

[12] In this I am following, among others, Deborah Harkness, and Peter Burke: Deborah Harkness, *The Jewel House: Elizabethan London and the Scientific Revolution* (New Haven and London, 2007); Peter Burke, *A Social History of Knowledge: From Gutenberg to Diderot* (Cambridge, 2000).

[13] From David Underdown, "Gentlemen, Players, and Media Moguls: Cricket and English Society Since 1600," plenary address given at the Pacific Coast Conference on British Studies, April 4, 1997, Mills College, Oakland, CA.

[14] Anthony Grafton, *Defenders of the Text: The Traditions of Scholarship in an Age of Science, 1450–1800* (Cambridge, MA, 1991), 3–4, 11–12.

common with other episodes of extreme, wide-scale instability – times of war and revolution, in other eras and other places – many of the customary social barriers did not hold. This abnormal social openness is usually one of the unintended consequences of conflict, one that creates opportunities for persons whose options are limited under normal circumstances. These are also doors that are soon closed, as social and cultural norms reassert themselves, and a certain amount of conservatism returns with the calm and quiet.

In terms of women's access to public discourse, religious activism, and political participation, this is a pattern that has had many forms and many repetitions. Thus the inclusion of women – as well as the inclusion of those men who would normally have been considered "outsiders" to learned discourse – came about because the opportunity existed. It was a synergistic moment, arising from the confluence of remarkable minds in a remarkable time. The force and variety of spiritual, intellectual, and scientific issues being discussed and promulgated in the mid-seventeenth-century republic of letters created a highly nutritive instability; and these agendas, combined with political and confessional conflict, gave rise to a situation in which a community of women intellectuals could flourish.

The answer to the second question, regarding the posthumous obscurity of this women's intellectual network, follows very closely on the chaotic situation described above. Political stability began to return to Europe and Britain after 1660. In a parallel process, the production of scientific knowledge outside the universities became institutionalized in various academies. Within these institutions, a certain level of social and epistemological homogeneity began to prevail.[15] The mid-century's plurality of religious and intellectual approaches resolved into something resembling mainstreams and margins, and subsequent historiography reified the triumph of rational, secular, latitudinarian learning. As this whiggish narrative unfolded, the outsiders disappeared.

Yet neither the original historiography nor its modern feminist corrective should be allowed to obscure this complex cooperative episode in seventeenth-century intellectual history. Gender was certainly an important constitutive element in the intellectual lives of Anna Maria van Schurman and her fellow female scholars of the early modern era. However, it was only one of many factors. In fact, if one were to choose the single factor most often responsible for limiting the shape and scope of women's learning, it would be social rank. The demands of survival on

---

[15] Theodore K. Rabb, *The Struggle for Stability in Early Modern Europe* (New York, 1975), 114–15.

one end of that scale, and of political and social obligations on the other, were usually quite effective in precluding the pursuit of learning – which often held true for men as well as for women. For instance, scholars of both genders who lived in areas removed from the easy circulation of books and colleagues would find their studies limited by their location, unless they also possessed the time and money for travel.

Female scholars, however, faced additional hurdles. And those women who were trying to construct lives of intellectual and religious activity – lives that were both collegial and visible – were contending with the entire weight of accepted Christian doctrine concerning the need for women to epitomize the Christian virtue of *modestia*. The meaning of *modestia* changed over time, and in translation between different languages, cultures, and confessional contexts. While it originally referred to the shared practice of chastity by men and women in early Christian sects, it quickly split into two streams; for men, chastity became a specialized practice forming part of monastic life, while for women, modesty and chastity became the stuff of everyday life.[16] Modesty was the public performance of a woman's private virtue. By controlling her behavior – her carriage, clothing, gestures, and glances – a modest woman could avoid inciting men to unchaste thoughts and immoderate actions. Female modesty was thus in many ways a woman's contribution to social control.

It is crucial, therefore, to consider gender as a factor in any analysis of early modern women's intellectual lives. However, it is equally important not to stop there. Van Schurman and dozens of other intellectual women managed to interact with numerous male scholars, acquire a high level of erudition, and participate in the republic of letters in a way that rendered these expectations moot – and they apparently did so without committing those transgressions of feminine modesty that would have resulted in their being labeled as viragos.

In attempting to reconcile these seemingly irreconcilable truths, Nicéron and a long list of other writers opted for the "beyond nature" explanation. In published works, emphasizing the singularity of a van Schurman or a Princess Elisabeth enabled gendered expectations to remain intact. These works, however – whether positive or negative, crafted by contemporaries or assembled by later generations of scholars – are indicators only of a

---

[16] Ruth Kelso, *Doctrine for the Lady of the Renaissance* (Urbana, IL, 1956); Elisabeth Schüssler Fiorenza, "Word, Spirit and Power: Women in Early Christian Communities," in *Women of Spirit: Female Leadership in the Jewish and Christian Traditions*, ed. Rosemary Ruether and Eleanor McLaughlin (New York, 1979), 29–70.

discourse. They do not give us access to the women themselves, nor to their functional role in learned Europe.

Yet modern analytical categories which foreground considerations of gender can be equally unhelpful in this case. In Joan Scott's formulation, gender as "a useful category of analysis" must include a consideration of gender as a discourse of power:

The core of the definition rests on an integral connection between two propositions: gender is a constitutive element of social relationships based on perceived differences between the sexes, and gender is a primary way of signifying relationships of power.[17]

But in the case under consideration here, we are not dealing with an established institution, a state, or a broad concept of early modern European culture. We are considering, rather, the actual work done by women in the republic of letters, an amorphous, egalitarian, and self-conscious community whose stated ideal was to transcend divisions in order to work together for the advancement of learning.[18] Relationships of power qualified as one of those divisive categories that the republic of letters explicitly tried to transcend. And indeed, the women in this study functioned within that republic on a level that would have been the envy of many male contemporaries. Thus neither the "beyond their sex" model of extreme praise on one hand, nor the repressive "hierarchies of power" approach on the other, is likely to result in a useful analysis of how the learned women in this study actually functioned in the seventeenth-century intellectual landscape. And the problem with both of these approaches would appear to be their primary focus on gender.

Considerations of gender were, for van Schurman and other female scholars, problems of a practical, instrumental nature. Membership in the female sex was attached to a number of circumstances, expectations, and limitations that needed to be dealt with in order to pursue a life of scholarship. Sex was not, however, the primary consideration for any of the women under consideration in this study. Thus our analytical approach should be based on their own approach to scholarship – and that was a focus on *practice*. If we foreground what these women actually did – what they read, said, and studied; the people they knew; how they crafted a network of connections; and how they structured their lives to

---

[17] Joan Wallach Scott, "Gender: A Useful Category of Analysis," in *Gender and the Politics of History*, rev. edn. (New York, 1999), 42.
[18] Françoise Waquet, "Qu'est-ce que la République des Lettres? Essai de sémantique historique," *Bibliothèque de l'École des chartes* 147 (1989): 473–502.

include a space for learning – then gender slips much further down the list of priorities. It certainly does not go away; but while it was always present, that presence was often part of the background.

Yet if the gendered membership of van Schurman's circle made theirs a different and distinct group within the republic of letters, then why did that feminine distinction not result in their being isolated, segregated, or minimized within that intellectual community? How did their female intellectual enterprise differ or not differ from the informal correspondence networks of their male contemporaries? How does one define that larger intellectual community, and how does one define the republic of letters?

THE REPUBLIC OF LETTERS IN THE SEVENTEENTH CENTURY

The seventeenth-century republic of letters was not a place, or a polity, or a club for gentleman scholars. It was rather a heterogeneous, multi-faith, transnational and inclusive group fuelled by a shared desire to advance learning, and to discover the best pathway to knowledge. The citizens of the republic of letters were philosophers, poets, doctors, linguists, and theologians from cities across Europe, who created a shared intellectual identity – they were collegial scholars, connected by friendship, pedagogy, patronage, and learning. They pursued their investigations in a variety of ways and places for a variety of reasons, but the shared desire to know was the engine of that republic. Thus the republic of letters was rather an impossible, ambitious, and inclusive *ideal.*[19]

Adherence to this ideal involved an understood agreement to set aside religious, political, and social differences when participating in the activities of that entity. These activities involved, to various degrees: the translation of Latin, Greek, and Hebrew texts; complete familiarity with the humanist encyclopedia of learning; Biblical exegesis and theological discussion; sharing information on scientific experiments, apparatus, and events in the advancement of learning; lending, sending, and reviewing books; and introducing and assisting other scholars.

---

[19] The majority of scholarship on the republic of letters, and almost all the synthetic work, has been published in either French or Dutch. Two notable exceptions in English are Dena Goodman's *The Republic of Letters: A Cultural History of the French Enlightenment* (Ithaca, 1994), and Anne Goldgar's *Impolite Learning: Conduct and Community in the Republic of Letters 1680–1750* (New Haven, 1995). In the present study, I am building on Goldgar's analysis of the republic of letters as a self-aware social network.

Inevitably, the inclusion of so many scholars with vastly different belief systems meant that the ideals and overall ethic of the republic of letters were continually challenged by internal disruptions and disputes. Indeed, the flow of controversies was constant. However, the ideal remained explicit and intact; it was known, acknowledged, iterated, and often used as a pole-star for resolving conflicts. In addition, the inflammatory rhetoric found in published works might be completely contradicted by the content of epistolary exchanges. For instance: in polemical publications, Protestants might call the Pope the anti-Christ; Catholics would decry Protestantism as heresy; and men might write that women had no souls – and yet in their learned correspondence, these very same Protestants would write courteous, friendly, informational letters to Catholics, these same Catholics would share scientific news with Calvinists, and these same men might mentor individual women.

It has been thought that intellectual women were excluded from this communal enterprise. Hans Bots and Françoise Waquet, for instance, have argued that the republic of letters was "an essentially masculine society" in the seventeenth century; but by the eighteenth century, with the emergence of a culture of powerful salon women and "a cultivated feminine public," things had changed.[20] This study takes issue with their assessment, on two levels: first, it argues that the collegial intellectual work of seventeenth-century female scholars is evidence that there were, in fact, women participating fully in this "essentially masculine" enterprise; and second, it argues that the evidence for a cultivated feminine public later on actually represents something completely different – namely a secondary, feminized, stream of the republic of letters. And the correspondence of leading male intellectual figures in the seventeenth century – men like René Descartes, André Rivet, Marin Mersenne, Claude Saumaise, Samuel Hartlib, and Constantijn Huygens – shows that they included these women in the central activities of the republic of letters. The women reviewed and recommended books, made vital introductions, analyzed theological controversies, discussed philosophy, translated ancient texts, and solved mathematical problems.

This book does not, however, argue that women in the republic of letters constituted a force at the epicenter of intellectual change – their numbers were too small for that. And certainly, if that center continues to be defined as gentlemanly, male, and politely Christian, then these zealous female scholars simply cannot be squeezed in. However, their zealous

---

[20] Hans Bots and Françoise Waquet, *La République des Lettres* ([Paris], 1997), 96–9.

male colleagues will not fit, either. It becomes clear, then, that this center will not hold. We must consider the intellectual, scientific, and spiritual activity of the mid-seventeenth century on its own terms, rather than projecting later developments backward into these formative years. What we then find in the learned correspondence is evidence that these supposed outsiders were definitely there, participating in the conversation at the center.

The women in van Schurman's circle were members of both the republic of letters, and of a gendered subset of that republic; however, this women's epistolary network was far from unique in being structured this way. In fact, the entire seventeenth-century republic of letters was composed of these smaller, overlapping subsets. The Republic of Women was just one of these smaller groups, each of which was concerned with its own particular agenda, as well as with the overall ethos of the republic of letters.

The structure of the seventeenth-century republic of letters is thus best understood as a palimpsest of translucent and permeable layers. These horizontal layers were the individual networks that centered around particular projects – such as scientific experimentation, metaphysics, mathematics, educational reform, classical humanism, and ecumenicism – or around particular identities, representing groups such as Catholics, Calvinists, Pietists, radical cults, Huguenots, Royalists, Parliamentarians, or women. Within these horizontal layers, scholars strategized and supported each other regarding their particular shared issues and agendas. However, no single particularized horizontal layer can itself be called "the" republic of letters – each layer was only a subset interwoven with other subsets within the whole. These layers must also be visualized as translucent, so that one can see the traffic of ideas traveling both horizontally and vertically. Horizontally, shared ideas were exchanged within the individual layers. The vertical traffic came with the exchange of other sorts of ideas, which connected members of different layers to each other, and created new subsets whenever it made sense for the project in question. Both sorts of exchanges were commensurate with the overall ethos of the republic of letters.

Thus the ethos and construction of the seventeenth-century republic of letters form a stark contrast indeed to the political and religious events of the era; and despite the confessional conflict, the multinational members of the republic of letters continued pursuing and communicating ideas about faith and knowledge outside the formal setting of the university. Yet this republic of letters was far from being secular, and it was not the worldly association of *lumières* that would follow in the eighteenth century. An urgent enquiry into God's plan for mankind was one of the primary engines driving the seventeenth-century republic of letters, thus their intellectual commonwealth overlapped with a variety of religious circles, including Huguenot ministers in exile, ecumenical and pan-Protestant activists, Jesuits, millenarian radicals, and Pietist sects. The women in van Schurman's intellectual circle mirrored this overlap and were active in many of these circles as reformers and religious leaders, as well as scholars.

This structure of permeable layers also enabled the vital interaction of what have previously been seen as either excluded or mutually exclusive groups. Thus the republic of letters was in fact a much larger and more inclusive domain than has previously been thought: it included women as well as men, radical religious sectarians as well as latitudinarians, and princesses and schoolteachers as well as gentlemen. As we reconstruct the story of this women's network, that expanded intellectual landscape will make itself apparent. We turn now to a sketch of that Republic.

CITIZENS OF THE REPUBLIC OF WOMEN

In 1673, an anonymous tract on women's education appeared in London. Entitled *An Essay to Revive the Antient Education of Gentlewomen*, it was the first treatise in English to argue that women could and should be educated in the full "encyclopedeia" of humanist learning.[21] This anonymous male author, however, turned out to be a woman – the scholar, educator, and linguist Bathsua Makin. Makin had employed a traditional humanist strategy in her treatise, providing an exhaustive catalogue of learned and virtuous female *exempla* to validate her claims. Yet it was clear that Makin had one favorite among the names on this list. This one exceptional woman appeared no less than six times, personifying the heights of feminine achievement in the fields of linguistics, poetry, oratory, logic, philosophy, and theology. She had also been Makin's correspondent since the 1640s; and that woman was the modest, erudite, and pious Anna Maria van Schurman.[22]

Our focus now shifts back in time, to The Hague in the 1630s. Princess Elisabeth of Bohemia, renowned for her love of study and philosophy, had outgrown her tutors. Elisabeth eventually found a philosophical mentor and correspondent in René Descartes, who in turn found the

---

[21] Makin, *Essay*, 24. [22] *Ibid.*, 12–16.

princess an apt and demanding pupil; however, she still had unanswered questions.[23] Elisabeth needed help reconciling Descartes' scepticism with her own Calvinist values. Where could an intellectual woman turn for guidance in balancing these rival knowledge systems, in addition to reconciling modest feminine virtue with rigorous intellectual activity? Elisabeth turned to an authority on these matters – a woman of international scholarly reputation, and a friend whom she would respect and support throughout her life. That woman was the "Star of Utrecht," Anna Maria van Schurman.

Moving forward, we find ourselves in Dublin in 1641. It was the eve of the Irish Rebellion, and the widow Dorothy Moore was experiencing an intellectual crisis of conscience. Moore was a woman of great piety and learning, a scholar who had mastered Hebrew.[24] In addition, her first marriage to Lord Arthur Moore had made her the aunt of Katherine Jones, Lady Ranelagh, the elder sister of the scientist Robert Boyle. Ranelagh, a religious activist, intellectual broker, and moral mentor, was a forceful and highly respected participant in the intellectual careers of John Milton, Henry Oldenburg, Samuel Hartlib, Robert Boyle, and John Dury, while also serving as the religious and ethical centre for her various networks. However, status and connections were not Moore's concern; she wanted to preach, and was enmeshed in a crucial and agonizing personal dilemma concerning her true calling. Moore's male friends and co-religionists were of limited help to her on this question; she needed to consult a female authority, one who had negotiated this territory herself. The authority to whom she turned was the scholar who had written to her a year earlier, offering complete support for Moore's pursuits – and that woman was Anna Maria van Schurman.

Now to France, in that same year of 1641. The French scholar Marie de Gournay, at the age of seventy-six, had just published the final version of her feminist treatise on *The Equality of Men and Women*.[25] Throughout her career, she had been an alchemist, a self-supporting author, the editor of Montaigne's *Essais*, and the hostess of a salon that suffered fatally from

[23] On their correspondence, see especially Princess Elisabeth, *The Correspondence between Princess Elisabeth of Bohemia and René Descartes*, trans. Lisa Shapiro (Chicago and London, 2007).

[24] On Moore, see especially *The Letters of Dorothy Moore, 1612–64: The Friendships, Marriage, and Intellectual Life of a Seventeenth-Century Woman*, ed. Lynette Hunter (Aldershot, 2004).

[25] Marie de Gournay's *L'Égalité des hommes et des femmes* was originally published in 1622. Gournay re-edited and repackaged the text with other works numerous times over the following two decades. Marie le Jars de Gournay, *Apology for the Woman Writing and Other Works*, ed. Richard Hillman and Colette Quesnel (Chicago and London, 2002); Michèle Fogel, *Marie de Gournay: Itinéraires d'une femme savante* (Paris, 2004).

her tight budget and terrible food.[26] While there were many who criticized the outspoken Gournay, the older scholar did have an admirer who had written to her in 1639, honoring her for her service to women, and praising her as "the Pride of Gournay," and "the defender of our sex." That admirer was the young Anna Maria van Schurman.

Lastly, our focus remains in France, but we move forward to 1646, where Madeleine de Scudéry was outraged over a perceived insult to the reputation of Joan of Arc. Scudéry, one of the most popular writers in Europe, also reigned over a highly respected literary and intellectual salon. She leapt to the defence of the Maid of Orleans, but was unsure about an intellectual engagement with André Rivet, the esteemed theologian who had disparaged Scudéry's hero. She hoped that Rivet's protégée, a woman with impeccable intellectual and moral credentials, would support her case – but fearing to contact her directly, she went instead to Marie du Moulin. Marie also had impeccable credentials. She was a Hebrew scholar, and the author of a tract on the education of princes – and she agreed to write on Joan's behalf to the woman she called "my learned sister." That "sister," the woman whose help Scudéry had wanted, but dared not ask for personally, was Anna Maria van Schurman.[27]

As indicated by the contours sketched above, van Schurman was an important component in the intellectual self-images of other female scholars for over forty years. Yet her significance for these other scholars did not derive from her assigned role in contemporary literature on exemplary women – that of an epitome, a paragon, and a miracle. What we are seeing here instead is a network of intellectual women relying on one other in a very practical and instrumental way, as resources to be consulted during the process of constructing a life of learning. Because of van Schurman's success, she emerged as one of the most effective and influential of these resources in her generation of female scholars. Thus in order to do justice to the practicality of this network, and the ways in which it mirrored and interacted with the networks of their male

---

[26] Margaret Ilsley, *A Daughter of the Renaissance: Marie le Jars de Gournay, Her Life and Works* (The Hague, 1963), 89.

[27] This episode is based on a volume of correspondence exchanged between André Rivet, Marie du Moulin, Valentin Conrart, and Madeleine de Scudéry, held in the collection of Rivetiana at the Library of the University of Leiden, Ms. BPL 290. Selections from this manuscript were published by Edouard de Barthélemy in *Un Tournoi de trois pucelles en l'honneur de Jeanne d'Arc: Lettres inédites de Conrart, de Mlle. de Scudéry, et de Mlle. du Moulin* (Paris, 1878). On Marie du Moulin, see Elisabeth Labrousse, "Marie du Moulin, Educatrice," *Bulletin de la Société de l'Histoire du Protestantisme Français* 139, no. 2 (1993): 255–68.

colleagues, this study employs a methodology based on the processes of intellectual work in the republic of letters.

METHODOLOGY: THE PRACTICES OF KNOWLEDGE

In an important 1989 essay, Françoise Waquet asked, "What is the Republic of Letters?"[28] Her answer identified a multinational community of learned men, whose stated ideal – always in tension with reality – was to transcend national and religious divisions in order to work together for the advancement of learning. Their activities covered nearly the entire range of seventeenth-century intellectual activity. And in furtherance of their desired ideal, these learned men engaged in "a system of exchanges":

> This circulation, which operated according to multiple modes, was built on vectors as diverse as letters, journals, travels, and the search for a common language. Finally, such exchanges were favoured by the existence of privileged places, such as universities, intellectual salons, and the shops of booksellers.[29]

One can readily see the difficulties inherent in placing learned women in this picture. The work of intellectual exchange required two kinds of circulation – lettered circulation, in terms of both correspondence and publications; and physical circulation, as scholars made contacts through travel and association in places of learning. Women at this time circulated in a circumscribed way. In terms of lettered circulation, they certainly engaged in correspondence, but appear to have published comparatively little, especially in the area of scholarly works and polemics. And in terms of physical circulation, it is true that some did travel; most, however, did not, and with the exception of salons, the "privileged places" of learning were off limits to them. However, salons served a somewhat different function from that of intellectual communities within the republic of letters. They certainly constituted places where educated women could associate with one another; the salons were always directed by women, who would choose the topics for discussion, and whose presence would set the tone. However, the salons were not intended to function as locations for female scholarship; they were rather a "sociocultural adaptive mechanism" in *ancien régime* France, wherein the newly ennobled *bourgeois gentilhomme* could acquire the culture, manners, and values of the nobility.[30]

---

[28] Waquet, "Qu'est-ce que la République des Lettres?"
[29] Bots and Waquet, *La République des Lettres*, 117.
[30] Carolyn C. Lougee, *Le Paradis des Femmes: Women, Salons, and Social Stratification in Seventeenth-Century France* (Princeton, 1976), 5, 212.

Yet an examination of learned correspondence reveals that, despite these limitations, female scholars were indeed participating in the system of exchanges that fuelled the republic of letters. Thus in order to make sense of this counterintuitive phenomenon, it is time to take the Bots and Waquet thesis a step or two further.

Building on their work, and on the social-network analysis of Anne Goldgar, this study considers the intellectual labor of the republic of letters through the lens of four major practices – correspondence, net-working, publication, and mentorship – that enabled these exchanges to take place. Female scholars employed all of these same practices: they used some in the same way that their male colleagues did, while they adapted others in order to create their own versions of those privileged places so important for facilitating scholarly exchange. The following section sets out the four constituent parts of this analytical framework, and then turns to a discussion of sources.

Correspondence. Correspondence is being defined here as the exchange of letters, and of the objects that were sometimes included with these letters. Those objects were primarily portraits and publications: the por-traits were an important item for far-flung scholars, who might never get the chance to meet, while the sending and lending of new publications was an essential backup to distribution systems that were vulnerable to the disruptions of war and the vagaries of censorship.[31] The letters themselves were both private and semi-public. A great deal of correspondence in the republic of letters was of this semi-public variety. Some letters remained in manuscript form, becoming part of the culture of scribal communi-cation, while others were eventually published.[32]

Did female scholars differ from their male colleagues in learned corres-pondence? Their letters discuss the latest developments in politics and science; they review and exchange new publications; and they take pos-itions in current debates over faith and philosophy. Their letters also contain personal news, reports of family illness and recovery, and spiritual

---

[31] On the ways in which the exchange of portraits served to solidify friendships in the *respublica litteraria*, see Lisa Jardine, *Erasmus, Man of Letters: The Construction of Charisma in Print* (Princeton, 1993).

[32] Harold Love, *Scribal Publication in Seventeenth-Century England* (Oxford, 1993), reprinted as *The Culture and Commerce of Texts* (Amherst, 1998), 180–1. For the Continental aspects of learned scribal communication, and its relationship with publication and journals, see Hans Bots and Françoise Waquet, eds., *Commercium Litterarium: La Communications dans la République des Lettres 1600–1750* (Amsterdam, 1993); and Françoise Waquet, "De la lettre érudite au périodique savant: les faux semblants d'une mutation intellectuelle," *XVIIe Siècle* 140, no.3 (July–September 1983): 347–59.

reflections. In all of these aspects, the correspondence of female scholars was practically indistinguishable from that of male scholars. Sometimes there were differences, but these arose when the issues being discussed were particular to their identity-specific subgroup within the republic of letters. Among these women, then, the content and imperilled continuance of their studies was a shared and important topic, constituting their particular "corporate ideology" – just as, for instance, French developments would constitute a topic for networks of Huguenot scholars, or English Royalists would discuss the ongoing struggles between Charles I and Parliament.[33]

Networking. I use the word "networking" here to designate the ways in which introductions were made among scholars in the republic of letters. The practice of making personal introductions – whether to further one's own learned career or to facilitate the careers of others – was the thread used to weave together the fabric of the republic of letters. Much of this was accomplished by letter, and on this level the women in the republic of letters deployed this practice in the same way as their male colleagues: they introduced themselves to each other, or to senior scholars, and they introduced other female scholars into various learned circles.

For face-to-face networking, however, adaptation was required. In the republic of letters, epistolary relationships were bolstered by face-to-face meetings as often as possible; and for young male scholars, the *peregrinatio academica*, or academic pilgrimage, was "a veritable rite." Outside the walls of the academy, and beyond the intellectual salon, young scholars would arm themselves with letters of introduction and recommendation from their mentors, then undertake an intellectual Grand Tour of Europe.[34] For example, when Zacharias Conrad von Uffenbach made his *peregrinatio academica* in 1710, he met at least seventy-two distinguished scholars on one trip.[35] It was in these *voyages érudits* that a younger scholar would finally emerge from the shadow of his mentor. From that point on, all doors to the republic of letters were opened for him, and erudition served as the only passport necessary.

For female scholars, however, the *peregrinatio academica* was a practical impossibility. The modesty required of a virtuous Christian woman was

---

[33] "Corporate ideology" is Harold Love's phrase for the agenda or identity particular to a specific scribal community. In Love, *Scribal Publication*.

[34] Hans Bots, "De la transmission du savoir à la communication entre les hommes de lettres: universités et académies en Europe du XVIe au XVIIIe siècle," in Bots and Waquet, eds., *Commercium Litterarium*, 112.

[35] Goldgar, *Impolite Learning*, 4.

of crucial importance, both personally and culturally; thus the scholarly practice of networking needed to fit within women's circumscribed orbits. The solution for female scholars was to create their own version of those "privileged places" named by Bots and Waquet, a location that could provide some of the same networking benefits that male scholars derived from the academy and the academic pilgrimage.

In other times and places, female scholars accomplished this through proposals adapting the model of the cloister for academic purposes – for instance, Christine de Pizan's 1405 *City of Ladies*, and Mary Astell's 1694 *Serious Proposal to the Ladies*.[36] But in the middle of the seventeenth century, these walls were not necessary; and in the 1630s, the female scholars in this study turned the Queen of Bohemia's exile court in The Hague into a concrete location for learning, meeting, and building a network of relationships.

Publication. Publication was a complicated and circuitous process for early modern female scholars. While there were quite a number of early modern women who published poetry or plays or sacred meditations, there were few who ventured into the realms of philosophy, theology, learned languages, or mathematics. However, of the seven female scholars at the center of this study, three – Anna Maria van Schurman, Bathsua Makin, and Marie de Gournay – published learned works under their own names. Bathsua Makin and Marie du Moulin also participated in the process of anonymous publication. Makin published her poetry under her own name, while her work on education was anonymous; Marie du Moulin published all her work anonymously, although her authorship of these treatises was an open secret in the republic of letters.[37] The writings of Dorothy Moore and Lady Ranelagh circulated by means of scribal publication only; and the philosophical letters of Princess Elisabeth, while also an open secret in the republic of letters, circulated only with her express permission.

Mentorship. In the process of intellectual mentorship, we encounter the greatest range of adaptations made by female scholars working in the republic of letters. For male scholars, mentoring was almost always based on relationships formed at the academy, whether it was a grammar school,

---

[36] Christine de Pizan, *The Book of the City of Ladies* [1405], ed. and trans. Earl Jeffrey Richards (New York, 1982); Mary Astell, *A Serious Proposal to the Ladies for the Advancement of their True and Greatest Interest, By a Lover of her Sex* (London, 1694).

[37] On the problematics of female authorship and anonymity, see Chapter 7, "Reading the Anonymous Female Voice," in Marcy L. North, *The Anonymous Renaissance: Cultures of Discretion in Tudor-Stuart England* (Chicago, 2003).

a seminary, a Protestant academy, a Dutch *école illustre*, or a full-fledged university. The mentoring was necessary for both intellectual networking and scholarly development. Without introductions, jobs, and friendships, erudition alone could not guarantee that a young scholar would be woven into the international web of new ideas, experiments, and arguments. For female scholars, then – without access to the academy, and unable to attend universities, seminaries, or any other establishment for higher learning – their mentoring relationships within the republic of letters were doubly important. Like their male peers, women in the republic of letters needed their mentors to guide their entrée into the world of learned correspondence. Beyond this, however, female scholars needed to construct their own extra-institutional educational programs if they were to acquire the advanced learning that the schools offered to men alone. Thus their mentors needed to be their tutors as well; and, as we learn from their correspondence, female scholars identified their intellectual needs, then sought out the individuals who might fill the gaps in their learning.

In addition, there were intellectual issues particular to the female scholar. These were primarily of two sorts. First, entitlement and purpose: female scholars needed to justify the time, resources, and possible moral perils of a life of study, a life which ultimately – since women could practice no learned professions – would have no worldly purpose whatsoever. And secondly, instrumentality: even assuming there were no problems regarding entitlement and purpose, *how*, exactly, could a woman go about constructing an intellectual life? What were her means, and where could she obtain this desired learning? The female scholars in this study solved their mentoring problem in one of two ways: through the unmediated solicitation of advice; and through the creation of an intellectual family. The construction of the intellectual family was simultaneously a form of networking, a type of mentorship, and the creation of an abstract "privileged place" for the formation of the early modern female scholar.

SOURCES

It is one of the contentions of this study that the real functioning of female scholarship in the republic of letters can only be discerned by returning to the learned correspondence itself – to the women's own letters, and to the numerous references to them throughout the correspondence of their male colleagues. Early modern printed works featuring discussions of exemplary women – whether pro or con – cannot by themselves be considered accurate or adequate sources for assessing female scholars as historical actors. These works were, on a certain level, rhetorical performances in the centuries-long *querelle des femmes*, and the truth cannot easily be disentangled from the art. Thus *Republic of Women* relies primarily on learned correspondence in two forms: manuscript letters in the archives, many of which were written in Latin, and have not been translated before; and the published correspondence of the most renowned names in the republic of letters, men such as René Descartes, Marin Mersenne, Constantijn Huygens, Claude Saumaise, Samuel Hartlib, Henry Oldenburg, Justus Lipsius, Gottfried Wilhelm von Leibniz, Nicolas Malebranche, André Rivet, John Evelyn, and Pierre Bayle.

Yet our concept of early modern female scholarship could also be distorted by reliance on correspondence alone. Many renowned male scholars would express one opinion on learned women in their printed works, and then manifest a completely different viewpoint in their actions and correspondence – thus we find conflicting ideas expressed by the same person. In the republic of letters, however, these variant stances were not seen as being contradictory at all. By using a combination of literary and archival documents, and reading them against one another to assess what is said in which type of source, this study demonstrates instead that these were manifestations of the seventeenth-century intellectual enterprise at work, a complex entity that functioned in different ways at different levels. *Republic of Women* not only locates these actors in the intellectual landscape of early modern Europe, but also considers the consequences of their posthumous obscurity.

It is, therefore, through examining this scholarly work – its content, its practice, and who was producing it – that one discovers an entirely new dimension to the intellectual landscape. Beyond the famous *érudits* whose names have been synonymous with the republic of letters, we find reformers, radicals, artisans, preachers, and – in surprising numbers – women. Using these knowledge practices as a lens, we encounter this past on its own terms, putting aside our notions of who these practitioners might have been, of which practices were important, and of where these practices of knowledge took place. The evidence then compels us to weave these historical actors back into the fabric of the republic of letters; and, in so doing, to restore the impressive breadth and depth of the early modern intellectual landscape.

CHAPTER I

Princess Elisabeth of Bohemia: an ephemeral academy at The Hague in the 1630s

Even Anna Schurman is said to be inferior to the Palatine Princess
Elisabeth, who is called the Star of the North.

Madame de Guebriant[1]

Late in 1634, a rather improbable conversation took place in The Hague.
The two participants were René Descartes, the French Catholic mathematician and philosopher, and John Dury, the itinerant Scottish minister
whose never-ending quest was a mission to unite all Protestants. The topic
under discussion was Truth, with Dury and Descartes each representing a
very distinct extremity of the seventeenth-century spectrum of thought on
this subject. In simplest terms, John Dury was an advocate of identifying
truth and eliminating doubt through the right interpretation of Scripture.
Descartes, on the other hand, was a rationalist, and in this conversation
was advocating for identifying truth and eliminating doubt through
mathematics. Dury's colleague, Samuel Hartlib, described the conversation in his work diary:

Cardes excellency lyes especially in the Mathematikes. Hee hase an Algebra Nova
by plus et minus to discover truths by false-hoods which also could bee easily
dived into . . . Hee discoursed with Mr Dury complaining of the Uncertainties of
all things, which Dury refuteth by the truths and certainty of those reports in the
Scripture and an infallible way of interpreting them which hee denyed. But being
brought to many absurdities left of.[2]

Unsurprisingly, then, Dury and Descartes ended the conversation by
agreeing to disagree.

---

[1] From Madame de Guebriant's report on meeting van Schurman in 1644. Guebriant was
accompanying Marie de Gonzague on her nuptial voyage from France to her new home in
Poland, where she wed King Wladislaus IV. Quoted in [Elizabeth Ogilvy] Benger, *Memoirs of
Elizabeth Stuart, Queen of Bohemia, Daughter of King James the First*, 2 vols. (London, 1825), II, 367.
[2] Samuel Hartlib, *Ephemerides* 1635, Part I, Sheffield University, Hartlib Papers (hereinafter "HP")
29/3/13B-14A.

The vocabulary of this conversation, involving certainty, doubt, Scripture, and science, was typical for correspondents in the republic of letters, thus it was not the content of the conversation that was improbable. The improbability lay rather in the setting itself. For this was far from being an academic debate – this was, in fact, a meeting of the minds organized and orchestrated by Princess Elisabeth, the sixteen-year-old mathematician, philosopher, and eldest daughter of the Queen of Bohemia.[3]

The setting was a court, and the hostess was a princess – however, conventional interpretations of this scenario do not apply here. The court of the Queen of Bohemia was impoverished and in exile, thus there was little hope of patronage for either Dury or Descartes. And their serious, studious, strictly Calvinist hostess was extremely unlikely to harbor ambitions to craft herself as a socially savvy Dutch *salonnière*. What, then, was the point of bringing Dury and Descartes together for this conversation at the exile court? What did Princess Elisabeth hope to accomplish, and what did these two men mean to her? The answer to these questions is suggested by another meeting that took place earlier that same year.

Even before she hosted Dury and Descartes – in that same exile court in The Hague, and in that same year of 1634 – Princess Elisabeth had met with another scholar to discuss these very issues. The questions regarded how to reconcile classical humanist erudition on the one hand with Baconian New Learning on the other, while avoiding potential pitfalls of heresy. There had, in fact, been some alarm in The Hague over the perilous and untrammelled catholicity of Elisabeth's studies.[4] It was thought that she needed the advice of a more traditionally humanist scholar, one whose erudition was grounded in classical texts, rather than modern experimentation and metaphysics. And in this case, the authority called in for consultation was a woman, the erudite Anna Maria van Schurman of Utrecht.

---

[3] Richard Popkin, *The History of Scepticism: From Savonarola to Bayle*, revised edn. (Oxford and New York, 2003), 174; Cornelius de Waard, "Un Entretien avec Descartes en 1634 ou 1635," *Archives Internationales d'Histoire des Sciences* 32, no. 22 (January–March 1953): 14–16.

[4] Recent work has begun to assess Elisabeth as a philosopher, as well as a royal. See especially *The Correspondence between Princess Elisabeth of Bohemia and René Descartes*. See also Beatrice H. Zedler, "The Three Princesses," *Hypatia* 4, no. 1 (Spring 1989): 28–63; Erica Harth, *Cartesian Women: Versions and Subversions of Rational Discourse in the Old Regime* (Ithaca, 1992); Anna Creese, "The Letters of Elisabeth, Princess Palatine: A Seventeenth-Century Correspondence" (Ph.D. dissertation, Princeton University, 1993); Deborah Tollefsen, "Princess Elisabeth and the Problem of Mind–Body Interaction," *Hypatia* 14, no. 3 (1999): 59–77; and a somewhat romanticized treatment by Andrea Nye, *The Princess and the Philosopher: Letters of Elisabeth of the Palatine to René Descartes* (Lanham, 1999).

It is clear, then, that the point of these meetings was not social advancement or economic security. The point was rather intellectual, a scholarly exchange on the most current concerns of the republic of letters. And what makes these conversations surprising is that they show us the supposedly all-male republic of letters functioning in a dually gendered way.

In this example, women are interacting with both women and men; and, going beyond their more circumscribed functions as hostesses, patrons, or acolytes, they are acting as participants, colleagues, and mentors. The 1634 conversation between Dury and Descartes would be recorded by Samuel Hartlib in his *Ephemerides*, while the exchanges between Elisabeth and van Schurman survive only in their correspondence. Both provide a fascinating window onto the republic of letters, revealing the shared and deeply felt concerns of scholars representing very different ideological and religious systems. However, the circumstances of these conversations open that window even wider. The fact that these meetings took place at the Queen of Bohemia's exile court in The Hague helps to demonstrate how Elisabeth and a handful of other female scholars were taking full intellectual advantage of the court's location at the crossroads of learned Europe. This was one of the ways in which a group of female scholars participated in and adapted the work processes of the republic of letters in the seventeenth century – turning the exile court in The Hague into a "privileged place" for scholarship in 1634.[5]

The exile court was a uniquely protected and productive space located at an intellectual crossroads, one that enabled the birth of a women's intellectual commonwealth. It was an environment that resulted from the intersection of Dutch religious tolerance, the republic of letters, and the political exile of the Queen of Bohemia in The Hague during the 1630s. An intellectual woman of the seventeenth century had no access to advanced study beyond the basic education provided for women of her rank. The daughters of kings and the daughters of schoolteachers were alike in that they could not attend a university, do research in a library, or travel to meet other scholars. Yet there were in fact a number of early modern women who were intellectually assertive, who were acute and insistent scholars. Some were models of humanist erudition and classical learning, with a command of languages and authoritative texts; others were "moderns," interested in metaphysics, mathematics, and philosophy – restless thinkers, exploring issues of ethics, experimentation, and science. Still others were biblical scholars, whose focus of study was Scripture and the revealed word. At the

---

[5] The phrase "*lieux privilégiés*" comes from Bots and Waquet, *La République des Lettres*, 117.

exile court in The Hague, courtiers, ministers, scholars, artists, princes, princesses, diplomats, ministers, and refugees met and mingled in the halls of the Wassenaer Hof, fleeing war and religious conflict in England, Ireland, Germany, and France. And it was here that a number of these intellectual women were introduced to each other.

This setting enabled these women to participate in the networking that was so necessary for their growth as scholars. At the exile court, they could engage with *érudits*, ideas, and each other. And, because the setting was so conducive to women's intellectual careers, it is here that we see a number of them undergoing a very similar three-stage development in terms of intellectual connection: first, the women are noticed individually as singular examples of feminine accomplishment in learning; second, they come to the attention of supportive men in religious and intellectual networks, who begin to introduce them into their collegial enterprise; and finally, these female scholars begin to hear about each other, reaching out to form their own network of correspondence and connection within the larger republic of letters.

This, in the 1630s, was the beginning of a female scholarly community. Of the seven women who will constitute the primary focus of this study – Anna Maria van Schurman, Marie de Gournay, Marie du Moulin, Princess Elisabeth of Bohemia, Dorothy Moore, Bathsua Makin, and Lady Ranelagh – four can be reliably placed at the exile court in The Hague during the 1630s. These four were van Schurman, Moore, du Moulin, and Elisabeth. The other three, Makin, Gournay, and Ranelagh, were closely associated with this court through their connections to intellectual men and women there.

One of the most important questions to be considered, then, is how this female intellectual community did or did not differ from that of their male colleagues. This also encapsulates the question of how individual female scholars did or did not differ from their male colleagues. Did gender make a difference? One way to approach this question is through the issue of intellectual consistency. For instance, Elisabeth's thinking would go through many changes. As far as is known, she never developed a full-fledged philosophical system of her own, although Lisa Shapiro has recently argued that we might read Elisabeth's side of her correspondence with Descartes as an emergent philosophical treatise in its own right – intellectually substantial, internally consistent, and committed to a clear position.[6] Elisabeth also went through a number of different religious

---

[6] *The Correspondence between Princess Elisabeth of Bohemia and René Descartes*, 4.

phases, from her strict Calvinist upbringing, to her extensive interactions with Quakers, to her final days as the director of a Lutheran abbey. Van Schurman's intellect also moved through many phases, from the relentless pursuit of humanistic erudition that characterized her youth, to the Pietist sect she helped found in her later years.

Yet the intellectual and religious lives of Elisabeth and van Schurman – together with the intellectual and religious lives of their fellow female scholars – were entirely consistent. I do not mean that their lives were consistent with those of the majority of early modern women; they were far from being that. However, the trajectories of their intellectual lives were entirely consistent with those of their male colleagues in the republic of letters in a number of ways.

First, within the unavoidable limits imposed by differences in social status and gender, these women selected their scholarly paths in precisely the same way male scholars did. They identified fields of interest, and then sought out mentors, teachers, and colleagues with whom those interests could be developed further. They were deeply religious, but struggling to absorb and accommodate all the new empirical findings, systems of knowledge, and schismatic sects that challenged the faiths into which they were born. Second, although they were highly influenced by people and events in their lives, by powerful mentors and recurrent adversity, they showed early evidence of strong minds and strong systems of belief. And although their knowledge and values were challenged and adapted over the years, these changes were the result of intellectual and spiritual evolution – not, as has been alleged, of surrender to more powerful souls. Third, the friendships among these women unfolded concurrently with their disagreements over matters of epistemology and faith – van Schurman and Elisabeth, for example, representing opposite sides of the debate between "ancients" and "moderns."[7] And fourth, the relationships between these women included explicit commitments to lifelong intellectual mentoring, as older generations gave their younger colleagues the benefit of their knowledge, connections, and advice in pursuing a life of learning.

These activities were all completely characteristic of the seventeenth-century republic of letters, but lacking the supportive environment of the university, these women interacted instead at the exile court. We turn now

---

[7] R. F. Jones, *Ancients and Moderns: A Study of the Rise of the Scientific Movement in Seventeenth-Century England*, 2nd edn. (St Louis, MO, 1961).

to an analysis of the setting in The Hague, and the beginnings of this scholarly community.

AT THE CROSSROADS OF THE REPUBLIC OF LETTERS

In 1637, René Descartes explained why he had chosen to leave France and live in Holland.[8] Holland was, he said, the perfect place in which to be intellectually productive, because he could count on being left alone. The Dutch were so weary of war, and so busy pursuing their own business, that they did not have time to pester a solitary thinker like himself; he could "lead a life as solitary and withdrawn as if I were in the most remote desert, while lacking none of the comforts found in the most populous cities."[9] Not everyone was convinced by Descartes' description of the Netherlands as a hideaway, or of himself as the retiring philosophical hermit cached within it. In 1651, for instance, the anti-Cartesian Cyriacus Lentulus insisted that Descartes' real craving had not been for seclusion, but rather for fame. He pointed out that no place on earth was better for garnering scholarly celebrity than the place in which Descartes had allegedly chosen to make himself invisible – a fact which, he insisted, Descartes knew better than anyone.[10]

Lentulus was neither the first nor the last to question Descartes' ingenuousness on this issue. However, the salient point in this argument is that the facts themselves were never in dispute. Knowledge does not just emerge – it is produced. So even in the abstract, correspondence-based republic of letters, knowledge always bore the imprint of its location.[11] And the Netherlands – geographically, culturally, and intellectually – constituted a location perfectly suited to the pursuit of a scholarly career, an environment that benefited both male and female scholars at the crossroads of learned Europe.

Geographically, Holland's location on the western edge of northern Europe made it easily accessible by both land and sea. The constant traffic of travellers from Scotland, England, Denmark, France, Italy, and Germany benefited trade and scholarship alike. In addition, the Dutch

---

[8] "*La Hollande, Carrefour de la République des Lettres*" is the phrase used by Paul Dibon in *Regards sur la Hollande du Siècle d'Or* (Naples, 1990), 1.

[9] From the conclusion to Part Three of *Discours de la Méthode*, in *The Philosophical Writings of Descartes*, trans. John Cottingham, Robert Stoothoff, and Dugald Murdoch, 2 vols. (Cambridge, 1985), I, 126.

[10] Cyriacus Lentulus, *Nova Renati Descartes Sapientia* (1651). Quoted in Dibon, *Regards*, 12.

[11] Here I am building on David Livingstone's argument regarding scientific knowledge. David N. Livingstone, *Putting Science in Its Place: Geographies of Scientific Knowledge* (Chicago, 2003).

East India and Dutch West India Companies combined colonization, commerce, and Calvinist proselytizing into a successful venture, enhancing the growth of an already large and affluent "middle" class. It was the "golden age" of the Republic, when a combination of new wealth, political power, and cultural enrichment combined to produce a short but brilliant era in Dutch history.[12]

The result was a Dutch culture characterized by moderation, tolerance, austerity, practicality, domesticity, and the somewhat untranslatable attribute of *burgerlijkheid*, denoting the hegemony of middle-class customs and values.[13] It may perhaps be due to this businesslike *burgerlijkheid* that religious differences and female visibility alike were tolerated in the Dutch Republic. This was not a simple formula, nor was this tolerance uncontested – in fact it was complicated and conflicted from the very beginning. For women, however, the practical and mercantile aspects of this culture combined to provide the seventeenth-century Dutch woman with a range of movement not available to her continental contemporaries; she could have a public presence, and was expected to be able to run a business.[14]

As for religious toleration, it was both implicit and explicit in the Dutch Republic. Article Thirteen of the Union of Utrecht (1579) stated that, "no body shall be persecuted or examined for religious reasons," and in a Europe being ravaged by confessional conflict and religious persecution, this was in itself a remarkable statement.[15] It appeared to express a lofty ideal of toleration quite out of keeping with the confessionally fuelled bloodshed that characterized the rest of Europe; and as Britain and the Continent were being torn apart by the French Wars of Religion, the Thirty Years' War, and the English Civil Wars, the streets of Calvinist Amsterdam thronged with Catholics, Calvinists, and Jews. Religious

---

[12] Johan Huizinga, *Dutch Civilisation in the Seventeenth Century and Other Essays*, selected by Pieter Geyl and F. W. N. Hugenholtz, trans. Arnold J. Pomerans (New York, 1968), 103–4. For a general discussion of this period, see Jonathan Israel, *The Dutch Republic: Its Rise, Greatness, and Fall 1477–1806* (Oxford, 1995).

[13] The range of dictionary definitions for the adjective *burgerlijk* also includes such terms as philistine, conventional, respectable, civilian, and smug. *Van Dale Groot Woordenboek Nederlands-Engels.*

[14] Els Kloek, "Introduction," in *Women of the Golden Age: An International Debate on Women in Seventeenth-Century Holland, England and Italy*, ed. Els Kloek, Nicole Tesuwen, and Marijke Huisman (Hilversum, 1994).

[15] M. E. H. N. Mout, "Limits and Debates: A Comparative View of Dutch Toleration in the Sixteenth and Early Seventeenth Centuries," in *The Emergence of Tolerance in the Dutch Republic*, ed. C. Berkevens-Stevelinck, J. Israel, and G. H. M. Posthumus Meyjes (Leiden and New York, 1997), 41. See also Ronnie Po-Chia Hsia, "Introduction," in *Calvinism and Religious Toleration in the Dutch Golden Age*, ed. Ronnie Po-Chia Hsia and Henk van Nierop (Cambridge, 2002), 1–7.

conversions of all types took place in all directions: Mennonites became Catholics, Jews became agnostic, and Calvinists became Pietists.

Yet it is likely that the Dutch Republic's position of religious tolerance arose less from an ideological stance than from the same pragmatic desire that had given Dutch women their relative freedom of movement – a desire to facilitate civic discipline and good business through the maintenance of social peace. As Sir John Reresby observed in 1657:

They admit persons of all countries and opinions amongst them, knowing well that this liberty draws people, numbers of people increase trade and that trade brings money.[16]

It was an arrangement that also found its detractors, as the English poet Andrew Marvell sneered in 1665:

> Hence Amsterdam Turk-Christian-Pagan-Jew,
> Staple of Sects, and Mint of Schisme grew.
> That Bank of Conscience, where not one so strange
> Opinion, but finds Credit and Exchange.[17]

Marvell's poem, ridiculing the Dutch for their religious pluralism while decrying their culture of commerce, expressed a not uncommon viewpoint among the English during the era of the Anglo-Dutch Wars, when England hoped to gain ascendancy over its only Protestant rival in trade.

Yet Catholic observers of Dutch culture were equally bewildered by the ways in which the Dutch focus on commerce led to a level of religious toleration that included Jews. Among these was the historian Jean le Laboureur, accompanying Marie de Gonzague, the consort of Wladislaus IV, on her nuptial voyage from France to her new home in Poland. It was a voyage that would include a visit to the erudite van Schurman, who met with much more approval from the party than did the city of Amsterdam itself:

All these streams of goods and foreign merchants are just as much composed of vices and of various religions, which the demands of commerce introduce into this City. Catholics there have less freedom than Jews, who are allowed to have public Synagogues.[18]

---

[16] From the travel journal of Sir John Reresby (1634–89), written during his Grand Tour of Europe in 1657. In C. D. van Strien, *British Travellers in Holland during the Stuart Period: Edward Browne and John Locke as Tourists in the United Provinces* (Leiden, 1993), 203.

[17] Andrew Marvell, *The Character of Holland* (London, 1665), 4.

[18] Jean le Laboureur, *Relation dv voyage de la Royne de Pologne … par la Hongrie, l'Avstriche, Styrie, Carinthie, le Frioul, & l'Italie. avec un discours historique de toutes les Villes & Estats, par où elle a passé …* (Paris, 1647), 71. The historian Jean le Laboureur (1623–75) later became a priest.

Thus even after 1619, when the Synod of Dort established strict reformed Calvinism as the official church of the Netherlands, the result had been the creation of the "central paradox" of the Dutch Republic – an officially intolerant Calvinist church, coupled with pragmatic *de facto* religious toleration.[19] Held together by a shared adherence to piety – in whatever form it was practiced – the Republic was simultaneously a haven of "interconfessional bliss" and a site for vitriolic pamphlet wars between opposing religious factions.[20]

This context of religious toleration and pluralism in the Netherlands had attracted fugitive scholars and theologians since the sixteenth century. The Dutch book trade, in particular, flourished with the influx of manuscripts that could not get past the censors in France, or Italy, or England. These human and literary exiles helped to create a flourishing intellectual environment, which can be seen in a number of related phenomena – Dutch universities, the Dutch book trade, Dutch intellectual salons, and the republic of letters – each of which helped create an environment that allowed for the emergence of a network of intellectual women.

The early Dutch Republic was less a nation than an alliance, comprising seven provinces. An alliance of forces interested in trade and Protestantism had risen up against Spanish rule in 1572, when Philip II instituted an excise tax, the infamous "tenth penny." The resulting Republic was led simultaneously by two very different heads of state: the Stadholder Prince Maurice of the House of Orange, who represented the Calvinist cause; and Oldenbarneveldt, the Landsadvocaat of Holland, who represented the interests of the wealthy and powerful merchant rulers of Dutch cities. Yet almost immediately, despite their differences, these leaders had agreed that universities would help anchor the amorphous new Republic.

From its founding in 1575, the University of Leiden was an international institution, an intellectual *pays sans frontières*. Eschewing strict confessionalism, Leiden permitted even Catholics to teach in its university. By the 1590s the library of the University of Leiden was one of the largest in Protestant Europe, and in the seventeenth century it was the largest international center for Protestants. At its height, between 1625 and 1650, over half the students at the University of Leiden were from countries other than the Dutch Republic. They came from Britain, Scandinavia, France, Hungary, Portugal, the German lands, and even

---

[19] Hsia and Nierop, *Calvinism and Religious Toleration*, 2.
[20] Judith Pollman, "The Bond of Christian Piety: The Individual Practice of Tolerance and Intolerance in the Dutch Republic," in *ibid.*, 53–71.

"the depths of Poland" to study theology, history, classical and oriental philology, Roman law, natural science, medicine, and Cartesian philosophy.[21] In his 1765 article on Leiden in the *Encyclopédie*, Denis Diderot wrote:

The academy of Leiden is the foremost in Europe. It seems that all the famous men of the Republic of Letters went there in order to make it flourish, from the time of its foundation right up to modern times.[22]

Among those famous *érudits* who came to Leiden as instructors and pupils were some of the foremost scholars in the republic of letters: Hugo Doneau, Joseph Scaliger, Hugo Grotius, Daniel Heinsius, Gerard Vossius, André Rivet, Pierre du Moulin, Frederik Spanheim, Charles Drelincourt, Johan Frederik Gronovius, Jean-Louis Guez de Balzac, Claude Saumaise, William Ames, and Pierre Bayle.[23]

However, Leiden's strength as a magnet for learned Europe did not depend on the University alone. Two dynasties of printer-publishers – the house of Plantin, and the house of Elsevier – were associated with the University of Leiden from its earliest years and throughout much of the seventeenth century. Christophe Plantin of Antwerp became official printer to the University of Leiden in 1583. Printers from France and Italy, attracted by Dutch religious tolerance and the quality of Plantin's press, fled censorship and religious repression to work with Plantin in Leiden. And the Elsevier dynasty, which had its greatest success under Bonaventure (1583–1652) and his brother Abraham (1592–1652), garnered a reputation in the republic of letters for both the beauty of their typefaces and the variety of their publications. Their fame as publishers and printers of classical and oriental texts, in addition to their productions of controversial contemporary works, attracted scholars to Plantin and *les Elsevier* from all over Europe; the group even included James Ussher, the learned Primate of Ireland.[24] The success of the University of Leiden was soon followed by the opening of three more

---

[21] Samuel Sorbière, *État des sciences en Hollande* (1660), in Bots and Waquet, *La République des Lettres*, 76.

[22] Denis Diderot, ed., "Leyde," in *Encyclopédie ou dictionnaire raisonné des sciences, des arts et des métiers*, 17 vols. (Paris, 1751–65), IX, 451.

[23] Dibon, *Regards*, 15–17; Hilde de Ridder-Symoens, *A History of the University*, vol. II: *Universities in Early Modern Europe (1500–1800)* (Cambridge, 1996), 423. Diderot's article in the *Encyclopédie* also added the names of Jan Dousa, Adrien Junius, Jean Cocceius, François Gomar, and Conrard Vorstius.

[24] On Plantin, see Dibon, *Regards*, 52. On the Elseviers, see A. Willems, *Les Elseviers*, in *Annales Typographiques* (Brussels, 1880); and David Davies, *The World of the Elseviers 1580–1712* (The Hague, 1954).

Dutch universities: Franeker (1585), Groningen (1614), and Utrecht (1636). In addition, the Netherlands founded a number of teaching academies, or *illustre* schools, which were universities in every respect save the privilege of awarding degrees.[25] Among the *érudits* tapped for governorships and professorships at *illustre* schools were Johann Friedrich Gronovius, Isaac Vossius, and André Rivet.

The presence of this international constellation of scholars meant that intellectual women in the Netherlands had access to a wide range of potential mentors. René Descartes, who would become the philosophical mentor of Princess Elisabeth, came from France to attend the University of Franeker in 1629. Gisbertus Voëtius, who would become van Schurman's religious mentor in the late 1630s, held the chair of theology at the University of Utrecht. André Rivet, van Schurman's other male mentor, fled the persecution of Huguenots in France to become a professor at the University of Leiden. Pierre du Moulin, the father of Marie du Moulin, was also a Huguenot and professor of philosophy at Leiden – and while he does not appear to have ever encouraged the scholarship of his daughter, he brought her into contact with Rivet, which led to her meeting those women who would indeed turn out to be her intellectual mentors.

Male scholars were also drawn to this geographical area as part of their participation in the scholarly world outside the walls of the Academy – the world of the republic of letters. And it is important to note that geography greatly facilitated these scholarly interactions. Amsterdam, Leiden, and Utrecht form a roughly equilateral triangle, with sides that are approximately 30 miles long. Moreover, The Hague lies less than ten miles southeast of Leiden, and the distance from Leiden to Endegeest, Descartes' hideaway, is less than three miles. Thus even in the seventeenth century, journeys between these Dutch cities and universities were easily accomplished. Samuel Sorbière, writing to Pierre Petit in 1657, recalled visiting Descartes in 1642:

I remarked with much pleasure the civility of this Gentleman, his retirement and his economy. He was in a little chateau in a lovely setting, at the gates of a grand and beautiful University, three leagues from the Court, and two short hours from the Sea ... He could spend part of the day in The Hague and then return to his lodgings, making the trip by the most beautiful route imaginable, passing fields and cottages, then the great forest that borders this Village [The Hague],

---

[25] Letters to André Rivet from Valentin Conrart of the Académie Française were addressed variously to the "Academy of Breda" and the "University of Breda." University of Leiden, MS. BPL 288, *Lettres de Conrart à A. Rivet, 1644–1650*.

comparable to the most beautiful Cities of Europe, and at this time superb due to the residence of three Courts.[26]

Thus for male students, and for members of the republic of letters making the *peregrinatio academica*, this particular part of the Netherlands was a rich and rewarding destination.

What, then, of the young female scholar? Given the early modern era's restrictions on appropriate public behavior for Christian women, there could be no attendance at university, and no *peregrinatio academica*. Where could she acquire a mentor, or a colleague, or even an acquaintance with other intellectual women? The answer, for a group of intellectual women in the 1630s, was the exile court of the Winter Queen at The Hague.

THE EXILE COURT IN THE HAGUE

Frederick V, the Elector Palatine, and his wife, Elizabeth Stuart, became known as the Winter King and the Winter Queen for a very good reason – their tenure as King and Queen of Bohemia had lasted only one winter. The largely Protestant Bohemian States had been chafing under the Habsburg yoke, and with the Holy Roman Emperor Matthias lying near death, the states had revolted against Habsburg rule on 23 May 1618. In the infamous Defenestration of Prague, Bohemian nobles flung two Imperial envoys from a window of the Hrdčany Castle. According to the Protestant version of the story, the envoys' lives were spared by a serendipitous manure pile; in the Catholic version, the envoy called upon Jesus and Mary as he fell, which "saved him from all harm despite his corpulent body."[27] The event proved to be the opening salvo of the Thirty Years' War, and the Bohemian States urged the Protestant Frederick V, the Elector Palatine, to accept the crown as King of Bohemia. Against the advice of almost everyone who might have helped his cause – including, most ominously, that of his father-in-law, King James I of England – Frederick accepted the crown. Thus, in November 1619, Frederick V and

---

[26] Letter 87, Sorbière à M. Petit, Conseiller du Roy et Intendant de ses fortifications, 10 novembre, 1657, in Samuel Sorbière, *Lettres et Discours de M. de Sorbiere sur diverses matieres curieuses* (Paris, 1660), 677. The three courts resident in The Hague at the time were those of the Prince of Orange, the States-General, and the exiled Queen of Bohemia.

[27] H. Schulz, ed., *Der Dreissigjaerige Krieg*, 1 (Leipzig, 1917), 31–2. See also Brennan C. Pursell, *The Winter King: Frederick V of the Palatinate and the Coming of the Thirty Years' War* (Aldershot, 2003), 43–8; and Henry Frederick Schwarz, *The Imperial Privy Council in the Seventeenth Century* (Cambridge, MA, 1943), 344–7.

his wife became the King and Queen of Bohemia – and one year later, in November 1620, Frederick's forces were crushed in the Battle of White Mountain and forced to flee. The King and Queen of Bohemia went into exile. They initially fled to the German lands, landing variously in Silesia and Brandenburg before settling in the Netherlands.

When "the unfortunate champion of the Protestant cause" arrived in The Hague, he and his Queen were granted the use of the Wassenaer Hof as a winter palace, in addition to a summer home at Rhenen.[28] In The Hague, Frederick and Elizabeth were received with all the ceremony befitting royal guests. With their retinue and royal display, they brought an unheard-of degree of glamor to the city. Their court attracted artists, scholars, and theologians from all over Europe. And, despite their status as heroes of the Protestant cause, the exile court also welcomed Catholic scholars, including René Descartes.

Frederick and Elizabeth had arrived in a part of the world already familiar with intellectual salons of various sorts. For example, the English Governor of Utrecht, Sir John Ogle, was hosting international gatherings in his home. His daughter Utricia, who would later correspond with van Schurman and Elisabeth, thus grew up in an intellectually challenging environment, one recalled with pleasure by the writer and tutor Sir Henry Peacham:

When I was in Utrecht, and lived at the table of that Honorable Gentleman, Sir John Ogle, Lord Governour, whither resorted many great Schollers and Captaines, English, Scottish, French, and Dutch, it had beene enough to have made a Scholler or Souldier, to have observed the severall disputations and discourses among many strangers, one while of sundry formes of battailes, sometime of Fortification; of Fire-workes, History, Antiquities, Heraldry, pronunciation of Languages, &c. that his table seemed many times a little Academie."[29]

In addition, the *Muiderkring*, or "Muiden Circle" was a literary and intellectual group that met near Amsterdam in the castle of Muiden between 1609 and 1625. The poet and historian Pieter Cornelis Hooft presided over the *Muiderkring* in self-conscious emulation of French salons, notably the *chambre bleue* of Mme de Rambouillet. Hooft assembled a glittering gathering of poets, musicians, artists, and scholars, in the hope that his coterie might become the nucleus of a reinvigorated Dutch culture. Pedantry was banished

---

[28] Jacques Bernot, *Les Palatins, Princes d'Europe* (Paris, 2000), 11–50; Marika Keblusek, "The Bohemian Court at The Hague," in *Princely Display: The Court of Frederik Hendrik of Orange and Amalia van Sohms*, ed. Marika Keblusek and Jori Zijlmans (The Hague, c.1997), 47–57.

[29] Sir Henry Peacham, *The Compleat Gentleman. Fashioning him absolut, in the most necessary and commendable Qualities* . . . (London, 1634), 231.

in accordance with the French example, but there was an extensive overlap between members of the *Muiderkring* and the republic of letters; for instance, the group also included two of the young van Schurman's earliest admirers – Constantijn Huygens, and Caspar Barlaeus.[30]

Thus a community of knowledge based primarily on *circulation* – the republic of letters – coalesced at one particular *locality* in time and space. That time was the 1630s, and that space was the exile court of the Winter Queen in The Hague. And in the midst of this heady mixture of artists and scholars at the crossroads of learned Europe, a group of intellectual women began to assemble. Together, they produced a formerly unnoticed and somewhat counterintuitive identity, one that was not individual, but rather collective and collegial – a network of female scholars who were members of the republic of letters.

First, of course, there was Princess Elisabeth herself. The exile court at The Hague was presided over by her mother, Queen Elizabeth of Bohemia. Then, in 1632, the Leiden professor and French theologian André Rivet became court chaplain and tutor to Prince William of Orange; and when Rivet came to The Hague, he did his utmost to ensure that the intellectual women of his acquaintance were introduced to one another. Foremost among these was the young woman who would become his *fille d'alliance*, Anna Maria van Schurman. Van Schurman was already a celebrated scholar in the republic of letters, but through Rivet she now was introduced to Elisabeth. In addition, Rivet brought his niece to court; this was Marie du Moulin, who would later be mentored by van Schurman and become a Hebrew scholar in her own right. The Scottish pastor John Dury was at the exile court as part of his constant peregrinations on behalf of ecumenicism; his co-religionist, fellow worker, and sister-in-Christ was Dorothy Moore. Through Dury and Rivet, Moore was introduced to the exile court, becoming friends with van Schurman.

Thus Elisabeth, van Schurman, Moore, and du Moulin were all physically present in The Hague, at the exile court, where they began to form an intellectual community in the 1630s. Gournay, Ranelagh, and Makin do not appear to have ever journeyed to the Netherlands in person. However, they were closely associated with the exile court through their

---

[30] Rosalie L. Colie, *"Some Thankfulnesse to Constantine": A Study of English Influence upon the Early Works of Constantijn Huygens* (The Hague, 1956), 55–7; Johannes Arend Dijkshoorn, *L'Influence Française dans les Moeurs et les Salons des Provinces-Unies*, Ph.D. dissertation, University of Groningen (Paris, 1925), 72–198; Thea van Kempen-Stijgers and Peter Rietbergen, "Constantijn Huygens en Engeland," in Hans Bots, ed., *Constantijn Huygens: Zijn Plaats in Geleerd Europa* (Amsterdam, 1973), 77–141.

connections to the intellectual men and women there. Ranelagh was both a friend of John Dury and a correspondent of Queen Elizabeth of Bohemia; most importantly, she was also the lifelong friend and patron of Moore. And Makin, who participated in John Dury's educational reform circles, was introduced to van Schurman through Sir Simonds D'Ewes, who corresponded with both Rivet and the Queen of Bohemia. Thus the exile court at The Hague was the initial magnet drawing these intellectual women together at the crossroads of the republic of letters.

The balance of this chapter will show how Princess Elisabeth adapted one of the crucial systems that constituted the engine of the republic of letters, turning the exile court in The Hague into a privileged place for the networking of intellectual women in 1634.

ELISABETH, PRINCESS PALATINE (1618–80)

In 1657, the French physician Samuel Sorbière described a visit he had made decades earlier to the exile court at The Hague:

> The Court of the Queen of Bohemia was that of the Graces, who numbered no less than four, since her Majesty had four daughters, around whom everyone in society in The Hague would gather every day, to pay homage to the wit and beauty of these Princesses.[31]

As Sorbière noted, the exile court was essentially a female-directed space: Frederick had died in 1632, and the Winter Queen's sons, Karl Ludwig, Maurice, and Rupert, were in residence at other courts, acquiring military and diplomatic skills. Although all four of the Princesses Palatine were lively and accomplished, Sorbière was most impressed with Elisabeth, the eldest of these four Graces:

> Wonders were told of this rare personage: that to the knowledge of languages she added that of the sciences; that she was not the least bit pleased with the trivialities of her schooling, but wished to understand things clearly; that for this pursuit she had a perfectly suited mind, and a solid judgment; that she took pleasure in listening to Descartes; that she read deep into the night; that she taught herself to perform dissections and experiments; that in her palace there was a minister who was considered to be a Socinian. It appears that she was about twenty years old; her beauty and commanding presence were truly those of a Heroine.[32]

---

[31] Sorbière, *Lettres et Discours*, 677.
[32] Samuel Sorbière, *Sorberiana: ou Bons mots, rencontres agreables, et pensées judicieuses* ... (Paris, 1694), 85–6.

This passage reflects both the praise that was accorded to Elisabeth and the constant level of concern raised by her wide-ranging investigations into philosophy and faith. Socinianism was a heresy in the Calvinist Netherlands; it was an anti-Trinitarian theology that attempted to apply a rational approach to Scripture, treating the sacraments as symbolic acts. Moreover, "dissections and experiments" were quite literally the cutting edge of Baconian New Learning – and while we have no further proof that Sorbière's claims were correct, these suspicions alone were cause for alarm. Socinianism and surgeries aside, however, this was a description with which everyone agreed.

Elisabeth was often known as "La Grecque" among her family members, both for her knowledge of Greek and for her devotion to the study of philosophy. This penchant for intellectual activity put Elisabeth somewhat out of step with the gaiety of her mother's court, where hunting was the favored pastime. Although she was a very cultivated woman, Queen Elizabeth of Bohemia had no interest in intellectual pursuits and had chosen to deal with adversity by being "of my old wild humor to be as merry as I can"; presumably, then, she was quite puzzled by her serious eldest daughter.[33] In her *Memoirs*, Sophie recalled the young Elisabeth, who apparently was a puzzle to her siblings as well:

Louise was lively and unaffected; Elisabeth very learned – she knew every language and every science under the sun, and corresponded regularly with Descartes. This great learning, however, by making her rather absent-minded, often became the subject of our mirth.

In true sisterly fashion, Sophie then goes on to focus on Elisabeth's worst feature:

My sister, who was called Mme. Elisabeth, had black hair, a dazzling complexion, brown sparkling eyes, a well-shaped forehead, beautiful cherry lips, and a sharp aquiline nose, which was rather apt to turn red. She loved study, but all her philosophy could not save her from vexation when her nose was red. At such times she hid herself from the world. I remember that my sister, Princess Louise, who was not so sensitive, asked her on one such unlucky occasion to come upstairs to the Queen, as it was the usual hour for visiting her. Princess Elisabeth said, "Would you have me go with this nose?" The other replied, "Will you wait till you get another?"[34]

---

[33] Elizabeth Godfrey, *A Sister of Prince Rupert* (London, 1909), 67–8; and Benger, *Memoirs of Elizabeth Stuart*, II, 356–7.

[34] Sophie of Hanover, *The Memoirs of Sophia, Electress of Hanover 1630–1680*, trans. H. Forester (London, 1888), 14–15. Sophia (1630–1714) married Ernst Augustus, the Duke of Brunswick; their

Elisabeth's brothers and sisters appear to have accepted her scholarly distraction. For the purposes of this study, however, Sophie's memoirs still raise a large and largely unanswered question: how and where did Elisabeth manage to obtain her undisputed depth of learning?

Elisabeth had been born at Heidelberg on December 26, 1618, into a chaotic, dispersed, and constantly expanding family. In eighteen years of marriage, the King and Queen of Bohemia produced thirteen children. Five of these were daughters, and Elisabeth was the eldest of the four surviving princesses. The children spent their early years at the courts of various relatives, and Elisabeth's mother had very little to do with her early upbringing. In fact, according to Sophie, "the Queen my mother . . . had her whole family brought up apart from herself, preferring the sight of her monkeys and dogs to that of her children."[35] Thus when Frederick and Elizabeth fled to the Netherlands, Elisabeth and her brother Karl Ludwig remained in Heidelberg. They were placed in the care of Frederick's mother, the dowager Electress Juliana van Stolberg, who then took them to Berlin to be raised by her daughter Elisabeth Charlotte, the children's aunt. In later years, Elisabeth would return to this place, describing it in a letter to Descartes as her only real home, "the house where I have been cherished since my childhood and where every one conspires to take care of me."[36] It was not until 1628, at the age of ten, that Elisabeth joined her parents in The Hague.

The education received by the Princesses Palatine was apparently a standard combination for Protestant women of their rank. Schooling in mathematics was reserved for the boys, while embroidery was reserved for the girls. All the royal children learned history, geography, drawing, lute playing, and dancing. On the one hand, this education inculcated strict Calvinist principles, while on the other hand the princesses became proficient in the French, dancing, and manners that were required at

---

son became King George I of England, the first of the Hanoverian line. "Louise" refers to their sister Louise Hollandine (1622–1709). Louise converted to Catholicism in 1658 and became the Abbess of Maubuisson in France.

[35] *Ibid.*, 3. I am quoting here from the delightful nineteenth-century English translation of Sophie's *Mémoires*, because it is both lively and accurate. The original French text can be found in Sophie de Hanovre, *Mémoires et Lettres de voyage*, ed. Dirk van der Cruysse (Mesnil-sur-l'Estreée, 1990). The autograph manuscript of this document is no longer extant. However, a seventeenth-century copy was made by Gottfried Wilhelm von Leibniz, Sophie's friend and correspondent, and the *Mémoires* survived among his papers. *Memoirs of Sophia*, xiv–xv.

[36] Princess Elisabeth, Berlin, to René Descartes, Egmond, 10 October [1646], in *The Correspondence between Princess Elisabeth of Bohemia and René Descartes*, 146. See also Keblusek, "The Bohemian Court at The Hague," 50–1.

court. Elisabeth has left no record of her education, but we may assume that it did not really differ from that given to her sister Sophie:

I learned the Heidelberg catechism in German, and knew it by heart, without understanding a word of it. I rose at seven in the morning, and was obliged to go every day *en déshabillé* to Mlle. Marie de Quat ... who made me pray and read the Bible. She then set me to learn the "Quadrains de Pebrac," while she employed the time in brushing her teeth; her grimaces during this performance are more firmly fixed in my memory than the lessons which she tried to teach. I was then dressed and prepared by half-past eight to endure the regular succession of teacher after teacher.

They kept me busy until ten o'clock, except when, to my comfort, kind Providence sent them a cold in the head. At ten o'clock the dancing-master was always welcome, for he gave me exercise till eleven, which was the dinner hour ... On Sundays and Wednesdays two divines or two professors were always invited to dine with us ... After dinner I rested till two o'clock, when my teachers returned to the charge. At six I supped, and at half-past eight went to bed, having said my prayers and read some chapters in the Bible.[37]

Unsurprisingly, Sophie goes on to tell us that her only object was "to give up study when I had acquired all that was necessary, and be no longer forced to endure the weariness of learning."[38]

Somehow, however, Elisabeth managed to transcend this dreary litany. Descartes' biographer Baillet, writing in 1691, described her learning this way:

This princess had been schooled in the knowledge of a great number of languages, and in everything that is comprehended under the name of *belles-lettres*. But the loftiness and depth of her genius did not in the least allow her to end her studies at this point, where the most accomplished wits of her sex, who wish only to shine, ordinarily call a halt. She wanted to move beyond, to those studies that demanded the most intense efforts of men, and she made herself adept in philosophy and mathematics ...[39]

Yet Baillet does not explain how Elisabeth might have managed to "make herself adept" in these unprincess-like subjects, and we have no explanation for the gap between Elisabeth's learning and that of her sisters. Elisabeth knew English, French, German, Dutch, Latin, and Italian, and her knowledge of mathematics, physics, and philosophy were such that

---

[37] "Quadrains de Pebrac" is a reference to the popular sixteenth-century educational work *Fifty Quatrains, containing useful Precepts for the Guidance of Man* by Gui de Faur Pibrac. See the introduction by H. Forester to *Memoirs of Sophia*, 4–6.

[38] *Ibid.*, 6–7.

[39] Adrien Baillet, *La Vie de Monsieur Descartes* [1691], 5th edn. ([Paris], 1946), 214–15.

she consistently challenged Descartes to clarify and refine his arguments. It seems most probable that she might have followed or been present for the lessons being given to her brothers, and then enhanced this second-hand education by reading voraciously on her own.

Baillet concludes by stating that Elisabeth's intellectual life was transformed at the point where she encountered the works of Descartes:

... having read the philosophical Essays of M. Descartes, she conceived such a passion for his doctrine, that she counted as nothing all that she had learned before, and placed herself under his tutelage in order to raise a new edifice to his principles.[40]

Descartes, of course, is one of the giants of intellectual history. He stands among those credited with having swept away the last vestiges of medieval superstition and "the smell of the schools," laying out the mathematical, objective, and secular path that knowledge-making would follow for centuries to come. In terms of its intellectual content, then, the relationship between Elisabeth and Descartes has been seen as clearly hierarchical; while Elisabeth is considered to have been the perfect pupil, she is deemed to have learned everything at the feet of this master:

Never did a master profit more from the docility, penetration, and at the same time the solidity of mind in a disciple. Having accustomed her imperceptibly to profound meditation of Nature's greatest mysteries, and having given her sufficient practice in the most abstract problems of geometry and on the most sublime problems of metaphysics, he had nothing to hide from her, and he had no trouble at all recognizing that he had never before found anyone other than she ... who had arrived at a perfect understanding of the works he had published up to that point.[41]

Following Baillet, scholars over the past 300 years have continued to characterize Elisabeth as Descartes' most apt pupil – his disciple, his would-be patron, and his muse. Her mind was a "magic mirror" in which Descartes' original masculine ideas were reflected back to him, cloaked now in "grace and femininity."[42] Suggestions that Elisabeth had a schoolgirl's crush on Descartes, who had been born in the same year as her late father Frederick, continue to be made even today. Elisabeth is alleged to have made improper and unwanted visits to Descartes in his retreat, and these visits are sometimes given as the reason behind his flight from Endegeest, near The Hague, to the more distant Egmond.

[40] *Ibid.*   [41] *Ibid.*
[42] Gustave Cohen, *Écrivains français en Hollande dans la Première Moitié du XVIIe Siècle* (Paris, 1920), 605.

These assumptions have in all likelihood been based on a misreading of one of Sorbière's anecdotes. In *Sorberiana*, under the heading "*ELIZABET DE BOHEME*," Sorbière recounted one of the entertainments invented by the high-spirited Princesses Palatine:

During my time there, which was 1642, court ladies in Holland would amuse themselves by going in boats from The Hague to Delft or Leiden, dressed like *bourgeoises*, and mingling with the crowds, so they could overhear what was being said about the Nobility . . . Elisabeth, the eldest of the Princesses of Bohemia, was sometimes of this party.[43]

It has been assumed that one of the destinations for these trips had been Descartes' home in Endegeest, and the anecdote is cited as proof that Elisabeth imposed herself on Descartes.

One is not overly surprised to find this assumption in older scholarship on Elisabeth and Descartes. For instance, Elizabeth Godfrey, writing in 1909, assumes these visits took place, although she views these supposed episodes through a lens of innocence and curiosity:

Would that a fuller record of these visits than de Sorbière's fleeting mention had survived! How much we should like to know on what lines the talk ran, what part the Princess bore in it, who were the other members of the company, and whether the Philosopher showed himself more the deep thinker . . . or the kindly host, the agreeable man of the world, drawing from the lighter store of his learning for the entertainment of his visitors. Well, we shall never know, and imagination here must be allowed some little play.[44]

And Gustave Cohen, writing in 1920, gives this unsubstantiated episode a further spin into melodrama, heartbreak, and intrigue:

[Descartes] was there, at Endegeest, he had only to traverse the woods of Wassenaer and The Hague in order to arrive at her feet, but precisely because he was too close to her, because she had visited him in a too-small house, he was afraid, and the fact that it was he who first ran away from her is precisely the proof of his love. This is not mentioned in the Treatise on the Passions, but it is inscribed for all eternity in the heart of man.[45]

Cohen then attempts a further qualification, turning the forbidden love between Elisabeth and Descartes into a Cartesian *amour intellectuel,* "where two minds came together and permeated each other with that hidden tenderness and sensitivity that possesses all the charm of love."[46]

---

[43] Sorbière, *Sorberiana*, 85–6.   [44] Godfrey, *A Sister of Prince Rupert*, 98–9.
[45] Cohen, *Écrivains français*, 605–7.   [46] *Ibid.*, 607.

It is, however, much more puzzling to see these assumptions repeated in modern scholarship. Vrooman's 1970 biography of Descartes uncritically repeats all of Cohen's assertions.[47] And Andrea Nye, in her 1999 philosophical analysis of the Descartes–Elisabeth correspondence, dismisses these suppositions concerning Descartes' flight as just that – suppositions. Yet Nye continually suggests that there may indeed have been a budding romance there. For example:

> Imaginary clandestine visits aside, perhaps this sober, rational man has caught a fleeting, tantalizing scent of romance as he sat in Egmond in yet another rented garden. Might he have savored it as he would the odor of a particularly fragrant old rose? Did he dream just a little that this young woman might indeed be the one ... had he finally the hope of finding the feminine "cogito," soul mate to the modern rational man?[48]

These allusions, old and new, are wholly unsubstantiated. There is absolutely no evidence of a forbidden romance between Elisabeth and Descartes. However, Descartes is still seen as having been much more than a colleague, teacher, friend, and mentor to his brilliant philosophical apprentice. He is cast as the magnetic master, while her role is that of the acolyte, the *tabula rasa* whose intellectual pliancy must be accounted as one of her greatest assets.

This simply was not the case. Elisabeth's strength of mind and powerful allegiances had been evident at an early age. From her earliest years to the very end of her life, there were three areas – scholarship, faith, and politics – with which she perpetually engaged. She had an acute and open-minded intelligence, interested in philosophy, ethics, and science; an abiding devotion to the Protestant faith; and a primary identification of herself as royalty, with both Palatine and Stuart blood and an unswerving dedication to the reinstatement of her family's former glory. Certainly, Descartes was an extremely powerful and important intellectual influence in the life of Princess Elisabeth. However, she was far from pliant, and it was often Descartes who was compelled to make adjustments, to refine his propositions in the light of Elisabeth's questions and criticisms. Moreover, Descartes was not the first scholarly mentor in Elisabeth's life, nor was he the last.

Elisabeth had formed connections to contemporary philosophers before she encountered Descartes, and she would correspond with other

[47] Jack R. Vrooman, *René Descartes: A Biography* (New York, 1970), 153–4; Elizabeth Haldane, *Descartes: His Life and Times* (London, 1905), 172.
[48] Nye, *The Princess and the Philosopher*, 20.

thinkers, such as Leibniz and Malebranche, after Descartes' death. In The Hague, at her mother's court, Elisabeth had begun working with another intellectual mentor to whom she would be close throughout her life – a woman, Anna Maria van Schurman And prior to her correspondence with Descartes, Elisabeth's neo-Stoicism was already evident in a letter she wrote to her cousin, commiserating with her on the loss of her father.[49] Elisabeth's own father had died in 1632, thus she was familiar with the pain that early loss could bring. Yet in addition to offering condolences, the seventeen-year-old Elisabeth encouraged her cousin to take a philosophical approach:

This, and the affection I have for you, Mademoiselle, obliges me to beg you as one of your servants, to moderate the justifiable suffering this affliction has caused you. I know the enormity of it through the experience which is still so fresh in my memory, and so I will not burden you with the reasons, which you already know.[50]

By suggesting that choosing to "moderate" her feelings would be the correct way for her cousin to deal with grief, Elisabeth is giving evidence of her engagement with Stoicism. Ten years later, in her correspondence with Descartes, Elisabeth will reveal the roots of this approach, when she discusses her extensive early reading of Seneca.

Although they had met earlier in The Hague, their epistolary relationship did not begin until after October 1642, when Descartes asked their mutual friend Alphonse Pollot to engineer a reintroduction and official visit:

I had before now already heard so many marvels concerning the excellent mind of Mademoiselle the Princess of Bohemia, that I was hardly surprised to learn that she reads works of metaphysics, since I consider myself fortunate in that having deigned to read those written by me, she gives evidence that she does not disapprove of them; and I think more of her judgment than that of those Doctors who, for laws of truth, prefer the opinions of Aristotle to the evidence of reason.[51]

---

[49] This cousin, Elisabeth Louise, would become the Abbess of the Lutheran abbey at Herford, Westphalia, in 1649. Princess Elisabeth would join her there in 1661 as coadjutrix, and then succeed her as Abbess upon Elisabeth Louise's death in 1667.

[50] Elisabeth to Elisabeth Louise, Pfalzgräfin von Zweibrücken. Rhenen, 3/13 October [1635], in Karl Hauck, "Die Briefe der Kinder des Winterkönigs," *Neue Heidelberger Jahrbücher* 15 (1908): 2–3. See also Creese, "The Letters of Elisabeth," 54–6.

[51] Descartes to Pollot, October 6, 1642. Letter no. CCLXXXIII in *Oeuvres de Descartes*, III, 577. Alphonse Pollot (*c.*1604–68), a Huguenot exile, worked as an administrator in the house of Orange in The Hague.

Descartes went on to say that he would come to The Hague to speak with the anti-Aristotelian princess just as soon as Pollot could set up the meeting. Pollot did as Descartes requested, and this philosophical friendship had begun.

Elisabeth was a very different sort of scholar from her friend van Schurman, in that the prime factor determining Descartes' high estimate of Elisabeth's mind was not her erudition, but rather her willingness and ability to embrace the new learning. The first extant letter from this correspondence shows, moreover, that Elisabeth was taking immediate advantage of her newfound ability to go directly to the Cartesian source. After a paragraph of courtesies, she launched right in with her questions concerning some problems with the theory of mind–body interaction in Descartes' philosophy:

> For it seems that all determination of movement happens through the impulsion of the thing moved, by the manner in which it is pushed by that which moves it, or else by the particular qualities and shape of the surface of the latter. Physical contact is required for the first two conditions, extension for the third. You entirely exclude the one [extension] from the notion that you have of the soul, and the other [physical contact] appears to me incompatible with an immaterial thing. This is why I ask you for a more precise definition of the soul than the one you give in your Metaphysics . . .[52]

Descartes was then forced to think this through again, and the tone was set.

There are fifty-eight extant letters in this correspondence, which lasted from 1643 to 1649, and Elisabeth's rigorous demands for clarification remained consistent throughout. She did not permit Descartes to remain vague or abstract. She insisted that Descartes explain his theories of extension and mind–body interaction in terms of real bodies, including real bodies gendered female. She also consistently raised moral and ethical issues, which formed a large segment of their correspondence. Her extensive involvement in state and family politics brought her face-to-face with urgent and complex questions – questions of how to weigh personal interest against the greater good, of how to overcome natural inclinations in order to follow a necessary path, and of needing to either use or ignore one's passions in order to arrive at rational judgments. These were not

---

[52] Elisabeth to Descartes, May 6, 1643, in *The Correspondence between Princess Elisabeth of Bohemia and René Descartes*, trans. Lisa Shapiro (Chicago and London, 2007), 61–2. Descartes, *Oeuvres*, ed. Adam and Tannery, III, 660–2. Shapiro points out that it was Elisabeth who first clearly articulated the mind–body problem, still a central issue in philosophy today.

puzzles for future reflection, but rather pressing realities requiring immediate action. And in response to Elisabeth's prodding, Descartes was
forced to clarify and refine his thoughts on all these subjects.

However, the conversation between Elisabeth and Descartes was not only
philosophical, but mathematical as well; and in 1645, when Descartes published his *Principia*, an explanation of his physics and metaphysics, he dedicated the work to Princess Elisabeth, as someone who had the rare ability to
understand all the multiple facets of his thinking. First Elisabeth is addressed as
a generic royal dedicatee, then she is addressed as a learned aristocratic woman.
In the next section, however, Descartes finally gets specific and addresses what
it is that sets Elisabeth apart from all other scholars:

you are the only person I have so far found who has completely understood all
my previously published works. Many other people, even those of the utmost
acumen and learning, find them very obscure; and it generally happens with
almost everyone else that if they are accomplished in Metaphysics they hate
Geometry, while if they have mastered Geometry they do not grasp what I have
written on First Philosophy. Your intellect is, to my knowledge, unique in
finding everything equally clear; and this is why my use of the term "incomparable" is quite deserved.[53]

Thus it was Elisabeth's remarkable breadth as a scholar, her ability to engage
with both philosophy and mathematics on a profound level, which set her
apart not only from other learned women, but from learned men as well.

Elisabeth was also part of a circle engaged in mathematical letter-writing,
in which problems were posed and correspondents attempted to find
solutions. She had learned her mathematics from Jan Stampioen (1610–90),
who was in The Hague to tutor Prince William of Orange and who
also instructed the young Christiaan Huygens. The brash young
Stampioen, however, had managed to offend Descartes in 1638 by publishing a treatise called *Algebra ofte Nieuwe Stel-Regel* [Algebra, or The New
Method], which Descartes interpreted as an attempt to tread on his own
computational turf.[54] A major mathematical quarrel ensued. It went on
for nearly two years, involving the mathematicians Golius, van Schooten,
Wassenaer, and Schotanus, as well as an alarmed Constantijn Huygens.
The quarrel was replete with challenges, a trigonometrical duel, wagers,
seconds, and – finally – the necessity of a signed and witnessed peace treaty.

[53] Dedication "To Her Serene Highness the Princess Elisabeth . . . " from René Descartes, *Principles of Philosophy*, in *The Philosophical Writings of Descartes*, trans. John Cottingham, Robert Stoothoff, and Dugald Murdoch, 2 vols. (Cambridge, 1985), i, 192.
[54] Stephen Gaukroger, *Descartes: An Intellectual Biography* (Oxford, 1995), 334–5.

Huygens wrote a rather long letter to Descartes on December 28, 1639, enraged at Stampioen's refusal to *signer le compromis*, and quite ashamed of himself over the fact that he had lost his own temper with this "impertinent and unjust squabbler."[55]

However, this same erroneous and detestable squabbler was the teacher from whom Elisabeth had apparently learned her mathematics. So after sending Elisabeth the famously difficult problem of the three circles, Descartes had second thoughts:

> I feel rather badly about having lately posed the problem of the three circles to Mademoiselle the Princess of Bohemia, because it is so difficult that I do not see how even an angel, who had had no lessons in Algebra other than the ones that Stampioen would have given her, could possibly solve it without some miracle.[56]

However, Elisabeth had already come up with her own solution. And while Elisabeth knew her solution worked, she also knew it could be better – so she had deliberately decided to push on, calculating that her solution would prod Descartes into responding with a demonstration of his new algebraic method. Her strategy worked. Descartes praised Elisabeth for a solution "so just that it is not possible to desire anything more," and was particularly pleased that "the calculation which your Highness used is entirely similar to that which I proposed in my Geometry." He then showed her how to solve it in a new way, giving her "the keys to my Algebra."[57]

This particular exchange became quite famous in the republic of letters, and the philosophical Elisabeth gained a new reputation as a hard-headed mathematician. Descartes' geometry was notoriously difficult. Voltaire, in fact, pointed out a century later that only two men in all of Europe had understood it:

> This Geometry . . . was so abstruse in his Time, that not so much as one Professor would undertake to explain it; and Schotten in Holland, and Fermat in France, were the only Men who understood it.[58]

---

[55] Huygens to Descartes, 28 December, 1639. Letter no. 2289 in *De Briefwisseling van Constantijn Huygens 1608–1687*, ed. J. A. Worp, 6 vols. (The Hague, 1911–17), II, 519–20. On the quarrel itself, see Charles Adam, *Vie & Oeuvres de Descartes: Étude Historique*, in Descartes, *Oeuvres*, XII, 272–80.

[56] Descartes to Pollot, October 21, 1643, in Descartes, *Oeuvres*, IV, 25–7. In the problem of the three circles, also known as Apollonius' problem, there are three given circles. The challenge is to find the radius of a fourth circle whose circumference touches the circumferences of the other three.

[57] Descartes to Elisabeth, November 29, 1643, in *The Correspondence between Princess Elisabeth of Bohemia and René Descartes*, 78; Descartes, *Oeuvres*, IV, 45–50.

[58] Letter XIV, "On Des Cartes and Sir Isaac Newton," in Voltaire, *Letters Concerning the English Nation, by Mr. de Voltaire* (London, 1733), 118. It should be kept in mind that Voltaire was overstating his case in order to make a point about contemporary anti-Cartesian attitudes.

Yet Voltaire had omitted the one woman who should have been added to this small list – Princess Elisabeth of Bohemia.

Another one of Descartes' quarrels – this time with van Schurman's mentor, Voëtius – serves to illustrate the functioning of the republic of letters, and Elisabeth's role within it. Descartes was an intellectual brawler; he was repeatedly involved in protracted disputes, such as the mathematical quarrel with Stampioen, that went on for years, and from which he refused to back down. Thus we find Andreas Colvius writing to Elisabeth in 1643 about their shared desire to bring an end to the *querelle d'Utrecht*, a fierce and bitter controversy between Descartes and Voëtius that lasted from 1639 until Descartes' death in 1650.[59]

Colvius, a minister in Dordrecht, had been connected with the *Muiderkring*, as well as the circle that gathered at Château Develstein, and it was here that he had first met the young van Schurman.[60] On June 9, 1643, Colvius wrote a letter to Descartes in which he was simultaneously blunt and heartbroken. Voëtius and Descartes were theological and philosophical leaders who had a duty to their fellow men; could they not see that this dispute was a large-scale tragedy that hurt everyone?[61] And on that same day, Colvius wrote a letter to Elisabeth. Although they had met twice before, he knew that he was being bold in doing this. However, he had heard from mutual friends that she would probably welcome an ally in her attempts to bring an end to the dispute, so he was sending her a copy of what he had just sent to Descartes.[62]

Moreover, as a bonus, Colvius sent Elisabeth something extra:

In addition, I am sending you something concerning astronomy, which was just sent to me from Maslines. The cappuchin De Rheita must answer for the problems that the learned Dr. Pell has put before him, or he will be taken for a dreamer or an impostor. I hope to have more news soon.[63]

---

[59] On the dispute, see René Descartes and Martin Schook, *La querelle d'Utrecht [Querela apologetica ad amplissimum magistratum Ultrajectinum]*, trans. Theo Verbeek (Paris, 1988); and J. A. van Ruler, *The Crisis of Causality: Voetius and Descartes on God, Nature and Change* (Leiden, 1995).

[60] G. D. J. Schotel, *Anna Maria van Schurman* ('S Hertogenbosch, 1853), 23. On Andreas Colvius (1594–1671), see C. Louise Thijssen-Schoute, "Een Correspondent van Descartes: Andreas Colvius," *Nederlands Archief voor Kerkgeschiedenis*, n.s., no. 38 (1952): 224–48.

[61] Colvius refers to Descartes' *Lettre Apologetique de M. Descartes, aux magistrats de la ville d'Utrecht, Contre Messieurs Voëtius, Pere & Fils*. Andreas Colvius to René Descartes, June 9, 1643. Letter no. cccvi in Descartes, *Oeuvres*, iii, 680–2.

[62] Colvius to Elisabeth, June 9, 1643, in C. Louise Thijssen-Schoute, *Nederlands Cartesianisme* (Amsterdam, 1954), 566–7.

[63] *Ibid.*

The "cappuchin De Rheita" was Anton Maria Schyrle von Rheita, a Czech astronomer and Capuchin friar who was circulating a letter claiming that he had found five new planets around Jupiter.[64] Von Rheita also developed a binocular telescope, called "Enoch's Eye," which was the precursor to modern binoculars. This letter makes it clear that Elisabeth was on the forefront of new developments in astronomy and optics, and that she was familiar with the work of Bathsua Makin's brother-in-law, the mathematician John Pell. It also presents us with a new side of Elisabeth's scholarship and another view of her vigorous participation in the advancement of learning. John Pell and Pierre Gassendi both received copies of the letter; both wrote critical responses. Gassendi asserted that the bodies Von Rheita had taken for planets were merely fixed stars; Pell, lacking a telescope of his own, instead raised a series of logical objections in a letter to Sir William Boswell. Von Rheita's letter, together with both sets of objections, had come to Colvius, and Colvius had sent them to Elisabeth.[65]

Elisabeth responded within weeks. First, she assured Colvius that she had indeed been happy to hear from him and was happy to have his help in trying "to introduce peace and reciprocal kindness among the learned." The war between Voëtius and Descartes was no less destructive, in her view, than the wars made by princes.[66] She then went on to give her opinion of the letter, and the new astronomical developments:

I could wish that its author (and Rheita, too) had helped us to understand his knowledge, before having us admire it. The Count of Arundel has heard so many wonders of this person, that he has resolved to go see his Enoch's Eye; and if he continues in his resolution to travel from Cologne to this country, I am certain that he will bring us the instrument itself, if it is for sale, or at least a more specific account of its construction, which I will send to you immediately, should it merit being seen by you.[67]

[64] Anton Maria Schyrle von Rheita (1597–1660) is known primarily for his work in optics, and he was the maker of Kepler's telescope. His 1643 letter was entitled *Novem stellae circa Jovem visae, circa Saturnum sex, circa Martem nonnullae* (Louvain, 1643).

[65] See Descartes' letter to Colvius of April 23, 1643, thanking him for the receipt of von Rheita's letter, and reporting Gassendi's objections, in Descartes, *Oeuvres*, III, 646–7. Noel Malcolm's interpretation of this exchange is that Princess Elisabeth received the letters first, and then circulated them among her friends, including Colvius. However, given the content of Elisabeth's response, it seems more likely that it was Colvius who possessed these letters first. Noel Malcolm and Jacqueline Stedall, *John Pell (1611–1685) and His Correspondence with Sir Charles Cavendish: The Mental World of an Early Modern Mathematician* (Oxford, 2005), 97–8.

[66] Elisabeth to Colvius, June 23, 1643, in Descartes, *Oeuvres*, VIII, part 2, 196–7.

[67] *Ibid.*

Thus Elisabeth, the mathematician and philosopher, was also a participant in scientific networks. She was concerned not only in the circulation of ideas, but in the circulation of scientific instruments, and their construction.

Elisabeth's tenacity as a scholar was consistent with other areas of her life, and a failed negotiation for her hand serves as another instance illustrating her independence of mind and unwillingness to compromise. This time, the issue was her faith; and despite the breadth of her spiritual explorations, her identity as a Protestant was clearly non-negotiable. As early as 1631, when Elisabeth was thirteen, negotiations had been underway for a match between the Calvinist princess and the Catholic Wladislaus IV, Prince of Poland; then, when Wladislaus succeeded to the throne, the suit was renewed. The tentative negotiations were carried on over a five-year period. Wladislaus desired the match in order to form an alliance with England; then, with England's support, he hoped to regain the throne of Sweden, a throne his father had lost when deposed by Gustavus Adolphus in 1599. However, it was highly unlikely that Elisabeth's mother, an icon of the Protestant cause, would ever have agreed to a scheme that involved deposing Queen Christina, the Lutheran monarch of Sweden, and this is confirmed by a letter she wrote to Sir Thomas Roe. The Queen often felt free to give voice to her opinions in writing to her old friend Roe, an English diplomat and scholar whom she had known since childhood.[68] Thus in February 1635, the Queen wrote: "For the Polish business, you may see by what I wrote to you by Mr. Dury, that his last proposition did much scandalise me, for I cannot find it in my heart to consent that [Gustavus Adolphus'] child should be disinherited, to whom we have had all so much obligation."[69]

It would have been an important match for the unfortunate family living in exile in The Hague. In fact, the Venetian Ambassador considered their poverty to be an insurmountable problem:

The lady is certainly full of grace and worthy to be the consort of any prince, however great; but the misfortunes and the weakness of her house render the affair improbable.[70]

---

[68] Thomas Roe had befriended Elizabeth during her childhood, when he was at the court of her father, King James I. On Roe, see Samuel Rawson Gardiner, *Letters Relating to the Mission of Sir Thomas Roe to Gustavus Adolphus, 1629–30*, Camden Miscellany, Volume 7 ([Westminster], 1875); and Michael Strachan, *Sir Thomas Roe, 1581–1644: A Life* (Salisbury, 1989).

[69] Queen Elizabeth of Bohemia to Thomas Roe, February 11/21, 1635, *CSPD* 1635, 509. This letter also shows that John Dury was already a trusted presence at the exile court in 1635. Mary Anne Everett Green, *Elizabeth, Electress Palatine and Queen of Bohemia*, revised by S. C. Lomas (London, 1909), 326–30; Creese, "The Letters of Elisabeth," 46–9.

[70] Franceso Michiel, Venetian Ambassador at The Hague, to the Doge and Senate. December 14, 1634, *CSPV* 1632–36, 305.

Yet despite the disparity in fortune, the Polish prince pursued the match. There was, however, a catch: the Polish people had made it clear to their king that they would not tolerate a Protestant queen. As Elisabeth's elder brother Karl Ludwig wrote to their mother: "Concerning the Polish business ... he needs not the States of Poland's consent to do it; but it seemeth he seeketh all means to do it with their good-will, and for that wishes she may be of their religion."[71] Thus Princess Elisabeth would have to convert to Catholicism.

The Polish Prince's wishes for Elisabeth's conversion would come to naught, since she resolutely refused to become a Catholic. And in the end, Elisabeth's mother was neither for the match nor against it; as far as she was concerned, Elisabeth's wishes were beside the point. In a letter to Roe, the Queen pointed out that she just wanted to make sure that everything worked out in the best interests of her son:

For myself, if it be found good for my son's affairs, and good conditions for religion, I shall be content with it; else, I assure you, I shall not desire it, my son being more dear to me than all my daughters.[72]

Despite the relative unimportance of Elisabeth in her mother's schemes, it appears that the Queen eventually supported her daughter's religious stand.[73] Indeed, it must have become a family joke, since in a later letter, Karl Ludwig wrote to the Queen: "I shewed both to the king & to the Archbishop that which you write about the Polish Ambassadours discours they made them selves very mery with it."[74] Ten years later, however, this family joke would have less than merry consequences.

In 1645, Elisabeth's beloved brother Edward married a French princess, Anne de Gonzague. In financial terms, it was a good match for the landless prince. But in terms of faith and family, the match was a disaster. Anne de Gonzague was fervently Catholic, and Edward had abjured in order to marry her. This was an enormous blow to his family on two levels. The first level was public, because of the Winter Queen's symbolic power as a

---

[71] The Elector Charles Louis [Karl Ludwig] to the Queen of Bohemia, 16 May, 1636, in Sir George Bromley, ed., *A Collection of Original Royal Letters, Written by King Charles the First and Second, King James the Second, and the King and Queen of Bohemia ... And Several other distinguished Persons; from the Year 1619 to 1665* (London, 1787), 69–71.

[72] Queen Elizabeth of Bohemia to Thomas Roe, February 11/21, 1635, *CSPD 1635*, 509.

[73] *Ibid.*, 380.

[74] Since Karl Ludwig was in England at this time, the king and archbishop being referenced here were his uncle, King Charles I, and Archbishop William Laud. Elector Karl Ludwig to the Queen of Bohemia, May 31, 1636, Victoria and Albert Museum Art Library, Forster Collection: Correspondence of Charles 1st and Sister Queen of Bohemia, 1617–58, MS. 48.g.25, f. 7.

Protestant heroine.[75] And on a more personal level, this was a blow to Elisabeth. His new bride Anne was the sister of Marie de Gonzague, who that same week had become the Queen of Poland – and she had done so by marrying Wladislaw IV, the suitor whom Elisabeth had refused years earlier on these very grounds of faith and forced conversion. The blow to Elisabeth was thus personal, political, and spiritual.

Then, to make matters even worse, the new Queen of Poland insisted that as part of her nuptial celebrations she really needed to meet the two most learned women in Europe: Anna Maria van Schurman and Princess Elisabeth. This was not surprising, perhaps, since Marie de Gonzague was an active and intelligent woman in her own right, and in 1652 she founded the first Polish newspaper, *Merkuriusz Polski*. Marie de Gonzague achieved her desired visit with van Schurman, and as the scene was quite breathlessly described by the young historian Jean le Laboureur, the Queen of Poland was extremely impressed by the exquisite detail and variety of van Schurman's artistic productions. However, she was even more impressed by van Schurman's command of languages, and actually tested the Dutch scholar's erudition by ordering her courtiers to converse with their hostess, one after the other, in Italian, Latin, Greek, and French.[76] Following this, the Queen's next stop would have been the exile court in The Hague, to see the learned woman least likely ever to welcome the visit. Fortunately for Elisabeth, time did not permit:

They speak with these same praises about the Palatine Princess Elisabeth of Bohemia. The entire North resounds with her glory; but the happiness of seeing her was missing from the happiness of our voyage, because she was living in The Hague, to which the Queen of Poland did not travel.[77]

Thus Elisabeth was spared one final indignity after her brother's abjuration.

There were other suitors for Elisabeth's hand, but she never married.[78] She remained at The Hague, reading philosophy, doing mathematics, and keeping close track of family alliances. It is here that Anna Maria van Schurman entered the story, and a women's scholarly community began to form in the exile court.

---

[75] See, for instance, the lament by Valentin Conrart to André Rivet, November 10, 1645, letter no. XIV in R. Kerviler and E. de Barthélemy, *Valentin Conrart, premier secrétaire perpétuel de l'Académie Française: Sa vie et sa correspondance* (Paris, 1881; reprint, Geneva, 1971), 295–8.

[76] Jean le Laboureur, *Relation du voyage*, 64–7.   [77] *Ibid.*

[78] Carola Oman, *Elizabeth of Bohemia* (1938; reprint, London, 1964), 402–3; also Creese, "The Letters of Elisabeth," 49–50.

CHAPTER 2

Anna Maria van Schurman: the birth of an intellectual network

because of a certain similarity in our studies, she embraced me with her distinguished favor.

Anna Maria van Schurman on Princess Elisabeth of Bohemia[1]

In 1673, nearing the end of her life, Anna Maria van Schurman published her last book, *Eukleria*. Partly a religious tract and partly an autobiography, the text analyzed the errors of van Schurman's past, and her scholarly celebrity. Yet despite the fact that she was repudiating this former pride, she still had fond recollections of the intellectual friendships that had formed at the exile court in the 1630s. Recalling Princess Elisabeth, she wrote:

Indeed, I believe that forty years have passed since, having abandoned the inanities or pleasures of other royal girls, she applied her mind to the more noble studies of the Sciences. And I have heard that because I had at that time a flattering reputation not only for piety, but also for learning, and because of a certain similarity in our studies, she embraced me with her distinguished favor – which she often testified to not only with her presence, but also with her obliging letters.[2]

Thus despite the enormous changes in the world around them, and despite the eventual disparity in their spiritual paths, these two female scholars had continued to honor the intellectual network they had formed forty years earlier at the exile court. This chapter examines the early life and career of Anna Maria van Schurman, and the path that led to her connection with Princess Elisabeth and other female scholars in The Hague.

ANNA MARIA VAN SCHURMAN (1607–78)

Anna Maria van Schurman was born in Cologne on November 5, 1607. Van Schurman's parents, Frederik van Schurman and Eva von Harff, had

---

[1] Anna Maria van Schurman, *Eukleria seu Melioris Partis Electio. Tractatus Brevem Vitae ejus Delineationem Exhibens* (Altona, 1673), VII, xv, 169.
[2] *Ibid.*

four children, of whom Anna Maria was the only daughter. Eva von Harff came from a wealthy and noble Protestant family in Germany; the family of Frederik van Schurman had originally come from Antwerp, but their conversion to Calvinism had forced them to flee to Cologne during the reign of the Duke of Alva. Given her mother's family wealth and the ennoblement of the van Schurmans in 1613, Anna Maria was well provided for and extremely marriageable; however, she would not have had to marry in order to survive, and there is no evidence that any of the men were ever required to follow a profession.[3]

However, the boys – Hendrik-Frederik, Johan Godschalk, and Willem – did receive a good education, and this fact proved to be of crucial importance for their sister Anna Maria. When the van Schurmans moved to the family seat at Dreiborn in 1610, the children were educated at home by a tutor; then, once they settled in Utrecht in 1613, Anna Maria briefly attended a French school. Her parents, however, quickly concluded that the education at this school was far too worldly. As van Schurman recalls in her autobiography:

An additional merit of my unusual education was that my parents did not send me to the French school until I was seven and then only for two months, so that I might suffer little corruption from childish games and from the contagion of impure words, which are easily imprinted on a delicate memory as on a blank slate. They preferred that I be taught the arts of writing and arithmetic, as well as both instrumental and vocal music, by tutors together with my brothers.[4]

Thus, as with so many of the erudite women who had come before her, a key factor in van Schurman's development as a scholar was the training provided at home by an attentive, admiring, and encouraging father.[5]

---

[3] For the early biography of van Schurman, see Mirjam de Baar and Brita Rang, "Anna Maria van Schurman: A Historical Survey of her Reception since the Seventeenth Century," in *Choosing the Better Part: Anna Maria van Schurman (1607–1678)*, ed. Mirjam de Baar *et al.* (Dordrecht, 1996), 2–21; and Pierre Yvon (1646–1707), "Abregé sincere de la vie & de la conduite & des vrais sentimens de feu Mr. De Labadie," in Gottfried Arnold, *Forsetzungen und Erläuterungen, Unpartheyische Kirchen- und Ketzerhistorie* (Frankfurt am Main, 1715), 1261–70. While the title of Yvon's essay mentions only Jean de Labadie, nine of its thirty-six folio pages – fully one-quarter of the essay – are in fact a biography of van Schurman.

[4] *Eukleria*, I, v. Translation by Joyce Irwin in Anna Maria van Schurman, *Whether a Christian Woman Should Be Educated: and Other Writings from Her Intellectual Circle* (Chicago, 1998), 82.

[5] On the role played by fathers in early modern women's intellectual accomplishment, see Ingrid A. R. de Smet, "'In the Name of the Father': Feminist Voices in the Republic of Letters (A. Tarabotti, A.M. van Schurman, and M. de Gournay)," in *La Femme lettrée à la Renaissance: Actes du Colloque international*, ed. Michel Bastiaensen (Brussels, 1997), 177–96; and Chapter 1, "Her Father's Daughter," in Sarah Gwyneth Ross, *The Birth of Feminism: Woman as Intellect in Renaissance Italy and England* (Cambridge, MA, 2009).

In *Eukleria*, written at the end of her life, Anna Maria van Schurman reviewed that education, along with her childhood, her fame, and the people who influenced her. The text is in part an explanation of why she eventually walked away from the secular limelight to join a religious community; thus she problematizes her unprecedented intellectual renown. She recounts how she was once swayed by the praises of "lying eulogists," listening to their "literary idolatry" and being "caught in this grossest of faults by certain extravagant singers of my praises. They exalted me to the heavens, though I am a mortal human being."[6]

Her language in *Eukleria* is angry and condemnatory, reflecting the pain of her lifelong struggle to reconcile her Christian humility with her intellectual pride. Throughout her lifetime, van Schurman was also highly praised as an artist and a woman of exemplary piety. However, her artistic accomplishments, while quite dazzling in their intricacy, variety, and perfection, were all in the amateur genres practiced by aristocratic women; and her religiosity, while admirable, would later become the subject of controversy and reproach. It was rather her remarkable skill as a linguist, rhetorician, poet, and classicist – in short, the portfolio of a humanist scholar – that astounded philosophers and men of learning throughout seventeenth-century Europe. Her erudition elicited paeans of awestruck praise, seeming to place her in a category not only beyond the reach of other women, but beyond nature itself.

She was "the Star of Utrecht," "the Dutch Sappho," "Minerva Batava," the "Utrecht Pallas," and "a miracle of our time." She surpassed the goddesses themselves, whose linguistic skills could not compare with hers. Even Pierre Yvon, her religious colleague and fellow Labadist, reported that: "To have been in Utrecht without seeing Mademoiselle de Schurman was like having been to Paris without seeing the king."[7] She was also, according to an early eulogist, "a miracle or monster of nature."[8]

This was an assessment with which van Schurman herself eventually agreed. However, she did not see herself, the human being, as the monster. It was rather the overall shapelessness of her early scholarship, the unbalanced, overpraised, and directionless pursuit of intellectual accomplishment for its own sake, with no practical or spiritual end in sight, which constituted the monstrosity:

---

[6] *Eukleria*, I, vi. In van Schurman, *Whether a Christian Woman*, 78.
[7] Yvon, "Abregé sincere," 1264–5.   [8] Jacob, "*Elogium eruditissimae*," 83–4.

I have not been either so prudent or so fortunate as always and everywhere to have separated abuse from use in the course of my studies, or to have observed equal proportion in all things ... On the contrary, if I were to observe diligently all the stages of my life along with the studies that occupied them and to expose to everyone the complete shape of the whole, it would be like a monster. But there are enough monsters in the world.[9]

Yet at the same time, van Schurman gave her reader every reason to believe that these fawning flatterers had been accurate in their assessments. She pointed out that she could read German at the age of three; picked up Latin at age eleven; outshone all others at the art of paper-cutting when she was only six; learned embroidery in only three hours at the age of four; and taught herself in a matter of days to carve amazingly lifelike images in wax and wood.[10] She quotes liberally from her own published works, as well as from more traditional authorities such as the Bible and Aristotle. Van Schurman also reveals how she consecrated herself to virginity while still a child, evincing a spiritual precocity in step with her intellectual advancement.

The choice of celibacy was, to say the least, a remarkable choice for the daughter of an aristocratic Calvinist family. It was a choice that completely precluded van Schurman from either continuing the family bloodline or raising Protestant children – the traditional social and religious contributions available to Protestant women. Even more startling is the fact that it was a choice urged on her at a very early age by her own father. As reported by van Schurman:

As a matter of fact, in order that I might not become heedlessly entangled in the snares of this world, around the time of his death he diligently and most passionately urged me especially to be on guard against the inextricable and (as is generally the case) degenerate bond of worldly marriage.[11]

While van Schurman evidently took her father's words to heart, and would remain celibate throughout her life, her father's role in this choice is somewhat puzzling. This was an aristocratic family, with a heritable name and fortune; thus, when Anna Maria's brothers died childless, the ultimate consequence of her father's advice was the extinction of their line. Since there are no extant writings by her father, we have only van Schurman's report regarding a choice that might easily have originated

---

[9] *Eukleria* I, vii, in van Schurman, *Whether a Christian Woman*, 79.
[10] *Eukleria* II, ii; II, vi; II, vii, in *ibid.*, 80–4.   [11] Eukleria, II, x, in *ibid.*, 87.

with her instead.[12] However, it was also a choice that was embraced wholeheartedly by the pious young scholar.

Throughout van Schurman's youth, frustrated suitors would be divided as to whether this problematic celibacy should be blamed on her scholarship, her piety, her filial devotion, or some incipient madness. There was even a brief period when Constantijn Huygens appeared to be seeking van Schurman's hand in marriage. After his wife died in 1632, Huygens wrote a large number of poems to van Schurman; in 1634 alone, he wrote ten poems in three languages on one of her self-portraits. Other members of the republic of letters chastised and teased him for his interest, since van Schurman's commitment to celibacy, sworn at her dying father's bedside, was unwavering. Then, when she chose the phrase *Amor Meus Crucifixus Est* ("My Love Has Been Crucified") as her personal device, her colleagues were finally convinced that she had made a life choice of celibacy in no uncertain terms – and the reasons for this choice lay in her piety, rather than her scholarship. The device inspired a number of poetic responses from members of the republic of letters, including Daniel Heinsius and Cornelius Böy.[13] Nicéron, writing a century later, chose instead to pair this choice of lifelong celibacy with her arachnoid diet, thereby making a clear statement about van Schurman's state of mind.

She took for her device these words from Saint Ignatius, the martyr: "My love has been crucified." They say that she very much liked to eat Spiders.[14]

How, then, should one assess van Schurman as an early modern female scholar? Does her astounding precocity in a wide array of accomplishments mean that she was indeed a freak or "monster"? Does this then render her unhelpful as a factor in analyzing early modern intellectual women as a category, since she was essentially a sample of one?

The answer is no. Certainly, the intellectual career of van Schurman would appear to be unique. Her fame as a female scholar was unprecedented, and her scholarship, in both its depth and its breadth, was quite breathtaking. According to her contemporary biographer Pierre Yvon, she had an excellent command of mathematics, geography, astronomy, and

---

[12] Yvon, however, confirms that this was her parents' choice. Yvon, "Abregé sincere," 1262.

[13] Some excerpts from these responses are preserved in the British Library (Sloane MS. 2764, f. 185). A published response, included in a collection of "Epigrammes, Dedicated to the Virtue of Mademoiselle, Mademoiselle Anne Marie de Schurman by the Gentleman des Hayons" characterizes her choice as a spiritual marriage. G. D. J. Schotel, *Anna Maria van Schurman*, 2 vols. in 1 ('S Hertogenbosch, 1853), II, 88.

[14] Nicéron, *Mémoires pour servir*, XXXIII, 22.

music, both instrumental and vocal; she was adept in drawing, painting, sculpting, paper cutting, etching, and embroidery; she mastered Latin, Greek, and Hebrew, and was proficient as well in Chaldaic, Arabic, Ethiopian, Flemish, German, English, French, and Italian.

However, it is also necessary to unpack the various elements of her accomplishments and her associations, placing each in its appropriate context. She was a childhood prodigy of humanist scholarship – but there were a number of other prodigies among her correspondents in the republic of letters. She was an extremely devout Christian and an ardent participant in theological debates – but this was also characteristic of many of her fellow scholars. She was a "node" of correspondence, sending and receiving learned letters at the crossroads of a number of different scholarly networks – however, the same was true of a number of men in the republic of letters, from Erasmus and Peiresc, to Mersenne, Oldenburg, Hartlib, and Huet. She was an extremely learned woman, whose intellectual accomplishments went far beyond what was common to her sex – but the same was true of dozens of female scholars even during van Schurman's lifetime.

The difficulty, then – both for van Schurman in her lifetime, and for scholars assessing her in the years to follow – lies in the fact that Anna Maria van Schurman figured so prominently in two contradictory currents of seventeenth-century scholarship. The first was the actual functioning of the republic of letters, that letter-based web of working relationships in the service of scholarship and faith. In that process, van Schurman was a colleague both to male scholars in the republic of letters and to the intellectual women who would form her female epistolary network. The second current, however, was the ongoing discourse on female excellence that had attracted the pens of learned men since the fourteenth century. In that polemical process, van Schurman's renown made her an instantly recognizable name, a scholarly celebrity whose reputation was often deployed in rhetorical displays whose real focus lay elsewhere.

Van Schurman's spiritual intensity and intellectual visibility caused her to become involved in numerous controversies – a common occupation in the republic of letters. As a Calvinist and staunch supporter of Voëtius, these disputes had her corresponding with Pierre du Moulin, Claude Saumaise, Frederick Spanheim, Pierre Gassendi, and John Cloppenburgh. At the same time, as a member of humanist and philological circles, van Schurman debated the various merits of Aristotelianism, Scripture, philosophy, and the empiricism of Baconian New Learning with René

Descartes, Henricus Reneri, Daniel Heinsius, Adolph Vorstius, Caspar Barlaeus, Constantijn Huygens, Johannes de Laet, Marin Mersenne, and Sir Simonds D'Ewes. Again, this was common in the republic of letters.

However, van Schurman's eulogizers wanted to focus instead on her rarity. When she considers, in *Eukleria*, how she has been misrepresented in works written by men of learning, she reflects that "perhaps they judged nothing worthy of observing and celebrating except what was rare in our sex and valued for that reason."[15] It was a process that rendered her fame unbearable, and it became one of the primary factors leading to her decision finally to choose her faith over her scholarship.

However, our concern here will be with the first process, the collegial workings of a scholarly network that included van Schurman as a participant. It is a process that allows us to see beyond her dazzling legacy to discern the fellow travellers, both male and female, who were her intellectual and religious colleagues. In reconstructing that process, we must begin with her earliest correspondence.

VAN SCHURMAN AND THE REPUBLIC OF LETTERS

Anna Maria van Schurman's entry into learned society had already taken place by the time she was thirteen years old. A poem dating from 1620 addresses the learned child as "Little Blossom." She is hailed as the possessor of prodigious abilities in learned languages, as a maiden who could easily have conversed with Greek and Roman scholars without needing an interpreter. This poem, however, was doing more than just celebrating a prodigy. The poet was the accomplished Anna Roemers Visscher, and she was embracing the young maiden as a future colleague among other learned women:

> In whose knowledge I take pride
> Whom I respect, and whom I love
> Whom I cherish as my friend:
> Who in the years to come . . .
> Will become the foremost of the maidens
> Who ever entered into science.[16]

This was a poem of welcome and friendship, and the thirteen-year-old van Schurman was being invited into the Dutch salon known as the

---

[15] *Eukleria*, ii, i, in van Schurman, *Whether a Christian Woman*, 80.
[16] "Aen Juffrouwe Anna Maria Schuermans" [1620], in *Gedichten van Anna Roemers Visscher*, ed. Nicolaas Beets (The Hague, 1925), 28.

Muiderkring. Certainly, the adolescent Anna Maria must have been flattered by the attentions of these scholarly and artistic luminaries, especially since they included the Visscher sisters, who were so willing to be her female mentors and chaperones.

Anna Roemers Visscher and her sister, Maria "Tesselschade" Visscher, were the two learned and accomplished daughters of Roemer Visscher (1547–1620), an Amsterdam merchant and author. Their home was a literary, philosophical, and artistic salon in the early decades of the seventeenth century, and the sisters had been given a humanistic education along the lines of the program provided by Sir Thomas More to his daughter, the English scholar Margaret Roper. Anna and Maria were accomplished at poetry, art, music, and languages, and were widely admired. They presided over the salon until they were joined to wealthy but unexceptional husbands, at which point they disappeared from the literary scene. Yet when Maria was widowed in 1634, she apparently re-established herself as a cultural presence.[17]

However, the thirteen-year-old van Schurman decided to keep her distance. She chose instead to associate with the more pious intellectual circle at the Château Develstein, whose center was the poet Jacob Cats. The Muiden circle, finally, was far too French. Its overtones of playful flirtatiousness and its rejection of religious debate were equally insupportable to the devout teenager, and she never set foot in Muiden castle.[18]

These discrepancies in style were visible from both sides. The beautiful Tesselschade Visscher, who was an accomplished poet but never wished to learn Latin, must have felt at some point that she was being compared unfavorably to the erudite van Schurman. In particular, she thought that Barlaeus was doing this, but Hooft rushed to reassure her:

[Barlaeus] thinks that Mademoiselle writes only with a feather drawn from the wings of Cupid, and he has just now told me … that he would place Mademoiselle's mind far above that of Mlle. van Schurman, because her work

---

[17] On the Visscher sisters, see Mieke B. Smits-Veldt, *Maria Tesselschade: Leven met Talent en Vriendschap* (Zutphen, 1994); James A. Parente Jr, "Anna Roemers Visscher and Maria Tesselschade Roemers Visscher," in *Women Writing in Dutch*, ed. Kristiaan Aercke (New York and London, 1994), 147–84; and Ria Vanderauwera, "Maria Tesselschade: A Woman of More than Letters," in *Women Writers of the Seventeenth Century*, ed. Katharina M. Wilson and Frank J. Warnke (Athens and London, 1989), 141–63.

[18] Dijkshoorn, *L'Influence française*, 189. Una Birch mistakenly concluded that van Schurman's non-participation in the *Muiderkring* was the result of arriving too late on the cultural scene. Una Birch [Constance Pope-Hennessy] *Anna van Schurman: Artist, Scholar, Saint* (London and New York, 1909), 33.

smells of the schoolmaster's domain, while yours is that of a superior intellect, bursting with sublime insights.[19]

The olfactory epithet – "smelling of the schools" – was being directed at many humanists in the seventeenth century, and was not specific to van Schurman alone. Scholarship based on ancient authorities and patristic sources was now considered dusty, dry, and old-fashioned by the denizens of salon culture. And even at the tender age of thirteen, van Schurman was casting her lot with the conservative "ancients" in the battle between ancients and moderns.

Nevertheless, she did not reject the friendship of learned women. In fact, by her early twenties van Schurman began to assemble a coterie of intellectual and artistic colleagues of her own, who would meet at her home and at the Château Develstein. These included Constantijn Huygens, Johan van Beverwijck, Jacob de Witt, Cornelius Böy, and the preacher Andreas Colvius. It also included the beginnings of a circle of intellectual women: among those women were the Hebrew scholar Margaret Godewijck, whose accomplishments would result in her reputation as "the second van Schurman," and the musician Utricia Ogle.[20]

Utricia Ogle, in particular, would become a lifelong friend. Utricia's father was the English colonel John Ogle, the governor of Utrecht. It was a post that must have suited him well, since the city of Utrecht became the inspiration for the names of two of his daughters, Utricia and Trajectina ("Trajectina" is the Latin name for Utrecht).[21] It would have been a stimulating environment for Ogle's daughter Utricia, who later would participate in her own "little Academie," and join the gatherings around Princess Elisabeth at the exile court in The Hague. Utricia Ogle was renowned for her lute playing and her beautiful voice, and there were musical evenings in Utrecht – possibly at the home of van Schurman herself – that apparently included Huygens, Ogle, Ogle's future husband William Swann, the theologian Gisbert Voëtius, and Anna Maria van Schurman and her brother.[22]

---

[19] P. C. Hooft to Maria "Tesselschade" Visscher, May 8, 1639, in Marcel van der Heijden, *'T Hoge Huis te Muiden: Teksten uit der Muiderkring*, Spectrum van de Nederlandse Letterkunde 8 (Utrecht, 1972), 234.

[20] Schotel, *Anna Maria van Schurman*, 1:23.

[21] On Utricia Ogle, later Utricia Swann-Ogle (1611?–74), see J. A. Worp, "Nog eens Utricia Ogle en de Muzikale Correspondentie van Huygens," *Tijdschrift der Vereeniging voor Noord-Nederlands Muziekgeschiedenis* 5 (1899): 129–36; Dijkshoorn, *L'Influence française*, 187–8; and L. Strengholt, *Constanter: Het Leven van Constantijn Huygens* (Amsterdam, 1987), 88–91.

[22] Constantijn Huygens reminisced about one of these musical evenings in a Latin poem dated October 10, 1650, which he translated into Dutch on October 21. Constantijn Huygens, *De Gedichten van Constantijn Huygens, naar zijn handschrift uitgegeven*, ed. J. A. Worp, 9 vols. (Groningen, 1892–9), IV, 240. It was to Utricia Swann-Ogle that Huygens dedicated his *Pathodia sacra et profana* (1647).

Here, in the life of the teenaged van Schurman, we see early evidence of her lifelong struggle to identify her appropriate peer group. Men, women, mystics, musicians, Calvinists, philosophers, preachers, princesses, and poets – all were eager to claim her acquaintance. However, she had no desire for an entourage; she wanted a community. Her search for like-minded associates, made difficult by her status as an aristocratic female scholar, resonates with the life of Princess Elisabeth. As scholars, Elisabeth and van Schurman followed very different paths. Elisabeth was a thinker. Her interests in science, philosophy, and new ideas identify her as a representative of the New Learning, constantly questioning everything she had ever been taught. Van Schurman, on the other hand, was extremely conservative. She was a scholar in the humanist tradition, who relied on scholastic authorities to validate her intellectual path. Van Schurman's search for scholarly and religious mentors continued through-out her life; and although her changes of life seemed confusing and abrupt to those around her, they were in fact entirely consistent with the complex mixture of intellectual pride and spiritual humility that she had exempli-fied from her earliest years.

In 1622 for instance, at the age of fifteen, van Schurman had written a poem in Latin to a popular poet and lawyer named Jacob Cats (1577–1660), whose works on the family extolled the virtues of domesticity as the cornerstone of an ordered society. Impressed with the young woman's erudition and reputation for virtue, Cats featured her three years later in a treatise on marriage – a rather odd choice given van Schurman's well-known commitment to a celibate life.[23] He introduced her to his readers by saying:

Miss Anna Maria Schuermans ... about 18 years old ... will undoubtedly, being set on the wings of Fame by divers learned pens, be a new and outstanding adornment to our century.[24]

Yet van Schurman, the adornment in question, had not waited for the learned pen of Jacob Cats to set her upon the wings of fame.

Several months after writing the poem to Cats, van Schurman had written a letter in Latin to Daniel Heinsius, Professor of Latin and Greek

---

[23] Agnes Sneller speculates that Cats felt a kinship with van Schurman based on his perception that they were two virtuous souls whose writings constituted their "paper children." A. Agnes Sneller, "'If She Had Been a Man ... ': Anna Maria van Schurman in the Social and Literary Life of her Age," in de Baar *et al.*, *Choosing the Better Part*, 142.

[24] Jacob Cats, *Alle de wercke* (Amsterdam, 1712), I, 332a. Cited in Sneller, "'If She Had Been a Man ...'", 141.

at the University of Leiden. Heinsius, like van Schurman, had been a child prodigy. He was Joseph Scaliger's favorite student, and at the age of fourteen he had enrolled in Greek studies at the University of Franeker, where his scholarship, literary skill, and mastery of classical languages gained him early renown in the republic of letters.[25] In her letter, the sixteen-year-old van Schurman presents herself as a "maiden just beyond childhood," whose ardent desire to contact the eminent Heinsius had been hindered up to this point by an excessive concern for her maidenly modesty. However, she had now been saved from this paralyzing primness by the voice of her faith. In booming tones, it had chided her for her foolishness and ordered her in the name of the gods to do honor to the man they had themselves singled out for blessings of virtue and learning. Thus despite her hesitation, she had finally decided to write, and to hope against hope that Heinsius would agree to correspond with her. Van Schurman took great pains to demonstrate and insist that, "only my faith, and my immense admiration for your divine virtue, have compelled this; it was not my pretentiousness."[26]

It was a pretty conceit, executed in an elegant Latin style, and the adolescent van Schurman reaped her reward in Heinsius' positive response and continuing correspondence with her. Yet in reconstructing the category of collegial female scholars, the importance of this letter consists in much more than either the prodigious scholarship of its young writer or the warm welcome she received from an older scholar in the republic of letters.

First, this letter is a clear example of a female scholar using the practices of networking and mentorship to advance her intellectual career. Second, there is an evident internalized struggle – between van Schurman's love of scholarship and pride in her accomplishment on the one side, and her deep faith and sincere Christian humility on the other – that goes far beyond a rhetorical device or cultural *topos*, and instead constitutes the real theme of her letter. It is a struggle that surfaces again and again in her writings, from her adolescent letters to learned men, to the religious and

---

[25] On Daniel Heinsius (1580–1655), see Paul R. Sellin, *Daniel Heinsius and Stuart England* (Leiden and London, 1968); *Correspondance de Jacques Dupuy et de Nicolas Heinsius (1646–1656)*, ed. Hans Bots, Archives Internationales d'Histoire des Idées 40 (The Hague, 1971), ix–lii; and Baerbel Becker-Cantarino, *Daniel Heinsius*, Twayne's World Authors Series, no. 477 (Boston, 1978).

[26] Anna Maria van Schurman to Daniel Heinsius, September 18, 1623. There are two seventeenth-century copies of this letter in the collection of the University of Utrecht; both are in letterbooks containing copies of learned correspondence from scholars in the republic of letters. Letterbook of Arnoldus Buchelius, HS 983, 7.E.7, f. 134; Letterbook of E. van Engelen, HS 1655, 5.H.40, f. 126.

autobiographical apology she published at the age of seventy. It is also a struggle that surfaces again and again in the correspondence of other female scholars, and indeed it is one of the major factors differentiating the content of the women's letters from those of their learned brethren. The republic of letters could not provide learned women with either a home or a profession, and beyond the borders of that idealized republic, feminine modesty was simply incommensurate with an intellectual presence. Eventually, this struggle would result in van Schurman's departure from the intellectual limelight of the republic of letters – but that moment was still many years in the future.

THE ARRIVAL OF ANNA MARIA VAN SCHURMAN

In 1629, six years after van Schurman's letter to Heinsius, the poet and scholar Caspar Barlaeus received a letter from a young medical student named Johan Godschalk van Schurman. Although Barlaeus had lost his position as Professor of Logic at the University of Leiden after the purge following the Synod of Dort, he had been befriended by Constantijn Huygens, and joined the scholarly and artistic circle of the *Muiderkring*.[27] Johan Godschalk was Anna Maria's older brother, and he had assumed responsibility for his sister's education after the death of their father in 1623. He also had aspirations to be known as a poet and a scholar, and hoped Barlaeus would be interested in the little poem he had just written. The young man's hopes would unfortunately come to nothing; he was, as René Descartes would later observe, "a man of little wit."[28] However, Johan Godschalk was particularly anxious to tell Barlaeus about his remarkable younger sister:

And I have one sister only, of the kind not averse to learned studies; I do not know whether her reputation, somewhat well known in other places, has reached you ... At some point I will write to you at length about her intellect, employments, and progress.[29]

Barlaeus was indeed impressed by the intellect of this young woman. Within the month, in fact, Barlaeus had written about her in turn to

---

[27] On Barlaeus (1584–1648), see Piet van der Sluijs, "Constantijn Huygens en de Muiderkring," in Hans Bots, ed., *Constantijn Huygens: Zijn Plaats in Geleerd Europa* (Amsterdam, 1973), 196–217; and F. F. Blok, *Caspar Barlaeus: From the Correspondence of a Melancholic* (Amsterdam, 1976).

[28] René Descartes to Marin Mersenne, November 11, 1640, in Descartes, *Oeuvres*, III, 231.

[29] Johan Godschalk van Schurman to C. Barlaeus, December 5, 1629, University of Leiden, MS. PAP 2.

Constantijn Huygens, a humanist, scholar, and courtier in the service of the House of Orange:

In Utrecht there is a maiden of rare character, Anna Maria van Schurman, and she is truly a Roman, not only because she has a forename, name, and surname, but because she in fact converses [in Latin] just like a Roman. She paints, she writes, she creates poetry, she reads Greek and understands it . . .[30]

Huygens was also impressed and began to correspond with this young Dutch "Roman." It was the beginning of an important, decades-long friendship between Huygens and van Schurman, who was twenty-two years old at the time.

This has also been considered the beginning of van Schurman's participation in the republic of letters, as Huygens and Barlaeus shared their knowledge of this precocious polymath with their circle of correspondents, and she then began to correspond with these other scholars in turn. However, van Schurman's reputation rested almost as much on her character as it did on her intellect, and much of the praise she received focused happily on her ability to exemplify *modestia* as well as *mens*. As the renowned Latinist Jean Louis Guez de Balzac remarked, voicing a typical sentiment:

I do not think that this Sulpitia who was so highly praised by Martial ever produced more beautiful or more perfect Latin: But how she possesses modesty and decency in addition to the grace and beauty of her poetry! How the virtue of her soul mingles pleasantly with the productions of her mind![31]

Indeed, it was thought that without the nudging and mentoring from renowned male *érudits* like Barlaeus and Huygens, the modest van Schurman's fame would never have reached beyond her circle of personal acquaintances. According to Père Nicéron, the chronicler of the republic of letters:

Her character was such that her merit and learning would have remained unknown, if Rivet, Vossius, and Spanheim had not pushed her almost in spite of herself onto the world stage. To these three theologians must be added the names of Saumaise, Beverwijck, and Huygens.[32]

This passage was taken almost verbatim from Pierre Yvon's biography of van Schurman, except that Nicéron somehow managed to substitute

---

[30] Caspar Barlaeus to Constantijn Huygens. January 8, 1630, in *De Briefwisseling van Constantijn Huygens*, I, 273.
[31] Jean Louis Guez de Balzac (1597–1654), quoted in Pierre Yvon, "Abregé sincere," 1265.
[32] Nicéron, *Mémoires pour servir*, XXXIII, 19–20.

Vossius, a theologian with Arminian leanings, for van Schurman's strictly Calvinist mentor Voëtius – a move that would presumably have horrified the subject herself.[33]

Yet Yvon and Nicéron were both mistaken. This "pushing" of the young woman was not what first launched her career in the republic of letters. In spite of her modesty, as we have already seen, the virtuous van Schurman had in fact launched herself into that learned community while still in her teens, seeking out mentors and correspondents like Heinsius and contacting them on her own. This misjudgment of van Schurman should come as no surprise. Her life exhibits, from beginning to end, a series of counterintuitive pairings: an intertwining of modesty with pride, of the desire for retreat with a longing for community, and of humanist erudition with revealed faith.

Yet these were conflicts she negotiated in common with her male colleagues in the republic of letters. Balancing modesty and pride was a conundrum for all Christian scholars. Deciding between community and retreat was also a familiar theme, certainly a primary consideration for Descartes; and the path from scriptural scholarship to the direct experience of God had been trod by other Pietists before her. Thus it was not the scope, nature, or performance of van Schurman's scholarly *practices* that led Nicéron astray. Nicéron, like his succeeding chroniclers of the republic of letters, erred rather in trying to interpret van Schurman's career through the lens of her gender.

It is not difficult to see why scholars made and continue to make this mistake. Van Schurman's most well-known publication grew out of an engaged correspondence with the French Protestant theologian André Rivet, and it was entitled: *Dissertatio de ingenii muliebris ad doctrinam & meliores litteras aptitudine,* or *An Argument concerning women's innate capacity for knowledge and higher learning.* Thus the tract was indeed focused on a question of gender, and it inspired a generation of intellectual women to believe that they could also aspire to lives that combined scholarship and virtue. However, the first words of the text are: *Problema practicum* – "a practical problem." And it is van Schurman, presenting herself here as a learned Christian woman negotiating the practical problems of scholarship, who points the way out of this analytical dilemma.

---

[33] Unfortunately, it is not possible to determine whether Nicéron's substitution was deliberate or accidental. Yvon, "Abregé sincere," 1263.

Considerations of gender were, for van Schurman and other female scholars, problems of a practical, instrumental nature. They certainly existed: there were instrumental difficulties associated with being a scholar and a woman, just as there were instrumental difficulties associated with being a scholar and coming from a poor family, or growing up in an isolated village, or living through a time of war, or being a member of a persecuted religious minority. All were problematic, and all needed to be dealt with – but gender was just one of these considerations, and in terms of the women being analyzed in this study, it was a consideration that does not appear to have been at the top of the list.

Nevertheless, the practical problem presented by being both a woman and a scholar was very real. It was a problem that required creative solutions, and it is here that we see an intellectual network taking shape in The Hague in the 1630s.

PRINCESS ELISABETH MEETS ANNA MARIA VAN SCHURMAN

In 1632, the Huguenot theologian André Rivet came to The Hague as tutor to Prince William of Orange; and when he did so, he brought with him a wealth of connections: to religious networks, to the republic of letters, and to a remarkable number of learned women, including his niece Marie du Moulin, and the Huguenot poet and heroine Princess Anne de Rohan. He also brought with him his obvious respect for these female scholars, and his sense that they would enjoy getting to know one another. And it was in this way, through Rivet, that van Schurman came to The Hague and met the Palatine Princess Elisabeth.

In 1631, van Schurman was only twenty-three years old, yet she had already spent ten years in the intellectual limelight of the republic of letters. It was a position that had never been comfortable for her. She was still looking for the right community in which to practice both her scholarship and her faith, and she was looking for a mentor who could help her find a way to integrate her intellect with her devotion. Although it is not clear precisely when or how the relationship began, a letter to Rivet reveals her belief that she had finally found someone whose piety would provide the perfect antidote to her fame:

Indeed, who would not rejoice at those [flattering] utterances, which are as obliging as they are friendly? Who remembers those utterances? On the contrary, then, to how much greater an extent do I rejoice at the warm affection animating your letters? I, in whom for several years already the sacred Theology has instilled love and respect toward you . . .

The letter of gratitude then closed on a more personal note:

Farewell, most excellent of men, and if it would not especially burden you, I long for the warmest greetings to be conveyed in my name to your dear Wife.[34]

Clearly, this was not their first contact, and the reference to Rivet's encouraging letters indicates that van Schurman had already been corresponding with this Professor of Theology from the University of Leiden. It is also clear from this letter that she was acquainted with Rivet's wife.[35] Van Schurman's relationship with Rivet and the women in his family would turn out to be powerful, supportive, intimate, and long-lived, and they were her first intellectual *famille d'alliance*. The correspondence with Rivet, whom she always called her "beloved Father in Christ," continued up until his death in 1651, and the correspondence with his niece, whom she called her "dear sister," continued until van Schurman's own demise. Yet while the evident deference and respect in this letter would be characteristic of their entire correspondence, the unfocused formality would give way almost immediately to a rather clear-cut agenda.

Several months after writing this letter, van Schurman wrote again to Rivet, telling him that she no longer wanted to conceal anything from him. The truth was that she was writing a book:

It is now a year or so since some person attempted to render my little book into French (because in truth the grace and elegance of that language accustom it to being accepted by young women as much as possible): in which I attempt to persuade these same young women (granted, by means of [the method's] effects, rather than its power) of the best method for making good use of our leisure.[36]

The "little book" in question was van Schurman's *Dissertatio*. The format was the traditional scholastic *quaestio*, and the question being debated was "A Practical Problem: Whether the study of letters is fitting for a Christian woman."[37] Apparently, her book had been rushed into

[34] Anna Maria van Schurman, Utrecht, to André Rivet, Leiden, July 20, 1631, KB MS. 133B8, no. 1. This is the earliest extant document of van Shurman's relationship with Rivet. It is possible that the original connection between Rivet and van Schurman was facilitated by Gisbert Voëtius, who was also a Professor at Leiden, and a family friend of the van Schurmans.

[35] In order to avoid confusion, the Marie du Moulin who was married to André Rivet will be referred to as Marie Rivet. Her niece, van Schurman's friend, will be referred to as Marie du Moulin.

[36] Anna Maria van Schurman, Utrecht, to André Rivet, Leiden, January 12, 1632, KB MS. 133B8, no. 3. Later printed in *Nobiliss. Virginis Annae Mariae à Schurman, Opuscula Hebraea, Graeca, Latina, Gallica: Prosaica & Metrica* (Leiden, 1648), 57–9. Also in van Schurman, *Whether a Christian Woman*, 39–40.

[37] The original text was in Latin, and it was published by the Elseviers in Leiden in 1641. The *Dissertatio*, along with some letters between van Schurman and Rivet on the same subject, was later

print in an unauthorized French edition, and she needed to deal with this other "practical problem."[38] But publication problems aside, the import of these sentences is clear. Van Schurman is not only seeking a mentor for herself, she is also crafting herself as a mentor, seeking to encourage other young women with the time and ability to lead lives of scholarship and study.

Rivet was clearly intrigued by this idea, which he and van Schurman would continue to discuss in their correspondence over the next ten years. This does not mean that they were in perfect agreement about van Schurman's desire to share her strategies with other would-be women scholars – in fact, Rivet felt that van Schurman was just far too exceptional in both her abilities and her piety, and other female scholars simply could not be judged by her standard. In Rivet's opinion, other women might indeed possess both the intellect and the social status that would provide them with the leisure for these pursuits; however, they could not be counted as well to possess the spiritual strength that was so necessary for negotiating the moral pitfalls of scholarship. Women simply could not lead lives of study without dangerously compromising their feminine Christian modesty.

Yet Rivet's published position on women's scholarship must be contrasted with his actions, as revealed in his correspondence. Based on his published statements, Rivet's attitude has been seen as ultimately restrictive; however, his actions operated powerfully to contradict his words in two ways: first, he continued to encourage van Schurman's desire to position herself as a model for other female scholars; and second, he introduced her and her writings to the many learned women of his acquaintance. In effect, it was Rivet himself who set the stage for the female intellectual mentoring that would characterize this network of intellectual women.

André Rivet was born in 1572, the year of the St Bartholomew massacre, into a Protestant family in Saint Maixent. After serving as a minister in Thouars, he spent twenty-five years as chaplain to the family of the Duc

---

incorporated into various editions of van Schurman's *Opuscula* ("Little Works"). A French version of the *Dissertatio* was published in 1646 under the title *Question celebre. S'il est necessaire, ou non, que les Filles soient sçavantes.* An English version, translated by Clement Barksdale, appeared in 1659 under the title *The Learned Maid or, Whether a Maid may be a Scholar. A Logick Exercise.* This was the second time the *Dissertatio* had appeared in English; the first appearance was an excerpt that constituted Chapter 3 of Samuel Torshell's *The Womans Glorie* in 1645. In the present study, all citations from the *Dissertatio* reference the 1641 Latin publication.

[38] This pirated French edition has never been traced.

de la Trémoille.[39] It was most likely his position at their court that led to his being familiar with the family of the Duc de Rohan, a Huguenot hero and the father of Anne de Rohan. Anne de Rohan was known as a poet, heroine, and scholar of the learned languages; she was later to become one of van Schurman's correspondents, and would appear in her *Opuscula*. Then, in 1620, Rivet's life shifted from France to the Netherlands.

After the academic purge of Arminianism that followed in the wake of the Synod of Dort, the University of Leiden found itself desperate for new faculty, for professors who had solid reputations for both their rigorous scholarship and their doctrinal orthodoxy.[40] So the curators at Leiden went to France in 1620, on a mission to procure Pierre du Moulin, the renowned Huguenot preacher and polemicist. Their repeated attempts to obtain his release from the Consistory of Paris were all met with failure; du Moulin was far too necessary to the Protestant cause at home. However, the curators' second choice was a man of almost equal stature, and one who was willing and able to make the trip. This man was André Rivet, who became from 1620 to 1632 the Professor of Theology at the University of Leiden. The only problem with the plan was Rivet's wife: she fiercely objected, and simply refused to move. Rivet eventually left for the Netherlands without her, and she died within months.

Rivet did not, however, remain single for long, and in 1621, Pierre du Moulin wrote a letter expressing his pleasure with Rivet's plans for the future:

Sir and honored brother:
I would indeed be a man deprived of his senses if I did not take it as a great honor that you seek my sister's hand in marriage, and if I did not recognize in this the providence of God, who in a time of great difficulty is preparing for this poor woman a refuge in which to end her days with honor and comfort. In making this choice, you also are acting as a virtuous man, who, without regard for either wealth or beauty, has gone in search of virtue, which you will find in abundance in this little woman; and I dare say that in her prudence and dextrous wit, she surpasses her sex; to which she adds a generous courage, governed by the fear of God.[41]

One hopes that the future Marie Rivet, the sister in question, never discovered that she had been the prize in a search conducted "without

[39] This discussion is taken from J. A. Bots, "André Rivet en zijn positie in de Republiek der Letteren," *Tijdschrift voor Geschiedenis* 84, no.1 (1971): 24–35.

[40] *Claude Saumaise & André Rivet: Correspondance Échangée entre 1632 et 1648*, ed. Pierre Leroy and Hans Bots (Amsterdam, 1987), xii–xxiv; Gustave Cohen, "Un Grand Théologien Orthodoxe: André Rivet (1620–32)," in *Écrivains français*, 293–310.

[41] Pierre du Moulin to André Rivet, July 21, 1621, University of Leiden, BPL 282, f. 151.

regard for either wealth or beauty." It is also worth noting here that Rivet's prospective bride was not about to "end her days." Although she was forty-seven years old, she was in fact two years younger than Rivet, and would survive him by several years.

This union between André Rivet and the sister of Pierre du Moulin was the first move in what might be seen as a multi-generational dynastic survival strategy, involving the merger of two of the most prominent Huguenot families of the seventeenth century. Eventually, the du Moulin clan would intermarry with the families of a number of other prominent Huguenot ministers: those of Pierre and Daniel Jurieu, Samuel Bochart, Samuel de l'Angle, and Jacques Basnage.[42] Yet despite this rather unromantic genesis, the marriage between André and Marie Rivet appears to have been a warm and happy one. And in 1632, when Rivet was appointed governor to the young Prince William of Orange, he and his wife moved to The Hague. The following year, they were joined by Marie, the daughter of Pierre du Moulin. It was in this way that the younger Marie du Moulin came to The Hague and was introduced to van Schurman and Elisabeth.[43]

Almost immediately after his arrival in The Hague, Rivet wrote to van Schurman about a new acquaintance:

I have delivered your French verses to the Princess Elisabeth, which, in my presence, she read and praised, and promised that she would, in her own hand, thank you for them. Moreover, since you are contemplating a little work in that same language, I ask that you not suffer me to be without it for long: I will read it with great eagerness.[44]

This mediation by André Rivet quickly led to a personal relationship between the two women.

It is possible that the relationship between van Schurman and Elisabeth took place only in correspondence for another two years, until 1634. It has been suggested that they met when van Schurman came to court to take art lessons with the celebrated painter Gerard van

---

[42] For a genealogical chart of the du Moulin family, see Carol Pal, "Republic of Women: Rethinking the Republic of Letters, 1630–1680" (Ph.D. dissertation, Stanford University, 2007), Appendix B.

[43] Bulckaert, following Voisine, asserts the reverse – that it was through the intervention of Marie du Moulin that Rivet first made the acquaintance of van Schurman. However, there is no evidence adduced to support this statement. Barbara Bulckaert, "L'Education de la femme dans la correspondance d'Anna Maria van Schurman (1607–78) et André Rivet (1572–1651)," in Bastiaensen, *La Femme lettrée*, 185–6; J. Voisine, "Un astre éclipsé: Anna Maria van Schurman (1607–78)," *Études Germaniques* 27, no. 4 (October–December, 1972), 510.

[44] André Rivet, Leiden, to Anna Maria van Schurman, Utrecht. March 1, 1632, *Opuscula*, 60–2. Also in van Schurman, *Whether a Christian Woman*, 40–1.

Honthorst. Honthorst, who had been invited to England in 1628 by King Charles I, was now in The Hague as court painter to Amalia van Solms, the Princess of Orange, and was also at the court of the exiled King and Queen of Bohemia, painting portraits of the family and teaching drawing to their children.[45] However, while van Schurman mentions in *Eukleria* that her brother showed her boxwood carvings to Honthorst, who declared that they were worth "at least a thousand florins," there is no direct evidence that van Schurman attended any of Honthorst's art lessons.[46] Instead, it is much more likely that the friendship between van Schurman and Elisabeth evolved from their shared devotion to their studies and their faith, and their introduction by Rivet.

Eighteen months after Rivet had first shown van Schurman's poems to the Princess, van Schurman was writing back to Rivet in turn. She was discussing the work on her book, but then took a moment to tell Rivet about her pleasure in this new colleague:

Here you have also our Princess, whose friendship I enjoy, and I do not know how anything could ever feel more blessed to me than the great inspiration of her genius.[47]

As we saw earlier, this same genius had often been a source of concern to those who knew Elisabeth. She was so widely read in the New Learning, so interested in science and medical experiments, and so willing to consider the viewpoints of writers representing an enormous range of spiritual and philosophical positions, that rumors had begun to circulate about her possible flirtations with heresy. Finally, Rivet appealed to van Schurman to help guide her younger colleague in terms of her rather heterodox approach to learning. In reply, van Schurman wrote:

It was most agreeably pleasant to understand from you how the Princess feels toward me: and to understand also that her Highness does not disdain to remember even her humblest acolyte. And finally, I will encourage her of whom

---

[45] On Gerard van Honthorst (1592–1656), see Marieke Tiethoff-Spliethoff, "Role-play and Representation: Portrait Painting at the Court of Frederik Hendrik and Amalia," in *Princely Display: The Court of Frederik Hendrik of Orange and Amalia van Sohms*, ed. Marika Keblusek and Jori Zijlmans (The Hague, *c.*1997), 168–77.

[46] *Eukleria* II, vii. Also in van Schurman, *Whether a Christian Woman*, 83. Nevertheless, several scholars have suggested this possibility. See, for instance, Katlijne van der Stighelen, "'Et ses artistes mains . . .': The Art of Anna Maria van Schurman," in de Baar *et al.*, *Choosing the Better Part*, 63. Una Birch also claims that Elisabeth and van Schurman became acquainted in Honthorst's studio, but places the studio in Utrecht. Birch, *Anna van Schurman*, 29.

[47] Van Schurman to Rivet, October 23, 1633, KB MS. 133 B 8, no. 4.

you write to a proper moderation in her studies; and may God bring it to pass that we might soon be permitted to enjoy our friendship in person.[48]

That pleasure would come to pass in that same year.

Elisabeth belonged to a royal family; it was a rank that created an enormous gap in status between the princess and the rest of the scholarly world, including the aristocrat van Schurman. However, the connection they formed in The Hague survived the ensuing decades of their lives, through changes in faith, nation, and intellectual allegiance. And van Schurman, who came to The Hague as Elisabeth's intellectual mentor in the 1630s, would in turn become the recipient of Elisabeth's kindness and shelter in the 1670s, when her religious community was in need of safety and refuge.

Thus, by 1634, a women's intellectual community had begun to form in The Hague. Eschewing their isolating and goddess-like reputations, the two hubs of this network – Anna Maria van Schurman, the "Dutch Pallas," and Princess Elisabeth, the "Star of the North" – had met and begun working together as colleagues and fellow members of the republic of letters.

EDUCATIONAL ADVICE FOR PRINCESS ELISABETH

Elisabeth, like van Schurman, cast her intellectual net as widely as possible. Their interests were very different – Elisabeth was engaged in politics, mathematics, and rationalist philosophy, while van Schurman pursued theology, linguistics, and classical scholarship – thus their intellectual paths were widely divergent. Yet it is clear that Elisabeth included van Schurman among her mentors.

Elisabeth was also extremely active in maintaining an ongoing and far-reaching network of philosophical correspondents throughout the many changes in her life. As a member of the republic of letters, Elisabeth worked toward the development of rational philosophical systems, in dialogue with such thinkers as Descartes, Leibniz, and Malebranche. And since her mother's exile court – a physical location completely accessible to both sexes – functioned as an intellectual destination point during this period, much of the work of philosophical networking and discussion would have been taking place at the level of face-to-face meetings, rather than in correspondence alone. Thus there is very little

[48] Van Schurman to Rivet, March 4, 1634, KB MS. 133 B 8, no. 12.

documentation of Elisabeth's intellectual development between 1634, when she first met van Schurman, and 1643, when she began her correspondence with Descartes. However, two extant documents from this period testify to Elisabeth's ongoing development as a self-directed scholar, engaging with a range of philosophers and philosophies.

The first of these comes from 1639, when a pamphlet entitled *A Treatise of the Passions and Faculties of the Soule of Man* was published in England. Its author, Edward Reynolds (1599–1676), was the Rector of Bramston, the future Bishop of Norwich, and a philosopher *manqué*. The pamphlet outlined his own approaches to the problem of right living, a "philosophicall Miscallany." Our interest here, however, is in the pamphlet's dedication to the Princess Elisabeth. In that text, Reynolds characterizes his treatise as the product of his youth, "a Blossome which put forth so much too soone," yet one which had had the felicity to fall into the hands of the philosopher-princess:

For so farre hath your Highnesse vouchsafed (having hapned on the sight of this Tractate) to expresse favour thereunto, as not onely to spend hours in it, and require a Transcript of it, but further to recommend it by your Gracious judgement unto publike view.[49]

While the date of the original treatise is never given, it was probably composed while Reynolds was at Merton College, Oxford, where he matriculated in 1616. The treatise would then have circulated in manuscript form among the members of philosophical circles, which is how Elisabeth would have first encountered it.[50] It is clear, then, that Elisabeth was reading, exploring, and engaging with philosophical debates long before she became the "disciple" of Descartes – and our evidence for this comes from the pen of van Schurman.

Rivet had been anxious enough over the possible moral dangers of these studies to have turned to van Schurman in 1634 for help in reining in the breadth of Elisabeth's interests. Van Schurman, as we have seen, responded with alacrity and pleasure, and the two women formed an intellectual bond. However, even a cursory glance at the ongoing evolution of Elisabeth's intellectual pursuits makes it clear that van Schurman

---

[49] Edward Reynoldes, *A Treatise of the Passions and Faculties of the Soule of Man. With the severall Dignities and Corruptions thereunto belonging,* 2nd edn. (London, 1640), n.p. On Reynolds, see Nathaniel Salmon, *The Lives of the English Bishops: From the Restauration to the Revolution* (London, 1731), 305–7; and Walter Simon, *The Restoration Episcopate* (New York, 1965), 22, 138.

[50] On the important, pervasive, and sophisticated phenomenon of early modern manuscript networks, see Love, *Scribal Publication.*

did not succeed at her original task. Nevertheless, over the following years, the princess would continue to turn to her for advice – which she probably ignored. At some point, Elisabeth herself solicited van Schurman's advice concerning what she should read and study. And in response, on September 7, 1639, van Schurman wrote an uncharacteristically long letter to the princess, outlining in some detail a program of reading and study for her younger colleague.

It is a uniquely valuable letter, allowing us a first-hand glimpse of how van Schurman translated her own theoretical discussions of women's learning into an actual syllabus, putting the idea of female intellectual mentorship into action. Elisabeth, of course, was far from representing what anyone would term a "typical" early modern female scholar. It is unclear how one might define typicality for an early modern female scholar – yet even among male scholars, royals were rare. Elisabeth was descended from two troubled houses, Stuart and Palatine; and although her family was currently out of power, this was a situation subject to momentary change during these years of war. Thus van Schurman's advice was clearly shaped by political and national considerations, as well as by her own intellectual prejudices – in favor of scholasticism, and opposed to both Baconian empiricism and Cartesian rationalism.

What is missing, however, is any consideration of gender. The writer and addressee are women. Some of the *exempla* are women. Yet apart from this, the sex of the student does not appear to have been a factor in this proposed reading program. What one sees here instead is a female mentor proposing a rigorous humanist course of study to a younger female colleague.

The letter begins formally: van Schurman praises Elisabeth's intellectual breadth, and expresses her pleasure at being asked to recommend a course of study:

Madame,

I cannot express the overabundance of joy and happiness I experienced upon reading the letter Your Highness was so gracious as to write to me. For beyond the inventiveness, wit, and phrasing, which could fill up the ears of the most learned, it was a marvellous pleasure for me to ponder within it the diversions of your broad-minded intellect.[51]

Yet the "diversions" of Elisabeth's "broad-minded intellect" were precisely the problem here. Thus the letter's opening compliments were immediately followed by conservative advice and admonitions.

---

[51] Anna Maria van Schurman to Princess Elisabeth, September 7, 1639, in *Opuscula*, 281–7; there is no trace of the original. Also in van Schurman, *Whether a Christian Woman*, 57–60.

The program van Schurman outlined for Elisabeth was composed in equal parts of what should and should not be pursued. Van Schurman makes it abundantly clear that Elisabeth should be reading history instead of philosophy. She provides a list of ancient historians whom she holds in high regard, and then gives the reasons why these studies are preferable:

If we care to move on to the usefulness that we derive from [History], and peel it back layer by layer, we find that it is almost infinite, especially in that its examples strike our senses and our imaginations more powerfully than do the precepts of Philosophy. In addition, the knowledge of matters in the past, acquired by means of this method, is impartial, and there is no danger of it leading to ruin, which is almost inevitable for those who allow themselves to be led by experience alone. We can see, as in a bright mirror, all the ages that have passed, and we can conjecture with real certainty about the ages to come.[52]

Van Schurman's argument is that, in comparison with philosophy, history communicates knowledge more powerfully and effectively; history also allows one to plan usefully for the future, based on sure and certain knowledge of the past. Most importantly, though, history is based on known, objective facts. It is therefore superior to philosophy, which – since it is based on conjectures concocted from the experience of the senses – contains the inherent peril of it "leading to ruin."

Van Schurman does not provide any explanation for her judgments concerning philosophy's disastrous potential; however, that explanation would presumably have been allied with the reasons why she exhorted Elisabeth to eschew astrology. Physics was "a little dreary," but had its good points – even Saint Augustine had written about it. The real danger came when one turned to the sky:

Now Astrology (I am not taking this word to mean Astronomy, as they were accustomed to do in ancient times; Astronomy is a noble science, and very worthy of our contemplation) goes further, and usually degenerates into super-stition, because it attributes more to secondary causes than is permitted in accordance with the order and fitness of Nature. For to say that human will and happenstance depend upon the configuration of the sky, or the aspects and conjunctions of the Planets, is to introduce into the world a necessity greater than that of the Stoics. Those causes that act freely and fortuitously do not allow themselves to be determined by natural causes, that is to say, by the influence of celestial bodies; but rather, due to their excellence, these causes are immediately dependent upon the first and supreme cause.[53]

[52] *Ibid.*   [53] *Ibid.*

Thus the problem with philosophy, as with astrology, is that it introduces extraneous layers into the celestial system of causation. Van Schurman believed that there was only one universal working force – and that was God. When van Schurman refers to what is permitted "in accordance with the order and fitness of Nature," she is referring to the Stoic maxim "to live consistently with nature." Given her references to Justus Lipsius, van Schurman was probably drawing on Lipsius' *De Constantia* (1584), considered to be a foundational statement of early modern Neo-Stoicism. In this text, Lipsius tried to reconcile Stoicism with Christianity, rejecting Stoic physics (materialism and determinism) while retaining the Stoic ethical system of virtue and self-knowledge. Interpolating other causes – such as the disposition of the planets, or empirically derived laws of nature – between God and Man would obfuscate human understanding of Divine Will, and lead inevitably to error.

Interestingly, however, van Schurman also appears to be saying that it is permissible, even within the bounds of her strict Calvinist principles, to try to predict the future. The issue arises not once, but twice. First, van Schurman tells Elisabeth that one may prognosticate using the lessons of history; based on them, "we can conjecture with real certainty about the ages to come." However, if one uses astrology to do the very same thing – "to predict future conditional events" – it becomes "no less dangerous than vain." Thus it is not the desire for future knowledge that is problematic, but rather the process one uses in fulfilling this desire.

Ultimately, however, van Schurman points out that no answers will be found on Earth; both the beginning and the end inhere in God, and van Schurman's citation of Isaiah makes this clear: "Remember the former things of old: for I am God, and there is none else; I am God, and there is none like me. Declaring the end from the beginning, and from ancient times the things that are not yet done."[54] Since there is no trace of Elisabeth's original letter, we cannot know how or why the issue of future events arose: was van Schurman responding to a particular query from Elisabeth? Or was this matter becoming a larger part of van Schurman's own thinking? But we do have, in this reply, some indication that the applications for this future knowledge would lie within the realm of politics.

In discussing the best use of history, van Schurman wrote:

Justus Lipsius outlined this method more completely in his book entitled *Admonitions and Political Examples*, demonstrating to certain people, and to

---

[54] Isaiah 46:9–10. Holy Bible, King James Version.

public figures, how they could make use of both ancient and modern examples. And in fact it seems to me that that the latter are in no way inferior to the former, if we consider less the force and eloquence of the Historians than their subject matter. I would dare to compare a single Elizabeth, who in her lifetime was Queen of England, or a single Jane Grey, to all the illustrious women of ancient Greece and Rome.[55]

Here we have van Schurman recommending Queen Elizabeth and Jane Grey – two learned women who ruled England – as models worth emulating. These are explicitly political *exempla*. It would appear, then, that van Schurman is creating in this letter an alternative to Vives' *De Institutione Feminae Christianae*, the severely limiting text on women's education that had been her *bête noire* in the correspondence with Rivet. Vives had written his treatise for Mary, a Tudor princess who would one day ascend the throne. Van Schurman was creating this program for Elisabeth, a Stuart-Palatine princess, related distantly to Mary Tudor, who might also one day ascend a throne.

Given Elisabeth's lifelong and extremely active involvement in politics, it is tempting to conjecture that this letter was a very specific response to Elisabeth's original query, which might have been: what course of reading and study would be most useful and appropriate for a learned female ruler? Without her original letter, this supposition must remain in the realm of conjecture. Nevertheless, van Schurman's response does provide telling evidence of Elisabeth's continuing drive to increase her own learning, to identify a philosophical path, and to acquire appropriate mentors.

Elisabeth made full use of her location at the crossroads of learned Europe, helping to turn her mother's exile court into a "privileged place" for women's intellectual networking. When van Schurman joined her there, the exile court also became a location for women's scholarly mentoring. The next chapter follows the development of this mentoring process, as it expanded outward from The Hague into the construction of the intellectual family – a network of adopted scholarly kin – which would include Marie de Gournay and Marie du Moulin.

---

[55] Van Schurman to Elisabeth, September 7, 1639. *Opuscula*, 281–7. Also in van Schurman, *Whether a Christian Woman*, 57–60.

CHAPTER 3

Marie de Gournay, Marie du Moulin, and Anna Maria van Schurman: constructing intellectual kinship

> Teach me, and instruct me in accordance with your modesty and wisdom ...
>
> Marie du Moulin to Anna Maria van Schurman[1]

In a letter dated March 18, 1635, Anna Maria van Schurman found herself needing to apologize to her mentor, André Rivet. She had been hiding herself away and had not told him why. It was not because she had been neglecting her studies; in fact, her excuse was precisely the reverse. Her studies had been eating up all her time. However, these were not the studies he had assigned to her. Moving beyond Rivet, she had been working with two other possible mentors – two scholars who represented polar opposites in terms of the seventeenth-century intellectual spectrum. First, as she explained to Rivet, there was the orthodox Calvinist Voëtius, who had been teaching her Hebrew:

> Now at last I have returned to myself, Respected and Beloved Father in Christ; up until this point I was pulled in many different directions by a succession and variety of studies. Wherefore ... I deemed that I owed my first letter to you. Indeed I had decided to address you in Hebrew, lest there be anything whatsoever keeping your paternal expectations and concerns concerning my progress in suspense for an even longer time.[2]

Since mastery of Hebrew would have allowed van Schurman to engage with the Old Testament in its original form, these were studies that made sense for the young Calvinist scholar; thus she was confident that Rivet would approve. But at the same time, van Schurman had been

---

[1] Marie du Moulin to Anna Maria van Schurman. Original in Hebrew. The letter is undated, except for "the fifth of the month, from Breda"; this places it sometime between 1647 and 1651, when André Rivet was curator of the College at Breda. University of Amsterdam, Gemeente Amsterdam archief handschriften, Diederichs Collection, 16 Ag.

[2] Anna Maria van Schurman, Utrecht, to André Rivet, The Hague, March 18, 1635, Universiteit Bibliotheek Utrecht, HS 8*F.19, f. 1.

investigating the pursuit of knowledge at another extreme – and, perhaps encouraged by her friend Princess Elisabeth, she had begun visiting the philosopher René Descartes:

Moreover, I did not wish to conceal from you that I have just visited Monsieur Descartes, a man of great, indeed unheard-of (as they say) erudition: a man who grandly deems the common or accepted progress of letters to be insufficient, saying that he sees none of this as contributing anything toward true Knowledge; moreover he himself has discovered an alternate path, by which route he arrives there far more quickly and surely.

In this case, however, she was still somewhat unsure of the reception her news would receive, since Descartes was already controversial. So van Schurman went on to defend her choice:

I consider the esteemed Professor Reneri to be an advocate for all this, and, as it were, the guarantor; however I reckoned that you ought to be consulted before any other as to what you think, since (as our very same Reneri asserts) you have been acquainted with the man.[3]

It is a letter that speaks to the affection, duty, respect, and shared intellectual interests that characterized van Schurman's relationship with Rivet. More importantly, however, this letter contains a wealth of information regarding the formation of female scholarship within the seventeenth-century republic of letters.

This chapter documents another stage in the process whereby these intellectual women were forming themselves into a network that functioned as other networks did within the seventeenth-century republic of letters – both on its own, as a small-focus group concerned with furthering a particular shared agenda, and as an integrated component of the larger intellectual enterprise. Despite their exclusion from the academy, it is clear from these exchanges that female scholars were utilizing fully the three primary work practices of the republic of letters – correspondence, networking, and mentorship – to further both their own intellectual development and that of their colleagues. And in particular, what these early letters demonstrate is the complexity of the process through which early modern female scholars constructed intellectual mentoring relationships – a process that involved not only friendship, faith, and kindness, but a sophisticated level of strategizing as well.

---

[3] *Ibid.* Henri Régnier (1593–1639) was known in the republic of letters as Henricus Reneri.

Van Schurman's letter of March 18 serves as an example of this process in action. According to this letter, one mentor alone was not enough for this female scholar. By 1635, van Schurman had been working for four years with Rivet, a man whose spiritual guidance and affection were evident from his status as her "beloved father in Christ." And beyond this, Rivet was fostering her development in two other ways: first, he served as her opponent in an epistolary quarrel over women's aptitude for learning, a friendly, rigorous, and rational discussion that led to her first and most enduring publication; and second, he used his position at the exile court in The Hague to introduce her to a number of other scholars, both male and female.

Yet in addition to Rivet, van Schurman was working with the orthodox Calvinist theologian Voëtius. This was a process that had begun about six months earlier, when van Schurman first wrote to Rivet that she was trying to improve her Greek:

Our most excellent and illustrious Professor Voëtius has most opportunely offered himself to me for the purpose of improving my acquaintance with the Greek language . . . And in fact he has also to some extent given me a taste of the Hebrew language, and has inspired in me no ordinary love for that holy tongue.[4]

She was also in touch with Reneri, a professor at the University of Utrecht and a friend of René Descartes. And she had been visiting Descartes himself, in order to learn more about his "alternate path" to true knowledge.

Descartes' path to true knowledge was controversial, and very different from the route followed by either Voëtius or Rivet.[5] In fact, Voëtius and Descartes were the primary combatants in the *querelle d'Utrecht*, a fierce and bitter controversy that lasted from 1639 until Descartes' death in 1650. The dispute began with Descartes' encouragement of Regius (Henri le Roy, 1598–1679), a physician, natural philosopher, and professor of medicine at the University of Utrecht. Regius had been disseminating Cartesian ideas at the school. When the alarmed theologian Voëtius tried to put a stop to this, Descartes wrote a public letter implying that Voëtius was using his

---

[4] Van Schurman to Rivet, November 21, 1634, KB MS.133 B 8, no. 9. In van Schurman's *Opuscula* there are two undated letters written in Hebrew to Voëtius and to André Rivet. The letter to Rivet is an echo of the Latin letter above, while the letter to Voëtius expresses her gratitude for this instruction. *Opuscula*, 158–9.

[5] On Descartes' relationships with Dutch scholars, see Theo Verbeek, *Descartes and the Dutch: Early Reactions to Cartesian Philosophy, 1637–1650* (Carbondale, IL, 1992); and Cohen, *Écrivains français*, 535–78 and 595–601. On Voëtius, see John W. Beardslee, *Reformed Dogmatics: J. Wollebius, G. Voëtius, F. Turretin* (New York, 1965).

theological authority as an excuse to meddle in other disciplines. The ensuing dispute expanded to involve many members of the republic of letters, including Martin Schook and Voëtius' son Paul Voët.[6]

This battle might easily have made matters awkward for van Schurman. Voëtius was famously intolerant; it has been pointed out that Voëtius hated Catholics, philosophers, and foreigners – and Descartes was all three.[7] However, as we saw in her letter to Elisabeth, van Schurman was solidly grounded in the older tradition of humanist scholarship; thus by the time the controversy erupted, it was already quite clear that she distrusted Descartes' method. Van Schurman, then, had proceeded on her own to set up a varied and inclusive educational program for herself in Greek, Hebrew, and philosophy. She had not relied on one mentor alone. And in addition to learning new languages, she had sought out teachers representing a wide spectrum of thought on issues of theology and metaphysics.

Mentoring, as has already been noted, was an essential component of both the structured environment of the early modern academy and the less-structured functioning of the republic of letters. In addition, there were intellectual issues particular to the female scholar; and in order to address these issues, women in the republic of letters created an additional layer of female mentorship to supplement the mentoring relationships they shared with their male colleagues. A number of intellectual women would turn to van Schurman in this capacity. And, as we have seen, van Schurman was already serving as mentor and model to other young female scholars, like Elisabeth. Yet van Schurman was still very young herself; she wanted a female role model of her own, someone to show her how a virtuous woman might negotiate her uniquely complicated path to scholarship. Thus van Schurman would decide to supplement her work with Rivet, Voëtius, and Descartes by turning to a female scholar from a previous generation, one whose frankly feminist work she had admired and defended for years.[8] That scholar was the French humanist Marie le Jars de Gournay.

---

[6] Descartes and Schook, *La Querelle d'Utrecht*; van Ruler, *The Crisis of Causality*.

[7] Vrooman, *René Descartes*, 153–4; Elizabeth Haldane, *Descartes: His Life and Times* (London, 1905), 202–4.

[8] In characterizing an early modern discourse as "feminist," I use the definition given by Siep Stuurman, who in turn draws on Nancy Cott and Karen Offen: "I distinguish three core components that together define a discourse as feminist: criticism of misogyny and male supremacy; the conviction that the condition of women is not an immutable fact of nature and can be changed for the better; and a sense of gender group identity, the conscious will to give a public voice to women, or 'to defend the female sex.' Using these criteria, we can characterize many early-modern writings as feminist in a nonanachronistic way, and without overstating the

MARIE DE GOURNAY (1565–1645)

Marie le Jars de Gournay was an impoverished female scholar of the sixteenth century who nevertheless managed to lead a very public life. She published widely, and was involved in a number of French literary controversies.[9] Gournay was frequently a topic of discussion among her intellectual contemporaries; and, although the praises of her admiring friends provide a counterpoint to the stories told by her derisive foes, all accounts are in full agreement on one point – "La Damoiselle de Gournay" was a very difficult woman. In fact, Gournay herself had no problem admitting that she was irascible, impatient, and hot-tempered. In *Peincture de moeurs*, a 1626 self-portrait in verse, Gournay wrote a list of her faults: "I have a fiery temperament, / I hardly ever forget a deeply-felt insult, / I am impatient and partial to rage."[10] Passionate, persistent, obstinate, and old-fashioned, she formed intense attachments to a select group of principles and people, then consecrated her life and career to an ongoing battle with the rest. Yet mixed in with her heartfelt devotion to the literary past was an equally uncompromising belief in the rights and abilities of contemporary women – and it was this heroic, eccentric, and insistent feminism that brought "*la vieille féministe*" to the attention of a very young Anna Maria van Schurman.[11]

Gournay lived from 1565 to 1645, a long life that began in the waning days of Renaissance humanism, and ended with the rise of French *pré-classicisme* and the birth of the Académie Française. She was born in Paris, one of six children of Guillaume de Jars, a member of a noble family and a treasurer in the court of Charles IX, and his wife Jeanne de Hacqueville. Guillaume died in 1577, and his widow, unable to afford the Parisian lifestyle, moved herself and the children to Gournay-sur-Aronde.

Gournay's father was dead, and her mother had no interest in learning; thus, while many early modern female scholars benefited from having

---

continuities with later feminisms." Siep Stuurman, *François Poulain de la Barre and the Invention of Modern Equality* (Cambridge, MA, 2004), 8.

[9] For contemporary views on Marie de Gournay, see Tallemant des Réaux, *Les Historiettes de Tallemant des Réaux*, ed. Georges Mongrédien, 8 vols. (Paris, 1932–4), II, 213–23; and Nicéron, *Mémoires pour servir*, XVI, 232–4. There is some interesting early twentieth-century scholarship on Marie de Gournay, notably: Théodore Joran, *La Trouée féministe* (Paris, 1909); and Mario Lodovico Schiff, *La Fille d'alliance de Montaigne, Marie de Gournay* (Paris, 1910). For modern assessments, see Ilsley, *A Daughter of the Renaissance*; Marie Le Jars de Gournay, *Fragments d'un discours féminin: textes établis, présentés et commentés par Elyane Dezon-Jones* (Paris, 1988); Gournay, *Apology for the Woman Writing*; and Fogel, *Marie de Gournay*.

[10] Schiff, *La Fille d'alliance de Montaigne*, 109.   [11] *Ibid.*, 47, 117.

fathers who doted on their talented daughters, or brothers whose lessons they could audit, the young Gournay had no resources other than her own determination. She was an autodidact, stealing moments away from household chores to teach herself Latin and Greek, a process she described in her third-person autobiography:

Under her mother's roof, and for the most part during stolen moments, she learned her letters alone, even Latin, without a grammar and without assistance, comparing the French translations of Latin works side-by-side against their originals … After someone showed her a Greek grammar, she learned that language, more or less, in very little time, but afterward she neglected it, finding the goal of perfecting it so far away that it would never be attained.[12]

Gournay also learned Spanish and Italian, and would eventually improve her Greek, although she would remain defensive about her imperfections in that language, and her lack of formal schooling. She had Latin, which was enough – everything else was old-fashioned and unnecessary – thus her critics were merely being stuffy:

a learned woman without Greek, without Hebrew, without aptitude for providing scholarly commentary on authors, without manuscripts, without Logic, without Physics or Metaphysics, Mathematics, or the rest? Let us add, without old medals in a cabinet, since possessing them is regularly set up as one of the chief accomplishments in our age.[13]

She does not say where she acquired her books, thus one must presume that they were part of the library at Gournay. However, her primary interests were not in linguistics and theology, as with van Schurman, or in philosophy and mathematics, like Elisabeth. Gournay's interests lay in the direction of traditional humanist scholarship on the one hand, and French language and literature on the other.

The defining moment of Gournay's life came in 1584, when at the age of nineteen she read the *Essais* of Michel de Montaigne for the first time. It was an experience she would later describe as a life-altering "transport."[14] She vowed to meet the author, and in 1588 Gournay made the trip to Paris. There she sent a letter to Montaigne, describing her profound respect and admiration for the man and his work. Montaigne responded

---

[12] From *Copie de la vie de la Damoiselle de Gournay* (1616), published as part of Gournay's 1641 *Les Advis ou les presens de la demoiselle de Gournay*. Gournay, *Fragments d'un discours féminin*, 138–9.
[13] From *L'Apologie pour celle qui escrit*. One of Gournay's many self-portraits, it first appeared in 1626 as one of two autobiographical components in *L'Ombre de la Damoiselle de Gournay*. Gournay, *Apology for the Woman Writing*, 126.
[14] From the Preface to her 1595 edition of Montaigne's *Essais*. Schiff, *La Fille d'alliance de Montaigne*, 3.

by showing up on her doorstep and offering to make the fatherless girl his intellectual daughter, or *fille d'alliance*. As Gournay developed her relationship with her adoptive intellectual father, she also began corresponding with the Belgian scholar Justus Lipsius, a humanist, antiquarian and philologist who taught law at the University of Leiden, and who was also an ardent admirer of Montaigne. This was additionally the beginning of her own writing career, when she was inspired by a stroll with her mentor to write *Le Proumenoir de Monsieur de Montaigne*. However, Gournay had no time to publish her work until nearly five years later; her mother had died in 1591, and Gournay had taken on the full responsibility for raising and supporting her siblings.

From this point on, economic hardship affected every part of Gournay's life. The need for money was likely a contributing factor to her ten-year project of alchemical research, from 1598 to 1608. While experimenting in alchemy was certainly consistent with Gournay's desire for knowledge, it was also true that the ability to produce gold would have been most welcome. Yet to set up a laboratory, and then to purchase equipment and supplies, required a considerable outlay of funds; thus once again, Gournay felt obliged to mount a defense:

> To that general condemnation of intellectual women, a particular point is added in my case – that is, my practice of alchemy, which they deem absolute folly in itself. Truly, whether that science is indeed folly, as they say, I do not know. But well I know this ... it is no small rashness to pronounce on occult subjects, negatively or affirmatively, or to prohibit the practice of them, if that practice lends itself to an exquisite consideration of nature, as does the practice of this one, which is therefore worthy of a curious mind, even if it has no utility but that alone.[15]

Economic hardship also affected Gournay's ability to fashion herself as a Parisian *salonnière*, since that project inevitably suffered from her tight budget and terrible food. According to one report: "[A]t one time a guest found the roast fowl so tough that it was uneatable, but her cat Donzelle finished the bird with gusto!"[16] Thus Gournay had neither the funds, the chef, nor the charm that would enable her to succeed with the brilliance she had envisioned. Her salon did have a success of sorts, and she developed her own intellectual circle; even John Evelyn came to visit

---

[15] Gournay, *Apology for the Woman Writing*, 127–9. See also Patricia Phillips, *The Scientific Lady: A Social History of Women's Scientific Interests 1520–1918* (London, 1990), 52–6.
[16] Ilsley, *A Daughter of the Renaissance*, 89.

the renowned *savante* when he was in Paris in the 1640s. But even at this early stage, her irascible nature and country manners were making her a prime target for practical jokes.[17] Yet the alchemical laboratory, the bare-bones salon, and the endless series of social squabbles do not define Marie de Gournay. She was first and foremost a writer, doing whatever she could to further her career while supporting herself and her siblings. Gournay had a real mentor in Montaigne while he lived, but this did not translate into either profitable patronage or perfect harmony – and in a letter from Gournay to Montaigne, introducing her *Proumenoir*, we have an instructive illustration of the complex ways in which male-to-female mentoring functioned in the republic of letters.

Gournay's letter appears to be a response to Montaigne's published opinions on female learning. In the *Essais*, he had asserted that women needed only to be charming, refined, and beautiful, in order "to do honor to the arts and to decorate decoration." There was little need for more, and there certainly was no use for higher learning in "well-born women":

When I see them intent on rhetoric, astrology, logic, and similar drugs, so vain and useless for their needs, I begin to fear that the men who advise them to do this, do so as a means of gaining authority over them under this pretext. For what other excuse could I find for them?[18]

It is not clear how or whether this opinion might apply to women of a different social rank, or whether Gournay's particular situation – that of a well-born woman who was now in severe financial straits – might have put her in a different category. Montaigne then went on to allow that if these women insisted on acquiring more book learning, they might derive some usefulness from poetry and history; however, philosophy might be best:

In philosophy, from the part that is useful for life, they will take the lessons that will train them to judge our humors and characteristics, to defend themselves against our treacheries . . . That is the most I should assign to them in the matter of learning.[19]

Thus according to Montaigne, "well-born women" really only needed to learn what was necessary for dealing with well-born men.

---

[17] See, for instance, Nicéron's description of an elaborate practical joke involving a visit to Gournay by serial impersonators of the poet Honoré de Bueil, Marquis de Racan. Nicéron, *Mémoires pour servir*, XVI, 232–4.

[18] Michel de Montaigne, "Of Three Kinds of Association," in *The Complete Essays of Montaigne*, ed. Donald Frame (Stanford, 1965), Book III, Essay no. 3, 624–5.

[19] *Ibid.*

This statement would certainly seem to have been contradicted by Montaigne's personal mentorship of Gournay. It was also contradicted by Gournay herself, in her introduction to the *Proumenoir*. Addressing Montaigne directly, she used this forum to belittle men's fears of female learning:

> whoever it was that first forbade learning [to women], claiming it was a torch that might ignite lasciviousness, I believe, my father, it was because he was so unfamiliar with letters that he feared he would be completely overcome by the second day of their studies. The vulgar say that in order for a woman to be chaste, she must not be so clever. Truly, it does too little honor to chastity to believe that only the blind could find it beautiful.[20]

In the *Essais*, then, it had appeared that Montaigne was concerned; he feared that women, under the guise of learning situations for which there was no point to begin with, might be susceptible to male manipulation and unwanted seductions. Gournay had responded, and flipped this around. She insisted to her *père d'alliance* that only a man – and further, a man who was ignorant, weak, and evil-minded – could possibly fear such a scenario.

It would therefore seem that Gournay had just issued a very harsh and very public rebuke to her mentor for his attitude toward learned women. However, another possible reading is suggested when we examine the way in which this same argument was mirrored by another *père* and *fille d'alliance*, André Rivet and Anna Maria van Schurman.

Since the very beginning of their epistolary relationship in 1631, van Schurman and her *père d'alliance* had been arguing about women's scholarship. There were two issues: virtue and erudition. In terms of virtue, they had both agreed that erudition came with potential moral pitfalls, and van Schurman herself had always felt that her spirituality was threatened by her worldly fame. In fact, it was Rivet who had pointed out that van Schurman's renown, although uncomfortable for her, might still be a good thing in three ways: first, she might inspire others; second, she would serve as a wonderful example of God's gifts; and third, she was living proof that what prevented women from attaining the heights of scholarly achievement was not a lack of intellect, but rather a lack of time. Most women were simply far too busy with "other and more humble occupations." And indeed, this was just as well.

---

[20]　This is taken from the 1594 Preface; it was removed from subsequent editions. Marie de Gournay, *Le Proumenoir de Monsieur de Montaigne. Par sa fille d'alliance* (Paris, 1594), 41v.

Erudition was fine for someone as special as van Schurman, but simply could not be considered appropriate for women in general.[21]

When van Schurman replied, she quoted Rivet's words back to him, agreeing that women with family obligations were simply too busy to pursue scholarship. The issue was time. But once that impediment was removed, van Schurman argued, there was no need to hold back

but if, on the other hand, we mean girls who have been endowed with a natural capacity, and who ought to be educated more liberally, of the sort that our age is producing as much as possible, I agree with greater difficulty. Immoderate veneration for knowledge, or for the justice of natural law, causes me to change my position, so that I will not consider as rare in our sex that which is most worthy of everyone's devotion.[22]

Schurman's authority for this assertion was Marie de Gournay, and Gournay's treatise *Égalité des hommes et des femmes*:

For if we are seeking evidence from antiquity, then not only the examples of every age, but also the judgment of the greatest men will prove the contrary; as the most noble glory of Gournay has made known no less charmingly than learnedly in the little book that she called *The Equality of Men and Women*.[23]

Interestingly, van Schurman's response is dated 1637, five years after Rivet's letter – and since the two corresponded regularly throughout the intervening years, it is not at all clear why she would have waited so long. This delay would make sense, however, if the considerations were strategic, and if these letters were being crafted with an eye toward future publication.

Meanwhile, Rivet was also unwilling to concede his point. Everything flowed from one basic question:

Which sort of learning, then, is appropriate for the sex to pursue? Indeed you will not be angry with me, however much Gournay opposes it, if I decree along with the Apostle that, "the woman is the weaker vessel."[24]

As St Paul had made clear, women were weaker, hence more vulnerable to moral and spiritual error – a fact which had held true ever since Eve ate

---

[21] André Rivet, Leiden, to Anna Maria van Schurman, Utrecht, March 1, 1632, in *Opuscula*, 60–2. Also translated by Joyce Irwin in van Schurman, *Whether a Christian Woman*, 40–1.

[22] Van Schurman to Rivet, November 6, 1637, KB MS.133 B 8, no. 14. Later published in van Schurman's *Opuscula*, 63–80, where it was printed with some minor changes and misdated March 15, 1638. Also in van Schurman, *Whether a Christian Woman*, 41–8.

[23] *Ibid.*

[24] Rivet to van Schurman, March 18, 1638, in *Opuscula*, 87. Also in van Schurman, *Whether a Christian Woman*, 48–54.

from the Tree of Knowledge in the Garden of Eden. Thus in order to avoid further disasters on a biblical scale, women still needed to be protected from confusing writings and morally precarious learning. Rivet suggested that perhaps the writings of Juan Luis Vives would be a better guide to women's education than those of Gournay. Vives' intellectual circle had included some of the most renowned female scholars of Tudor England, such as Margaret Roper and Lady Jane Grey. However, his approach to the education of his royal female pupils had been conservative, the aim being to "fence them in with holy counsels," so that they – and by extension those for whom they were responsible – would not be harmed by questionable knowledge.[25] So while Rivet did not begrudge van Schurman her justifiable pride in exemplary women, the point was that they needed to remain just that – exemplary: "not, perhaps, because there could not be more of them, but because it might not be useful, nor in the public good."[26] The real issue, then, was not female learning *per se*, but social control.

Society's most basic institutions, such as government and the church, had at their core an assumption that men and women would continue to perform the roles traditional to their gender. Everyone was agreed that, for good or ill, women had been, and continued to be, excluded from access to higher learning. Even though numerous *exempla* were brought forth time and time again to show that there had always been exceptions, the general case still held true. What, then, might happen if this general case were suddenly to change, if women were to be granted what they had never been granted before – an equal opportunity to participate in the world of scholarship?

Rivet's point was that these basic social institutions would then be severely threatened; and on that point, van Schurman appeared to acquiesce. She apologized for any lack of clarity that might have led Rivet to suspect that she wanted women to supplant men. Moreover, she did not agree with absolutely everything Gournay had said, either:

Just as I can by no means disapprove of the most noble Gournay's little treatise *De l'egalité des hommes et des femmes* due to its elegance and charm, so too I would neither wish nor even dare to approve of it in all respects.[27]

---

[25] Juan Luis Vives, *The Instruction of a Christen Woman*, ed. Virginia Beauchamp, Elizabeth Hagemen and Margaret Mikesell (Urbana, 2002).

[26] Rivet to van Schurman, 18 March, 1638, in *Opuscula*, 87. Also in van Schurman, *Whether a Christian Woman*, 48–54.

[27] Van Schurman to Rivet, March 14, 1638, KB MS.133 B 8, no. 16. Later printed in *Opuscula*, 91–5. Also in van Schurman, *Whether a Christian Woman*, 54–6. The dates here do not make sense, since this would mean that van Schurman's letter of March 14 was a response to Rivet's letter dated four

The more conservative Vives was indeed a sensible guide, whom she would henceforth try to follow.

Yet, for both Gournay and van Schurman, these arguments over female erudition were grafted onto another layer of apparent contradiction and conflict with their mentors. Rivet's public stance regarding learned women emerges as somewhat anxious and conservative, while at the same time he was encouraging Schurman to attain the heights of erudition. And when Montaigne had decried higher learning in well-born ladies, he had simultaneously been mentoring the well-born Gournay in a very public way. How can these conflicting positions be reconciled in a way that helps us to understand the real functioning of mentorship in the republic of letters, and the *famille d'alliance* in particular?

I would suggest that these seeming contradictions may not have been perceived as a problem at all. Instead, these variant stances were understood as manifestations of the seventeenth-century intellectual enterprise at work, functioning in different ways at different levels. Thus while the Rivet–van Schurman and Montaigne–Gournay examples are separated by significant distances in terms of nation, faith, and the passage of fifty years, the similarities are both striking and instructive. And if we turn to examine the formats in which these statements on female learning were expressed, then these apparent contradictions emerge as evidence for the interplay of large-scale and small-scale intellectual agendas within the republic of letters.

On the large-scale level of print, there is always a certain concern for order. The inequalities had been so basic, and of such long standing, that the possible consequences of disorder, dissolution, and moral chaos seemed unavoidable. But in the republic of letters, reputations and relationships were no less important than printed works.[28] Thus when we turn to the agenda of the small-scale community – in this case, the *famille d'alliance* – the threat of chaotic consequences seems to dwindle. Through the epistolary circulation of correspondence and the personal circulation of scholars on the *peregrinatio academica*, Rivet and Montaigne would have been just as well known for their personal support of their *filles d'alliance* as they were for their published reservations concerning higher learning for women in general. And on an even smaller scale, that

---

days later, on March 18. Irwin suggests that this might have resulted from a confusion of dates in two different calendrical systems – the "new-style" Gregorian and the "old-style" Julian – which were ten days apart.

[28] Goldgar, *Impolite Learning*, 4–7.

of the one-on-one functioning of mentoring relationships, the threat
disappears entirely. Neither Rivet nor Montaigne feared earth-shaking
consequences from their support for their chosen *filles d'alliance*.

However, since a male scholar could so easily come down on both
sides of the fence in the quarrel over learned women, it is also true
that the early modern female scholar could find herself in a rather
precarious and vulnerable position. Thus we find, in the republic of
letters, that female scholars with supportive *pères d'alliance* still needed
to seek out female mentors as well. And this is precisely what van
Schurman did.

When van Schurman ceased the public argument with Rivet over
female erudition, she had also appeared to acquiesce. Appearances, however, can be deceiving – and acquiescence is not agreement. In fact, van
Schurman's private approval of Gournay's treatise appears to have continued unabated. She wrote a ringing paean of praise and sent it to Marie
de Gournay:

> Anna Maria van Schurman congratulates
> the great and generously spirited
> Heroine Gournay
> for bravely defending the cause of our sex.
> You bear the arms of Pallas in battle, courageous woman warrior;
> And in order to wear the laurel, you bear the arms of Pallas.
> Thus it is fitting that you plead the cause of our innocent sex,
> And the guilty men have their own weapons turned against them.
> Lead on, glory of Gournay, we will follow your standard:
> Indeed your cause, mightier than oak, goes before you.[29]

The martial overtones here are inescapable. Van Schurman, whose
reputation for modesty, manners, and Christian humility was equalled
only by her intellectual glory, had done a complete turnabout. Casting
off her mantle of goddess-like perfection, van Schurman portrays
herself here as a lowly but eager foot soldier in the *querelle des
femmes*. The war is being fought over women's right to study – and
in the ranks of an avenging army of women, this demure Calvinist
maiden is following an elderly Catholic Minerva into battle against

---

[29] The poem is undated; however, given the dates of their correspondence, it was probably sent in
1638 or 1639. Gournay's response appeared in the 1641 edition of her *Égalité*, and the poem itself
was eventually published in van Schurman's 1648 *Opuscula*. Also translated by Pieta van Beek in
"*Alpha Virginum*: Anna Maria van Schurman (1607–1678)," in *Women Writing Latin: From Roman
Antiquity to Early Modern Europe*, ed. Laurie J. Churchill *et al.*, 3 vols. (New York and London,
2002), III, 289.

armies of disdainful men. Privately, however, this was a much more practical offering – and it was one which Gournay accepted.

When van Schurman's poem reached Gournay, it had been fifty years since the French scholar had last tried to expand her *famille d'alliance*. Like van Schurman, Gournay had been strategic about her position in the republic of letters, and had multiplied her avenues of entrée by acquiring more than one mentor. Thus in 1588, she had written to the Belgian scholar Justus Lipsius, hoping to form a second mentoring connection with him. Her letter must have given ample evidence of her erudition; Lipsius had responded with complete amazement:

Who are you, who writes to me thus? A maiden? I can scarcely credit that fact. Is it possible that these things – I will not even mention the reading and the talents, but the prudence and judgment – fall to the lot of that sex, in an age such as ours? Maiden, you have unsettled me: and I do not know whether to rejoice on behalf of our age, or grieve on behalf of my sex . . . Certainly I, who am unacquainted with you, love you; and although I render affection to very few, I admire you.[30]

They continued to correspond, based on their shared admiration of Montaigne, and a shared devotion to philology and Latin texts. Indeed it was Lipsius who had the sad task of telling Gournay in 1593 that her *père d'alliance* had died some months earlier. And in the conclusion of that letter, he had offered to become a second mentor to the grieving girl:

This is enough for now. I love you, Maiden, but chastely, in the same way that I love knowledge. Return that same love to me, and since your father has left this life, consider me to be your brother.[31]

It was a kind and much-appreciated offer. It was also an offer that Gournay took to heart. She sent numerous tracts, poems, and revisions to her *frère d'alliance*, in order to get his advice and guidance. And, since Montaigne's widow had pleaded with her to oversee the publication of her

---

[30] Justus Lipsius, Leiden, to Marie de Gournay. Undated, but probably 1588 or 1589, based on surrounding letters in the text. Gournay's original letter does not appear to be extant. Epistola IX in Justus Lipsius, *Epistolarum Centuria Secunda* (London, 1590), 52.

[31] Justus Lipsius to Marie de Gournay, May 24, 1593. Epistola XV from "Justi Lipsi Epistolarum Selectarum Centuria I ad Belgas," in Justus Lipsius, *Justi Lipsi Epistolarum Selectarum Chilias* ([Leiden?], 1618), 516–17. For a French translation of this letter, see J. F. Payen, "Recherches sur Michel Montaigne. Correspondance relative à sa mort," *Bulletin du Bibliophile et du Bibliothécaire* 15 (1862), 1310.

late husband's work, Gournay especially wanted Lipsius' advice on her editions of Montaigne's *Essais*. When she asked for this advice, she reminded him of the brotherhood he had offered to her:

I am ambitious and eager to be in your good graces – a compensation of sorts for my great sorrow. Would you want to deny me this, which I know I have earned as the daughter of that great man, and which I enjoy as your sister? You will not have forgotten that you gave me that title, at a time when it only boiled down to you because of my need and the honor that it bestowed upon me.[32]

Thus Gournay's *famille d'alliance* had expanded to include an intellectual older brother, who stepped in to fill the shoes of her departed mentor Montaigne.

Yet this second mentoring relationship, while initially powerful, was not destined to survive. Lipsius eventually soured on his *sœur d'alliance*, although the reasons for this are unclear. It is possible that Lipsius had never really seen himself as a long-term mentor to Gournay, although even as late as May 1597, Lipsius was still addressing her in his letters as "maiden and sister" (*virgo et soror*) – thus the break in their relationship must have occurred between June 1597 and December 1601.[33]

Whatever his reasons, Lipsius' dissatisfaction emerges obliquely, in a 1601 letter to his friend the printer Jean Moretus. Moretus had apparently written to Lipsius about the possibility of publishing a book of Latin poetry by a young English Latinist, Elizabeth Jane Weston. Weston, the stepdaughter of the scryer Edward Kelley, lived in Prague, and was being hailed on the Continent as *Virgo Angla*. In the early seventeenth century, she was the best-known Anglo-Latin poet of either gender in Europe, and although Weston's works were never published in England, she was known to English scholars.[34] Moretus had some interest in publishing her, but Lipsius discouraged him with these words:

Monsieur, I read the letter sent from Prague about publishing the poems of that English girl. I am definitely of your opinion, that they will not sell by the

[32] Gournay to Lipsius, Leiden, November 19, 1596. University of Leiden MS. LIP 4, f. 190.

[33] Lipsius to Gournay, May 5, 1597. Epistola xxvii from "Justi Lipsi Epistolarum Selectarum Centuria Singularis ad Germanos & Gallos," in *Justi Lipsi Epistolarum Selectarum Chilias*, 329–30.

[34] On Elizabeth Jane Weston, see *Elizabeth Jane Weston: Collected Writings*, ed. Donald Cheney and Brenda M. Hosington (Toronto, 2000); Donald Cheney, "Virgo Angla: The Self-Fashioning of Westonia," and Brenda M. Hosington, "Elizabeth Jane Weston and Men's Discourse of Praise," in Bastiaensen, *La Femme lettrée à la Renaissance*, 107–18 and 119–28; and R. J. W. Evans, *Rudolf II and His World: A Study in Intellectual History 1576–1612* (Oxford, 1973), 150–1 and 218–28.

thousands, as they write, or even, I fear, by the dozens. You must do what seems best to you. As for me . . . I once praised that French girl, and now neither I nor (perhaps) others are very happy with my judgment. It is a deceitful sex, more shine than substance.[35]

It is possible that Gournay, "that French girl," never knew about this development. Yet despite the tensions that may have arisen with Lipsius, Gournay clearly welcomed the contact from van Schurman, and the opportunity to expand her *famille d'alliance* into the next generation.[36]

Since Gournay was active in scholarly networks, she could not have avoided hearing about this learned young woman in Utrecht; thus by the time van Schurman's poem arrived, Gournay had already developed some opinions as to how her colleague should proceed in her career. Her reply to van Schurman began with some rather convoluted prose expressing Gournay's admiration and gratitude. Then, once these formalities were out of the way, Gournay got right down to business:

Might I venture, in passing, to tell you Philosophically a little word of advice? Languages occupy too much, and for too long a time, a mind such as yours, which is capable of doing other and better things. Neither does it serve you to say, as you do, that you want to read everything in the Original, because their translations are not as good. For everything that literature might contain that is truly worthy of the efforts of a soul such as yours, can be found in Latin, or at the most in Greek, to which you might with little effort add Italian, Spanish, and above all French, which the *Essais*, among other things, have rendered necessary to the whole world.[37]

Gournay's reference here to a statement van Schurman made about "reading everything in the Original," suggests that van Schurman had probably accompanied her poem of praise with a letter of self-introduction. Interestingly, Gournay, at the age of seventy-four, is repeating here the very advice she had received from Lipsius almost fifty years earlier. Gournay had asked for Lipsius' help in improving her self-taught skills in Latin and Greek. Lipsius had agreed to help

---

[35] Justus Lipsius to Jean Moretus, December 27, 1601. Letter no. 109 in *La Correspondance de Juste Lipse conservée au Musée Plantin-Moretus*, ed. A. Gerlo and H. D. L. Vervliet (Antwerp, 1967), 134–5.

[36] Michèle Fogel, however, deems Gournay to have been permanently mistrustful of everything and everyone originating from the United Provinces, with the exception of Daniel Heinsius. Fogel, *Marie de Gournay*, 367, n. 116.

[37] Marie de Gournay to Anna Maria van Schurman, October 20, 1639, KB MS.133 B 8, no. 76. This is not the autograph letter from Gournay, but rather a copy in the hand of van Schurman. Gournay's original does not appear to be extant.

with the Latin, but had counselled her to "omit the Greek." Latin would be more than sufficient for the work she wanted to do.[38]

Gournay had apparently taken this advice to heart; thus when Gournay addressed her treatises on the *Institution du Prince* to the son of Henri IV, her suggested program of education was typically hard-headed and practical. The focus was on virtue, and the prince would need to be educated in edifying *exempla* from ancient times. In order to do this, he would have to know some Latin, in addition to his native French – but that was all. She knew this was not a popular stance, but she insisted there was no need whatsoever for Greek or Hebrew:

> But what is the reason behind such a choice, and such an excess of study? These impertinent times in which we live, when in order to enquire into a man's learning and ability, one ascertains how many languages he knows, as if languages *were* learning and ability, rather than simply one of the legs on which one travels from one thing to another – and a leg without which one can still arrive at one's goal, provided one at least has Latin.[39]

Gournay's advice to the son of the king was precisely the same advice she would give decades later to van Schurman, her own *fille d'alliance*. And the solution was also identical – to read the *Essais* of Montaigne, where one could find everything one really needed to know. The issue was therefore not pedagogy *per se*, but rather the effort to convince others in the world of learning that Montaigne's careful, balanced approach to all things scholarly – rather than a slavish devotion to the traditions of humanist erudition – was the proper path for all to follow.

However, these linguistic limitations were certainly not to van Schurman's taste. The young Dutch scholar was absolutely determined to read theological sources in their original languages. She was learning Hebrew, Chaldaic, Ethiopian and Arabic, and the possibility of linguistic overload was a concern for others besides Gournay. Even Arnoldus Buchelius, a humanist, lawyer, and family friend of the van Schurmans, wrote in his diary for 1635 that her Hebrew script was so beautiful it looked like it had been done by a printer – but when he heard she was learning Arabic as well, he wrote: "I worry whether something might prove to be too much, and in the end she might

---

[38] Lipsius to Gournay, *c*.1589. Epistola LX in Lipsius, *Epistolarum Centuria Secunda*, 52.
[39] Marie de Gournay, *Abregé d'institution, pour le Prince Souverain*, in *Les Advis, ou, les Presens de la Demoiselle de Gournay (1641)*, ed. Jean-Philippe Beaulieu and Hanna Fournier (Amsterdam, 1997), 201–2. These tracts were originally written in 1608 and published as *Bienvenue de monseigneur le duc d'Anjou.*

finally overwhelm herself."[40] So it seems that Gournay was in good company when she reproached van Schurman for her insistence on mastering Hebrew and Arabic in order to study the Bible in its original tongues.

Nevertheless, Gournay concluded her letter with a personal promise: "If I live yet another few years, I will send you a new edition of my *Advis*, where you will be able to read your name."[41] Thus Gournay was clearly welcoming van Schurman into the fold as a fellow female scholar in the republic of letters. But Gournay was also giving her advice that she simply could not follow – so van Schurman needed a little time to consider how she should respond. Weeks after receiving Gournay's letter, when van Schurman wrote to Rivet to discuss her correspondence with Claude Saumaise, she also included this note: "I have not yet answered the Most Excellent Maiden Gournay; however, as soon as time permits, I will take up the task, in order to repay this foreign debt."[42] In the meantime, however, she was proud of the contact. She was showing off Gournay's letter to her friends and family, and in Buchelius' diary, we find the following entry for February 1640:

The lady Marie de Gournay, who is still living, wrote to Miss Anna Maria van Schurman in a very friendly way, saying that she was keeping her writings in her heart, and provided that some life still remained to her, she would reissue her works, and in them she would leave her a memorial to their love and mutual support. Her brother revealed these things to me.[43]

But in the end, the issue of Hebrew studies was one on which van Schurman would stand firm – and from the ensuing exchange between Gournay and van Schurman, it is clear that this was an issue on which the parties would have to agree to disagree.

Two months later, van Schurman finally had an answer for Gournay. Like Gournay's letter, van Schurman's response began with some complex and formal flattery; she thanked the elder scholar for her praise, for her offer to make her approval public, and for "the advantages that your heroic virtues have procured for our sex."[44] Then, again like Gournay, van

---

[40] Entries dated May 1635 and September 1635 in Arend van Buchell, *Notae Quotidianae*, ed. J. W. C. van Campen (Utrecht, 1940), 40, 48, 65. On Buchelius, see Judith Pollmann, *Religious Choice in the Dutch Republic: The Reformation of Arnoldus Buchelius (1565–1641)* (Manchester, 1999).

[41] Gournay to van Schurman, October 20, 1639, KB MS.133 B 8, no. 76.

[42] Van Schurman to Rivet, December 12, 1639, KB MS. 133 B 8, no. 19.

[43] Buchell, *Notae Quotidianae*, 101.

[44] Van Schurman to Gournay, February 18, 1640, KB MS. 135 D 79. Also in van Schurman, *Whether a Christian Woman*, 70–1. Van Schurman's response to Gournay was printed in the *Opuscula*, 318–20, where it was misdated January 16, 1647; Gournay, however, had died two years earlier, in 1645.

Schurman got down to business. She simply could not comply with Gournay's advice.

In an elegant defense, van Schurman argued that Hebrew was completely necessary, and insisted that she was really quite rational about the amount of time she spent in language study:

> As to the matter on which you expressed your opinion, that I amuse myself too much in the study of languages, I can assure you that I only do this in my leisure hours, and sometimes only after long intervals, providing that you allow me to except my study of the Holy Tongue. For besides the fact that its subject is the word of God, who must be the foremost object of our thoughts, and the fact that there is no translation whatsoever that expresses so well the innocence and emphasis of these Holy Mysteries, [Hebrew] has qualities and beauties that cannot be equalled by all the elegancies of Greek and Latin.[45]

For van Schurman, who spent her entire life working toward achieving the most immediate experience of God, the ability to engage with sacred texts in their original form seemed an essential ingredient for achieving her spiritual goals. The choice to persist in her study of Hebrew, the Sacred Tongue, was a metaphor for her choice between a life lived in the presence of God and a life lived on the intellectual stage of the republic of letters. Thus van Schurman's letter ended with an apology:

> It is an infallible proof to me of your good graces that you believe my intellect was born for good things. For me, if I cannot live up to the great plans you have made for my abilities, I will at least try at all times to conform to your good advice.[46]

Van Schurman would not, of course, conform to Gournay's "good advice" regarding language study – and it was clear from her letter that this would be the case. Nevertheless, it appears that from this point on, Gournay's mentorship of van Schurman not only continued, but grew into an even stronger bond. And our evidence for this comes from a letter van Schurman wrote to Rivet, dated October of that same year. In that letter, van Schurman again discussed her correspondence with Saumaise, as well as their plans for publishing their epistolary exchange on women and learning. Then, she revealed the developments in her relationship with Gournay.

Gournay had apparently just written to her, making the astounding and explicit offer to be her *mère d'alliance*; thus van Schurman was begging Rivet to give her permission to proceed:

[45] *Ibid.*　　[46] *Ibid.*

In a written communication, your noble lady of Gournay has recently appealed to me for a closer covenant, namely that of a mother and daughter, creating a powerful bond between us that I must fortify. Wherefore I beg you, urgently, again and again, to indicate as soon as possible what I must arrange with respect to this matter in accordance with your fatherly judgment and discretion.[47]

This was clearly a heartfelt plea from the usually restrained and formal van Schurman. Gournay had just offered to make van Schurman her protégée, to adopt her as a member of the intellectual family that had included the renowned Montaigne. And, since Rivet was van Schurman's intellectual "father," his permission was, of course, required.[48]

Van Schurman's letter to Rivet is explicit in referring to a level of female intellectual mentorship that has not heretofore been documented. Here we see evidence of female scholars in the process of constructing a chain of intellectual kinship from generation to generation within the republic of letters; and the relationship Gournay offered to van Schurman – that of acting as her *mère d'alliance* – was the female scholar's adaptive mirror of inter-generational male mentoring relationships within the republic of letters. Rivet's and Voëtius' mentoring relationships with van Schurman would not have been supplanted, but rather supplemented by her alliance with the older female scholar. But even within the same generation, female scholars were forming more mentoring relationships, and van Schurman's *famille d'alliance* soon expanded to include a sister.

MARIE DU MOULIN (C.1613–99)

When Marie du Moulin first came to The Hague, it was not to facilitate her career as an author, or to initiate her schooling in learned languages. Marie, one of eighteen children in her family, came to keep house for her aunt and uncle, Marie and André Rivet. Her father was Pierre du Moulin, the renowned and multifariously prolific Huguenot theologian, who in a ninety-year lifespan produced over eighty-two religious tracts and eighteen children.[49] Thus Marie's job in the family was to take care of her much younger siblings, the fruits of her father's second marriage, and she

---

[47] Van Schurman to Rivet, October 4, 1640, KB MS. 133 B 8, no. 23.
[48] Unfortunately, the letters documenting the subsequent communication between van Schurman and Gournay do not appear to be extant. There is also no trace of Rivet's response to this plea.
[49] Pierre du Moulin (1568–1658) had two wives, Marie de Colignon and Sarah de Gelhay. Eight of his children survived into adulthood. For genealogical information on the du Moulin family see Pal, "Republic of Women," 157, and the chart in Appendix B. See also Eugène and Émile Haag, *La France Protestante* (Paris, 1886), v. 5, cols. 800–830; and Labrousse, "Marie du Moulin, Educatrice."

would likely have remained in her father's home until she married. However, when the Rivets moved to The Hague, they requested that the young woman come live with them. Both father and daughter embraced this opportunity, and Marie's life was changed forever.[50]

Never a wealthy man, Pierre du Moulin had raised his daughters quite traditionally, to be good housekeepers and good Protestants. While it does not appear that Pierre du Moulin was opposed to having his daughters schooled – indeed, in his 1633 letter regarding Marie's move, du Moulin had written to Rivet that: "she would not know how to find herself a better school than yours, or a better example than my sister on which to model herself" – he had probably expected this schooling would consist primarily of lessons in virtue and domesticity.[51] Instead, Marie du Moulin encountered a group of scholars and educators in The Hague. It was a network that eventually included a number of *érudits* from both the Netherlands and France, men such as Constantijn Huygens, Valentin Conrart, and Pierre Bayle. And it was also a group that included female scholars, such as Princess Elisabeth and Anna Maria van Schurman, whose intellectual and religious ambitions extended far beyond the family hearth.

Van Schurman and Marie du Moulin began their relationship as *sœurs d'alliance* very soon after Marie's arrival in the Netherlands. The first mention of Marie in van Schurman's correspondence occurs in a letter dated May 30, 1634; then, six months later, van Schurman wrote again to Rivet:

I most gladly understood that you still promise to make mention of me to Mlle. du Moulin. I beg you at the same time, if it is not too much trouble, to testify as to my most sincere feelings toward her, and my admiration for the perfection of her talents.[52]

And almost immediately, van Schurman began pushing her domestically burdened young friend to do more – to study, and to learn the sacred tongue. It was a warm and supportive friendship of mutual admiration that lasted throughout their lives; it was not, however, an alliance of

---

[50] Because of the large number of du Moulins in this study, referring to Marie du Moulin by her last name might lead to some confusion – thus, unlike her colleagues, she will be referred to here by her first name. Her brother Pierre will be referred to as Peter in order to avoid confusion with their father Pierre du Moulin, the patriarch of the clan.

[51] Pierre du Moulin to André and Marie Rivet, February 16, 1633, University of Leiden, BPL 282, f. 152.

[52] Van Schurman to Rivet, November 21, 1634, KB MS 133 B8, no. 9. Also van Schurman to Rivet, May 30, 1634, KB MS 133 B8, no. 6.

equals. Although van Schurman was only six or seven years older than Marie, she was always in the position of mentor, advising, encouraging, and inspiring her less-educated "sister." Marie, in fact, would sometimes find herself in the role of gatekeeper, keeping van Schurman's unwanted correspondents at bay and giving excuses for the learned maiden's increasing silences.

Marie was initially hesitant about undertaking Hebrew studies. But ten years later, based on the encouragement of her "learned sister," her frustration with her inadequate education, and her own desire to read Scripture in its original tongue, Marie du Moulin began teaching herself Hebrew.[53] And just as van Schurman had kept this study a secret from Rivet until she was ready to reveal her progress, Marie kept her Hebrew studies secret from van Schurman until she sent her the following letter, written in a beginner's Hebrew script. It began with a lament over the deficiencies of her education, the passage of time, and her own lack of scholarly courage:

My honored sister,

I remember the days gone by, when I was in your house, when I lay on your breast, and you instructed me, saying: "Get wisdom, get understanding, because they will become life and delight for you." But I said I could not do that, because from the time of my youth I have been brought up just like the young girls in my fatherland, to do housekeeping, to prepare all sorts of appetizing foods, to fashion all sorts of handiwork from linen, wool, and dye, and to embroider all sorts of coverlets.[54]

Marie then went on to explain what had finally changed her mind:

Yet I myself never took your words to heart, until I was in my native country, in my father's house, when he lay ill. And it was then, as the hand of the Everlasting lay heavily upon him, that he said to me: "My daughter, do take the Bible and read me some fortifying passages." I answered: "See, I do not understand this Bible. I have acquired no understanding of it."[55]

It was well known that Pierre du Moulin "had a particular love for the holy tongue," and according to Marie's *Account* of her father's last hours, published immediately after his death in 1658, it was the language he

---

[53] The phrase used was "*ma docte sœur.*" Marie du Moulin to Valentin Conrart, n.d. Surrounding material places the letter between December 1646 and February 1647. University of Leiden, MS. BPL 290, f. 26. Also in Barthélemy, *Un Tournoi,* 47.

[54] Marie du Moulin to Anna Maria van Schurman, c.1647–51. University of Amsterdam, Gemeente Amsterdam archief handschriften, Diederichs Collection, 16 Ag.

[55] *Ibid.*

wanted to hear when he lay on his deathbed.[56] As a devout Protestant and dutiful daughter, Marie felt very keenly her inability to read the Bible in Hebrew, the language of the Psalms:

> Then my master became saddened, and increased the pains of my heart, while I thought, how I have scorned good advice, and not listened to the voice of my sister! For if I had [listened], I could now be my father's comfort. My father spoke: "Do not let it distress you, my daughter. I will instruct you and be your teacher."[57]

However, this opportunity for Hebrew instruction had not arisen until the moment alluded to in this letter, when Pierre was too old and ill for the offer to be realistic. So Marie finally decided to do something about it herself:

> But as I would busy myself now and then with these studies, my eyes were opened to the beauty of the Hebrew tongue, as if discovering it in the twilight. And now I have the daring to address my sister, even though she is an ornament of wisdom and I am merely a rank beginner. My errors will not remain hidden from you, but still I beg and implore this of you, do not tell me to be done with it! Teach me, and instruct me in accordance with your modesty and wisdom, and my lips will sing your praises without ceasing.[58]

Thus Marie had selected van Schurman to be her Hebrew mentor.

This letter gives us yet another glimpse into two processes: first, the intellectual formation of the early modern female scholar; and second, the functioning of overlapping networks in that scholar's career. In terms of the first, individual process, the task at hand was the acquisition of knowledge without formal schooling. Marie's disparaging remarks about her education, one that left her prepared for nothing more than cooking, cleaning, and needlework, certainly appear to have been accurate. And yet, Marie became an author, with at least three published tracts on educational and religious subjects to her credit.[59] How, then, was her extra-domestic learning acquired?

---

[56] [Marie du Moulin], *An Account of the Last Hours of Dr. Peter du Moulin, Minister of God's Word, and Professor of Divinity at Sedan . . . Translated into English out of the French Copy printed at Sedan* (Oxford, 1658), 11–12. Since Peter du Moulin had been the English translator for his sister's treatise on the education of princes, he may also have been the anonymous translator for this English version of her *Récit des dernières heures de Monsieur du Moulin* (Sedan, 1658).

[57] Marie du Moulin to Anna Maria van Schurman, c.1647–51. University of Amsterdam, Gemeente Amsterdam archief handschriften, Diederichs Collection, 16 Ag.

[58] *Ibid.*

[59] These were: *Les dernieres heures de Monsieur Rivet, vivant. Ministre de la Parole de Dieu, Docteur & Professeur honoraire en Theologie en l'Université de Leyden, & Curateur de l'Eschole Illustre, & College d'Orange à Breda. Fidelement receüillies* (Delf, 1651); *De la premiere education d'un Prince, Depuis sa*

Marie's Hebrew letter to van Schurman provides one possible answer. Marie's formal education had been lacking – indeed, she even mentioned that fact again in the Preface to her tract on the education of princes, where she confessed: "I beg you to tolerate the crudeness of my style, and do not be surprised if its deficiencies break through, since I have never studied languages or sciences."[60] So she had turned to a colleague, a female mentor and intellectual "sister," to fill the gaps in her learning. In keeping with the unique characteristics of the intellectual family – combining complete support with very limited compliance – Marie had ignored van Schurman's advice, just as van Schurman had ignored the advice of Marie de Gournay. However, this letter also attests to a level of intellectual collegiality that functioned in the same way that male mentoring relationships functioned in the republic of letters: as a practice designed to foster the education and careers of younger scholars beyond the walls of the academy.

MARIE DU MOULIN, EDUCATOR

Marie du Moulin wrote about education, and was a teacher as well; however, all her publications were anonymous. Unlike many of the more aristocratic women whose manuscripts circulated in literary networks, the key factor in Marie's choice of anonymity was neither gender nor social status. Her choices were governed rather by her identity as an expatriate Huguenot, and more particularly as a member of an extremely visible, engaged, and contentious dynasty of Huguenot preachers. Thus it was a specific configuration of the seventeenth-century nexus of politics and religion that determined Marie's choice to publish anonymously.

Marie wrote and published at least three works on educational and religious subjects: her treatise on educating princes, her account of the last hours of André Rivet, and her account of the last hours of her father, Pierre du Moulin. And despite her choice of anonymity, we can

---

naissance jusqu'a l'aage de sept ans. Traitté tres-utile non seulement aux grands, mais encor a tous ceux qui desirent de bien élever leurs enfans (Rotterdam, 1654); and Récit des dernières heures de Monsieur du Moulin. Marie's tract on education was printed again in 1679 as De l'Education des enfans. Et particulièrement de celle des princes. Où il est montré de quelle importance sont les sept premières années de la vie (Amsterdam, 1679). Two of her works were also translated into English by her brother Peter. They appeared as: An Account of the Last Hours of Dr. Peter du Moulin; and Directions for the Education of a Young Prince. Till Seven Years of Age. Which will serve for the Governing of Children of all Conditions. Translated out of French by Pierre du Moulin (London, 1673).

60 Marie du Moulin, De la premiere education d'un Prince, n.p.

determine her authorship in two ways: internally, through the content and references in the texts themselves; and externally, through references in the correspondence of other scholars in the republic of letters. In the letters of Constantijn Huygens, Pierre Bayle, André Rivet, Anna Maria van Schurman, and Claude Saumaise, there are discussions of all three works by Marie du Moulin, and references to her problems with licensing and publication. In fact, Marie's status as the author of these works was an open secret in the republic of letters; their authorship was veiled with a transparent anonymity, which has only become opaque with the passage of time.

Marie was also very active in polemical correspondence, and Bayle's *Dictionnaire* quotes her as a reference in several articles, including very lengthy excerpts from her letters to explain the origin of some doctrinal disputes – another instance of scribal publication in the careers of these female scholars.[61] And despite the fact that, as a woman, she could not join the men of the du Moulin family in the pulpit, it appears that Marie du Moulin was equally eager to jump into the fray of religious and political controversy conducted through pamphlets and correspondence. This is illustrated by a dispute that erupted in 1678 between her brother Louis and their nephew, Pierre Jurieu, on the subject of ecclesiology. Marie had been appalled; Louis was seventy-three years old, and the English Revolution had ended long ago. She wrote to remonstrate with her brother over his insistence on beating a dead horse and on his misspent life, still "hammering on the same nail, despite the fact that it has been buried up to its head for over twenty years now." Louis, in retaliation for this letter, had it published along with his response in *La tyrannie des prejugez ou reflexions sur le fragment d'une lettre de Mademoiselle Marie du Moulin*.[62]

Marie was also involved in a much kinder and gentler epistolary exchange, involving Rivet, van Schurman, Valentin Conrart, and Madeleine de Scudéry. The topic under discussion was the virtue of Joan of Arc, and the occasion here had been the publication in 1646 of *Question*

---

[61] This incident involved a dispute over the anti-orthodox Calvinism of Moïse Amyrault (Amyraldus) at Saumur. Pierre Bayle, *Dictionnaire historique et critique de Pierre Bayle*, 16 vols. (Paris, 1820–4), III, 464–79, s.v. "Blondel, David."

[62] [Louis du Moulin], *La tyrannie des prejugez ou reflexions sur le fragment d'une lettre de Mademoiselle Marie du Moulin … pour servir de Response a Monsieur Jurieu* (London, 1678), 10. For a contemporary's analysis of the dispute, see the letter from Pierre Bayle to Jacob Bayle, November 26, 1678, no. 160 in *Correspondance de Pierre Bayle*, ed. Elisabeth Labrousse et al., 3 vols. (Oxford, 1999–2004), III, 85–7.

celebre, Colletet's French translation of van Schurman's Latin *Dissertatio*. In the last of the *Dissertatio*'s letters from Rivet to van Schurman, Rivet had been discussing inappropriate fields of endeavor for women; and foremost among those was women engaging in battle on the field of combat. It had been done by biblical heroines like Deborah, but that sort of thing simply did not work any longer – not even for Joan of Arc. As Rivet wrote, "I know equally well that the greatest admirers of her valor, and those who are the most fiercely attached to her glory, cannot speak of her honor and chastity without a great deal of incertitude."[63] It was Rivet's use of the word "incertitude" in referring to Joan's virtue that had outraged Madeleine de Scudéry.

Scudéry had wanted to talk to van Schurman about this insult, but she feared to disturb the reclusive maid of Utrecht. So she had contacted Valentin Conrart, who was equally reluctant to barge uninvited into van Schurman's circle. However, since Conrart was already in touch with Marie du Moulin, he asked her if she would agree to put the issue before her "learned sister." Marie agreed to do so, and a lively correspondence ensued.[64]

However, the entire uproar was little more than a rhetorical performance in the vocabulary of the *querelle des femmes*, and it was being used as a pretext for what Conrart and Scudéry really wanted. Conrart and Scudéry were both hoping to insinuate themselves into van Schurman's circle of correspondents. Van Schurman herself appears to have participated very minimally in the debate. However, there were two very positive consequences from this attempt – Conrart and Rivet began to correspond regularly, and a warm collegial relationship was formed between Scudéry and Marie du Moulin.

For Scudéry, this had been a completely unexpected outcome. It was Marie who had finally explained Rivet's thinking, assuring Scudéry of her uncle's real respect for strong and virtuous women. It had been a very impressive letter, and in the middle of a long disquisition on Joan of Arc, Scudéry had paused to mention this to Conrart:

In all honesty, I have never seen anything more courteously thought out, or more nobly expressed, than what this excellent person wrote to you; and the character

---

[63] Van Schurman, *Question celebre*, 59–61. Latin text in van Schurman's *Dissertatio*, 66–7, and her *Opuscula*, 87–8.

[64] This episode is based on a volume of correspondence exchanged between André Rivet, Marie du Moulin, Valentin Conrart, and Madeleine de Scudéry, held in the collection of Rivetiana at the Library of the University of Leiden, MS. BPL 290. Selections from this manuscript were published by Edouard de Barthélemy in *Un Tournoi*.

of this letter is so easy, so kind, and so spiritual, that I am not at all surprised if Mlle. van Schurman made the woman who wrote it her *sœur d'alliance*.[65]

As the furor died down, the burgeoning friendship among these intellectual women was cemented by one of van Schurman's self-portraits, which Marie sent to Scudéry in faraway Marseilles. Scudéry was very moved, and expressed her gratitude for this connection, especially when she was so distant from them. Marie responded with a promise of intellectual friendship, and a bond that would not break:

Be my friend, and I will be yours; indeed, we will be one, and the Ocean that separates us will not prevent this union of intellect.[66]

While there are no further extant letters in this correspondence, one hopes that this was indeed the case.

Marie's publication history had begun in 1651 with *Les dernières heures de Monsieur Rivet*, which recounted the piety and devotion of her uncle's final days. Then in 1654, several years after this first work, her *De la premiere education d'un Prince* was published in the Netherlands. The anonymity of the author was addressed in the Preface, wherein it was playfully asserted that this had resulted from the writer's modesty. Since then, this anonymous educational treatise, in all its French editions, has been attributed to Marie's cousin, Frédéric Rivet.[67] The text next appeared in 1673, in an English translation by Peter du Moulin; and at that point, the work was attributed to Marie's brother.[68] However, both internal and external evidence point convincingly to Marie du Moulin as the author of this tract.

In terms of content, this was a tract on educating the sons of royalty during early childhood, before the age of seven. The care of infants and small children was not a task that royalty assigned to male guardians or educators; thus the tract focused exclusively on the requisite qualities and

---

[65] Undated extract of a letter from Madeleine de Scudéry to Valentin Conrart [1646], University of Leiden, MS. BPL 290, f. 32. Also in Barthélemy, *Un Tournoi*, 67.

[66] Marie du Moulin to Madeleine de Scudéry, [1647]. The letter is undated, but it is a response to Scudéry's letter of August 21, University of Leiden, MS. BPL 290, f. 38v. Also in Barthélemy, *Un Tournoi*, 93.

[67] A handwritten notation on the Bibliothèque Nationale's copy of this work reads "*par Rivet.*" Based on this note, and on the process of elimination (André and his brother Guillaume had already died), Barbier concluded that it must have been written by Frédéric Rivet. A.-A. Barbier, *Dictionnaire des ouvrages anonymes*, 3rd edn., ed. Olivier Barbier and René and Paul Billard, 4 vols. (Paris, 1882), III, col. 998.

[68] Peter du Moulin dedicated his translation to Ranelagh's sister-in-law, "the Right Honourable Elizabeth, Countess of Burlington & Cork." When Peter du Moulin lost his living in 1646, the Earl had hired him as a tutor for his sons.

training of the sort of woman who should be hired for this position, on her birth, morals, judgment, kindness, and learning. And since the author states that the following remarks "are based more in practice than in theory," it appears that the author must have been a woman with practical experience in this area.[69]

In the dedication, moreover, the author stated that "a great princess," who was awaiting the birth of her first child, had requested this educational information. That princess was Mary Stuart, the wife of William II of Orange, and the occasion was the impending birth in 1650 of William III. This is confirmed in Peter du Moulin's own words. In the dedication to his translation, he had stated that:

The Wisdom of the Counsels of this Discourse, is justified by the Experience of many Ages: And the particular occasion of it was on the birth of the Prince of Orange, by a Judicious Person of Quality living then in the Court of The Hague.[70]

Peter du Moulin might reasonably have been termed "a Judicious Person of Quality" – however, he would scarcely have described himself that way. Moreover, he had at no time lived at the exile court in The Hague. Marie, on the other hand, had spent a great deal of time there. And in addition to being the dedicatee for this educational tract, Princess Mary would later act as patron for Marie's refuge for Protestant women in Harlem.[71]

Further, we have the issue of the weak memory. In the conversation in which Rivet had asked Marie to take on the task of recording his final days, she had responded by referring to a very specific problem that would affect, but not preclude, her ability to become a published author. Marie had worried because she was "incapable of remembering and recapitulating in writing such an abundance of holy remarks."[72] And in the preface to her treatise on educating Princes, Marie had begun by apologizing for her lack of learning, and for her archaic and inelegant French; she had then gone on to relate all her deficiencies to a lifelong problem with memory:

---

[69] Marie du Moulin, *De la premiere education*, n.p.
[70] This passage also makes it clear that Peter du Moulin never claimed to be the author of this tract. Marie du Moulin, *Directions for the Education*, 3–4.
[71] The institution flourished from 1683 to 1770. The Princess of Orange was also the patron of similar institutions in Schiedam, Rotterdam, and The Hague. D. Allégret, "Société des dames françaises de harlem,"*Bulletin de la Société de l'Histoire du Protestantisme Français* 27 (1878): 315–22; 518–24; 557–63.
[72] Marie du Moulin, *Les dernieres heures de Monsieur Rivet* (1651), 25–6.

Since the weakness of my memory, which has been apparent since childhood, resulted in the opinion that I would never be able to succeed at those pursuits, the conversation of reasonable people has been the only textbook I ever studied.[73]

None of these remarks could apply in any way to Frédéric Rivet. He was a courtier, who spent years in London as ambassador from the United Provinces, then returned to be secretary to the dowager Princess Amalia van Solms. Frédéric had no experience whatsoever in educating the children of the nobility, nor were there any problems with his French – on the contrary, his employment as a courtier demanded excellent language skills.

However the reference to an alarmingly weak memory does resonate strongly with the words of Peter du Moulin. In a 1657 letter to his cousin Samuel Bochart, Peter had responded to Bochart's invitation to preach in France, explaining with regret why he could not accept:

I will be honest with you, and admit to my infirmity, which has prevented me from preaching the Holy Word in France. You know that in my youth I had a very poor memory, and it has scarcely improved since then.[74]

French tradition required preaching for hours without notes; in England, however, ministers could bring notes into the pulpit, thus enabling Peter du Moulin to have a career in the Anglican Church. One possible interpretation, then, would identify the forgetful Peter du Moulin as the author of this educational text. However, while Peter du Moulin had been employed as a tutor to the sons of Richard Boyle, Lady Ranelagh's older brother, this was during their adolescence, not their infancy. Moreover, he possessed none of the other factors – experience in teaching very young children, residence at the exile court, and a deficient education – that were referred to in the preface.

And finally, Marie's authorship is confirmed by a 1679 letter from Pierre Bayle to his brother Jacob. He laments that he is too busy to write more; nevertheless, there is something his brother should know:

However, I will not forget to inform you that the treatise *De l'Education des enfans* which you will find in the package that I have sent to M. Carla is a work by Mademoiselle Marie du Moulin, who because of her modesty is not worried that anyone will know it.[75]

---

[73] Marie du Moulin, *De la premiere education*, n.p.
[74] Peter du Moulin, Oxford, to Samuel Bochart, Caen, July 15, 1657. Autograph letter in the collection of the Yale Medical/Historical Library.
[75] Pierre Bayle to Jacob Bayle, June 15, 1679, letter no. 172 in Bayle, *Correspondance*, III, 184–5.

The conclusion, then, is that Marie was the author, and the problem of poor memory was quite likely a shared trait in that particular generation of the du Moulin family. She had written this tract at the request of the princess in The Hague, giving evidence for the interrelationship of publication, pedagogy, and the continuing interconnections of this network of female scholars.

Beyond the model of the intellectual family, and personal mentorship, we can also see in Marie du Moulin an example of the way in which female scholars created networks to further more businesslike goals. This appears to have been the case with Marie and the princesses at the exile court in The Hague. When Rivet had brought his niece with him to The Hague in 1632, he might have envisioned a position for her in the royal household. However, given Marie's country upbringing and her old-fashioned speech, she would not have been considered appropriate for such a position. In fact, in the preface to her treatise on educating princes, Marie had referred to her archaic and inelegant French:

I beg you to forgive me if my French is old-fashioned; I learned it from old *gaulois*, and I have not visited Paris since the Académie refined the language.[76]

Yet Marie did form relationships with the scholarly Princess Elisabeth and her sisters, a connection that would endure throughout their lives. After the English Restoration in 1660, she would turn once again to her Palatine connections to seek help for her brother Louis, the hotheaded Independent; and in 1687, when Marie was in her seventies, she was using this early connection to try to raise funds for a project that sheltered Huguenot noblewomen whose lives had been devastated by the Revocation.[77] Thus the unlikely connections forged at The Hague between the Palatine princesses and the Huguenot minister's daughter were still forming the basis for successful networking over fifty years later.

And in terms of the ways in which the women's network intersected with other levels of the republic of letters, we can turn to a letter representing a different facet of the intellectual family. Van Schurman's alliance with Marie du Moulin had allowed her to become part of yet another *famille d'alliance*, supplementing her relationships with André Rivet and Marie de Gournay – but this time it was based more on faith

---

[76] Marie du Moulin, *De la premiere education*, n.p.
[77] The evidence for this comes from letters Marie wrote to Elizabeth of Bohemia in 1660, and to Princess Elisabeth's sister Sophie in 1687. Marie du Moulin to Elizabeth, Queen of Bohemia, October 16/26, [1660], BL, Add. MSS 18,744, f. 29; and Marie du Moulin to the Duchess of Brunswick and Lüneburg, June 29, 1687, BL, King's MSS 140, f. 141b.

than on gender or intellectual allegiance. A 1635 letter from van Schurman to Marie's father, Pierre, attests to the way in which the bond of intellectual sisterhood had been acknowledged and accepted by the patriarch of the du Moulin family, just as the family of Michel de Montaigne had acknowledged and accepted Marie de Gournay as his *fille d'alliance*:

The honor that you believe has been accorded to Mademoiselle your daughter through our fond and dedicated alliance has been considerably more advantageous and profitable to me than to her ... In addition to which it seems that by an action so free and spontaneous you wanted to take into consideration the narrative of my praises, by means of which it has pleased my dear sister and others among my good friends to acquire for me your good favor, and to balance out the unevenness on my side.[78]

But in the next portion of this letter, van Schurman revealed that she had ambitions that reached beyond moulding herself on learned women:

I have always harbored the ambition to follow your example. And in fact, if I could bring myself to be jealous of Mademoiselle your daughter, it would be for this, that she has this advantage over me, that in such an ambitious pursuit, the proximity of blood and the order of nature are favoring her. In conclusion, you can assure yourself that the double bond of the love I bear toward her will never be in danger of being broken, since I love her not only for her own sake, but also for the sake of such a father.[79]

It appears, then, that even though Pierre du Moulin was from a very different world, van Schurman saw him as someone on whom she could model herself. Although the bulk of Pierre du Moulin's writings and activities were centred on his identity as a Huguenot, he was also a teacher of philosophy and a scholar of Greek, whom Spanheim called the keenest and most learned of theologians (*acutissimus et eruditissimus theologus*). Thus gender was not the determining factor in this relationship, but rather faith and learning.[80]

Thus by adapting the practices of networking, correspondence, and mentorship for use within the limited orbits of early modern women, a network of female scholars had begun to form within the republic of letters. Van Schurman and Marie du Moulin had joined Elisabeth in The Hague, creating a dually gendered intellectual nexus at the exile court.

---

[78] Anna Maria van Schurman to Pierre du Moulin, March 20, 1635, in *Opuscula*, 277–80.

[79] *Ibid.*

[80] Pierre du Moulin's first publication, on the *Elements of Logic* (1596), ran to thirteen editions. Pierre du Moulin, "Autobiographie de Pierre du Moulin, d'après une copie manuscrite," *Bulletin de la Société de l'Histoire du Protestantisme français* 7 (1858): 182, 336.

In addition, van Schurman participated in two intellectual families – one descended from Montaigne through his *fille d'alliance* Marie de Gournay, and another descended from Pierre du Moulin through van Schurman's *père d'alliance*, André Rivet, and her *sœur d'alliance*, Marie du Moulin. Using these practices, they were able to pursue their philosophical, linguistic, educational, and spiritual work in the republic of letters; they enhanced their learning, acquired learned languages, furthered their publishing careers, and interacted with multiple networks of male scholars. The next chapter concentrates on how this network of female scholars expanded through participation in the work of moral reform. Thus the focus shifts across the Channel to Britain in the momentous decade of the 1640s, and the work of Dorothy Moore and the Hartlib circle.

CHAPTER 4

Dorothy Moore of Dublin: an expanding network in the 1640s

Let us join together to trade and to acquire knowledge ...
Anna Maria van Schurman, Utrecht to Dorothy Moore, Dublin[1]

In the decade spanning the mid-1630s to the mid-1640s, the scholarly scenario in The Hague began to get much more complicated. Despite the fact that it was a court in exile, the onset of the English Civil Wars and the Irish Uprising of 1641 made the Winter Queen's court an increasingly important location. As we have seen, it had already been functioning as an intellectual crossroads. Now, however, it was also becoming a strategic destination for the members of various radical Protestant sects in need of connections and funds. For the male and female scholars who had formed collegial networks at The Hague, this increased religious activity did not supplant their intellectual relationships; instead, it added another layer to the palimpsest that was the republic of letters in the seventeenth century. For the female scholars already in The Hague – Princess Elisabeth, Anna Maria van Schurman, and Marie du Moulin – these developments brought them into contact with new networks of activists working for a blended agenda of religious reform and the advancement of learning.

This networking activity, however, only makes sense in the context of the tumultuous upheavals in politics, religion, and knowledge-making that characterized the decade. These events were more than just the background for the women's intellectual activity. These events shaped, enabled, and justified much of the work being done, and the picture becomes increasingly complex in the realms of scholarship and faith. Political and commercial relations between Britain and the Netherlands, Europe's two officially Protestant nations, were contentious. Culturally, the English and Dutch

---

[1] "To the city of Dublin, to the honorable Lady Dorothy Moore, widow of Ben Horim Moore from the city of Utrecht, from Anna Maria van Schurman, in the city of Utrecht." Original in Hebrew. Printed in *Opuscula*, 160. See also translations by Joyce Irwin in van Schurman, *Whether a Christian Woman*, 61–2; and by Lynette Hunter in *The Letters of Dorothy Moore*, 1.

took turns sneering at one another. The English thought the Dutch were unrefined "butterboxes," completely obsessed with money; the Dutch, on the other hand, had thought for centuries that the English were morally lax, and scandalously deficient in terms of their hygiene.[2] Yet learned connections across the Channel were continually iterated and enacted, constituting a deep and powerful current that carried scholars, refugees, publications, and correspondence in both directions. Thus these conversations and correspondences took place against a background of war, revolution, and religious violence that repeatedly reconfigured the intellectual and spiritual landscape of Britain and the Continent.

Throughout this decade, Britain's political and religious situation became increasingly unstable, leading finally to the English Civil Wars (1642–51). These events were closely monitored and analyzed by the international scholarly community, whose members looked to Britain with equal portions of hope and horror. And although Protestantism had been officially tolerated in France since the Edict of Nantes in 1598, the situation for French Huguenots continued to worsen, until finally the Edict would be revoked in 1685. Thus the ranks of voluntary travellers were swollen by refugees. During the ascendancy of William Laud, Archbishop of Canterbury, Puritans fled from Britain to the Netherlands; then the situation reversed during the Interregnum, when Royalists went into exile. And Huguenot ministers, who had been circulating between France, England, and the Netherlands, were finally evicted from France in the diaspora of the Revocation. Men and women in the international community of learning interacted to incorporate and interpret these events on both sides of the Channel, as groups with varying political, spiritual, and reformist agendas were being woven into the fabric of intellectual connections formed in the 1630s.

The female working group from The Hague was part of this expansion across the Channel, and it is at this point that Dorothy Moore connected with the working group in The Hague.[3] In a letter from 1639, van Schurman had suggested to Princess Elisabeth that she might do well to emulate two highly erudite Englishwomen: Queen Elizabeth and Lady Jane Grey. Jane Grey in particular was a powerful figure in van Schurman's

---

[2] For instance, in a 1524 letter to John Francis, Cardinal Wolsey's physician, Erasmus had attributed English outbreaks of the plague to the appalling filth of English homes. Letter no. 1532 in *Opus Epistolarum Des. Erasmi Roterodami*, ed. P. S. Allen, 12 vols. (Oxford, 1906–55), v, 613–4.

[3] On Moore see especially *The Letters of Dorothy Moore*. See also G. H. Turnbull, *Hartlib, Dury and Comenius: Gleanings from Hartlib's Papers* (London, 1947), 219–99 *passim*; and James G. Taafe, "Mrs. John Dury: A Sister of Lycidas," *Notes and Queries* 207 (1962): 60–1.

personal pantheon of learned women, and she had used her as an *exemplum* in her debate with Rivet over female learning:

Let me lay claim to one example that is always present in my mind. The one example, I say, of the incomparable Princess Jane Grey: to whom no nation, no age (since I have said this with everyone's permission) will be supplying an equal ... nothing in her entire life was as dear to her as the fact that she had knowledge of the three languages which they call learned.[4]

In van Schurman's eyes, these two learned female role models had given grace and glory to sixteenth-century England. Sadly, however, their like had not been seen in that realm for a hundred years.

Then, less than a year later, it appeared that van Schurman had changed her mind about the dearth of female scholarship across the Channel. And in 1640, van Schurman wrote a letter in Hebrew to the Anglo-Irish Dorothy Moore, whom she had not yet met, rejoicing that an inheritor had finally been found for the dusty mantle of Tudor England's renowned female humanists:

I have heard a great deal about you, my beloved friend, honorable lady, and I was happy and I rejoiced, for one of the good things to come down to us from heaven in our days has been the renewal of the honor of your nation. Because in my ignorance, I had said that wisdom has remained hidden from the women of England since the deaths of Lady Jane Grey and Queen Elizabeth, may their memory be blessed. But wisdom has entered your heart, and knowledge has comforted your soul.[5]

The letter continued, bestowing compliments on Moore with passages taken from the Hebrew Bible. Then van Schurman got down to the real business of her letter – adding a member to her network of female scholars:

Let us join together to trade and to acquire knowledge, because the process is better than silver, and the yield is better than fine gold. And now, if I have found favor in your eyes, please let me know about all your pursuits. You are blessed in the eyes of God, and a glorious splendor to your nation.[6]

This letter, written in Hebrew, documents another stage in the formation of this working association of female scholars. As they grew more sophisticated in their networking, the group that had formed in The Hague

---

[4] Anna Maria van Schurman to André Rivet, November 6, 1637, KB MS 133B8, no. 14. Later printed in van Schurman's *Dissertatio*, 43–59, and *Opuscula*, 63–80. In the printed sources, the letter is misdated March 8. Also in van Schurman, *Whether a Christian Woman*, 41–8.

[5] Van Schurman to Moore, *Opuscula*, 160. Also in van Schurman, *Whether a Christian Woman*, 61–2; and *The Letters of Dorothy Moore*, 1. Lynette Hunter dates this letter August 8, 1640.

[6] *Ibid.*

reached out to incorporate scholars across the English Channel. The women were reading one another's publications and hearing reports about each other through mutual contacts – both in the larger republic of letters, and in various smaller groups such as ecumenical activists, Huguenot ministers, or the intelligencing network of Samuel Hartlib. And while this letter also provides a further example of van Schurman's respect for the intellectual Englishwomen of an earlier generation, it more importantly shows female scholars in the active, practical process of furthering their own intellectual pursuits by networking across the English Channel and Irish Sea.

The following section picks up the thread of Hebrew studies. It was a pursuit that was crucial for van Schurman, a joy for Marie du Moulin, and somewhat suspect to Marie de Gournay, while being intolerable to many others in the republic of letters; yet it was also a key point of connection linking the Anglo-Irish Dorothy Moore to female scholars in The Hague.

CHOICES AND CHANGE: SHIFTING ALLIANCES

The issues surrounding van Schurman's Hebrew studies – the purpose they would serve, the controversy they ignited, and the notoriety they created – open a useful analytical window onto the ways in which male and female scholars might strategically negotiate multiple networks in the republic of letters. In the republic of letters, expansion in some areas meant contraction in others, and the overlap of intellectual and religious networks would sometimes create friction at the points where they met. The scholarly trajectory of Anna Maria van Schurman is particularly illustrative of this process. Van Schurman was distancing herself from the precepts of Cartesian philosophy, while still participating in the literary exchanges of its adherents; she stayed close to many orthodox Calvinists, while still moving inexorably toward Pietism; and she continued to nurture her relationships with other female scholars, despite their many intellectual and religious differences. This was not a mode of functioning peculiar to the female scholar – it was rather a mode of functioning that mirrored the careers of van Schurman's male peers, who, like her, were simultaneously and variously active in multiple layers within the fabric of the republic of letters.

By the late 1630s, Gournay and van Schurman had overcome their differences regarding the study of Hebrew. In spite of their disagreement, Gournay had included a reference to van Schurman in her 1641 edition of *l'Égalité des hommes et des femmes*, and Montaigne's *fille d'alliance* had included her own *fille d'alliance* in an expanded catalogue of learned women:

If Tycho Brahe, the famous astronomer and Danish Baron, had lived in our times, would he not have commemorated this new star – let us call her thus – Mademoiselle van Schurman, who has just recently been discovered in his part of the world, the rival of these illustrious Ladies in eloquence, and of their lyric poets as well, even in their own Latin language, and who, besides this, possesses all the other languages, ancient and modern, and all the liberal and noble Arts?[7]

However, the holy tongue would soon emerge as the thin edge of a spiritual wedge separating van Schurman from her other scholarly colleagues. She had already begun trying to reduce her seemingly endless obligations to the republic of letters, and letters sent to her went unanswered for months. Most of van Schurman's mentors and friends – notably Rivet, Huygens, and Descartes – were alarmed by this. Another, Voëtius, attempted to shape and control it.

At first, these Hebrew studies had helped to augment and solidify van Schurman's status as a scholarly celebrity, and while her lessons with Voëtius had initially been a private matter, this changed with the opening of the new University of Utrecht in 1636. When the University opened its doors on 16 March, Voëtius invited van Schurman to write an inaugural ode for the opening ceremonies. The Latin ode gave high praise to both the city and the school; however, it also contained a rather pointed message. In her ode, the question, "But yet (perchance you ask) what are those concerns that are troubling your heart?" was answered with: "This Sacred place cannot be penetrated by the Virgin chorus."[8] It was a thinly veiled critique, taking the new university to task for allowing everyone except women to imbibe the Nectar of Knowledge in its "holy precincts." Yet either despite or because of this poem, the directors of the university responded by allowing Voëtius to smuggle his most famous pupil into his Hebrew lectures.

A small cubicle with a latticed opening was created for van Schurman at the rear of Voëtius' classroom. There, able to see without being seen, she could benefit from lectures without endangering her modesty. Van

---

[7] In Mario Lodovico Schiff, *La Fille d'alliance de Montaigne, Marie de Gournay* (Paris, 1910), 79.
[8] *Inclytae & Antiquae Urbi Trajectinae Nova Academia nuperrime donatae gratulatur Anna Maria a Schurman*, in *Opuscula*, 262–3. See also the translation by Pieta van Beek in "Alpha Virginum: Anna Maria van Schurman (1607–1678)," in Churchill *et al.*, eds., *Women Writing Latin*, III, 286–7.

Schurman thereby became the first woman to "attend" university in the Netherlands.[9] This stealthy scholarship was in fact an open secret in the republic of letters. Caspar Barlaeus made a joke about it when writing to Huygens about how much more sensible life would be if van Schurman were a man; Descartes joked to Regius about the possibility of sneaking into van Schurman's cubicle in order to secretly attend Voëtius' public disputation of Cartesianism; and even fifty years later, when Pierre Bayle was gathering facts for his *Dictionnaire*, he was pressing his informants for more information about van Schurman's "loge."[10]

Thus the open secret of van Schurman's presence at the University of Utrecht magnified her visibility on the intellectual stage, and when she was documenting her choice of a spiritual retreat over a career in the republic of letters, van Schurman identified that year of 1636 as one of intellectual and secular excess:

Indeed I considered it my duty to preserve carefully the little honor of my fame as a common good of the Republic of Letters and, as much as modesty would permit, to increase it, so that among the other great lights I too, as a star of the sixth magnitude, might contribute some brightness to that sphere of vast knowledge or Encyclopedia.[11]

Van Schurman is explicit here in referring to her membership in the republic of letters. This passage leaves no room for doubt – not only did she consider herself to be a full participant, but she was aware that others were counting on her in that regard.

But by the time van Schurman was corresponding with Gournay in 1638, she had already begun to withdraw from the republic of letters. She had been extremely active; indeed the theologian Johannes de Laet complained to Buchelius that "because she had involved herself in scholastic disputes, Miss van Schurman had wretchedly disturbed all her studies."[12] Descartes agreed, writing to Marin Mersenne that:

---

[9] This cubicle was to the north of the rostrum in the hall designated for theological lectures. It was replaced by a staircase in 1825. S. Muller, *De Universiteitsgebouwen te Utrecht* (1899), 20–1, quoted in Cohen, *Écrivains français*, 536 n. 4.

[10] Letter no. 1382, Caspar Barlaeus to Contantijn Huygens, April 30, 1636, in *De Briefwisseling van Constantijn Huygens*, II, 164. Lettre CXC, Descartes to Regius, May 24, 1640, in Descartes, *Oeuvres*, III, 70. Pierre Bayle to J. G. Gravius, December 26, 1692, in *Lettres Inédites de Divers Savants: de la fin du XVIIme et du commencement du XVIIIme siècle*, ed. Émile Gigas, 3 vols. (Copenhagen, 1890), I, 96.

[11] A. M. à Schurman, *ΕΥΚΛΗΡΙΑ seu Melioris Partis Electio: Tractatus Brevem Vitae ejus Delineationem exhibens* (Altona, 1673), II, xi. Translation by Irwin in van Schurman, *Whether a Christian Woman*, 87.

[12] In Buchelius' diary for February 1640. Buchell, *Notae Quotidianae*, 102–3

This Voëtius has also ruined Mademoiselle van Schurman ... he has possessed her so completely that she concerns herself with nothing but Theological controversies, and it has caused her to lose touch with all reasonable people.[13]

Huygens also worried about van Schurman's failure to answer his letters; he wrote to Rivet, whose response made it clear that he shared Descartes' opinion:

As to the rest, do not be surprised at the silence of Mlle. van Schurman ... Mons. Voëtius burdens her spirit so heavily, and cuts her off from the world so much, that she is his alone, and to be frank with you, I am afraid that he is overwhelming that mind that wants to know everything, and to know it exactly.[14]

Yet Rivet, Descartes, and Huygens were all mistaken. Voëtius may have indeed been burdening his pupil, but he was far from controlling her. Interwoven with these other networks was a burgeoning network of female scholars; and as van Schurman withdrew from the demands of humanist and theological circles, she continued to involve herself with an international and multi-faith group of women. It was an eclectic group – including Catholics and Cartesians – of whom Voëtius would certainly *not* have approved. And among these new contacts was Dorothy Moore of Dublin.

DOROTHY MOORE (C.1612–64)

Van Schurman was explicit about wanting to introduce the Anglo-Irish Dorothy Moore into her network of scholarly correspondents. She wanted "to establish contact between us for the sake of wisdom and exchange of knowledge," and she wanted to do it immediately. Although she had yet to meet Moore in person, van Schurman was ready to move ahead on this project based on the reports of mutual friends, including Voëtius, Elisabeth, and the ecumenicist John Dury. Indeed van Schurman had already begun facilitating Moore's intellectual career several years earlier, when she convinced Beverwijck to include Moore in the 1639 edition of his text *On the Excellence of the Female Sex.*

---

[13] René Descartes, Leiden, to Marin Mersenne, Paris, November 11, 1640. This letter was published in the collected correspondences of both Descartes and Mersenne. Letter no. ccxiv in Descartes, *Oeuvres*, iii, 231; and letter no. 938 in Le Père Marin Mersenne, *Correspondance du P. Marin Mersenne, Religieux Minime*, ed. Mme Paul Tannery and Cornelis de Waard, 2nd edn., 17 vols. ([Paris], 1960–88), x, 224.

[14] André Rivet to Constantijn Huygens, September 26, 1639, University of Leiden, MS. HUG 37. Also published as letter no. 2247 in *De Briefwisseling van Constantijn Huygens*, ii, 502–3.

Johan van Beverwijck was a physician from Dordrecht and Deputy to the States General, and at his request van Schurman had written a treatise on the timing of the end of life entitled *De vitae termino*.[15] Beverwijck's *On the Excellence of the Female Sex*, however, was a monumental work arguing for the superiority of women, and, in over 700 pages, he marshalled 700 female exempla to prove his point. It had been circulating since 1636 in learned networks as a Latin manuscript; yet when Beverwijck informed van Schurman that he was going to publish the book in Dutch, she begged him to reconsider.[16] Publication in a vernacular language would mean exposure to an exponentially larger public, and van Schurman was acutely aware that the praise accorded to intellectual women did not always redound to their benefit or their credit. She feared the backlash, and she did not fear it for herself alone – she foresaw unfortunate consequences for the hopes of all aspiring female scholars. However, she did concede that there might be some benefits, if Beverwijck's book were to inspire other women:

Nevertheless, since your path has been illuminated by the light coming from both every kind of learning and from the wisest women of antiquity ... I believe scarcely anything is more worthy of your concern than, as I write in a certain public place, you both asserting the dignity of our sex, and also kindling the desires of our more high-born maidens toward this sort of life that they ought to embrace.[17]

It is also worth noting here that van Schurman's arguments concern only "our more high-born maidens." In van Schurman's analysis, access to education ought to be open to both sexes, but limited by considerations of social rank and familial responsibility. Nevertheless, if Beverwijck could adequately portray the intellectual capabilities of women, the book might be of benefit for the republic of letters as a whole:

Nor have I desired this so much for myself, as for the sake of the entire Republic of Letters, to which for a long time now you have not hesitated to devote yourself entirely.[18]

---

[15] It was published by Beverwijck in two forms: in Latin, as part of his *Epistolica quaestio, de vitae termino fatali, an mobili?: cum doctorum responsis* (Leiden, 1639); and in a Dutch translation as *Paelsteen vanden tijt onses levens ... In Latijn aen d'Heere Johan van Beverwyck geschreven door de Edele, Deught-en-Konst-rijcke Joffrouvv, Joffr. Anna Maria van Schvrman* (Dordrecht, 1639).

[16] The Latin version was apparently never published, and the book did not appear in print until the Dutch version came out in 1639 as *Van de Wtnementheyt des Vrouwelicken Geslachts, verciert met kopere platen; ende verssen van Mr. Corn. Boy*. A second edition was published in Dordrecht in 1643.

[17] Anna Maria van Schurman to Johan van Beverwijck, January 21, 1638, in *Opuscula*, 184–7.

[18] *Ibid.*

According to van Schurman, then, women as a group – not just she herself – had an important role to play in the republic of letters.

However, for the sake of working toward their shared intellectual goals, it was important that she not be singled out. Beverwijck did not agree; in fact, beyond including her as one of his *exempla*, he wanted to dedicate the entire book to her. Van Schurman was horrified:

> I have seen your treatise, most Illustrious Man, which you entitled *On the Excellence of the Female Sex*. Beware, then … particularly since you have raised so many examples of illustrious women to such an exalted peak of renown that you might seem to have discussed them more for the purpose of ill-will than for the purpose of emulation.

She then ended with a plea:

> Therefore, since this is the case, I vehemently implore you, nay rather by the faith of our inviolable friendship I do solemnly beseech you, do not persist … in dedicating this book to me.[19]

She knew Beverwijck was well-intentioned; however, she needed to point out that he was also being dangerously naïve:

> Surely it has not escaped your notice with what envious eyes the majority of men (here I am speaking less about men of the lowest rank, whom it is easy to hold in contempt, than I am about men of great esteem) regard that which is favorable to us – to the extent that they judge themselves to have acted obligingly toward us, while thus far we have merely obtained pardon for aspiring to these higher studies.[20]

This was, in fact, the second time van Schurman had conveyed these same sentiments to Beverwijck.[21] She was convinced that any publication focusing on her as an exception would be both distorted and counter-productive for the shared work of international scholarship.

So on behalf of the intellectual community at large, and for the good of female scholars in particular, van Schurman ended the letter by supplying Beverwijck with the names of three other intellectual women. One was a noblewoman, a "heroine" skilled in languages and literature; she was probably known personally to van Schurman, but her name was removed from the published letter.[22]

---

[19] Anna Maria van Schurman to Johan van Beverwijck, 1639, in *Opuscula*, 187–90.   [20] *Ibid.*

[21] Anna Maria van Schurman to Johan van Beverwijck, January 21, 1638, and [n.d.], 1639. Both letters were printed in van Schurman's *Opuscula*, 184–7 and 187–90.

[22] Anna Maria van Schurman to Johan van Beverwijck, 1639, in *Opuscula*, 187–90. It is most likely that "N. N.", the anonymous, noble, and learned female heroine being proposed here, was Anne de Rohan, a noted Hebraist and poet.

The other two were already van Schurman's correspondents – Marie le Jars de Gournay and Dorothy Moore.[23]

Van Schurman was destined to fail in her attempt to have Beverwijck remove her from the uncomfortable and unwanted pedestal he had constructed for her. And, despite her heartfelt plea, she was singled out in the dedication to his work. Although Beverwijck was a noted pro-female voice in the *querelle des femmes*, he still insisted on seeing Anna Maria van Schurman as one of a kind, and in the Dedication, he wrote:

> But as the light of the sun shines above all the stars and with its bright splendor dulls the sparkling starlight, so the learned light of these other ladies stands, as it were, in the shadow because of the incomparable young lady Anna Maria van Schurman.[24]

Nevertheless, van Schurman did succeed in having Beverwijck publish the praises of Dorothy Moore. In 1639 Beverwijck described Moore as:

> the widow of an English nobleman, not yet twenty-seven years of age, adorned with all the graces of body and soul. In a short time she learned Italian and French to such an extent that she could read works written in both languages and spoke French fluently. This encouraged her to study Latin, which she also mastered soon. Not stopping there, she embarked on the study of Hebrew, in which she progressed so far in a few months that she could read the Bible in that language. In addition, she is so devout that, in between her studies, she sets aside a special time each day to spend piously, reading and meditating.

Then Beverwijck provided some details of Moore's introduction to van Schurman:

> A little while ago, she wrote a letter in Hebrew to the most learned maid that ever lived, who needs no further introduction here.[25]

When Beverwijck says "the most learned maid that ever lived," he means Anna Maria van Schurman. According to Beverwijck, then, it was in fact Moore who had first written to the maid of Utrecht, displaying her skills in Hebrew and inspiring her to respond with the offer to include her in

---

[23] Cornelia Niekus Moore, "Not by Nature but by Custom: Johan van Beverwijck's 'Van de wtnementheyt des vrouwelicken Geslachts,'" *Sixteenth Century Journal* 25, no. 3 (fall 1994), 641.

[24] Quoted in Joyce Irwin, "Anna Maria van Schurman: From Feminism to Pietism," *Church History* 46, no. 1 (March 1977), 48.

[25] Beverwijck, *Van de Wtnementheyt des Vrouwelicken Geslachts*. Translation from Cornelia N. Moore, "Anna Maria van Schurman," in *Women Writing in Dutch*, ed. Kristiaan Aercke (New York and London, 1994), 226–7. Although there is ample evidence of Moore's skills in French and Hebrew, there is no extant evidence of her mastery of either Latin or Italian.

her intellectual network.[26] Thus Moore – like Gournay, van Schurman, Elisabeth, and their male colleagues in the republic of letters – had been seeking to expand her network of scholarly connections by introducing herself to possible mentors.

Dorothy Moore, the meditative and multilingual subject of this passage by Beverwijck, was born in Dublin in 1612 or 1613. She was one of the nine children of Sir John King, a wealthy Irish administrator, and Catherine Drury.[27] Moore and her sisters Margaret and Mary were all spoken of as being learned. Their brother Edward King was also a scholar, a schoolmate of John Milton and Henry More at Cambridge. When Edward was tragically drowned in a shipwreck at the age of twenty-five, a book of elegies appeared in tribute; and, while John Milton's contribution immortalized the young man as his "Lycidas," it was clearly one of Edward's less talented elegists who praised his sister's learning with these unfortunate words:

> To us he's dead, he lives in you;
> All his vertues in your breast . . .
> Who sees, would say you are no other
> But your sex-transformèd brother.[28]

Yet even before this posthumous transformation, the King sisters had somehow acquired a highly unusual degree of learning.

The Kings, like their neighbors the Boyles, belonged to a social rank that did not value the education of their daughters. The girls were all raised to marry early, and marry well, while their brothers were educated at Cambridge.[29] Certainly, the King sisters did not receive any schooling of their own beyond the basic noblewomen's curriculum; in fact, Moore later wrote a short treatise on the education of girls, in which she lamented this regrettable education. As she recalled her own schooling, it had functioned only to instruct her in "daucing and curious workes" and to "fill the fancy with unnecessary, unprofitable and proud

---

[26] I have so far been unable to trace this first letter from Moore to van Schurman.

[27] Throughout this study, I refer to her by her first married name, Dorothy Moore; this was the name used most often in her correspondence.

[28] Christopher Bainbrigge, "To His Vertuous Sister," in *Justa Edovardo King* [1638], ed. E. C. Mossner, published for The Facsimile Text Society (New York, 1939), 17–18. One of the "*sorores, foeminas lectissimas*" is clearly identified as Margaret; the other would presumably be Dorothy. On Milton and Edward King, see David Masson, *The Life of John Milton: Narrated in Connexion with the Political, Ecclesiastical, and Literary History of His Time*, 7 vols. (London, 1873–94), I, 647–59.

[29] Nicholas Canny, *The Upstart Earl: A Study of the Social and Mental World of Richard Boyle, first Earl of Cork 1566–1643* (Cambridge, 1982), 88–9, 103.

imaginations."[30] However, references to his daughters being "learned" suggests that Sir John King – even if he cannot be considered in the same paternal league as a Sir Thomas More or a Frederick van Schurman – was at the very least amenable to having his female children audit their brothers' lessons at home. And apart from the unfortunate skills she lamented, Moore had somehow acquired proficiency in multiple languages, and was particularly adept as a Hebrew scholar; both John Dury and Samuel Hartlib would refer to her in correspondence as "Mrs. Aethiop."

Moore's comments, then, become interesting on several levels. First, for what they most clearly leave out: for if Moore's education had been so deficient, then how did she manage to become so learned? And second, her comments are remarkable for the ways in which they resonate with those of Marie du Moulin. Marie's Hebrew letter to van Schurman had also disparaged her education, one that left her prepared for nothing more than cooking, cleaning, and needlework. Although Marie and Moore had emerged from very different social ranks – Moore was a member of the Anglo-Irish gentry, while Marie belonged to a family of dispossessed Huguenot preachers – neither of their families had made provisions for educating their daughters beyond what was needed for household management.

And yet, both Dorothy Moore and Marie du Moulin became scholars. While neither would ever acquire the level of learning exhibited by a van Schurman or a Bathsua Makin – women whose fathers had made a point of schooling their daughters as rigorously as others schooled their sons – each was able to master some of the learned languages, including Hebrew, and each was highly active and respected in her respective religious networks. One must assume, then, that although the families of Dorothy Moore and Marie du Moulin were quite different in terms of social rank and nation, they were aligned by some surprisingly strong similarities in attitudes toward learning. Both families had probably allowed their daughters to audit their brothers' lessons in Latin, and perhaps in other subjects as well.

Dorothy King's formal education and proxy lessons would both have ended in the late 1620s, when she was still in her teens. It was then that she married Arthur Moore, the younger son of Garrett Moore, Earl of Drogheda.[31]

---

[30] BL, Sloane MS. 649, ff. 203–5.
[31] Sir Garret Moore (c.1560–1627), Baron Moore of Mellifont and Viscount Moore of Drogheda, left his estate Drumbanagher, in Co. Armagh, to his fifth son, Arthur. Anne [Moore], Countess of Drogheda, *History of the Moore Family* (Belfast, 1902), 44.

This marriage also made her the aunt of Katherine Jones, Lady Ranelagh, although the two women were contemporaries who had probably been acquainted since their childhood in the Anglo-Irish community of Dublin.[32]

Little is known of Arthur Moore. We know that he represented County Armagh along with Dorothy's brother Sir Robert King at the 1634 Irish Parliament. He also, apparently, had a reputation for conviviality among his fellow Irish statesmen, and this emerges in a letter written to Edward, Second Viscount Conway, by his secretary George Rawdon, who was managing the estate in Conway's absence.[33] After reporting on the comings and goings of visitors, the dog's new puppies, and the choice between bream and pike for the new fishpond, Rawdon mentioned that: "Mr. Arthur Moore has been drunk often enough remembering your Lordship's health in the good wine."[34] A number of scholars have cited the first eight words of this entry as a complaint being lodged against Arthur Moore for his behavior in Parliament, one that further suggests Dorothy Moore's husband was a drunkard. But this entry in fact has nothing to do with Parliament. It is entirely domestic, and Rawdon appears to be making the report for two purposes: first, to let Conway know that his friends remember him; and second (perhaps more importantly) to account for some unexpected attrition in the wine cellar.

Arthur Moore may also have been involved in Protestant reform movements, which brought him to Utrecht in the early 1630s. Certainly, there is no other record explaining why he became what van Schurman would later call "a Freeman of Utrecht."[35] He died in the late 1630s, leaving Dorothy a widow in Dublin with two young sons, Charles and John. A petition on behalf of Charles and John Moore to the House of Lords on September 4, 1648 states that: "they were left fatherless when one of them was four and the other but two years old, a few years before the rebellion in Ireland, by which they and their mother were

---

[32] Arthur Moore's sister Frances and her husband, Roger Jones, had two children – their son, Arthur Jones, married Katherine Boyle.

[33] On George Rawdon, see Anne Conway, *The Conway Letters: The Correspondence of Anne, Viscountess Conway, Henry More, and their Friends 1642–1684*, ed. Marjorie Hope Nicolson, revised edition by Sarah Hutton (Oxford, 1992), 127. George Rawdon would later marry Conway's daughter Dorothy. Conway's son, also Edward, Third Viscount Conway, married Anne Finch, who later gained renown as the scholar and philosopher Anne Conway.

[34] Entry dated October 8, 1634, CSPI 1633–47, 81.

[35] From van Schurman's Hebrew letter to Moore, dated August 8, 1640, in *Opuscula*, 160.

despoiled of all their estate."[36] This suggests that Charles was born around 1635, and John followed two years later.

It was during this period, in the late 1630s, that Moore began to associate with a network of Protestant reformers in the Netherlands. As a subset within the republic of letters, this group included scholars who were intricately integrated with several other networks – networks whose aims were very different, but whose memberships overlapped for purposes of knowledge and learning. These included Royalist exiles living on the Continent, reformers associated with Parliament during the Interregnum, Anglo-Irish Protestants who fled Ireland during the Rebellion of 1641 to sit out their exile in London, young men in Europe for their Grand Tour, and an ever-circulating cadre of Huguenot ministers. The members of these groups frequently travelled back and forth across the Channel, carrying news reports, correspondence, and newly published books and treatises. They included John Dury, Lady Ranelagh, Robert Boyle, Benjamin Worsley, Samuel Hartlib, Pierre, Peter, Louis, Cyrus, and Marie du Moulin, and the brothers Gerard and Arnold Boate.

It was also during this period that Moore must have been introduced to the Hartlib circle, a reforming network whose aim was nothing less than the remaking of the world and the reuniting of Christendom. The twin engines of this network were the erudite and indefatigable Samuel Hartlib and John Dury. From this point on, Moore's intellectual and spiritual life was completely entwined with the shared aims of the Hartlib circle – a group whose interests ranged from agricultural reform to a universal language system, from building a better beehive to the conversion of the Jews, and from a revolution in pedagogy to the Invisible College.

By 1641, she was in London, and was staying at the home of the learned physicians Gerard and Arnold Boate when John Dury addressed a letter to "Mistris Moore at the house of Dr. Boot" on 6 July.[37] Indeed it may have been Moore's connection with the Boates that initiated her Hebrew studies, since Arnold Boate was a noted Hebraist. Gerard (1604–50) and Arnold Boate (1606–53) were Dutch physicians from Leiden; Arnold was

---

[36] Historical Manuscripts Commission, *Seventh Report*, Part 1 (London, 1879), 50. Lodge mistakenly states that Charles Moore was born in 1629. See John Lodge, *The Peerage of Ireland: or, A Genealogical History of the Present Nobility of that Kingdom*, revised and ed. Mervyn Archdall (London, 1789), s.v. "Moore, Earl of Drogheda," 99.

[37] HP 2/5/1A-2B. The Hartlib Papers are now available in two forms – as transcriptions and as reproductions of the sources themselves – in an electronic archive on CD-ROM, produced by the Hartlib Papers Project at Sheffield. Moore's correspondence from the Hartlib Papers has been published in a very complete edition by Lynetter Hunter in *The Letters of Dorothy Moore*.

physician to both the erudite Archbishop Ussher and the unfortunate Thomas Wentworth, Earl of Strafford, while Gerard's patients included Robert Boyle, Lady Ranelagh, and King Charles I.[38] And a letter Moore received while staying with the Boates shows that she was beginning her work with both the reforming activities of the Hartlib circle and the network of intellectual women in The Hague.

The letter came from John Dury; he addressed her as "Most entirely beloved friend," and was writing to inform her about his efforts to have her sons board with Voëtius while they were attending the Latin school in Utrecht:

> The account that I can give you is this; that I have spoken to Dr. Voetius to know whether or no hee could receive your Children into his house & upon what conditions hee would doe it? to the first hee answered that at this present there was no roome in his house at all, because hee hadde 13 boorders which tooke up all the house, & so could not possiblely receive them till place should bee made . . . therefore I have prepared the waye that in due tyme it may bee effected.

The postscript to the letter read:

> Mris schurmans & hir Brother who salute you kindly, wish much your arrivall.[39]

It appears, then, that van Schurman was in contact with at least one member of the Hartlib circle; and when van Schurman had written Moore in 1639 to say, "I have heard a great deal about you," her source of information had most likely been John Dury.

CREATING A CAREER: DOROTHY MOORE
IN THE NETHERLANDS

In spite of Dury's warnings that Voëtius' house was full, Moore abruptly arrived in Utrecht at the beginning of August, 1641. Dury and Moore began working together as brother and sister in Christ, and they would eventually marry in 1645. From this point on, Dorothy Moore was involved with learned networks in The Hague as much as with the Hartlib circle and the Anglo-Irish networks in London. The Scotsman John Dury (1596–1680) was her colleague in several of these networks, though of

---

[38] On the Boates, especially Gerard, see Charles Webster, *The Great Instauration: Science, Medicine, and Reform 1626–1660* (London, 1975), 64–6; also T. C. Barnard, "The Hartlib Circle and the Cult and Culture of Improvement in Ireland," in *Samuel Hartlib and Universal Reformation: Studies in Intellectual Communication*, ed. Mark Greengrass *et al.*, 281–97 (Cambridge, 1994).

[39] John Dury, Utrecht, to Dorothy Moore, London, July 19/29, 1641, HP 68/7/1B. Also *The Letters of Dorothy Moore*, 6–7.

course he was not a member of either the Anglo-Irish circle or van Schurman's expanding group of female scholars. However, Dury's combination of scholarly and spiritual goals played a large role in determining the shape and scope of Moore's own intellectual interactions.

Throughout John Dury's long and peripatetic life, his unwavering goal was to achieve ecclesiastical peace.[40] With the fluctuating support of princes and prelates, he travelled throughout Europe on a mission that went far beyond the bounds of reconciling Lutherans and Calvinists. He dreamed of bringing Anglicans together with Independents; he anticipated welcoming Jews into the fold, and even held out hope that Catholics might one day join him in this work. Throughout the 1640s and 1650s, these aims were entertained, if not necessarily embraced, by a wide range of actors on the political, religious, and scholarly scene. From the Queen of Bohemia to the Queen of Sweden, from Archbishop Laud to Oliver Cromwell, and from René Descartes to William Penn, many found reasons to praise and support Dury's mission.[41] His quest was, of course, an impossible ideal, and after the Restoration, almost all of Dury's erstwhile supporters found a reason to create as much distance as possible between Dury and themselves. Yet those who had been closest to Dury's ecumenical mission continued believing that this shared ideal should override individual interest. It was a close-knit group that had included men like his fellow travellers Samuel Hartlib and Jan Amos Comenius. The group had also included a range of female fellow travellers: from Dury's sister in Christ, the Hebraist Dorothy Moore; to his supporter Lady Ranelagh; to his co-educationalist Bathsua Makin; to his lifelong friend the scholarly Princess Elisabeth.

Dury had probably first been introduced to the exile court in The Hague by his patron and supporter, Sir Thomas Roe. In 1634, Roe wrote to the Queen of Bohemia, telling her that Dury was coming to The

---

[40] The best full-length study of Dury is still J. Minton Batten's *John Dury: Advocate of Christian Reunion* (Chicago, 1944). Earlier sources include two eighteenth-century dissertations written in Germany: G. H. Arnold, *Historia Joannis Dvraei* (Wittenberg, 1716); and Carolus Iesper Benzelius, *Dissertatio Historico-Theologica de Johanne Dvraeo, Pacificatore Celeberrimo, maxime de actis eivs svecanis* (Helmstadt, 1744). There is also valuable information in T. A. Fischer, *The Scots in Germany: Being a Contribution Towards the History of the Scot Abroad* (Edinburgh, [1902]), 174–85, and the excellent study by Gunnar Westin, *Negotiations About Church Unity 1628–1634: John Durie, Gustavus Adolphus, Axel Oxenstierna*, Uppsala Universitets Årsskrift, Teologi 3 (Uppsala, 1932). A more recent full-length treatment is Thomas H. H. Rae, *John Dury and the Royal Road to Piety* (Frankfurt am Main, 1998).

[41] Batten's long list of Dury's erstwhile supporters included scholars, churchmen, Continental divines, and heads of state. Batten, *John Dury*, 7.

Hague to inform her about his mission, and to beseech her letters and favors. Roe then entreated her to agree to help Dury:

for he is an excellent man, honest, zealous, & indefatigable; one whom I beleeve God hath raysed to be an Ante-Joseph and Instrument of the greatest treatye that hath honored this Age.[42]

Although the Winter Queen always had money woes, she had also initially supported Dury's mission, writing to Roe on February 21, 1635, that "Mr. Durie she will help all she can." She could not provide much in the way of funds; however, Dury wrote to Roe eight months later to tell him that he was wintering in Amsterdam, in the hopes that "what the Queen of Bohemia has bestowed upon him through Mr. Dineley will sustain him until the spring."[43] Dury had already spent some time in Utrecht, where he conferred with Rivet, and where he probably met van Schurman for the first time around 1633.[44] Now, thanks to his increased access to the exile court, Dury's ecumenical mission could move forward together with his other project, the advancement and reformation of learning. These were not, of course, separate endeavors. In 1631, long before the English Revolution, Dury had sought a way to combine Christian unification with a revolution in knowledge of the "Arts and Sciences Philosophicall, Chymicall and Mechanicall."[45]

A third project for Dury was apparently the widow Dorothy Moore. A week after telling Moore that Voëtius had no room for her sons, Dury wrote again to his "most sweet & loving friend" to elaborate on the various charges that would be entailed should her sons enroll in Voëtius' school. There would be costs for food, bedding, linens and laundry, and "at their first entrie to the house each of them useth to give a peece of gold unto the hostesse as a present according to his affection." Also, the French schoolmaster needed to be paid separately from the Latin master. In short, her sons' education would probably cost her 150 pounds sterling a year. Added to which, the house was still full – so Dury reiterated, "therefore yow should make no haste, this I doe repeat lest if the first advertisement,

---

[42] Roe to Queen Elizabeth of Bohemia, April 24, 1634, PRO SP 16/266, f. 44. In Westin, *Negotiations*, 170.

[43] Elizabeth to Roe, February 21, 1635; Dury to Roe, November 21, 1635. Sir John Dingley was the Queen of Bohemia's secretary. *CSPD* 1634–5, 509–10; *CSPD* 1635, 459–60.

[44] In Dury's *A Summarie Relation*, he recounted a visit with Rivet in 1633. Since van Schurman was Rivet's neighbor, friend, and *fille d'alliance*, it seems nearly impossible that Dury could or would have missed meeting her on this occasion. Westin, *Negotiations*, 275. See also letters from Dury to Rivet in the collection of *Rivetiana*, Universiteit Bibliotheek Leiden, BPL 285 II, ff. 16–18.

[45] John Dury, *The Purpose and Platforme of my Journy into Germany*, BL Sloane MSS 654, ff. 247r–249v.

concerning these thinges, should miscarrie."[46] In spite of this, Moore landed in Utrecht immediately afterward; then, less than a month later, Dury had to bring her back to London himself, since "shee was in a strait & could not helpe hir selfe out of it."[47] Moore finally relocated to The Hague some time prior to May 30, 1642.

Moore's move was occasioned in part by the need to see to the schooling of her sons. As she wrote to a kinsman in 1640, seeking his help in procuring a godly tutor, "the youth of this Kingdome are not trained up soe strickly, as els where" – and apparently that "elsewhere" was the Netherlands.[48] She was also, however, pursuing her own agenda, hoping to build a network of supporters in order to create a spiritual career for herself. Moore felt she was destined for something much larger and much more public than a traditional role in the family, and she refused to be satisfied with such a subordinate position. As a woman, however, Moore had no clear professional path to follow. She spent a great deal of time and energy trying to discern the precise nature of what she referred to as her "calling," the role God truly wanted her to play in serving "the advance of Christs kingdome."[49]

More than anything else, Moore wanted to preach. She wrote to Ranelagh, her kinswoman and colleague, about the anguish of trying to determine how this could be done. Apparently, there had been setbacks, but Moore was undaunted:

yett I repent not my Omissions; my preachings being governed then according to the light I had to cleere my way and such it represents my Actions still.[50]

Moore's model was the primitive church, the original apostolic commu-nity of St. Paul. Unlike the deutero-Pauline letters that mandated silence for women in church, Paul's authenticated letters describe a ministry that included women as co-workers and equals.[51] His Christianity was an apoca-lyptic faith, whose adherents eagerly awaited the end of this "present age"

---

[46] Dury to Moore, July 11/August 1, 1641, HP 2/5/5A-B. Also in *The Letters of Dorothy Moore*, 8–9.
[47] *The Letters of Dorothy Moore*, 9, fn. 15.
[48] [Dorothy] Moore to Sir William Moore, August 23, [1640], Huntington Library, Loudon MSS, LO 10378.
[49] Moore to Ranelagh, May 5, 1645, HP 3/2/119A. Also in *The Letters of Dorothy Moore*, 73–4.
[50] Moore to Ranelagh, July 8, 1643, HP 21/7/1A-2B. Also in *The Letters of Dorothy Moore*, 17–20.
[51] The commonly evoked admonitions in the letters of St Paul come from 1 Corinthians and 1 Timothy. Scholars now agree that the pastoral letters to Timothy and Titus were probably written around 100 ce, many decades after Paul's death. Elaine Pagels, *Adam, Eve, and the Serpent* (New York, 1988), 23.

of sin; thus traditional marital ties were rejected. Whether married or virgin, all women and men were required to live a life of celibacy in the apostolic church. Women served alongside the men as equals in common cause, and in fact sixteen of the thirty-six co-workers named by Paul in Romans 16 were women. The women's ministry was not limited to women nor to specific gender roles and functions, and Paul used terms such as "co-worker," "brother/sister," "*diakonos*," and "apostle" to refer to the women who labored with him in the cause of the gospel.[52] Writing to Ranelagh, Moore explained that this was precisely what she wanted for herself:

Thus Madame rudely and briefly I lay before you my conception concerning that Aime which I conceive every Member of Christ ought to propose unto themselves as theire Duty without excluding our Sex ... many are apt to thinke us alltogeather incapable of such service as I now speak off, but untill you can proove us incapable of that honor of being Members of that body I must beleive that every Member in his owne station may bee proffitable to the rest.[53]

However, Moore was still unsure whether she was truly attending to God's call, or only listening to the sound of her own wilfulness and desire. She awaited a sign. In the meantime, as she told Ranelagh, she was willing to wait And while she was waiting, she was willing to entertain several other options; she might seek a position at the exile court, or "take up a course of Instructing youth, of my owne Sex."[54]

Moore's commitment to the Hartlib circle's reformationist agenda, coupled with her own refusal to accept the limitations imposed on her sex, had led her to develop some ideas for changes in women's education. She jotted these down and sent this short treatise on the education of girls to Ranelagh, who had apparently requested it "as the instrument of others."[55] In the accompanying letter, she lamented her own regrettable education in the traditional skills of young noblewomen:

Upon this ground I have in this litle draught, left out the teaching of youth dauncing and curious workes; both which serve onely, to fill the fancy with unnecessary, unprofitable and proud imaginations. My experience as well as my

---

[52] Fiorenza, "Word, Spirit and Power," 33–6. On early Christian ascetic communities, see Peter Brown, *The Body and Society: Men, Women, and Sexual Renunciation in Early Christianity* (New York, 1988).

[53] Moore to Ranelagh, July 8, 1643, HP 21/7/1A-2B. Also in *The Letters of Dorothy Moore*, 17–20.

[54] *Ibid.*   [55] BL, Sloane MS. 649, ff. 203–5. The treatise itself does not appear to be extant.

reason tells me this; for my owne education was to learne both, and all I got by them was a great trouble to forget both, that so I might stand lesse in opposition to the simplicity of the Gospell in my affections and practice.[56]

Thus for Moore, the goal was not educational reform *per se*. Her goal was rather to make women's education conformable to a godly reformation – a goal toward which she and her colleagues in the Hartlib network were devoting so much of their energies. In their Comenian approach to educational reform, boys and girls would both be trained toward the same end. Virtue and practical skills came first, while those of either sex who had intellectual abilities for more learned pursuits would be encouraged to pursue them. Their approach to educational reform was quite unlike that espoused by Milton. Although Milton dedicated his own tract *Of Education* (1644) "To Master Samuel Hartlib . . . a person sent hither by some good providence from a far country to be the occasion and incitement of great good to this island," he did not share Hartlib's belief that the whole world needed to be remade in order to fix certain problems. And in describing his own methods, Milton had specifically targeted Comenius, saying: "to search what many modern *Januas* and *Didactics* more than ever I shall read, have projected, my inclination leads me not."[57]

Yet Moore did not really want to become an educator. She was still focused on becoming a preacher and was awaiting God's call; but until that day arrived, she knew she could still be involved in both God's work and the advancement of learning by becoming a teacher. The possibility of Moore teaching comes as no surprise; however, her idea that she might become a court attendant strikes one as astoundingly inappropriate for this impulsively outspoken would-be preacher. The likelihood is that Moore was desperately searching for some gainful employment that would enable her to stay at the court in The Hague, where she had the company of van Schurman, Elisabeth, Dury, and Marie du Moulin. A decade later, she was still searching for gainful employment, and was exploring the idea of a chemical career. The key objection to Moore's having a career of this sort would not originate with her gender, but rather with her social rank.[58] But in attempting to establish herself in any of these

---

[56] *Ibid.*

[57] *John Milton: A Critical Edition of the Major Works*, ed. Stephen Orgel and Jonathan Goldberg (Oxford, 1991), 226–7 and 252; Christopher Hill, *Milton and the English Revolution* (London, 1977), 146–9.

[58] In a letter to Hartlib, the chemist Benjamin Worsely discussed a range of possibilities available to Moore in terms of a career in chemistry. Worsely to Hartlib, June 22, 1649, HP 26/33/1A-3B.

possible careers – preacher, court attendant, educator, or chemist – Dorothy Moore drew on every possible connection in her various networks.

The most important connections, as one might expect, were Moore's radical Protestant colleagues: Dury, Hartlib, and Ranelagh. However, support also came from an unexpected quarter – the scholastically and religiously conservative Anna Maria van Schurman of Utrecht. The following sections will analyze Moore's connections with Dury, van Schurman, and Rivet, in order to explore another example of a female scholar establishing herself and furthering the advancement of learning through intellectual networking.

First, there was the unswervingly loyal John Dury. Dury appears to have been in love with Moore since at least 1640, when he first began addressing her as his "most entirely beloved friend," and rescuing her from the long series of scrapes occasioned by her impulsive behavior and uncensored opinions. As mentioned above, Moore had thought she could be useful in service to "some greatt Person." Thus once she relocated to the Netherlands, she began to frequent the exile court of the Queen of Bohemia in The Hague. Here she would have associated with the learned women who used the exile court as their place of intellectual networking – van Schurman, Elisabeth, Marie du Moulin, and Utricia Ogle.[59]

Dury was already at the exile court, and would eventually be appointed chaplain to eleven-year-old Princess Mary Stuart when she arrived in The Hague in 1643. Princess Mary, the daughter of King Charles I, had come there as the bride of Rivet's pupil, Prince William of Orange. The position required the godly Dury to conform to the doctrine of the Church of England.[60] However, he never accommodated himself to either the glamor of court life or the laxity of the courtiers' spiritual devotions; and with his preaching style, both verbal and sartorial, he appears to have made his disapproval conspicuous. As he wrote to Hartlib, "entering upon my Charge, I preached in my Clocke before the Princesse; & made them singe a psalme all which was considered as a strange matter amonst

---

[59] While there are letters documenting Moore's personal and epistolary relationships with van Schurman, Rivet, Voëtius, Princess Sophie, Utricia Ogle, and Queen Elizabeth of Bohemia, there is no extant correspondence documenting her relationships with Elisabeth or Marie du Moulin. However, they were all part of the same tight-knit circle in The Hague, and were physically present there at the same time.

[60] Charles I wrote, in his order appointing Dury, that "our expresse Will & Command is, That yow precisely observe the Method of the Liturgy & sence of the Articles received & practised in the Church of England," April 7, 1642, HP 5/5/10B-11A.

them."[61] However, Dury found his time at the exile court strategically advantageous for the same reasons that it was advantageous to learned women – because there were so many scholars and reformers there. Thus, despite his discomfort, he did not resign immediately:

for besides that I am in a high place to bee taken notice of; I have a dore of entrance into many public Relations opened unto me for Correspondencie, for Printing & proposing of matters which no where I can have with so good conveniencie; if only I hadde meanes to subsist by, which I confesse are to bee exceeding scant.[62]

Moreover, Dury thought this position would enable him to obtain employment for Moore as a tutor to the princesses at the exile court in The Hague. Elisabeth was by this time a grown woman of twenty-four; however, her sisters Sophie and Henriette-Marie were still in their teens, and Princess Mary Stuart was only eleven years old. Lady Roxborough, the governess to the royal children, was about to be replaced by Lady Stanhope, and it was hoped that Moore would be her second-in-command for the education of the princess.[63] Dury was greatly in favor of this development, and wrote to Hartlib:

to morrow God willing I am to go with Mistris Moore to Utrecht; shee doth intend to staye there with her Children a few weekes; some meanes have beene used to bring hir to our family. praye to God to give a blessing to them for wee have need of persons of hir spirit amongst the woemen kind which are with our Princes.[64]

This plan, however, was undone by premature rumors of a marriage between Dury and Moore.

These rumors were not, perhaps, the only problem with having Moore at court. She was opinionated and impatient; she had very strong feelings about her faith, and she was outspokenly opposed to the political conduct of Charles I. Moreover, she did not hesitate to express these opinions openly, even in the court of Charles' sister. Deeming Elizabeth's chaplain Samsson Johnson far too morally lax – hence responsible for the fact that

---

[61] Dury to Hartlib, May 30, 1642, HP 2/9/1A-2B. Also in *The Letters of Dorothy Moore*, 99–101.

[62] Dury to [Hartlib], June 26, 1642, BL, Sloane MS. 1469, ff. 2v–4r. This is from the copy in Dury's letterbook; in the Hartlib Papers, this letter is dated 27 June. HP 2/9/6A-7B.

[63] When Parliament appointed the Calvinist Lady Vere, a patron of Godly ministers, to work with Lady Stanhope, this had seemed like a very opportune circumstance for Moore. Dury to [Hartlib], June 27, 1642, HP 2/9/6A-7B; also Margaret Clotworthy to John Dury, June 30, 1643, HP 2/10/3A-4B.

[64] Dury to Hartlib, August 20, 1642, HP 2/9/13A-B. The phrase "our family," refers to the Protestant royal houses currently represented in The Hague: the Palatines, Stuarts, and the House of Orange.

the Lord was still afflicting the luckless Palatine family – Moore had gone so far as to call him a "dumbe dogg" and "a barking kurr."[65]

It was an outburst that could hardly have promoted her plan to obtain a position at court; yet it was finally the marriage rumors which undid Moore's plans. Using Moore's nickname of "Mistress Aethiop" – a reference to her skills in Hebrew – Dury complained about these rumors to Hartlib:

as for Mistris [Ae]thiop. & the matter of my marriage; that is here so bruited that all is full of it; shee is not troubled at it nor I otherwise; but that it not beeing so & poeple beeing willing to beleeve it, [they] looke otherwise upon us then is fitte they should doe . . . & in another kind it is prejudiciall to hir because it doth hinder that which I otherwise could intend to doe; to bring hir in about the person of Princesse, which now by reason of this rumour & suspicion I cannot doe in respect that it will bee thought I seeke my self in the businesse.[66]

Moore and Dury published their denials everywhere, at court and in the republic of letters. Moore even wrote a letter in French to Albert Joachimi, the Dutch ambassador in London, in which she simultaneously denied and justified the marriage:

M. Dury is a particular friend of mine, a friend to whom I am very much obliged, and on whom I have very often relied. If I were to see any possibility of glorifying God more in that state than in my present condition, I assure myself that, being fully satisfied of my affection for this person, my resolution would find no difficulty or impediment in choosing him, or in making an open declaration of my choice. I am firmly determined to please myself in this matter, and have no intention whatsoever of complying with other peoples' whims.[67]

In a perfect world, then, Dorothy Moore would have pleased herself by remaining single, "which condition my inclinations preferred before the other incomparably."[68] Only then could she have followed her chosen path to the ministry. However, this longed-for world was still in the planning stages for these ambitious reformers – and in the real world, circumstances conspired to make the marriage necessary.

Although Dury and Moore cared a great deal for each other, and continued to do so throughout their lives, Moore's vision of their relationship was that of brother and sister in Christ. Dury, perhaps the more

---

[65] Moore to Hartlib, August 24, 1642, HP 21/5/1A-2B. Also in *The Letters of Dorothy Moore*, 9–11.
[66] Dury to Hartlib, June 27, 1642, HP 2/9/6A-7B. Also in *The Letters of Dorothy Moore*, 101–5.
[67] Moore to Ambassador Joachimi, n.d., HP 21/4A-B. Original in French. Also translated in *The Letters of Dorothy Moore*, 12–14.
[68] Moore to Ranelagh, May 5, 1645, HP 3/2/118A-121B. Also in *The Letters of Dorothy Moore*, 69–73.

realistic of the two, wanted to form a more earthly union with his spiritual partner. He even wrote to Ranelagh, pleading with her to help argue his case before the reluctant widow Moore. In the letter, he begged Ranelagh's pardon for the importunity, but also insisted that this was a vital request. He began by confessing that he had never before experienced any particular need for women in his life, that "the silly weaknesse, and want of capacitie, which doth appeare in most of the Female kind . . . hath kept me at a distance."[69] However, knowing Moore had completely changed his mind. She was intelligent, strong, and devout; and, like him, she had committed herself to a life lived "unto the Communion of Saints." They had become close friends:

I found that she was capable, not onely of a Morall, but of a Spirituall friendship: And therefore upon her departure into Ireland, after that I had beene in Holland, I proposed unto her the heads of a Covenant of spirituall friendship, to be maintained for the Aimes of publike and mutuall Edification, as well at a distance as when we should be neere at hand.[70]

Now, however, this "Covenant of spirituall friendship" was threatened by social restrictions. As unmarried spiritual partners, they could not live together in the same house, and this had begun to hinder God's work. To Dury, the solution was clear: they had to get married. But Moore was not convinced, so Dury had turned to Ranelagh for help in convincing the reluctant widow.[71] The appeal worked, and Dury and Moore were married in February 1645.

Thus it was not, perhaps, surprising that these marriage rumors abounded. What was surprising, however, was the source of those rumors – for they appear to have originated with the usually circumspect and supportive André Rivet. Rivet's son, the courtier Frédéric Rivet, had apparently told his father about the impending match, "& the Father having given it out here amongst all those of note; it is like to bee a prejudice to us both if it should bee fully beleeved either here or there."[72]

Rivet and Dury worked together in The Hague, but Rivet also had a separate relationship with Moore. This had been a relationship of potential mentoring, modelled on Rivet's position as van Schurman's *père*

---

[69] Dury to Ranelagh, December 4/14, 1644, HP 3/2/92A-94B. Also in *The Letters of Dorothy Moore*, 114–17. This letter, together with two others written by Dury and two written by Moore, was printed by Hartlib in a pamphlet whose title is the first line of the letter: *Madam, although my former freedom* [London, 1645].
[70] *Ibid.*   [71] *Ibid.*
[72] Dury to Hartlib, May 30, 1642, HP 2/9/1A-2B. Also in *The Letters of Dorothy Moore*, 99–101.

d'alliance. In fact, it was van Schurman herself who had set the wheels in motion, using her position in the learned network at The Hague to try to help Moore achieve her goals. However, things had not gone as well as one might have wished.

DOROTHY MOORE, ANDRÉ RIVET, AND ANNA MARIA VAN SCHURMAN

Moore and van Schurman had been corresponding since 1638 or 1639, but they probably did not meet in person until Moore's first brief stay in Utrecht in 1641. As noted earlier, the republic of letters was based on relationships; and, while these relationships were carried on primarily in correspondence, they were reinforced by face-to-face meetings as often as possible.[73] Thus when Moore returned to the Netherlands in 1642, van Schurman took the next step and began to facilitate Moore's introduction into the world of face-to-face intellectual networking.

In a letter to Rivet from November of that year, van Schurman wrote to express concern for Pierre du Moulin, who was seriously ill, bemoaning the fact that there appeared to be many in the republic of letters who would probably be happy to see the cantankerous old man expire.[74] She then went on to express her eagerness to read Rivet's new response in the ongoing controversy with Grotius, whom she deemed an amateur treading on treacherous theological ground.[75] Finally van Schurman made a request on behalf of "the most noble lady Dorothy Moore":

I powerfully desire for you to admit her to the innermost temple of your friendship: first because I know extremely well how much she esteems and honors you and your Virtues, and second because, due to her uncommon piety, the sweetness of her nature, and the other extraordinary endowments of her intellect, my friendship with her is by no means commonplace.[76]

Van Schurman did not say what precisely she meant by the "innermost temple" of Rivet's friendship; but given the correspondence that followed,

---

[73] Goldgar, *Impolite Learning*, 4–7.

[74] Anna Maria van Schurman, Utrecht, to André Rivet, The Hague, November 19, 1642, KB, MS. 133 B 8, no. 28.

[75] Rivet's treatise was *Andreae Riveti apologeticus, pro suo de verae & sincerae pacis ecclesiae proposito. Contra Hugonis Grotii Votum, et id genus conciliatorum artes, pro fucata & fallacy pace ecclesiastica* (Leiden, 1643). Van Schurman's aggressive tone in this polemical dispute matched that of Rivet and Grotius themselves, and was repeated in a poem she wrote on the same subject. KB MS. 133 B 8, no. 59.

[76] Van Schurman to Rivet, November 19, 1642, KB, MS. 133 B 8, no. 28.

it is likely that van Schurman was referring practically and specifically to those various networks in which both she and Rivet were participants – the court circle in The Hague, the vast network of expatriate Protestants from Ireland and France, and the republic of letters at large. It also seems possible that van Schurman hoped to have Moore become a second *sœur d'alliance*, with Rivet as their mutual mentor. It is clear, however, that van Schurman was working to expand her network of intellectual women, encouraging Moore's theological pursuits by introducing her to the Rivet–du Moulin nexus of theologians. And indeed, this introduction yielded results.

Shortly after van Schurman's letter of introduction, Moore began her own correspondence with Rivet. The issue at stake was the role that women could play in serving God. In many ways, this correspondence, together with the issue under discussion, was modelled on van Schurman's correspondence with Rivet regarding the *Dissertatio*. Like van Schurman, Moore was arguing an issue at the very core of her being, and hoping to get validation for her quest. Unlike van Schurman, however, Moore was not able to be gracious or subtle, nor could she concede a point. Moore's exchange with Rivet thus serves as a useful counterpoint to van Schurman's correspondence with the same person, arguing a very similar issue. An examination and comparison of these two epistolary exchanges illustrates two important aspects of female scholarship in the early modern republic of letters: first, the practice and consequences of intellectual networking; and second, the range and diversity of ideas and approaches that fuelled the intellectual lives of these active, learned women.

In September 1643, Moore wrote the first of the five extant letters in French that constitute this epistolary exchange.[77] She began quite deferentially; then the letter continued in Moore's forthright style, demanding clear answers to what she felt were clear theological questions:

I have often asked myself a question with regard to our sex ... The question is firstly this: to ascertain, Monsieur, whether those Christian women who are united in Christ, and consequently members of his body, should have as their primary purpose ... serving the rest of that body in the communion of saints – yes or no.

---

[77] The extant correspondence consists of three letters from Moore, and two replies from Rivet. Copies of these letters, some in Moore's hand, and some in what appears to be Dury's hand, are preserved in HP 21/3/1A-13B. The letters were calendared by Paul Dibon in *Inventaire de la correspondance d'André Rivet (1590–1650)* (The Hague, 1971). Also translated in *The Letters of Dorothy Moore*, 21–35.

And if the answer to that question must be yes, then the second question must be this: namely, Monsieur, to ascertain by what path can or should the female sex pursue that goal without transgressing the modesty required in our sex, and without overstepping the boundaries that bar women from the public administering of justice in a Republic, or of the word of God in the Church – that is, the role that belongs to women in this union.[78]

Moore is certainly clear about what she wants: first, to know whether Rivet thinks she is right about godly women having a responsibility to serve in the communion of saints; and second, to know exactly how women might best perform that service without transgressing cultural or ecclesiastical codes of feminine behavior. What she was not making clear, however, was the fact that she was unwilling to accept any answer that might prevent her from following through on what she already believed was her call to the ministry.

Rivet's reply came six days later. He was honored by Moore's request, but still a little confused as to what she really wanted. Nevertheless, he assured her that, "I will try not to take what you ask as a subject for controversy."[79] The response to Moore's first question was easy; Rivet had no problem agreeing that the primary goal of women in "*l'Eglise militant*" was to glorify God by serving the rest of its members.[80] But problems immediately arose in regard to Moore's second question:

But here is where you lay the grounds for your principal difficulty, deeming that since your sex is incorporated in Christ, it must not be excluded from the public administering of justice in a Republic, or from the administering of the word of God in the Church … If that were truly the case, then not only women, but also the majority of Christian men would be unable to serve God in his members according to your definition of service.[81]

The problem lay with Moore's intent to take her private faith, and transform it into a public career. So as evidence for his point that women should not preach in public, Rivet reminded Moore of the admonitions of St Paul.[82]

It was clear to Rivet that women were never intended to preach. He acknowledged that the Pauline church had certainly included women as

---

[78] Moore to Rivet, September 23, 1643, HP 21/3/1A-2B.
[79] Rivet to Moore, September 29, 1643, HP 21/3/3A-6B.   [80] *Ibid.*   [81] *Ibid.*
[82] The relevant passages are from 1 Corinthians and 1 Timothy: "The head of every man is Christ; and the head of the woman is the man," and "Let your women keep silence in the churches" (1 Corinthians 11:3, 14:34); "Let a woman learn in silence with all submissiveness," and "I suffer not a woman to teach nor to usurp authority over the man, but to be in silence" (1 Timothy 2:11–12).

deaconesses; however, this had only been because Christian converts in those days were baptized as adults, thus women had needed to be baptized by other women in order to preserve the chastity and propriety of the process. As Rivet pointed out, times had changed, and today's church required no such service.[83] Biblical prophetesses were one thing; but a contemporary woman preaching would indeed be a transgression:

I am speaking of the order established and received in the communion of saints, which must not be transgressed, even when devout women possess the talents . . . Our Lord did not even give that power to his own mother, as has so often been noted by the elders.[84]

Ultimately, then, Rivet's advice to Moore was to be patient, and perhaps to look for a position as an educator of women. At some point, God's plans for her would be made clear.[85]

As we have seen, Rivet was very far from discouraging women's intellectual and religious activities, particularly in the field of education. Yet Rivet was also an orthodox Calvinist, anxious to preserve the current structure of the church; he had no interest in radical ecclesiology, or in women preaching. The comparison here with his responses to Anna Maria van Schurman's arguments in the *Dissertatio* is inescapable. Rivet is the same kindly but conservative correspondent with both women; however, these two female scholars and friends were very different people, working toward two very different goals in terms of their public and intellectual lives.

Van Schurman's *Dissertatio* had been a closely reasoned and highly formal syllogistic argument that began with the premise that "the study of letters is fitting for a Christian woman." First, van Schurman had defined which studies, and which women. Nearly all fields of knowledge were appropriate, but the range of women under consideration was somewhat limited. They needed to be as free as possible from daily chores, and exempt from the worries of public business – in other words, unmarried women of high social rank, with no need to work and no children to care for.[86] Yet once these criteria were met, she argued, the whole encyclopedia of learning should be opened to them. Van Schurman then constructed a series of possible objections, which she answered, and concluded the *Dissertatio* by stating:

Consequently, our thesis stands firm. The study of Letters is fitting for Christian Women. From which we elicit this logical consequent.

---

[83] Rivet to Moore, September 29, 1643. HP 21/3/3A-6B.
[84] *Ibid.*   [85] *Ibid.*   [86] Arguments IV and V in van Schurman, *Dissertatio*.

Women can and ought to be called upon to embrace this mode of life by the best and most powerful considerations, by the testimonies of the Philosophers, and finally by the examples of illustrious women; especially, however, those women who are prepared for the study of Letters in advance of others due to their leisure and other means and resources.[87]

Van Schurman had wanted to apply her own particular good fortune – that of being a highly educated woman blessed with both the leisure and the means to pursue a life of learning – to every woman who might be in a similar situation. The *Dissertatio* was therefore based on something van Schurman already possessed. Moore, on the other hand, was trying to create something that did not yet exist – a ministry of women and a career for herself as one of those ministers. Both Moore and van Schurman were arguing for the validity of some very ambitious intellectual and spiritual goals for women, and both felt they had a possible source of male support in Rivet.

Rivet was indeed supportive. However, he also thought that both women were being too ambitious, albeit for very different reasons. In the case of van Schurman, the point for Rivet was that she was in a league of her own. Moreover, Rivet was convinced that van Schurman had misjudged women as a group. Not only was her educational plan a threat to the general order of things, it was also something he was quite sure would be of no interest to the majority of her sex:

Forgive me if I say that reality will not conform to your words, nor will you be able, even if you obtain from us that which you strive for, to lure the feminine world into your way of thinking. And so either you will battle on alone, or with a select few, abandoned by everyone else whose character or mind does not incline toward such things.[88]

Instead, Rivet had recommended that van Schurman endorse Vives' much more limited educational plan for women, and in her reply, van Schurman had apparently acquiesced.[89]

But when Dorothy Moore received her own career-dampening response from Rivet, acquiescence was evidently not an option. Instead, Moore decided that Rivet simply had not understood her correctly. So she tried again:

I must tell you that I find myself extremely obliged to you for your very extensive and courteous response, which would have been more useful to me if my obscure

---

[87] *Dissertatio*, 36. Also in van Schurman, *Whether a Christian Woman*, 36–7.

[88] André Rivet to Anna Maria van Schurman, March 18, 1638, *Dissertatio*, 60–9. Also in van Schurman, *Whether a Christian Woman*, 48–54.

[89] Van Schurman to Rivet, March 4, 1638, KB MS.133 B 8, no. 16; later printed in *Opuscula*, 91–5.

explanation of my meaning had not given you occasion to misunderstand me. I am going to correct this, hoping thereby to lure you into giving me a more specific response, so that I can find a clearer path for rendering unto God the best service that I can, in my present condition.[90]

She and Rivet had no problem agreeing on her first question, wherein she wanted to know whether women had a responsibility to serve; that answer had been yes. But then problems had arisen, so Moore persisted: "Now I must clear up a great injustice arising from the second question ... I insist on knowing the path by which the female sex can or must pursue this goal." She was not persuaded by Rivet's argument that the functions performed by women in the primitive church – assisting at baptisms, and performing a semi-ecclesiastical role as deaconesses – were no longer necessary. In fact, Moore thought it was high time for them to be reinstated:

are they not now a part of the design which we ought to have today, if only the church were willing to choose some women to be Deaconesses, so that they could help the Ministers in governing and instructing the feminine sex?[91]

Then finally, Moore got to her real point. She admitted that the Dutch Republic and the church had no current public functions for women to perform. And she had noted Rivet's suggestions, which in her mind boiled down to cultivating an acceptance of women's permanently subordinate role in serving the common good. Yet "subordinate" was not acceptable to Moore; she insisted on "equal." If women were barred from doing what men did, then her logic told her this meant there was something women could do better, and which men could not do at all:

I hope that now you understand my meaning in this matter, wherein I hope to find a rule by which to govern our studies and the employment of our minds in the most excellent and most spiritual pursuits; not for our own happiness, or to please ourselves, but to serve the public good in accordance with what is proportionate to our line ... and in order to resolve this uncertainty, it would be useful to know:

First, the exclusive role of our sex in the spiritual communion of saints; that is, the role we can fill more distinctly and essentially better than the men.[92]

Rivet had urged her to take under consideration what Paul had written in his epistle to the Galatians: "There is neither Jew nor Greek, there is

---

[90] Moore to Rivet, October 8, [1643], HP 21/3/7A-9B. Moore's specification of her "condition" is a reference to her being an unmarried woman.
[91] *Ibid.*   [92] *Ibid.*

neither bond nor free, there is neither male nor female: for ye are all one in Christ Jesus."[93] Thus there was no need for women to be looking for a special, exclusive role, because the soul had no sex.

Moore, however, had her own take on the message of the Apostle. In her analysis, Paul's words were of course correct, but they applied only to "the interior." Moore's concern was with the exterior, "the public arena," wherein bodies were clearly gendered. Thus women needed to use their equally valuable souls to preach God's word in an equally valuable – yet different – way:

> This makes it appear that there is something that belongs most distinctly and essentially to women, rather than to men ... and this is why [your answer] does not satisfy me – because I suddenly realized that the aim of our sex should be something on a larger scale, principally in regard to the employment of our spiritual gifts, a pursuit which we are advised to follow just as much as the men are, however much our methods may differ.[94]

On one level, Moore is arguing for the validity of her own chosen career path. On a deeper level, however, Moore is raising an issue that was also under discussion at the opposite end of the seventeenth-century intellectual spectrum. At the core of Moore's argument was a difficult problematic: how to reconcile the theoretical egalitarianism of sexless souls on the inside with the very real restrictions that limited bodies gendered female on the outside. This same issue constituted a philosophical problematic in Elisabeth's correspondence with Descartes. Elisabeth's experience of inhabiting a body gendered female, and the inevitable interactions of this female body with her allegedly asexual mind, gave her continuing grounds for challenging Descartes on his theory of mind/body dualism. Thus these two disparate examples exemplify the multilayered republic of letters at work. First, we see the essential interaction of otherwise separate networks, as the radical nexus of Dury, Hartlib, and Moore interacted at The Hague with the courtly and Catholic philosophical networks of Descartes, and with van Schurman's expanding network of intellectual women. And second, we see how intellectual work was carried out in learned Europe, as one specific question came under discussion for the very different contexts that defined smaller networks within the republic of letters.

The letter above was the final item in the Moore/Rivet correspondence. There may have been other exchanges between Moore and Rivet, but these are likely to have taken place in person; they had a number of close

---

[93] Galatians 3:28.   [94] Moore to Rivet, October 24, 1643, HP 21/3/10A-11B.

friends in common, such as van Schurman, Voëtius, and Dury, and they both frequented the exile court in The Hague. But it is abundantly clear that neither one had been convinced by the other's arguments: Rivet continued to believe that women should accept their current role in the church, while Moore continued to insist that women's pastoral role – *her* pastoral role – was simply awaiting clearer definition.

This outcome would at first seem very different from the deferential way in which van Schurman ended her educational dispute with Rivet. Yet despite their very different paths and scholarly styles, both Moore and van Schurman continued to pursue their personal and professional goals long after receiving Rivet's advice to let them go; they advanced in terms of their own intellectual and religious development, and persisted in expanding their network of female scholars. Van Schurman had turned to Marie de Gournay, praising her as a "courageous woman warrior," and ultimately becoming her *fille d'alliance*. And while Moore had been arguing over her pastoral career, she had simultaneously been working on her network of political connections, seeking to improve relations between Britain and the exile court in The Hague. The next chapter focuses on this combination of intellectual, religious, and political work in early modern intelligence networks, with particular attention to the career of Moore's chosen instrument for political negotiations – the "incomparable" Lady Ranelagh.

CHAPTER 5

Katherine Jones, Lady Ranelagh: many networks, one "incomparable" instrument

she made the greatest Figure in all the Revolutions of these
Kingdoms for above fifty Years, of any Woman of our Age . . .
Gilbert Burnet on Lady Ranelagh, 1691[1]

When Dorothy Moore turned her attention from preaching to politics, her aim was to heal the many breaches in the Protestant world. In particular, her focus was on the end of the civil wars in England, and the restoration of the exiled Queen of Bohemia. Moore deplored the Queen's poverty, and the fact that her birth nation had done so little to help her; and rather than sit on the sidelines, she decided to contact everyone in her network who might be able to help. Writing to the intelligencer Samuel Hartlib, she bemoaned the fact that the exile queen had been all but abandoned by her countrymen:

Mr Hartleb. I have heertofore intreated mr Durye, to acquaint you with the present condition of the Queen of Bohemiah, which is soe sadd in all respects, that it cannot be related or heard, without great sence of her miserye, by any who can trewly compationat the afflictions of others but alas! most men are such lovers of themselves, and the rest are now so involved in publicke and privet distresses, as 'tis hard to finde any to whom probably an effectuall application can be made for her advantage.[2]

The exiled queen was in dire financial straits. Moore blamed Parliament, and she especially blamed the inadequacies of Elizabeth's chaplain Johnson, the "dumbe dogg" of an earlier letter.[3] So she decided to begin these negotiations herself, with little success:

---

[1] *A Sermon Preached at the Funeral of the Honourable Robert Boyle; at St. Martins in the Fields, January 7, 1691/2. By the Right Reverend Father in God, Gilbert Lord Bishop of Sarum* (London, 1692), 32–4.
[2] Dorothy Moore to Samuel Hartlib, March 17, 1643, HP 21/5/3A-4B. Also in *The Letters of Dorothy Moore*, 14–17.
[3] Moore to Hartlib, August 24, 1642. HP 21/5/1A-2B. Also in *The Letters of Dorothy Moore*, 9–11.

I must tell you I have negotiated in her Majestys behalf, with sume of members of the howses, who say there is little hope of . . . receiving any help from them.[4]

Yet Moore's political negotiations did not end there. A year later, she was still working to effect change through a closer relationship between Britain and the Palatine house, but she was now approaching from another direction; and this time, she was addressing herself directly to the Queen of Bohemia's son, Karl Ludwig, Elector Palatine, urging him to present the "enclosed paper" to the appropriate body.

Your Highness being upon the place will easily discerne how convenient it may bee to make the subject of this Discourse a request as also where to make it, whither to the Committee of both kingdoms or Parlament and Assembly.[5]

However, there is yet another facet to Moore's political networking, because on the same day that she wrote to Karl Ludwig, Moore wrote the following letter to Hartlib:

I have a great desire to bringe an acquaintance to pass between the Prince Elector and my Lady Ranalaugh; and therfore I thincke it very expedient that you give her my Leter to his Highness, that shee may give him oppertunity to make his acquaintance.

The point of bringing Ranelagh and the Elector together was not social; it was, in fact, political:

Which being done you will finde her very capable to be instrumentall, for the effecting faithfully and prudently, whatsoever shall be by you or others committed to her trust; eyther concerning the busines therin inclosed or any other, that shall heer after bee fitt to communicate to his Highnes.[6]

Thus it is not the Elector who can be of use to Ranelagh, but rather Ranelagh who can be of use to the Elector. Moore obviously deemed Ranelagh to be an effective "instrument" for political negotiation, and felt certain that it would be of benefit to Karl Ludwig to get to know her – so certain, in fact, that she was making Ranelagh the intermediary for the letter itself. And Moore was not the only one to have this opinion. In fact, Ranelagh's effectiveness in the realms of politics, religion, and revolution was well known and highly respected.

---

[4] Moore to Hartlib, March 17, 1643, HP 21/5/3A-4B. Also in *The Letters of Dorothy Moore*, 14–17.
[5] Moore to Karl Ludwig, Prince Elector, September 29, 1644, HP 21/6A-B. Also in *The Letters of Dorothy Moore*, 49.
[6] Moore to Hartlib, September 29, [1644], HP 21/5/16A-B. Also in *The Letters of Dorothy Moore*, 50. A misprint in Hunter erroneously references the letter as HP 1/5/16A-B.

This chapter, focusing on the work of intelligencing networks in the 1640s, is, of course, greatly concerned with Samuel Hartlib. The Hartlib Papers, which contain nearly 200 items relating to Lady Ranelagh, are an excellent source for analyzing her career in politics, religion, education, and science. But Hartlib, placed at the hub of a vast network of correspondence, was not only working with his own correspondents; he was also working with other intelligencing "hubs" like himself. These were the scholars who directed traffic in other correspondence networks within the republic of letters, men like Marin Mersenne, Constantijn Huygens, and Henry Oldenburg. Considering intelligencing as a coherent group of practices furthering the advancement of learning, I will be suggesting that Ranelagh was much more than just another correspondent. In fact, Ranelagh emerges from the evidence as a "hub" in her own right, the center of a network of Anglo-Irish activists working for political, religious, educational, and scientific reform. Thus as we examine the development and expansion of a female intellectual network within the republic of letters, it also becomes important to trace the prehistory of another network, whose engine was the "incomparable" Lady Ranelagh.[7]

THE INCOMPARABLE LADY RANELAGH (1615–91)

Katherine Jones, Lady Ranelagh, lived a long and productive life.[8] For fifty years, she was involved in politics, ethics, education, medicine, and godly reform. She associated with preachers, poets, Parliamentarians, royalty, and practitioners of experimental science. She was known as a passionate partisan in terms of faith, an indispensable ally and patron to the members of her circle, and a force to be dealt with in the business of politics. And among all of these, the epithet used to refer to her was always "the incomparable." It was a term that made her very much her father's daughter, and the ubiquity of "the incomparable Lady Ranelagh"

---

[7] On Ranelagh, see Kathleen M. Lynch, "The Incomparable Lady Ranelagh," in *Of Books and Humankind*, ed. John Butt (London, 1964), 25–35; R. E. W. Maddison, *The Life of the Honourable Robert Boyle* (London, 1969), *passim*; Hunter, "Sisters of the Royal Society"; Alan Cook, "Ladies in the Scientific Revolution," *Notes and Records of the Royal Society of London* 51, no. 1 (January 1997): 1–12; and Ruth Connolly, "'A Wise and Godly Sybilla': Viscountess Ranelagh and the Politics of International Protestantism," in *Women, Gender, and Radical Religion in Early Modern Europe*, ed. Sylvia Brown (Leiden, 2007), 285–306.

[8] Throughout this study, I will be referring to her as Ranelagh, since this was the name most commonly used in the letters of the Hartlib circle. She was born Katherine Boyle, and in 1631 she married Arthur Jones, thus becoming Katherine Jones. Her husband succeeded to the title of Lord Ranelagh in 1643.

resonates with that of "the great Earl of Cork" – "great" being a seemingly unavoidable adjective when referring to the patriarch of the Boyle clan. As Sir John Leeke remarked, in speaking of young Katherine: "Believe it ould Corke could not begett nothing foolish."[9]

This incomparable woman was born into a wealthy Anglo-Irish family, one of the fifteen children of Richard Boyle (1566–1643), the great Earl of Cork, and his second wife, Catherine Fenton.[10] Cork was a New English landowner who amassed a fortune in Ireland and secured it through strategic dynastic marriages for most of his fifteen children. But even in a remarkable family, Katherine's remarkable abilities were noticed at an early age. In 1638, when Sir John Leeke came to visit his cousin Alice Barrymore, he met Alice's sister Katherine for the first time. Describing her to Sir Edmund Verney, Leeke said:

You shall likewise find with her a sister Katherin, my deere cossen, a more brawnie wench or a Braver spiritt you have not often mett with all. She hath a memory that will hear a sermon and goe home and penn itt after dinner verbatim. I know not how she will appear in England, but she is most accounted of att Dublin.[11]

Thus in the 1630s, at least five years before moving to London, the young Katherine Boyle was already well known in Dublin for both her remarkable mind and her engagement with the church.

It is difficult, however, to ascertain the source of the future Lady Ranelagh's learning. Among the eight sisters in the Boyle household, Katherine appears to have been the only one to achieve any degree of scholarship; this makes it highly unlikely, then, that her education took place in the family home. Dorothy Moore, who moved in the same Dublin circles, had probably audited her brother's lessons. Katherine, however, was betrothed at the age of six to Sapcott Beaumont and immediately sent off to live with her fiancé's family.[12] She resided with them for six years, after which the marriage alliance fell through and she returned home in 1628. Her father appears to have disapproved of the ways in which she had been shaped by her time with the Beaumonts, and

[9] Sir John Leeke to Sir Edmund Verney, September 13, 1638, in Frances P. and Margaret M. Verney, *Memoirs of the Verney Family During the Seventeenth Century*, 3 vols. (London, 1925), I, 124.

[10] For the genealogy of the Boyle family, see Lodge, *The Peerage of Ireland*; and Maddison, *Life of Boyle*, 289–313. On the great Earl, see Canny, *The Upstart Earl*.

[11] Sir John Leeke to Sir Edmund Verney, August 11, 1638, in *Memoirs of the Verney Family*, I, 123. Leeke was related to the Barrymores, the family of Alice Boyle's husband.

[12] Sapcott Beaumont was the son of Lord Beaumont of Coleorton. For details regarding this betrothal, see Dorothea Townshend, *The Life and Letters of the Great Earl of Cork* (London, 1904), 157.

in a letter to Sir Thomas Stafford he lamented that Katherine had "lost the foundations of religion and civility wherein she was first educated."[13] Given this timing, however, it may very well have been the family of her betrothed who provided Katherine with her further education.

Nevertheless, the collapse of this match did not deter the great Earl of Cork. There were many suitors for his daughters, including a young Lucius Cary, son of the Lord Deputy of Ireland; and while the Carys were not wealthy enough to meet Cork's standards, Ranelagh and the future Lord Falkland remained friends until the latter's untimely death at the age of thirty-three. Sir Edward Villiers, brother of the Duke of Buckingham, was also hoping to ally his family with the Boyles – a plan that foundered on the same shoals of finance.[14] Yet despite Cork's highly complex and hard-headed dynastic strategies, he still managed to select some spectacularly bad spouses for his daughters. Lettice Boyle's husband George Goring, the Earl of Norwich, was a drunkard, a gambler, and a cheat, of whom Clarendon said, "dissimulation was his master-piece."[15] Cork tried to help by purchasing a commission for Goring in the army of the Prince of Orange. Given that the Queen of Bohemia referred to him as "that rogue Goring" in her correspondence, it appears that this move may not have been universally appreciated in The Hague.[16] However, it did have the inadvertent but happy side effect of introducing several members of the Boyle clan into the orbit of the exile court.

But Cork may have done even worse in selecting Arthur Jones, Lord Ranelagh, as the husband for fifteen-year-old Katherine.[17] In describing the marital situation of the young Lady Ranelagh, John Leeke had noted:

She is keapte and longe hath bine by the foulest Churle in the world; he hath only one vertu that he seldom cometh sober to bedd."[18]

---

[13] Cork to Stafford, March 20, 1632, Chatsworth, Cork Letter Book 1, f. 448. Quoted in Canny, *The Upstart Earl*, 60. Thomas Stafford was the stepfather of Elizabeth Killegrew, one of the Queen's maids of honour, and future wife of Ranelagh's brother Francis.

[14] Kenneth G. Murdock, *The Sun at Noon: Three Biographical Sketches* (New York, 1939), 48–51; and Townshend, *The Great Earl*, 140–2.

[15] Edward Hyde, Earl of Clarendon, *The History of the Rebellion and Civil Wars in England, Begun in the Year 1641*, ed. W. Dunn Macray, 6 vols. (Oxford, 1888), III, 444–5 [Book VIII, 168–71]. George Goring (1608–57), Earl of Norwich, was a courtier and Royalist soldier.

[16] Elizabeth of Bohemia to the Duke of Buckingham, August 13/23, [1627]. BL, Harleian MSS. 6988, f. 35. The letters of Constantijn Huygens, secretary to the Prince of Orange, also contain numerous references to the perfidious Goring.

[17] Arthur Jones (c.1617–70) was the son of Roger Jones, first Viscount Ranelagh, and Frances Moore. Frances Moore was the daughter of Sir Garret Moore of Drogheda, and the sister of Arthur Moore, the first husband of Dorothy Moore.

[18] Sir John Leeke to Sir Edmund Verney, September 13, 1638, in *Memoirs of the Verney Family*, I, 124.

Like George Goring, then, Jones was a gambler and a drunkard. In fact, both Ranelagh and her sister Lettice would often find themselves writing to Cork to ask for money to cover their respective husbands' gambling debts, and were sometimes reduced to finger-pointing as each one tried to point out that her husband was at least no worse than her brother-in-law. For instance, Cork received two letters on the same day, 13 October, 1640. The letter from Lettice complains about her sister, and asks about some money her father has sent to her husband Goring. The letter from Ranelagh also refers to her husband's need for money, and admits that he is "guilty of play," but then goes on to point out that Goring is "at least as faulty as he."[19]

After their marriage in 1630, Ranelagh and her new husband went to live in the grim Anglo-Norman keep of Athlone Castle, where two of their daughters were born.[20] It was at Athlone Castle that Ranelagh may have been stricken with smallpox. A letter from her father-in-law to the great Earl informs him that "my daughter kate is fled to Ceashell, from the small poxe, which is come within the walls of this Castle." Then, a year later, Sir John Leeke wrote that, "my pretious Katherine is somewhat decayed from the sweetest face I ever saw (and surely I have seene good ones)."[21] The castle was besieged in the Uprising of 1641, and the family was held prisoner for the entire winter. This would ultimately, however, prove propitious for Lady Ranelagh. She negotiated safe conduct for herself and her children, left her churlish spouse behind, and fled to London.

Ranelagh thus took up residence in London in late 1642 or early 1643, and the evidence shows that her life from that point on was entwined with the activities of a number of different groups of reformers, scholars, and activists. Among these was a group to which she was already connected through Dorothy Moore, a group whose members were convening in London from Moravia, Scotland, and Prussia. This was the millennial "band of brothers" – Hartlib, Dury, and Comenius.

---

[19] Chatsworth House, Lismore MSS., Bundle 21, articles 59 and 61, October 13, 1640.

[20] Ranelagh had four children. All three daughters predeceased her: Catherine Jones (1633–75); Elizabeth Jones, who caused scandal by eloping with a footman; and Frances Jones (1639–72). Her son Richard Jones (1641–1712) was first Earl of Ranelagh, and a pupil of John Milton and Henry Oldenburg. Richard became vice-treasurer of Ireland, and used his position to embezzle funds.

[21] Lord Ranelagh to Cork, 9 May 1637, Chatsworth, Lismore MSS., bundle 19, article 3; and Sir John Leeke to Sir Edmund Verney, September 13, 1638, in *Memoirs of the Verney Family*, I, 124.

A BAND OF BROTHERS: HARTLIB, DURY, AND COMENIUS

In 1641, a Prussian, a Scotsman, and a Moravian met together in London and swore out a pact of eternal brotherhood. In this *foedus fraternus*, Samuel Hartlib, John Dury, and Jan Amos Comenius formally consecrated themselves to each other; as Dury would later put it, "for though our taskes be different, yet we are all three in a knot sharers of one anothers labours." And their shared "knot" was the Herculean task of bringing about a new Christian kingdom on Earth, a kingdom secured and nourished by "the Reformation of studies in true Knowledge."[22] In dedicating their lives and efforts to this task, they also dedicated themselves to a chimera; thus Hartlib, Dury, and Comenius would appear to have been the quintessential intellectual outsiders, whose scriptural interpretation of the world put them on the margins of seventeenth-century intellectual events. However, they did not struggle alone, nor were their struggles without very real effects. They were intimately connected with Descartes, Huygens, Mersenne, and many other scholars and scientists in the republic of letters. And their work produced several very real scientific networks, from which the religiously moderate and empirically oriented Royal Society – the quintessential insider of early modern science – would eventually emerge. Moreover, this was more than a band of brothers alone, because it also included women like Ranelagh and Moore.

Yet in order to understand their shared work, it is necessary first to understand these three in terms of the individual paths that led them to London in 1641. As we trace these routes, we will see how the projects of the Hartlib circle emerged from their connections to learned Europe. The circle centered on Hartlib, Dury, and Comenius thus serves us in two ways: first, as an example of the diversity and function of intelligencing practices in the republic of letters; and second, as one of the networks through which women interested in godly reform got connected to van Schurman's circle of erudite women in The Hague. The Scotsman in this band was Moore's co-worker and future husband, John Dury; the Moravian was Jan Amos Comenius, and the Prussian was Samuel Hartlib.

Comenius was fated to be a wanderer and a survivor.[23] He was born into a family of Moravian Brethren, evangelical Christians who

---

[22] John Dury, *A Motion Tending to the Publick Good of This Age, and of Posteritie.* Published by Samuel Hartlib [1642], 41–2. On the pact, dated London, March 3/13, 1642, see *HDC*, 460–1.
[23] On Comenius (1592–1670), see Robert Fitzgibbon Young, *Comenius in England: The Visit of Jan Amos Komenský (Comenius) the Czech Philosopher and Educationist to London in 1641–1642*

followed the Bohemian priest Jan Hus. A persecuted sect in their homeland, they were dispersed and became extinct in the seventeenth century. For Comenius, this disaster was quickly followed by others, including the burning of his library, and the loss of his wife and children during an outbreak of plague. However, his tale of woe has another side – for as a consequence of the Bohemian Protestant diaspora, Comenius came into contact with a network of scholars and reformers in Germany, England, Sweden, Poland, and America. His sojourn in Germany resulted in his studying under the celebrated encyclopedist Johann Heinrich Alsted (1588–1638) in Herborn. Then in the 1630s, heavily influenced by Alsted, Jan Amos Comenius began to publish his own tracts on the reformation of learning; his all-inclusive *pansophia* carried on Alsted's encyclopedic approach, as well as his advocacy of learning for boys and girls alike.[24] And while Comenius' pansophic knowledge would remain an ambitious and amorphous ideal, it enabled the wanderer Comenius to find an intellectual home among the members of the republic of letters. The serious pastor who might never have left Moravia now had a name known throughout Europe, and invitations to work in locations as disparate as the royal court in Stockholm and the presidency of newly founded Harvard College in the colony of Massachusetts.

Like Bacon's *Great Instauration*, Comenius' pansophia, or "universal knowledge," was not limited to education alone. For intertwined with these educational goals was a revolution in every possible concept of knowing – of what should be known, and how it should be known, and by whom. Thus the pedagogical revolution was necessarily a political revolution as well, and in the final analysis, a plan to reform the entire Christian world. Some of his publications, like the *Janua Linguarum Reserata* and *Didactica Magna*, were meticulously detailed programs for teaching through "things, not words." However, his pedagogical approach then led him further on; and with pansophia, he aimed at producing "some general book which though single, should so exhibit all things

(London, 1932); Matthew Spinka, *John Amos Comenius, That Incomparable Moravian* (1943; reprint, New York, 1967); *HDC*, 342–464; and Dagmar Čapková, "Comenius and His Ideals: Escape from the Labyrinth," in *Samuel Hartlib and Universal Reformation: Studies in Intellectual Communication,* ed. Mark Greengrass, Michael Leslie, and Timothy Raylor (Cambridge, 1994), 75–91.

[24] Comenius' works included *Didactica Magna* (1628–43); *Janua Linguarum Reserata* (1631); *Physicae ad lumen reformatae Synopsis* (1633); *Conatuum Comenianorum praeludia ex Bibliotheca S[amuel] H[artlib]* (1637); *Pansophia Prodromus* (1639); *Via Lucis* (1641); *A Reformation of Schooles* (London, 1642); *Janua Rerum reserata sive Universalis Sapientiae Seminarium* (1643); *Tabula Pansophica* (1646); *Schola Pansophica* (1651); and *Orbis pictus* (1658).

necessary, that nought could rest to our shame unknown."[25] Comenius jotted down these pansophic ideas in a rough draft that he sent to an interested friend in London in 1636. After that, he heard nothing for months, and thought the manuscript had been lost. However, he had not counted on the drive and presumption of his London correspondent:

> receiving no answer for three whole months I began to think either it had been lost on the journey or was slightly looked upon. But lo! there cometh back to me at length a certain large bundle of books which had been sent from Dantzic: the which on opening, I perceive to be *Praeludia Conatuum Pansophicorum Comenii* ["Harbinger of Comenius' Pansophic Designs"], copies printed at Oxford – with a preface setting forth the reasons for its publication.[26]

The man responsible for that preface was also the correspondent responsible for surprising Comenius with the publication itself; and that man was Samuel Hartlib.

During his lifetime, it could truly be said that "everybody knew Hartlib."[27] He was "the Marin Mersenne of Protestant England," an intelligencer whose network of correspondence crossed the English Channel and the Atlantic Ocean, as he gathered and disseminated information from England, Ireland, Scotland, Germany, Prussia, Poland, Scandinavia, America, Jamaica, Bermuda, and the Low Countries.[28] Hundreds of names surface again and again in his work diary, *Ephemerides*, a remarkable document covering twenty-six years, from 1634 to 1660. In his *Ephemerides*, Hartlib cites everything he has learned from his contacts – tidbits that ranged from angelic conversations to agricultural innovations, from the atomism of Gassendi to the iatro-chemical experiments of Jan Baptista van Helmont, and from the theology of Archbishop Ussher to the medical tricks of whore-masters, from whom he learned that "in Horse-dung there are mighty secrets."[29]

---

[25] From an autobiographical fragment written by Comenius and inserted into his *Continuatio admonitionis fraternae de temperando charitate zelo ad S. Maresium* (Amsterdam, 1669). Translation by Young, *Comenius in England*, 31.

[26] Comenius, *Continuatio*, part 48. Translation in Young, *Comenius in England*, 35. The full title of the work was *Conatuum Comenianorum praeludia ex Bibliotheca S. H.* (1637).

[27] Masson, *The Life of John Milton* III, 193. The best source on Hartlib (*c*.1600–62) is still Turnbull, *HDC*. See also: Webster, *The Great Instauration*, *passim*; Stephen Clucas, "Samuel Hartlib's *Ephemerides*, 1635–59, and the Pursuit of Scientific and Philosophical Manuscripts: the Religious Ethos of an Intelligencer," *The Seventeenth Century* 6, no. 1 (spring, 1991): 33–55; and the very useful introduction to Greengrass *et al.*, *Samuel Hartlib and Universal Reformation*.

[28] Mark Greengrass, "Samuel Hartlib: 'Intelligenceur' Européen," in *Diffusion du savoir et affrontement des idées 1600–1770* (Montbrison, 1993), 213–34.

[29] *Ephemerides*, 1648, HP 31/22/31A.

Hartlib was an intelligencer and intellectual broker who was described by his lifelong friend John Dury as "the hub of the axletree of knowledge," the perfect person to function as the hub of an early modern information network. As Dury wrote to a potential backer:

The truth of this testimony which I give him, is knowne by all such as are familiarly acquainted with him, who perfectly also cann give wittnesse, of his abilityes and fittnesse, to be imployed in matters of intelligency, and correspondency, for gathering in of all manner of helpes, in learning and sciences, and for solliciting carefully, and laboring indefatigably in good purposes.[30]

The conclusion, according to Dury, was obvious: "and therefore it were a fitte and equitable thing, that hee should bee sette uppe as a conduit pipe of things communicable."[31]

The work of intelligencers in the seventeenth-century republic of letters was quite different from the work of intelligencers in the employ of governments or nobles – for instance, the espionage of Sir Francis Walsingham – and that work is not under consideration in the present analysis. Government intelligencers had paid positions, directed from above, with direct military and diplomatic consequences; thus their work was in a completely different category from those functions performed by intelligencers such as Hartlib, Mersenne, and Oldenburg. In the republic of letters, the work of intelligencers included: the collection of news, information, and reports of new advances in learning; the organization and systematizing of that information; and finally its distribution. Concurrent with these was the practice of putting like-minded scholars and activists in touch with one another, in a more far-flung version of the face-to-face networking that characterized the republic of letters. There were also other intelligencers operating as informational "conduit pipes" during these years, each directing epistolary traffic at the center of one of the smaller networks under the rubric of the republic of letters; one thinks, for instance, of Marin Mersenne, Constantijn Huygens, or Henry Oldenburg. They shared certain skills and characteristics: they knew multiple languages in addition to Latin, and they were completely dedicated to the tasks of sharing and advancing knowledge. In addition, these intelligencers possessed prodigious amounts of energy, such that they

---

[30] BL, Sloane MSS 654, ff. 250–1, 345–8, 350. Each is a letter from John Dury to a potential backer, praising Hartlib's qualifications as an intelligencer. These letters have also been printed as an Appendix in G. H. Turnbull, *Samuel Hartlib: A Sketch of His Life and His Relations to J. A. Comenius* (London, 1920), 74–9.
[31] *Ibid.*

would sometimes wear out their correspondents. Mersenne, for instance, would often fire off half a dozen letters in response to every communication he received from Descartes.[32] Descartes did not complain about his old friend's epistolary hyperactivity; however, Huygens had felt compelled to warn Anna Maria van Schurman about it when he first introduced her to Mersenne, writing: "I predict that your natural disposition is about to be exercised, worn out, and overwhelmed by letters, questions, and daily problems."[33] And Hartlib's own industry was such that John Dury needed two amanuenses in Frankfurt just to keep up with that one correspondence alone. As he wrote to Nathaniel Rich:

> From [Hartlib] you shall be able to know all that I have hitherto learned, or shall learn hereafter, for I have not only taken a course to have my letters addressed to him ... but also have obliged at Frankfort two to keep correspondence with him, the one for common current news, and the other for matters of greater moment.[34]

For a brief period, Hartlib lived in Chichester, where he worked with Bathsua Makin's brother-in-law, the mathematician John Pell, to establish "a little Academy for the Education of the Gentry of this Nation, to advance Piety, Learning, Morality, and other Exercises of Industry, not usual then in common schools."[35] However, the promised patronage never materialized, and the school failed after several months. Hartlib then returned to London, where he lived until his death on March 10, 1662. A flurry of letters written in 1635 discussed the possibilities that might materialize for Hartlib as an intelligencer working for Princess Elisabeth, should the Polish match have succeeded. Hartlib's network of contacts, and fluency in Polish, would have made him an ideal agent for the future Queen of Poland. However, when the Calvinist Princess refused to convert to Catholicism, the marriage was off, and despite the best efforts of Dury and Roe, that possibility came to naught.[36]

---

[32] Adam, *Vie & Oeuvres de Descartes*, in Descartes, *Oeuvres*, XII, 233–4.

[33] Contantijn Huygens to Anna Maria van Schurman. August 26, 1639. Latin Letterbook of Contantijn Huygens, KB MS, KA 44, f. 342. Also published with several errors of transcription as no. 2218 in *De Briefwisseling van Constantijn Huygens*, II, 489. Mersenne's published correspondence runs to 10,000 pages.

[34] John Dury to Nathaniel Rich, April 13, 1633. HMC VIII, Appendix II, 51a. Quoted in Turnbull, "Samuel Hartlib," 15–16.

[35] From Hartlib's Petition to the House of Commons (n.d., probably late 1660), in Turnbull, "Samuel Hartlib," 15.

[36] Dury to [?], August 20, 1635, BL Sloane MSS. 654, ff. 345–8; and Roe to Dury, December 16, 1635, HP 14/4/40A-44B.

The Chichester school and the hoped-for post with the Princess were not the only possible sources of income that failed for Hartlib. For the entire span of Hartlib's life and career in England, he was involved in a constant struggle for funds. Dury, who was often in the same straits, wrote countless letters trying to obtain support for Hartlib, avowing that without Hartlib's help as conduit and intelligencer, his own ecumenical efforts were doomed to fail:

> I cannot but say the truth in this, that without this action and negotiation to second my meane endeavours, and correspond with mee whiles I am abroad, I know not how to proceed or worke any thing in my purpose of pacification. Therefore if he fall to the ground, and for want of charity be deserted, I must allso resolve to give over my negotiation, and sit downe in sadnes.[37]

Promises poured in from patrons and Parliaments, but the flow of funding was never more than a trickle.

But it was in 1641 that the three projects dearest to Hartlib's heart – universal knowledge, practical education, and ascertaining and aligning with God's providential design – first came together in a real on-the-ground effort. He finally brought Comenius to London to attempt a pansophic project with the blessing of Parliament – indeed, there was even talk of giving Chelsea College to Hartlib, Dury, and Comenius for this purpose. And at the same time, Hartlib issued the group's ideas in a utopian tract entitled *A Description of the Famous Kingdome of Macaria.*[38] *Macaria* in fact became Hartlib's personal metaphor for the entire range of reforms "whose scope it is most professedly to propagate religion, and to endeavour the reformation of the whole world."[39]

But several days later, all had changed. The 1641 Uprising in Ireland began on the night of October 22. Wild rumors began to reach London, some alleging that barbarous Irish Catholics had massacred hundreds of thousands of Protestants overnight. The Uprising was real; the numbers, of course, were inflated and inflammatory. Nevertheless, for Comenius, who had already survived so many sieges and massacres, this was the signal

---

[37] Dury to [?], November 2, 1635. Quoted in *HDC*, 113–15.

[38] Since *Macaria* was published anonymously, under the aegis of Hartlib, it was long assumed to be his work; however, the actual author was Gabriel Plattes (*c.*1600–44). On Plattes, an expert on agriculture and mining, see Charles Webster, *Utopian Planning and the Puritan Revolution: Gabriel Plattes, Samuel Hartlib, and "Macaria"*, Research Publications of the Wellcome Unit for the History of Medicine, no. 11 (Oxford, 1979); and *idem*, "The Authorship and Significance of *Macaria*," in *The Intellectual Revolution of the Seventeenth Century* (London and Boston 1974), 369–85.

[39] Samuel Hartlib to Robert Boyle, November 15, 1659, in *The Correspondence of Robert Boyle*, ed. Michael Hunter, Antonio Clericuzio, and Lawrence M. Principe, 6 vols. (London, 2001), I, 385.

to leave.[40] Yet as Comenius was fleeing London to get away from the Ulster Uprising, others were entering London for the same reason. Anglo-Irish refugees began to convene, working on projects that were both parallel to and intertwined with those being promulgated by Hartlib, Dury, and Comenius. And among these exiles were Dorothy Moore and Lady Ranelagh.

TEACHING AS A TOOL FOR CHANGE: LADY RANELAGH AND EDUCATIONAL REFORM

In 1660, when an old friend wrote to Samuel Hartlib to recall those heady days of the 1640s, she characterized London in 1642 as "the beginning of our professions to a reformation." It had been a shared moment of possibilities, when it had seemed as though they might be able to bring real life to Bacon's *Instauratio Magna* – but the revolution had slipped through their fingers. The lament was over the failure of their educational reforms; and the friend, as Hartlib wrote to John Worthington, was "Mr. Boyle's incomparable sister the Lady Vicountess Ranalagh."[41]

Hartlib's production line of scribal publication immediately went into action. An extensive culture of scribal publication, bridging the gap between correspondence and print, was coeval with printed literature in early modern knowledge-making.[42] Small armies of scribes would copy and excerpt learned correspondence under the direction of intelligencing "hubs" like Hartlib. These items would then recirculate. Sometimes they circulated as extensive excerpts in correspondence; and sometimes as publications under a particular imprimatur, a name which would label that text as the product of an ideologically identifiable group. This was part of Hartlib's work as an intelligencer. His syndicate worked in script and print and correspondence; it distributed the works of authors who were both individual and corporate; it published both men and women; and it covered the entire range of early modern politics, religion, and knowledge-making.

---

[40] M. Perceval-Maxwell, *The Outbreak of the Irish Rebellion of 1641* (Montreal, 1994); Thomas Bartlett, "A New History of Ireland," *Past and Present* 116 (1987): 206–19; and Kathleen Noonan, "'Martyrs in Flames': Sir John Temple and the Conception of the Irish in English Martyrologies," *Albion* 36, no. 2 (summer 2004): 223–55.

[41] Samuel Hartlib to John Worthington, January 30, 1659/60. Cambridge University Library. Baker MSS 29, ff. 203–5. Ranelagh's original letter does not appear to be extant. Also printed in *The Diary and Correspondence of Dr. John Worthington. Remains Historical & Literary Connected with the Palatine Counties of Lancaster and Chester*, ed. James Crossley (Manchester, 1847–86), XIII, 162–77.

[42] Love, *Scribal Publication*.

Ranelagh's letters, discussing politics, religion, and reform, were an important component of Hartlib's scribal community. Thus her letter of 1660 was copied, excerpted, and annotated, and within two days it was being distributed among Hartlib's still-vast network of correspondents. As he wrote to Worthington: "No longer then two days ago, I received a missive from her in these words":

And if in the beginning of our professions to a reformation in these last 18 years we had fallen to this practice, and paid as many schoolmasters as we have done military officers ... we had by this time reaped better fruits of our labors and expences, then disappointment, division, poverty, shame and confusion, all which are in great letters upon the present frames of men's spirits, and posture of our affairs.[43]

Their plans had been literally global in extent, and had embraced a diverse array of projects, ranging from politics, preaching, and finance to agriculture, medicine, and mining. However, Ranelagh had also been involved in another reformationist project that has yet to be examined. This other project was crucial to the advancement of learning, since that endeavor could not proceed without its corollary: the advancement of *teaching*.

Practical education and pedagogical revolutions were central to the plans of Baconian empiricists, Comenians, and Hartlib's vast network of contacts. And in Ranelagh's letter, we see the centrality of education to her own revolutionary plans:

I do indeed expect a meeting here this afternoon of the two good men you mention ... and my brother Boyle, & another ingenious person, in order to the carrying on of that work (Education of Children), which tho' it may seem small & contemptible to those who judge according to appearance, cannot but be esteemed truly great by those who are assisted to judge righteous judgment.[44]

The "two good men" were Robert Wood and William Potter, economic reformers interested in introducing decimalization and paper currency to Britain. Ranelagh felt strongly that if only this one educational aspect of the revolution had succeeded eighteen years ago, that generation of children would now be a generation of enlightened, virtuous adults, to whom they could safely entrust their weary world. Ranelagh herself was never an educator, nor did she write specifically on the subject of pedagogy. However, as a scholar and activist involved in working for

---

[43] Hartlib to Worthington, January 30, 1659/60. Cambridge University Library. Baker MSS 29, ff. 203–5; also in *The Diary and Correspondence of Dr. John Worthington*, xii, 162–77.
[44] *Ibid.*

advancement of learning, she was clearly aware that teaching was the ultimate tool for change.

Ranelagh was active as a promoter of educational reform throughout her career, and she had begun by making the personal political, hiring John Milton as a tutor for at least two family members. First, in 1646, she arranged for Milton to instruct her nephew Richard Barry, the second Earl Barrymore; then, Ranelagh sent her own son Richard Jones to Milton's school.[45] Richard stayed with Milton until 1656, when he became the pupil of a young Henry Oldenburg, first secretary of the Royal Society. Unfortunately, Ranelagh's son Richard does not appear in any measure to have possessed the combination of intellect and piety that so brilliantly characterized both his mother and his uncle Robert Boyle. Even as Milton was handing over the reins of Richard's' education to Oldenburg, he wrote to his former charge to castigate him on several accounts – first for a rather casual attitude toward his studies; and second, for an apparent infatuation with majesty and military celebrity. As Milton put it: "I would not have you, as the disciple of philosophers, regard such things with too much admiration."[46] Richard may indeed have been "the disciple of philosophers," but this did not, unfortunately, result in his becoming a man of virtue; instead, he turned out to be somewhat of a rake, and embezzled nearly £900,000 while serving as Paymaster for Ireland.

Yet Ranelagh's choice to hire both Milton and Oldenburg as tutors allows us to view another aspect of how she functioned in her multiple networks. Ranelagh was able to identify the potential collaborators close by, and then put them to work in her various intellectual circles. Ranelagh found tutoring positions in noble families for struggling scholars and reformers. She filed petitions with Parliament for Hartlib and others. She put activists in touch with the most useful and influential politicians she knew, using her network of "intimacy and power."[47] She funneled books, letters, funds, ideas, and proposals to the right people and places, and a series of letters written by Robert Wood to Hartlib between 1656 and 1659 shows how Ranelagh had been functioning in this regard. Wood refers to Ranelagh receiving manuscripts, texts, and Latin translations, for work in the areas of financial, agricultural, and educational reform. She

---

[45] Although the date is not certain, Barrymore was sent to study with Milton at the poet's house in the Barbican – thus it must have been 1646 or 1647. Masson, *The Life of John Milton*, III, 658.

[46] John Milton to Richard Jones, September 21, 1656, in *Milton: Private Correspondence and Academic Exercises*, trans. Phyllis B. Tillyard (Cambridge, 1932), 37–8.

[47] William Hamilton to Hartlib and Dury, July 22, 1650, HP 9/11/21A-22B.

then assessed their worth, and finally decided whether and where to send them on.[48] She cured the sick, and disseminated medical information; she provided a haven for visiting preachers, fugitive Huguenots, and neophyte chemists; and she was the hub of an intelligence network that connected English and Palatine royalty with the hardscrabble Hartlibean web. In short, like a Théophraste Renaudot, she functioned as a one-person *bureau d'adresse*.

Realizing, then, that the advancement of teaching was crucial for the advancement of learning, Ranelagh put her network to work for peda-gogical reform. Ranelagh's name was "a passport to the highest intellec-tual circles," the key to Henry Oldenburg's entrée into the *sociabilité savante* of Paris when he first arrived there with Richard Jones in tow.[49] And in 1656, she also apparently tried to get Oldenburg a position with the sons of her older brother Richard, who had succeeded their father as Earl of Cork. The boys had been in the care of Marie du Moulin's brother Peter since childhood, but now they were heading off to Oxford, and were about to leave du Moulin's tutelage. However, Lady Cork eventually decided against Oldenburg, perhaps due to his as-yet imperfect English.[50] Then, in addition to operating on behalf of educators, it seems that Ranelagh also became a pupil. Like Moore, van Schurman, and Marie du Moulin, Ranelagh decided to learn the holy tongue, Hebrew.

Learning Hebrew was especially significant for Protestant reformers, since the holy tongue was revered as the language in which God first spoke to the world.[51] Ranelagh apparently decided to start learning Hebrew in the early 1650s, according to two tracts on Hebrew self-education pub-lished by the Scottish grammarian William Robertson. Robertson was a "pedagogical revolutionary," who published six works on the study of Hebrew and the Hebrew bible between 1653 and 1656.[52] His *A Gate or Door to the Holy Tongue, Opened in English* and the following *Second Gate, or the Inner Door* were both dedicated "To the Right Honorable the Lady

---

[48] Robert Wood to Samuel Hartlib, May 13, 1656, HP 33/1/1A-2B; April 8, 1657, HP 33/1/13A-14B; June 17, 1657, HP 33/1/17A-18B; May 26, 1658, HP 15/4/5A-B; February 9, 1659, HP 33/1/44A-B.

[49] *The Correspondence of Henry Oldenburg*, ed. A. Rupert Hall and Marie Boas Hall, 13 vols. (Madison, 1965), I, xxxvii. On the seventeenth-century *sociabilité savante* of Paris, see Simone Mazauric, *Savoirs et philosophie à Paris dans la première moitié du XVIIe siècle: Les conférences du bureau d'adresse de Théophraste Renaudot (1633–1642)* (Paris, 1997).

[50] In Oldenburg's letter to Lady Cork, he expresses his disappointment, while referring to himself as "both a stranger and an inferior." Oldenburg to Lady Cork, September 3, 1656, in Oldenburg, *Correspondence*, I, 107–8.

[51] G. Lloyd Jones, *The Discovery of Hebrew in Tudor England: a Third Language* (Manchester, 1983); Aaron L. Katchen, *Christian Hebraists and Dutch Rabbis* (Cambridge, MA, 1984).

[52] On William Robertson (fl. 1651–85), see Page Life, "Robertson, William," *ODNB*.

Vice-Countesse Ranalaugh." Robertson thanked her for her encouragement, her friendship, and above all for her successful acquisition of Hebrew, which had confirmed for him the efficacy of his method. He, of course, did not take all the credit for Ranelagh's success – that was due to "the eminency of your parts, to the constancy of your diligence, and to your industrous resolution." However, her success in teaching herself Hebrew using his texts had also confirmed for him a long-held suspicion:

> that not onely the Female sexe is, fully, capable enough of this kinde of learning; of which I had often before in my own thoughts perswaded my self . . . but that to the attaining thereof, the Latine tongue is not any ways necessary, nor absolutely prerequired thereunto.[53]

The politics here, in terms of both social status and gender, are inescapable. Women and boys below a certain social rank did not normally acquire Latin or Greek; it was not a question of ability, but rather of utility, cost, and custom. Since neither group could ever hope to put those linguistic skills to good use, Latin and Greek were considered the province of educated elites. Thus to free the acquisition of the holy tongue from being yoked to Latin made it a revolutionary spiritual skill indeed. Linguistic adepts like van Schurman and Makin had acquired all the learned languages in childhood; however, Moore and Marie du Moulin did not acquire Hebrew until adulthood, and, as far as we know, they did not become Latinate first. It may in fact have been Moore's success that had inspired Ranelagh to learn Hebrew herself. It is not known how Moore acquired her Hebrew learning, although it may have been in the 1640s, when she was living in London at the home of the noted Hebraist Arnold Boate – a process which would be further evidence for the strength of Anglo-Irish networks in London.

LADY RANELAGH, ANGLO-IRISH NETWORKS, AND THE INVISIBLE COLLEGE

While it is well known that Ranelagh supported the many projects and endeavors of the Hartlib circle over the years, the 1660 letter referenced above is one of many providing evidence for Ranelagh's activities at a very different level. When she refers here to her own participation in "our professions to a reformation," she is placing that reformation eighteen years previously, at the beginning of 1642. This predates her arrival in

---

[53] William Robertson, *A Gate or Door to the Holy Tongue, Opened in English* (London, 1653), A2–3.

London. This letter suggests, then, that when Ranelagh first appeared on the London scene, she did so as a member of an already-existing network of Irish natural philosophers and reformers. It further suggests that her work with the Hartlib circle was her own, and that it was an outgrowth of her earlier activities – thus it was not, as has been supposed, the fortuitous result of her having provided a home for her brother Robert Boyle, who at this time was still a youth of fifteen on his Grand Tour of the Continent.

In fact, many of Ranelagh's London associates appear to have been old friends from Ireland. Dorothy Moore, Benjamin Worsley, Gabriel Plattes, and the Boate brothers were there. And Lord Falkland, the failed suitor to the Boyles from a decade earlier, was yet another of Ranelagh's connections from her early years in Ireland. When she arrived in London, she found that her friend Lord Falkland had become the center of an English intellectual and literary salon that gathered at his estate in Great Tew. The Tew circle was essentially one of those "privileged places" that facilitated learning for a select group of scholars outside the walls of the academy.[54] As John Aubrey described Falkland's circle, "his House was like a college, full of Learned men."[55] Ranelagh was connected to this circle both through Falkland himself, and through another friend and associate: Edward Hyde, later Lord Clarendon.[56] Although she does not appear to have been as actively involved with the Tew circle as she was with the Hartlib circle, her continuing connections with Falkland and Hyde are further evidence for the breadth of her intellectual engagement and political engagement at both ends of the political spectrum.

Ranelagh thus settled in by early 1643, and a group of Anglo-Irish exiles began to gather and meet at her house in Pall Mall. It appears, however, that their agenda encompassed much more than the comforts of friendship and the accents of home. Networks focused on scientific, political, medical, and religious issues immediately became active among these refugees, with an alacrity that suggests they were not beginning at the beginning, but rather continuing activities that they had already been pursuing in Ireland.

---

[54] Bots and Waquet, *La République des Lettres*, 117.
[55] In *Aubrey's Brief Lives*, edited from the original manuscripts by Oliver Lawson Dick (reprint, Ann Arbor, 1957), 56. See also Hugh Trevor-Roper, "The Great Tew Circle," in *Catholics, Anglicans and Puritans: Seventeenth Century Essays* (London, 1987).
[56] It is not clear when Ranelagh first met Hyde. They were both close to Lord Falkland, and in 1665, Ranelagh's niece Henrietta Boyle married Clarendon's son Laurence Hyde, fourth Earl of Rochester.

Scholars have customarily considered Ireland to have been an intellectual *tabula rasa* prior to the Restoration and the founding of the Dublin Philosophical Society. In this argument, credit is given to the Hartlib circle for importing their zeal and learning during the Interregnum, thus kick-starting a moribund Irish intellectual culture.[57] Yet while there is a strong practical, personal and theoretical relationship between Irish science and the activities of the Hartlib circle, this causal explanation does nothing to illuminate the instantaneous intellectual fertility of the Anglo-Irish exiles who landed in London after the Uprising of 1641. We are much more usefully served by seeing Anglo-Irish intellectuals, the Hartlib circle, Protestant exiles from the Palatinate, and those who frequented the exile court in The Hague as contemporaneous co-workers, whose learned collegiality had always been an undercurrent of their intellectual activity and geographical displacement.

Among these interlinked groups was a mysterious entity that has come to be known as the Invisible College. The phrase occurs in several letters Boyle wrote to his former tutors Isaac Marcombes and Francis Tallents in 1646. In these letters, Boyle described the activities of a group of men with a very Baconian agenda – utilitarian, utopian, and scientific. They also welcomed young Boyle to their meetings, and he used the third person to effusively praise the men "of the invisible, or (as they term themselves) the philosophical college."[58] Thus the character of the Invisible College appears to resonate powerfully with the interests of the Hartlib circle. However, it does not appear that Hartlib himself was ever a member of that ghostly group. Early in 1647, Boyle had written to Hartlib, requesting "an account of the projects and successes of that college, whereof God has made you hitherto the midwife and nurse.[59] Then weeks later, Boyle wrote to Hartlib again to congratulate him on his progress in obtaining funding from Parliament:

---

[57] See, for instance, K. T. Hoppen, *The Common Scientist in the Seventeenth Century: A Study of the Dublin Philosophical Society 1683–1708* (London, 1970); and T. C. Barnard, "The Hartlib Circle and the Origins of the Dublin Philosophical Society," *Irish Historical Studies* 19, no. 73 (March 1974), 56–71. For a rather angry discussion of this scholarship and its disservice to Irish intellectual culture, see "Conclusion: the Boyles, Ireland and the 'New Science," in Canny, *The Upstart Earl*, 139–50.

[58] Boyle to Marcombes, October 22, 1646, and Boyle to Francis Tallents, November 21, 1646, in Boyle, *Correspondence*, 1, 42, 46. On the Invisible College, see Charles Webster, "New Light on the Invisible College: The Social Relations of English Science in the Mid-Seventeenth Century," *Transactions of the Royal Historical Society*, 5th Series, vol. 24 (1974): 19–42; idem, *The Great Instauration*, 57–67; and Thomas Leng, *Benjamin Worsley (1618–1677)* (Rochester, NY, 2008), 26–8.

[59] Boyle to Hartlib, [early 1647], in Boyle, *Correspondence*, 1, 51.

besides this, I say, you interest yourself so much in the Invisible College, and that whole society is so highly concerned in all the accidents of your life, that you can send me no intelligence of your own affaire, that does not (at least relationally) assume the nature of Utopian.[60]

In the first letter, then, Boyle is referring to a "college" that is clearly Hartlib's own project; but in the second letter, the Invisible College is something in which Hartlib has expressed an interest, so Boyle is providing him with information. Clearly, Hartlib could not be acting in 1647 as "midwife and nurse" to a project that had already been flourishing in 1646 – thus Hartlib's college and the Invisible College were two different entities.

In the correspondence of the Hartlib circle and their world of contacts, the word "college" was used to refer to a number of very different entities. The reference here to Hartlib's "college" probably concerns his plans for the Office of Public Address, which was being promoted in 1647, and was very often called a "colledge" in the correspondence between Hartlib and his supporter Sir Cheney Culpeper.[61] The informal salons of French intellectual culture at this time, including that of Mersenne, were also referred to as *académies*. This was characteristic of the years between the closing of the French Royal Academy in 1580 and the founding of the Académie Française in 1635.[62] Thus what we are seeing here is evidence for a diverse, interconnected, and apparently contradictory collection of agendas and practices. The intellectual culture of mid-seventeenth-century London was a virtual Venn diagram. And within these overlapping circles, many elements were using the same word – "college" – to refer to some very different projects. Thus problems will inevitably arise whenever we attempt to craft a streamlined narrative for this moment in intellectual history, a moment for which the evidence actually documents the analytical opposite of that story.[63] The Invisible College was neither the Hartlib circle, nor a precursor of the Royal Society; rather, it was probably the name given to a group of Baconian thinkers with no institutional home, thus rendering them "invisible" – a specific, local subset of the republic of

---

[60] Boyle to Hartlib, May 8, 1647, in Boyle, *Correspondence*, 1, 58.

[61] See letters from Culpeper to Hartlib, November through December, 1645. HP 13/279A, HP 13/117A-118B, HP 13/295B. On Culpeper, see *The Letters of Sir Cheney Culpeper (1641–1657)*, ed. M. J. Braddick and M. Greengrass, Camden Miscellany XXXIII, Fifth Series, vol. 7 (Cambridge, 1996).

[62] Josephine de Boer, "Men's Literary Circles in Paris 1610–1660," *Publications of the Modern Language Association of America* 53 (1938): 730–80; Mazauric, *Savoirs et philosophie à Paris*.

[63] Michael Hunter, "Restoration Science: Its Character and Origins," in *Science and Society in Restoration England* (Cambridge, 1981), 8–31.

letters. And as evidenced by a letter Ranelagh wrote in 1657, the Invisible College was still active ten years later.

In the Hartlib Papers there is a letter from Ranelagh to an unknown correspondent, dated Dublin, November 3, 1657. The letter begins with a lament that Ranelagh's correspondent has been out of touch. Combining the vocabularies of science and faith, it also mentions the Invisible College by name:

> I still wish with gladness to express my friendship for you, and would be pleased, at your convenience, to hear something of the news regarding your Invisible College, since in the visible ones one finds little more than that which gives us cause to complain and to long for improvement.[64]

Thus it would appear that in 1657 the Invisible College was still a working name for a group of scientists with an agenda of improvement, rather than the purely scientific pursuits of the Oxford group that would become one of the nuclei of the Royal Society.

There was another group, comprising Anglo-Irish exiles, deeply involved in politics, Protestantism, and practical science. The members included Benjamin Worsley, Miles Symner, the Boate brothers, Robert Boyle, and Ranelagh herself. It may in fact have been Ranelagh who brought her younger brother into this group. In 1646, Boyle was only nineteen, and his sister Katherine was the one with the connections, power, and reputation. Indeed, even as late as 1648, the scientist Robert Boyle was still being referred to as Ranelagh's younger brother.[65] Boyle's own network of chemical correspondents at this time was not extensive, and the most prominent among them was the chemist Benjamin Worsley. Boyle looked up to the older Worsley, who became a mentor; he helped to develop Boyle's belief that science was much more than an academic exercise, and in fact had a duty to advance the common good through the improvement of trades. And Ranelagh was much more than a patron or salon hostess for these exiles. She was providing intelligence to Boyle and Sir Cheney Culpeper on the progress of Worsley's saltpeter project, and may have been the first to put Worsley in touch with her brother.[66]

---

[64] The letter is in German, and the phrase used is "*unsichtbahren societt.*" Ranelagh to [?], Dublin, November 3, 1657, HP 39/2/56A. In the Hartlib Papers there are six German copy extracts of letters written by Ranelagh, dated between October 20, 1656 and January 18, 1657.

[65] On March 26, 1648, Sir William Waller, an army officer and parliamentarian, wrote to Hartlib from Leiden. He described a conversation he had had with "Mr Boyle (the brother of that noble Lady Raynello, unto whome I desire to have my most humble service presented)," HP 32/2/26A.

[66] In a 1646 letter to Worsley, Boyle discusses Ranelagh's report on Worsley's petition for a new method of making saltpeter. Boyle to Worsley, *c.* November 21, 1646, in Boyle, *Correspondence*, 1, 42–4.

We turn now to a discussion of Ranelagh's work in medical, political and scientific circles, in order to reconstruct the diverse array of networks in which she was active.

THE MEDICAL NETWORKS OF LADY RANELAGH

Ranelagh was well known for her expertise in medicine, and for over fifty years she was an active participant in medical manuscript networks. Throughout northern Europe and Britain, the circulation of medical receipts was a widespread and long-lived phenomenon.[67] It involved men as well as women from many walks of life, from the nobility to the middling classes. For instance, a name frequently mentioned in Ranelagh's medical correspondence is that of Sir Kenelm Digby (1603–65), a Catholic recusant, medical writer, and natural philosopher. In a letter to Hartlib in 1658, Ranelagh reported: "The One of these enclosed receipts I have experienced for sharpe hott humors, the other was given me by Sir Kenelme Digby, with most Extraordinary Commendation from his owne experience against festers & inflammation."[68] In Hartlib's correspondence and in his *Ephemerides* Ranelagh is asked to provide her medical recipes, and to compare and assess the remedies of other practitioners; she is also involved in discussions of how to obtain the necessary ingredients, asking her brother Robert Boyle for certain chemicals, and noting where to find healing herbs. In addition, when medicine runs out, she has a new batch concocted herself.

Some sense of the scope of her medical activities can be gleaned from a series of letters written to her brother Richard; Richard's wife Elizabeth was ill, and Ranelagh was mustering resources to help cure her:

On Worsley, see Leng, *Benjamin Worsley*; Charles Webster, "Benjamin Worsley: Engineering for Universal Reform," in Greengrass *et al.*, *Samuel Hartlib and Universal Reformation*, 213–35; and idem, *The Great Instauration*.

[67] Recent scholarship has established the involvement of female medical practitioners in medical manuscript networks at every social level, in both manuscript and print. See Jennifer K. Stine, "Opening Closets: The Discovery of Household Medicine in Early Modern England" (Ph.D. dissertation, Stanford University, 1996), esp. Chapter 4; Elaine Leong, "Medical Remedy Collections in Seventeenth-Century England: Knowledge, Text and Gender," (Ph.D. dissertation, Oxford University, 2005); and Alisha Rankin, "Medicine for the Uncommon Woman: Experience, Experiment, and Exchange in Early Modern Germany," (Ph.D. dissertation, Harvard University, 2006).

[68] HP 66/8/1A-B, September 11, 1658. Two books of Ranelagh's medical receipts in the Sloane MSS in the British Library also contain several items attributed to Digby. See *Severall receipts copied out of the booke of Mad. Iones. 1681*, Sloane MS. 1289, ff. 65–75b; and *My Lady Rennelaghs choice receipts: as also some of Capt. Willis who valued them above gold*, Sloane MS. 1367.

[April 27] My brother Robin has given me two smale Botles of sperit of Sal Armoniacke for her . . . he wishes she may use sperit of Harts horne but was soe destetute of any thereof that when the other day Prince Robert sent to him to begg some for himselfe upon the Experience he had found of its haveing donn him much good for his head, he was faigne to beg a litle to send him, but if out of your Parkes you would send up hornes either of stags or Buckes old or new I would have sperit made for & sent to her.[69]

"My Brother Robin" refers to Robert Boyle; in Ranelagh's letters he is almost always "Robin" or "the dear squire." And "Prince Robert" is Prince Rupert of the Rhine, the brother of Princess Elisabeth; thus Ranelagh's medical network had connections across the channel with the exile court. Ranelagh eventually obtained the necessary ingredients; she was able to concoct the new batch of spirit of hart's-horn, and her sister-in-law made a full recovery. Moreover, another medical correspondence, this time between Ranelagh and a different sister-in-law, suggests the degree to which Ranelagh identified herself as a serious practitioner of medicine.

In a letter sent to Margaret, Countess of Orrery, Ranelagh's concern was for the health of her brother Roger, the Countess' husband. Roger was apparently suffering from indigestion, gout, and a steadfast reluctance to take medical advice. The letter was accompanied by a packet of medicines Ranelagh had concocted herself – "sperit of wormewood & Plaister of Caranna" – along with explicit directions concerning their use:

The Black thing on the top of it is the chimical oyle 2 or 3 drops of which upon a good lumpe of sugar taken in a morneing fasting & fasting an houer or 2 after is what I hope wil help his stomack against the Clogg of Fleam that now opresses it, provided he doe it for a good many days together, the plaister is but to be warmed & layd to his stomack.[70]

This is followed by more instructions, this time in regard to changes Roger should be making in terms of diet and exercise.

For our purposes, however, the most fascinating part of this letter comes next, when Ranelagh turns her focus from the patient to the practitioner. Addressing herself to her sister-in-law, Ranelagh discussed another item that she had included in the packet of medicines:

---

[69] BL, Althorp Papers, B4. The letters give no year, but they have been given a provisional date of 1667. "Sister Warwick" is Ranelagh's sister Mary Rich. Lees was the estate of her husband Charles, the fourth Earl of Warwick.

[70] The letter is undated, although the archivist has assigned a provisional date of 1672. Petworth House Archives, West Sussex Record Office, Chichester. Orrery Papers, MS. 13,219, folder 24. No foliation.

I send you Dr. Boates Booke to write out for your owne use but must beg you that noe Dr nor Apothecary may have any thing out of it, because he has a sonn of his owne that is studdying towards being of his fathers proffesion, & therefore for him I would reserve the assistance of his fathers Experiments from al other Drs. but our selves. Yet to further your practise I hasten it to you.[71]

This passage is significant on a number of levels – and first among these is the fact that Ranelagh refers to herself here explicitly as a "Doctor." She is placing herself squarely in the company of prominent physicians like Gerard Boate, whose book she is sending along for the use of her sister-in-law alone.[72] Since Boate had performed all the medical "experiments" and done all the science himself, he deserved to be the one controlling the distribution of his hard-won knowledge. It was apparently a question of professional ethics, and Ranelagh was including herself as a member of this profession.

Additionally, however, this passage opens up a window onto the world of medical networks – a world whose functioning is being specifically addressed by Ranelagh. She states that she would reserve this medical knowledge for doctors like "ourselves." But how might Ranelagh be defining that "we" who were entitled to this information? The answer, like the republic of letters itself, has many levels.

On the most immediate level, one looks to family. After all, Ranelagh had written this letter to her sister-in-law. However, a Boate is not a Boyle. Perhaps, then, since the book was written by Gerard Boate, the "we" might refer to the members of Ranelagh's Anglo-Irish network. The Boates and Boyles were both members of this group; thus she might possibly have been defending the property of a network under siege for political and religious reasons. And on another level, Ranelagh might also have been speaking as a member of the Hartlib circle. Ranelagh was intimately familiar with Hartlib's tendency to publish first, and ask permission later. And an entry in Hartlib's *Ephemerides* for 1653 reported that the Cambridge Platonist Henry More "Hath gotten from Mr Boyle the Stirk's Balsam of Vegetables. Also the choicest secrets of Dr Gerard Boate."[73] Thus Ranelagh might have wanted to be especially careful with the "choicest secrets" in this particular book.

---

[71] *Ibid.*

[72] I have no further information as to what "book" is being referred to here. Both Gerard and Arnold Boate were physicians, and both had passed away by this date; however, Gerard was the only one with sons still living. See Elizabeth Baigent, "Boate, Gerard," *ODNB*.

[73] *Ephemerides*, 1653, HP 28/2/57A. Baigent misreads this entry as an indication that it was Hartlib himself who was in possession of these medical receipts. Baigent, "Boate, Gerard," *ODNB*.

It is also possible that the "we" in this case referred to female medical practitioners – specifically, to a network of women involved in the circulation of medical manuscripts. Bathsua Makin was a participant in this network, and it is possible that Dorothy Moore was also involved.

Moore, always searching for gainful employment in The Hague while trying to craft her career as a preacher, had apparently lit upon the idea of a chemical career. It is not clear precisely what form this career would have taken. Concocting, refining, mixing, and distributing various substances might take place under the rubric of what we now consider alchemy, chemistry, medicine, pharmacy, or cookery. The substances themselves might have been perfumes, medicines, or alcoholic spirits. And certainly, Moore's close relationship to the Boyles meant that she had a constant connection to all of these activities via Ranelagh's medical networks and Robert Boyle's scientific circles. All we know from the surviving evidence is that Moore was considering embarking upon a chemical venture and that the idea met with something less than universal approval.

In 1649, Hartlib had written to Worsley, apparently relaying Moore's request for help with this new project. Worsley had responded by affirming his desire to serve the Durys in whatever way possible, writing: "I am so farre both glad, and do thank you, that you would give me a hynt wherein I might serve Mrs Dury."[74] However, Worsley had very real concerns. First, he needed to know precisely what *sort* of chemistry Moore was talking about:

Yet [I] do not plainely perceive your meaning, you talking of distilling in the generall, under which you must comprehend eyther the whole of Chymia, or that comon one of hott waters, or some choyce one which may be used by a gentlewoman, or any for the eliciting or neat distilling of spiritts.[75]

The problem was one of propriety, of what was appropriate to Moore's social rank and to Dury's profession as a minister. The first two categories – "the whole of Chymia," or the distillation of common "hot waters" – would not do. The third, however, was certainly a possibility. Moore could concoct and sell choice distillations. Thus Worsley began immediately to provide helpful suggestions to get Moore started:

I did pitch upon this imployment, as most fitt for her; and shall give her the best skill I know, hyding nothing from her, how to destill spiritts which shall really indeed, and in a true valew, be first much more rich, & excellent, & perfect secondly more healthfull & comendable then any whatsoever, I have ever knowne and yett not much deerer or more chargeable. Which I will now show you by example.[76]

[74] Worsley to Hartlib, June 22, 1649, HP 26/33/1A-3B.   [75] *Ibid.*   [76] *Ibid.*

Worsley was as good as his word, and the next few pages were filled with chemical receipts for Moore to use in her new venture. Others, however, did not distinguish between one sort of chemistry and another in judging the propriety of this career; and William Hamilton, a Scottish scholar and co-worker with Hartlib, Dury, and Comenius, was simply aghast at the prospect.[77]

Yet two pieces of evidence suggest that Moore's attempt at a chemical career might have had some real results. In a 1658 letter to Robert Boyle, Hartlib wrote: "That glass, with whatever was in it, I did deliver very carefully to Mrs. Dury, according to my lady's direction."[78] "My Lady," in Hartlib's correspondence, refers to Ranelagh. Thus it would seem that Ranelagh had prepared a medical concoction, and had asked Hartlib to deliver it to Moore. And in a letter to Anne Conway in 1659, Henry More discusses his recent illness; it had been a serious one, but he was now feeling much better, thanks to a network of female scholars – a network that included Dorothy Moore and Princess Elisabeth of Bohemia:

I have returned the Princess letter, with my thanks to Mrs Dury, that she would be pleased to trouble herself so much in reference to me, but the greatest is due to your Ladiship, without whose intermediating nothing had been done.[79]

Although we cannot be certain, this letter suggests that Conway had contacted both Moore and Elisabeth on Henry More's behalf – and that Moore might have shared her chemical expertise. And further, while it is known that Conway and Elisabeth were connected on a different level, through shared interests in philosophy and Quakerism, this medical consultation would give a new valence to that relationship. It is also yet another illustration of how women's intellectual networks continually intersected with philosophical, religious, and medical networks in learned Europe.

It is not possible, therefore, to determine which of these concerns most closely defined the "ourselves" to which Ranelagh was referring. What is most important, however, is that the various possible definitions were very far from being mutually exclusive. In fact, I would suggest that the reverse was true. The very process which renders the "ourselves" of Ranelagh's letter so difficult to pin down – that is, her simultaneous participation in so many disparate networks – is the selfsame process that defines Ranelagh

---

[77] William Hamilton to Samuel Hartlib, December 17, 1649, HP 9/11/18A-20B. Hamilton was a later signatory to Hartlib, Dury, and Comenius' *foedus fraterni* of 1641, *HDC*, 263.

[78] Hartlib to Boyle, April 27, 1658, in Boyle, *Correspondence*, I, 263–9.

[79] Henry More to Anne Conway, May 10, 1659, BL, Add. MSS 23,216, f. 222. My thanks to Paul Seaver for the transcription of this letter. Also printed in *The Conway Letters*, 158.

as a member of the republic of letters. Family, physicians, Anglo-Irish exiles, scientists, Protestant reformers, and intellectual women – each of these constituted a network in which Ranelagh was one of "us." Moreover, Ranelagh's "us" possessed further layers of complexity due to her extensive involvement in the politics of these tumultuous times. The following section examines Ranelagh's networking activities at both ends of the political spectrum in seventeenth-century England.

THE POLITICAL NETWORKS OF LADY RANELAGH

In addition to being a member of the Anglo-Irish aristocracy, Ranelagh was a member of the inner circle of Hartlib's reformationist network. And since the Hartlibean agenda for the advancement of learning included medical knowledge, we should not be surprised to see that medical and political networks crossed paths at Ranelagh's home in Pall Mall. Because her home was also the physical setting for so much activity – such as meetings of the Hartlib circle, book exchanges, and her brother Robert's experiments – scholars have generally characterized Ranelagh's role in these projects as that of a "hostess" or "patroness." However, a closer look at the evidence demonstrates that these labels are both inadequate and inaccurate.

The bulk of Ranelagh's parliamentary activities took place between 1647 and 1659. She of course petitioned on her own behalf, and on behalf of her family, for the restitution of lost income resulting from the 1641 Uprising. This level of political activity in noblewomen is not surprising. But Ranelagh was also politically active on a national level. In addition to her efforts on behalf of Worsley's saltpeter project, documents in the Hartlib Papers show that Ranelagh was involved in trying to pass a bill on commodities, and was being consulted for her advice on the matter. A 1648 letter from Dury to Sir Cheney Culpeper references "Mr. Pruvosts" ordinance for staple commodities and a Corporation for trade, which was being opposed by monopolists. Ranelagh had some concerns, which Dury relayed to Culpeper. Culpeper answered those, but then added:

But now this Answer leads me to another Question which I made to my Lady [Ranelagh] ... The Question is this. How the certainty per centum which is disigned to the private adventurer, and the surplusage which is designed to the parliament will be secured to them, at least till time and experience have raysed a good opinion of what is proposed.[80]

---

[80] John Dury to Cheney Culpeper and reply, September 25 and 26, 1648, HP 12/23A-26B.

While there is no record of Ranelagh's reply to Culpeper's questions, his letter makes it clear that she was expected to be in command of the economic and political facts that would help propel this proposition to a successful conclusion.

In addition, Ranelagh was engaging Culpeper with some questions of her own, having to do with legal, political, and moral issues. She sent the questions to Hartlib, asking him to "get a Resolution to these Questions from Sir Cheney". It was a long list, concerning the balance of power between King and Parliament, and the legality or moral force of laws and oaths. For instance:

Quest. Whether according to the Fundamentalls of this Kingdome the two Houses of Parliament have power to declare the Law without appeale, without the King joyne with them to make a Declaration of the Law indisputable points by an Act of Parliament? . . .

Quest. Whether that Clause of the oath formerly administered to the Kings of England whereby they are bound as well To make such Law's as the People shall desire In Parliament as to keepe those made, ever remitted by any act of the People or only neglected thorough the Corruption of Our Kings and those that should have administered it, which not having beene administered to this King? *Quest.* Whether the People can justly clayme it from him?[81]

We do not know how Culpeper replied. Yet this was not the first time Ranelagh had engaged with questions regarding the legal rights of Parliament and crown, and supporters of the parliamentary side were not the only ones with whom she engaged on these issues. In fact, Ranelagh had already been active on the national level in attempting to formulate a new basis for reconciling King and Parliament – but this time she had been working with Royalist friends.

After Falkland's death fighting for the Royalist cause at the Battle of Newbury, on September 20, 1643, Ranelagh had written to their mutual friend, Edward Hyde, Lord Clarendon. And in Falkland's name she had exhorted him to take this opportunity to convince the King to acknowledge Parliament, "calling a company of people by the same name you have given them all this while to no purpose, and refuse to give them now it cannot be given but to so many happy purposes". As Ranelagh pointed out, this made no sense whatsoever:

They ask, if they be no Parliament, why you send to treat with them? Why you do not only send them the offer of a pardon? . . . If they be such uncoloured

---

[81] Undated, but with surrounding materials from 1648. HP 26/13/1A-2B.

traitors as they must needs be, if they be not a Parliament, where are the Houses, whereof you call yourselves members, if they be not they? And if they be, will you rather undo the Kingdom than call them so? Either, I beseech you, stop their mouths from these discourses by the desired message, or give your servants here something to answer them.[82]

Although matters did not turn out as Ranelagh might have wished, the letter was endorsed in the hand of Hyde: "A very sensible letter from Lady Ranelagh."

And apart from Clarendon and Falkland, Ranelagh's aristocratic political contacts included the Sydney family, Earls of Leicester and Lords Lieutenant of Ireland from 1641 to 1647. The evidence comes from a 1650 letter to Hartlib and Dury from the consistently disapproving William Hamilton. Hamilton began by upbraiding Dury for wasting his time in educational reform, then moved on to his own problems, which he blamed on "the base carriage and provocations of that nip of the devil, Sydney, of our house." And apparently, he was holding Ranelagh partly responsible for exacerbating the situation:

By his familiarity with Mr King, & the intimacy and power (if I be not deceived) that I heard my lady Reynola say, shee hath with his brother Coronell Sydney . . . I guesse at part of his spyte.[83]

Hamilton's particular problem in this letter is not made clear. However, it is abundantly clear that he considers Ranelagh to be a person who can achieve political results through the deployment of her "intimacy and power" with members of the aristocracy. In this he concurs with the judgment of Hartlib, who described his friend Ranelagh as a woman of "piety and parts, with power and interest, which she hath and will always have with all the great ones, let them change never so often."[84]

Thus Ranelagh was already collaborating with Hartlib and radical supporters of Parliament such as Cheney Culpeper, while also trying to influence important Royalists like Hyde. She continued to interest herself

---

[82] The original letter is held in the Bodleian Library, Clarendon SP MSS 23, ff. 113–15. The printed version is taken from a copy of the original made by Hyde's secretary, Mr Edgman, and also endorsed by Hyde: "Lady Ranelagh to me, after the death of my Lord Falkland." Calendared as No. 1748 in *Calendar of the Clarendon State Papers*, ed. Ogle and Bliss (Oxford, 1872), 1:248. My thanks to Dr. Ruth Connolly for this reference.

[83] HP 9/11/21A-22B. "Colonel Sydney" was Algernon Sydney (1623–83), and his brother was Philip Sydney (1619–98), who had briefly succeeded his father as Lord Lieutenant of Ireland. "Mr King" may refer to Dorothy Moore's brother, Sir Robert King.

[84] Hartlib to Worthington, January 30, 1659/60. Cambridge University Library, Baker MSS 29, ff. 203–5.

in these legal and political questions, and was apparently preparing a tract on legal reform in 1659; this was, according to Hartlib, "an argument concerning the reformation of English laws and lawyers."[85] Lady Ranelagh was especially active, however, in promoting the projects of the Hartlib circle, a fact that can be illustrated by her efforts on behalf of Hartlib's Office of Public Address.

The plans for an Office of Public Address are probably the clearest manifestation of the Hartlib circle's intensely systematic approach to knowledge. It was an approach that caused some intellectual division in the republic of letters, because inherent in this systematizing effort was the belief that knowledge should be put to work, and that learning should be used *for* something.[86] Among those in favor of this systematizing were the reformers one would expect to find – Hartlib, Dury, and Comenius, Worsley and Culpeper, Plattes, Petty and Pell. Yet the support also came from less expected quarters – such as Father Marin Mersenne, and the Cambridge Platonist Henry More. The Comenian plans for a pansophic college had never materialized, and the Invisible College was a local network with a particular focus. The Office of Address, on the other hand, was to be a state-funded organization, reaching throughout the British Isles.

The idea was derived in part from the *bureau d'adresse* of Théophraste Renaudot, a physician and journalist from Montpellier. Renaudot's bureau was part of the *sociabilité savante* of seventeenth-century Paris, which included assemblies such as the cabinet Dupuy, the mathematical meetings at the home of Descartes in 1626, the *"academies"* of Montmor and Mersenne, and the assembly directed by Marie de Gournay.[87] Yet Hartlib's Office of Address was more than just an English take on Renaudot. In fact, the multiple functions and varied supporters for this project serve as an instructive example demonstrating how disparate networks intersected within the republic of letters, and how women were active in their learned work.

Hartlib's 1648 proposal, entitled *A further Discoverie of The Office of Publick Addresse*, evolved from a 1643 proposal by John Dury, a three-page pamphlet entitled *A Faithfull and seasonable Advice, or, The necessity of a*

---

[85] Hartlib to Boyle, May 31, 1659, in Boyle, *Correspondence*, I, 357–9.
[86] Clucas, "Samuel Hartlib's *Ephemerides*," 36.
[87] Howard M. Solomon, *Public Welfare, Science, and Propaganda in Seventeenth Century France: The Innovations of Théophraste Renaudot* (Princeton, 1972); Mazauric, *Savoirs et philosophie à Paris*; Harcourt Brown, *Scientific Organizations in Seventeenth Century France (1620–1680)* (New York, 1934), 17–40.

Correspondencie for the advancement of the Protestant Cause. As the title suggests, the function of this state-sponsored program would have been to establish an international network of correspondents who would stream-line the flow of intelligence, and unite the fractured Protestant landscape. From the Scots to the Swedes, Britons could join with their brethren on the Continent to defeat the Hapsburg hordes and restore the Palatine house.

Yet by 1647, this became a much more elaborate project for furthering the advancement of learning; moreover, it was no longer focused on one goal, or even on one faith. It now included an Office of Address for Communications, which was apparently descended from a marriage between Dury's ecumenical projects and Comenius' pansophic college. Thus in addition to the Office of Address' scheme for the advancement of learning, the anti-Catholic valence of the religious agenda had given way to a more ecumenical expediency. Hartlib himself was noting in his *Ephemerides* how useful it would be to have his own "correspondencie" intersect with those of the great intelligencers of Europe – Huygens, Saumaise, and Mersenne, a Catholic monk. In his *Ephemerides* for 1639, Hartlib had written:

Hugens a great Correspondent in matters of Learning. Also Mersennus the whole Cloister maintaining the charges . . . Salmesius a mighty Correspondent writes all with his owne hands and no Amanuensis.[88]

Clearly, Hartlib was quite impressed by Mersenne's economic finesse in having the Minims foot the bill for his intelligencing network. But when it came to putting his own schemes into action, Hartlib had no "Cloister" to support him, and obtaining support from Parliament was a constant struggle. As Culpeper remarked to Hartlib:

your resolution to persist in your office of addresse showes me your life of faythe, & how in this (as in the rest of your life) you wrastle not onely without but againste hope."[89]

It appeared, then, that real political savvy was required – so Hartlib turned to Ranelagh.

In fact, it may have been Ranelagh who first introduced Hartlib's *A Further Discoverie* to Parliament as part of that attempt. A letter to

---

[88] *Ephemerides*, 1639, HP 30/4/7A. Renaudot was born into a French Protestant family, but converted to Catholicism in 1626. Solomon, *Public Welfare*, 93–4. "Salmesius" is a reference to Claude Saumaise (1588–1653).
[89] Culpeper to Hartlib, February 24, 1646, in Webster, *Great Instauration*, 68–9.

Ranelagh from John Sadler reports that he had "presented the litle booke to Mr soliciter with those arguments most likly to move him, which were your Ladyships." He then laments that he was given "litle groundes of hope." Ranelagh's reply is full of her annoyance "that those Publick aymes by which Mr Hartlib is rendred more Considereable than the other professing Christians amongst whom he lives should be a scarr Crow to the Parliament." But she then goes on to suggest a very practical and detailed plan by which Hartlib could be given a place at Oxford, with an income derived from Dean's and Chapter lands. This would certainly have solved some financial problems. Nevertheless, Ranelagh was also quite sure that Hartlib "will not think himselfe cared for unlesse his Public motions bee hearkned to."[90]

Ranelagh was clearly frustrated by her lack of success in this political effort. Yet in addition to the ups and downs of her work for political and religious reform, Ranelagh had a surprisingly strong presence among those adamantly opposed to the aims of the Hartlib circle – the Stuarts and the exile court in The Hague. And in this case, we are informed by two letters in which these royal connections are specifically referenced.

Ranelagh's work with royal informants may have begun when she was still in her early twenties. In 1640, she wrote a letter to her father, relaying news of political events:

I presumed your Lordship would receive Inteligence of all occurrents in the north, imediatly from thence, but in obedience to your Command I now send a perticular of such Passages, as came last to the Queens notice, which I had from a very good hand.[91]

It is clear here that there was an expectation of receiving political intelligencing reports from Ranelagh; it is also clear that her network of informants was somehow connected to the court. She is passing on information that she had received from a "very good" informant, who was passing on knowledge that had come to the Queen. We do not know who this other informant might have been, or which queen is being referred to; however, this would most likely have been Henrietta Maria, the wife of Charles I.[92]

---

[90] John Sadler to Lady Ranelagh and her reply, November 3, 1648, HP 46/9/12A–13B. "Mr soliciter" was Oliver St John, the Solicitor General. John Sadler (1615–74) was a reformer, political theorist, and Cambridge Platonist.

[91] Ranelagh to Cork, October 13, 1640. Chatsworth House, Lismore MSS, Bundle 21, articles 59 and 61.

[92] Ranelagh's interaction with the court of Charles I and Henrietta Maria had begun with family connections. In 1638, her brother Francis, Lord Shannon, married Elizabeth Killigrew, one of the Queen's maids of honour, and Ranelagh was in attendance. Townshend, *The Great Earl*, 338–42.

In that case, however, another letter, written six years later to the Queen of Bohemia, must serve as an indicator that Ranelagh was involved in conveying intelligence on diplomatic and military matters to more than one queen.

In July 1646, Charles I was in Scottish custody in Newcastle. In a negotiation for his freedom, Parliament had presented Charles with a series of propositions, which included a covenant to establish a Presbyterian form of church government and hand over control of the army. Charles had dragged out the discussions for several months, but finally the terms of the Newcastle Propositions were completely unacceptable to him. Apparently, however, Charles' sister had not been kept apprised of these major events. That task fell to Ranelagh:

> Madame
> I beleeve that your Majesties former inteligences have soe informed you that the affayres of this kingdome are now at a Determining point, & that your good nature & Christianety will make you willing to know what resolution they are put to by his Majestys answere to the propositions. And therefore I very saucylie venture to present your Majesty with as much satisfaction in that poynt as my information of matters here makes me able to doe though I have soe lately adressed my selfe to your Majesty in one of those troubles, that it were fitter for me to beg a pardon, than fall to a repetition so sudenly.[93]

Ranelagh proceeded to relate her news about the relative health and safety of Elizabeth's nephew and niece: James, the Duke of York, and the Princess Harriet. Then she got to the meat of her dispatch, reporting on the king:

> From Newcastle the news is that his Majesty has given by way of answere to the Parliament Comitees a paper wherein he complaynes of the want of his servants & espetially of his counsell when he was to resolve of a buyssenes of soe huge a concerne, & therefore desiers he may be permited to come up to the Parliament where he may have his counsell & then folowe their advices. Its sayd the Comitees would not send this to the Parliament as not thinking they would receive what was noe direct answere to their propositions, which in fine he refuses to grant saying that some of them he could not in Conscience nor others of them in honor grant & that he would rather loose his kingdomes than give them away & part with three crownes than hurt his conscience.[94]

Ranelagh's reporting was not neutral, nor did she hold back on her judgments. The letter then ended with a stern and pious reflection, hoping that the Queen might "be secured from a share of our ruine,"

---

[93] Katherine Ranelagh to Queen Elizabeth of Bohemia, August 7, [1646]. National Art Library, Victoria and Albert Museum, Forster Collection, MS. 454, Pressmark 48.g.25, f. 74.
[94] *Ibid.*

while pointing out that this same ruin might actually benefit her "if God be pleased to make up to your soule what he takes from your Estate."[95]

This letter is remarkably informative on a number of levels. First, we learn that this was not the first time Ranelagh had written to the Winter Queen on political matters. Although there are no other extant letters in this series, Ranelagh's apology for writing yet again, after having "so lately addressed" herself to the Queen, makes it clear that there were others.

Second, despite the apology, Ranelagh states that she will "very saucily" present Elizabeth with the latest intelligence. In a letter to a monarch, this is astounding language indeed, and is indicative of an easy, informal relationship. It is not clear when Ranelagh and the Winter Queen became acquainted, although we have already seen that Moore had been active in maintaining relations between Ranelagh and the exile court in The Hague. And third, Ranelagh is also using this intelligencing report as an opportunity to give her opinion. She is critical of Charles' obstinacy, and quite certain that God is punishing England with this war because the king is so "unmouvable." Moreover, she is apparently quite fearless in relaying these opinions to the monarch's sister.

These two letters – taken together with Moore's earlier suggestion that the Prince Elector would do well to contact Ranelagh for help in negotiating with Parliament – suggest that Ranelagh constituted a well-known and frequently utilized link between royal circles, the exile court, and the Hartlib circle. She appears to have arrived in London in 1643 with her noble networks, medical contacts, and Anglo-Irish associations already fully functional. She was well known as a writer among the members of her various networks, and her work was read on both sides of the Channel. Furthermore, while she never appeared under her own name in print, her work was identified, translated, excerpted, copied, and distributed widely throughout the international community served by scribal publication.

Thus when Ranelagh is viewed through lenses derived from other models of female intellectual activity – such as aristocratic patroness, mother hen, or *salonnière* – the result is distortion. Ranelagh was a female scholar and activist who was quite emphatically the product of her revolutionary times. In essence, then, she followed no real model whatsoever; she was truly "incomparable," and had a career that would seem to put her in a league of her own. But as a member of the Republic of Women, connected to other learned and active women, Ranelagh's

---

[95] *Ibid.*

activities formed one sort of answer to the issue with which they were all grappling – how to define the work of a scholar in the middle of the seventeenth century. The following chapter examines a practical way in which the members of the Republic of Women answered that question for themselves, by doing their work for the advancement of learning through their involvement in both the theory and practice of pedagogy.

CHAPTER 6

Bathsua Makin: female scholars and the reformation of learning

the greatest scholler, I thinke, of a woman in England.
Sir Simonds D'Ewes on Bathsua Makin[1]

The seventeenth-century advancement of learning was a project that could not go forward into the next generation without the simultaneous advancement of teaching. Thus the scholars in this network of intellectual women were all engaged with the practical issue of educational reform; however, their reasons for doing so varied widely, as did the manner of their participation. For instance, Lady Ranelagh and Dorothy Moore wanted to use education to change the entire world; Marie de Gournay wanted to instill virtue while curbing linguistic excess; Marie du Moulin saw education as a way to strengthen Protestant values and virtues; Princess Elisabeth wanted to help disseminate Cartesian philosophy; and Anna Maria van Schurman wanted to ensure that women had full access to the heights of humanist scholarship. Each of these female scholars – in her own way, and in concert with male scholars in their various networks – was engaged in doing the pedagogical work of the republic of letters.

Foremost among the educators in this network was Bathsua Makin. Like the others, she saw educational reform as an essential component of larger projects, and argued for the recognition of female scholars; but unlike her more aristocratic colleagues, she also needed quite desperately to earn a living. This chapter, focused primarily on the 1650s, examines the method, purpose, and content of Makin's pedagogical work, considering her career as an illustration of how the female scholars in this network represented the entire range of educational activity in the seventeenth-century republic of letters.

---

[1] *The Diary of Sir Simonds D'Ewes, 1622–1624: Journal d'un étudiant londonien sous le règne de Jacques 1er*, ed. and trans. Elizabeth Bourcier (Paris, 1974), 68–9.

A LIFETIME IN EDUCATION: BATHSUA MAKIN (C.1600–C.1681)

In 1673, an anonymous tract on women's education appeared in London. Entitled *An Essay to Revive the Antient Education of Gentlewomen*, it was the first treatise in English to argue that women could and should be educated in the full "encyclopedia" of humanist learning: rhetoric, grammar, logic, mathematics, Latin, and Greek. This made sense, the author argued, because Nature had clearly endowed the female sex with minds and souls that were "nothing inferior to those of men."[2] The *Essay* was loosely modelled on the scholastic disputation, and the author positioned himself as a "Champion" of the female sex. The author also claimed that this educational program for women would be of benefit to the male sex, since men would naturally wish to improve themselves in order to retain their pre-eminence. After all, the author pointed out, "I am a Man my self, that would not suggest a thing prejudicial to our Sex."[3]

An Objector then weighed in to reproach the author for a rather obvious absurdity. Young gentlewomen would be in school for far fewer years than young gentlemen; yet their Champion was claiming that in this short space of time girls could be taught their traditional feminine courses in needlework, dancing, music, and French, in addition to the full masculine complement of arts and sciences. It seemed quite impossible.[4]

However, our author had two answers to this objection. The first was a detailed description of his revolutionary pedagogical program. The second response was a more traditional humanist strategy: an exhaustive catalogue of 127 illustrious and virtuous female *exempla* to prove his point. Thus the author was making a case for women's education on both practical and rhetorical grounds. The *Essay*, then, emerges as a fascinating document located at the intersection of humanist scholarship and the new learning, of traditional gendered restrictions and their complete opposite. However, further investigation into the *Essay* reveals a deeper story, and an even deeper engagement with these same issues – for much of this document was not what it appeared to be.

First, the anonymous male Champion of the female sex was not a man at all. He was a woman named Bathsua Makin, a scholar, educator, and linguist who at the age of sixteen knew six languages.[5] Second,

---

[2] Makin, *Essay*, 23, 42.   [3] *Ibid.*, 5.   [4] *Ibid.*, 36.
[5] For a contemporary's view of Makin, see Sir Simonds D'Ewes, *The Autobiography and Correspondence of Sir Simonds D'Ewes, Bart., during the Reigns of James I. and Charles I*, ed. James O. Halliwell, 2 vols. (London, 1845). Among the more important recent studies on Makin are: Jean

Makin's revolutionary pedagogical program was not truly new. It was rather a gendered variant of the one developed by Jan Amos Comenius and promoted during the Interregnum by the members of the Hartlib circle. And among the many names in Makin's enormous roster of exceptional women – a somewhat standard list in the *querelle des femmes*, mixing the historical with the mythical, and combining biblical queens with pagan goddesses – we find a very familiar name. The name was that of Anna Maria van Schurman, one of Makin's correspondents. Appearing in Makin's catalogue no fewer than six times, van Schurman illustrated the possibilities for female achievement in the fields of linguistics, poetry, and oratory, as well as logic, philosophy, and theology. Makin insisted that: "Those who read *Schurman's* Decertations, will conclude she understood the Principles and Practice of Logick very well,"and "The works of *Anna Maria Schurman*, that are extant, declare how good a Divine she was."[6]

The connection between Makin and van Schurman, coupled with the way in which that connection came about, can provide us with another window onto the functioning of multiple networks within the seventeenth-century republic of letters. We see a group of female scholars reaching out to find other intellectual women like themselves; we see a network of educators sharing their goals, techniques, expertise, and pedagogical theories; and we see the republic of letters as a whole, forming unlikely connections to help promote the advancement of learning. Makin and van Schurman, like their male colleagues, participated in learned correspondence with two sorts of goals in mind. On the one hand, they used correspondence as a practical tool for networking and pursuing their individual careers; and on the other hand, they participated in the overall project of scholarly exchange for the advancement of learning. The synergistic interaction of these goals constituted a practical tool for the female scholars doing their pedagogical work in the republic of letters. But as they performed this more

R. Brink, "Bathsua Makin: Educator and Linguist," in *Female Scholars: A Tradition of Learned Women Before 1800* (Montreal, 1980), 86–100; Pieta van Beek, "'One Tongue Is Enough for a Woman': The Correspondence in Greek between Anna Maria van Schurman (1607–78) and Bathsua Makin (1600–167?)," *Dutch Crossing* 19, no. 1 (summer 1995): 24–48; Vivian Salmon, "Bathsua Makin (1600-c.1673): A Pioneer Linguist and Feminist," in *Language and Society in Early Modern England: Selected Essays 1981–1994* (Amsterdam, 1996), 239–60; Frances Teague, *Bathsua Makin, Woman of Learning* (Lewisburg, 1998); and Anne Leslie Saunders, "Bathsua Reginald Makin (1600–75?)," in *Women Writing Latin: From Roman Antiquity to Early Modern Europe*, ed. Laurie J. Churchill *et al.*, 3 vols. (New York and London, 2002), III, 247–70.
[6] Makin, *Essay*, 12–16.

general intellectual labor, female scholars were simultaneously grappling with an issue that was central to their intellectual identity – the
question of how to *be* a female scholar in the middle of the seventeenth
century. Makin's own answer to this question was worked out through
a lifetime in education.

We first encounter Bathsua Makin in an anecdote from the court of
James I. In 1616, an English schoolteacher named Henry Reynolds
brought his sixteen-year-old daughter to court to meet King James
I. Reynolds was an expert in cipher, and his daughter described him as
"a schoolmaster and language lover."[7] He was not, however, a notable
scholar; that honor, according to Sir Simonds D'Ewes, truly belonged to
his daughter Bathsua.[8] Sir Simonds D'Ewes (1602–50) was a Parliamentarian, antiquarian, and Anglo-Saxon scholar, who is remembered chiefly
for his important work in compiling the parliamentary journals from the
reign of Queen Elizabeth.[9] D'Ewes had been a pupil at Reynolds' school
in St Mary Axe parish in London, where he observed that Reynolds had "a
pleasing way of teaching," but that his real claim to fame was the
remarkable Bathsua:

> He had a daughter named Bathsua, being his eldest, that had an exact knowledge
> in the Greek, Latin, and French tongues, with some insight also into the Hebrew
> and Syriac; much more learning she had doubtless than her father, who was a
> mere pretender to it; and by the fame of her abilities, which she had acquired
> from others, he got many scholars which else would neither have repaired to him
> nor have long staid with him.[10]

Now, at the age of sixteen, this prodigy was to meet the King. Bathsua did
not arrive empty-handed; she presented James with her first published
work, a collection of original encomia written in six languages, and
bearing the title *Musa Virginea*, or "The Virgin Muse." John Collet, a
seventeenth-century diarist, described the scene in his commonplace-
book:

---

[7] From the title page of Bathsua's first publication, where Makin identified herself as "Bathsua
R. (daughter of Henry Reynolds, Schoolmaster and Language Lover in London)." Bathsua
Reynolds (Makin), *Musa Virginea Graeco-Latino-Gallica, Bathsuae R. [filiae Henrici reginaldi
Gymnasiarchae et philoglotti apud Londonienses]. Anno aetatis suae decimo sexto edita* (London,
1616). "Reginald" is the Latinized spelling of Reynolds; in this study the English spelling will be
used, since that was the one most often employed in correspondence.

[8] At this point in her life, she was Bathsua Reynolds; her marriage to Richard Makin took place on
March 5, 1622. For the sake of simplicity, she will be referred to by her married name in this study.

[9] Sir Simonds D'Ewes, *Journals of all the Parliaments during the Reign of Queen Elizabeth* (London,
1682).

[10] D'Ewes, *Autobiography*, 1, 63.

When a learned maid was presented to King James for an English rarity, because shee could speake and write pure Latine, Greek, and Hebrew, the King ask'd, – "but can shee spin?"[11]

No reaction to this witticism is recorded, although Collet's editor speculates that James shared the opinion of Martin Luther, who wrote, "There is no gown nor garments that becomes a woman wors than when shee will bee wise."[12]

Yet upon further examination, this incident illustrates more than the linguistic virtuosity of the young Bathsua Makin, and more than James' known antipathy toward learned women – although James had also reportedly spurned and mocked the encomiastic Latin poems he received from another female scholar, the Latinist Elizabeth Weston.[13] This incident more importantly illustrates how the skills of a female scholar were being deployed at a much different level from those of the aristocratic van Schurman. In presenting his daughter to James, Henry Reynolds was presumably hoping for patronage, and his daughter Bathsua was the most persuasive argument he could put forward. Indeed, Bathsua's *Musa Virginea* gives her own name in small print, while the name of her father is the featured item on the page. Thus beyond bearing out D'Ewes' assessments, this incident established a precedent for Makin's entire career as an educator and a scholar. While her scholarship in philology and languages may indeed have rivaled that of van Schurman, Makin needed to use these skills in order to earn a living – the leisure hours requisite for an extensive correspondence, or for the experimental pursuits of the *virtuosi*, were never hers to choose. Thus despite the fact that Makin embraced a strongly feminist stance, documented in her *Essay* of 1673, her studies may have been circumscribed by social rank even more than they were by gender. From her 1616 *Musa Virginea*, which advertised her father's skills as a teacher, to her 1673 *Essay to Revive the Antient Education of Gentlewomen*, which advertised her own, Makin's publications were always intended to help her in earning a pedagogical income.

[11] John Collet, "Commonplace-Book," in *Anecdotes and Traditions, Illustrative of Early English History and Literature, Derived form MS. Sources*, ed. William J. Thoms (London, 1839), 125.

[12] *Ibid.* James was quoted as saying: "It hath like operation to make women learned as to make Foxes tame." *Wittie Obervations Gathered from our late Soveraign King James in his ordinarie Discourse* (London, 8 November, 1643), 2.

[13] *Elizabeth Jane Weston: Collected Writings*, ed. Donald Cheney and Brenda M. Hosington (Toronto, 2000), 169–83.

Since Makin's *Musa Virginea* identifies her as a sixteen-year-old, we know that she was born around 1599 or 1600. Her sister Ithamar was christened a year later, followed by a third sister, Mespira.[14] Their names followed a fairly common custom among families in the godly community, and were variants on Old Testament names; Ithamar was one of the sons of Aaron, and Bathsua is a variant of Bathsheba. While we have very little information about Mespira Reynolds, some emerges from a letter she wrote to her sister Ithamar in 1636. Mespira was married to a Mr. Rogers, and although she was working as a seamstress, she appears to have been in some financial difficulty. Itemizing her expenditures for cloth and thread, she admitted her indebtedness to her sister: "I am a greate deale more then that Comes to; behind hand with you"; yet in a postscript she added: "I should wish I had a peice of Bacon if you have any."[15]

Their father, Henry Reynolds, came from Suffolk. It is certain that Bathsua's father was Henry Reynolds the schoolteacher, and it is quite likely that he was also the same Henry Reynolds who served in some capacity at the court of King James I. Earlier scholarship averred that Bathsua's father was also the "Dearely-Loved friend Henery Reynolds Esquire" to whom Michael Drayton addressed a poem recalling winter evenings when they "past the howres contentedly with chat."[16] However, Drayton's Henry Reynolds was the poet who wrote *Mythomystes*, a dense work of neo-Platonic literary criticism. The themes of this work and the leisure hours recalled by Drayton seem somewhat incommensurate with the life of a godly Suffolk schoolteacher. Most tellingly, however, *Mythomystes* was dedicated to "my ever-honor'd Lord, Henry Lord Matravers." This was Henry Frederick Howard, fifteenth Earl of Arundel, and second Earl of Norfolk.[17] Like most of the Howards, Henry's faith was located somewhere along a spectrum

---

[14] Baptismal records for January 1600/1 for St Dunstan's, Stepney, record: "Ithamar daughter of Henry Reignolds of Bowe scholemr baptised the xi day." London Metropolitan Archives, Baptismal Records, 1568–1656.

[15] Mespira Rogers to Ithamar Pell, March 7, 1636. BL Add. MSS. 4416, f. 25v.

[16] For this identification of Makin's father, see Vivian Salmon, "Henry Reynolds," *Pelliana* 1, no. 3, new series (privately printed, 1965), 11–18; and Mary Hobbs, "Drayton's 'Most Dearely-Loved Friend Henery Reynolds Esq',*" The Review of English Studies*, new series, 24, no. 96 (November 1973): 414–28.

[17] Since 1377, it had been a family custom for the sons of the family to assume the courtesy title of Lord Maltravers. J. T. Peacey, "Howard, Henry Frederick," *ODNB*; and H[enry] R[eynolds], *Mythomystes. Wherein a Short Survay is Taken of the Nature and Value of the True Poesy ...* (London, [1632]).

that had crypto-Catholicism at one end and outright recusancy at the other; it is therefore highly unlikely that the poet Henry Reynolds, with a Catholic patron, could be identified with the godly Henry Reynolds who was Bathsua's father and an associate of the Hartlib circle.

Bathsua would have grown up in an environment that was scholarly, Royalist, and godly – a combination that would continue to characterize her networks of association throughout her life. By 1614, the Reynolds family was in London, and Bathsua was helping out at her father's school. Henry Reynolds was apparently a kind man who preferred the carrot over the stick, and as D'Ewes later recalled:

And yet he had a pleasing way of teaching, contrary to all others of that kind; for the rod and ferular stood in his school rather as ensigns of his power than as instruments of his anger, and were rarely made use of for the punishment of delinquents; for he usually rewarded those who deserved well with raisins of the sun or other fruit, if the season of the year afforded it; and he accounted the privative punishment of not rewarding the remiss and negligent equipollent to the severest correction.[18]

Since there is no documentation of Bathsua Makin's education, we can only assume that she was proficient in all the subjects she was helping to teach at her father's school – Greek, Latin, French, mathematics, and grammar – and that her father had been her teacher. The quality of that instruction must have been quite good. Certainly Bathsua was a shining example; and although D'Ewes averred that Bathsua had acquired her abilities from unnamed "others," he still credited Henry Reynolds with having given him a first-rate education:

I lost not my time altogether at this school, but amended much my Latin tongue in respect of prose ... I made also a good entrance here into the Greek and French tongues, and learned to write a good Roman, secretary, and Greek hand.[19]

There is also some indication that the instruction in learned languages at Reynolds' school may have been supplemented by some lessons in alternative forms of writing – ciphers, secret codes, and the practice of shorthand.

D'Ewes claimed to have invented his own cipher with a friend while still a student in Reynolds' school in 1616, "a strange handwriting consisting of an alphabet of strange letters, which afterwards I altered also to mine own use." He used this same cipher as an adult in writing his diaries.[20] Yet in fact, this may have been yet another linguistic debt that

---

[18] D'Ewes, *Autobiography*, 1, 63–4.   [19] *Ibid.*, 1, 94–5.   [20] *Ibid.*, 1, 95–6.

D'Ewes owed to his teacher Henry Reynolds. Reynolds was the author of a number of pamphlets on alternative forms of writing: a 1604 work on ciphers and communication over long distances, using bells, pigeons, fireworks, or guns; and several versions of *Macrolexis*, "An Invention for brief speedie and secrete Intelligence."[21] Thus ciphers may indeed have been taught in Reynolds' school. Moreover, Reynolds' 1627 *Macrolexis* is of interest because it refers to a shorthand code called "Radiography" – a code which may not have been his invention at all, but rather the creation of his daughter Bathsua.

Less than two years after publishing *Musa Virginea*, Bathsua appears to have published a pamphlet outlining a new shorthand system. Nothing survives of her 1619 *Index Radiographia* except for the title page, which gives a small sample of her system of strokes, dots, and semi-circles.[22] In her dedication of the work to Anne of Denmark, Bathsua pointed out that it included: "the Invention of Radiography, which is a speedy and short writing, with great facility to be practized in any language, viz. in far less tyme, than the learning of the first Secretary letters do require." It is well known that Makin's 1673 *Essay* would be the first treatise in English to argue that women could and should be educated in everything being learned by men – but *Index Radiographia* is evidence that her career of "firsts" may have been initiated before her nineteenth year. And Bathsua was more than just "the first lady shorthand inventor"; her Radiography was in fact the earliest known example of the "stave" system of shorthand by any author.[23]

Alternative writing – shorthand, ciphers, and universal language systems – served a number of different purposes in the middle of the seventeenth century. Coded letters were necessary for the exchange of information in wartime, and various ciphers emerged during the Thirty

---

[21] H. Reynolds, *Architectiones seu Inventiones Sex* (1604), BL, Add. MSS. 4384, two copies, ff. 67–82. H. Reynolds, *Macrolexis, seu Nuncius Volucris* (1625). BL, Lansdowne MSS 684, ff. 5–15, and idem, *Macrolexis: an Invention for briefe speedie and secrete Intelligence without messenger or Letters sent* (1627), BL, Sloane MSS 4403, ff. 154–63. On this second copy of *Macrolexis* is a note in the hand of John Pell, indicating that it had been a gift from Reynolds himself ("*ex dono soceri*"). Further discussion of these texts can be found in William Poole, "*Nuncius Inanimatus.* Seventeenth-Century Telegraphy: the Schemes of Francis Godwin and Henry Reynolds," *The Seventeenth Century* 21, no. 1 (spring 2006): 45–72; and Malcolm and Stedall, *John Pell*, 35–8.

[22] *Index Radiographia*'s dedication to Queen Anne places its publication before 1619. Although John Westby-Gibson claimed to be in possession of a 1617 manuscript version of the entire text, it disappeared when his collection was dispersed after his death. John Westby-Gibson, *The Bibliography of Shorthand* (London, 1887), 188. The title page of *Index Radiographia* survives as Plate IV in R. C. Alston, *Treatises on Short-hand* (London, c.1866).

[23] E. H. Butler, *The Story of British Shorthand* (London, 1951), 212–14.

Years' War and Civil War. Descartes and Elisabeth had even considered using a code for their correspondence, although Elisabeth deemed the code Descartes had proposed to be far too easy to decipher.[24] Universal languages and alphabets were also included among the Hartlib circle's many projects for the advancement of learning.[25] In addition, shorthand was used by members of the godly community to record sermons in church. Each one of these uses, however, was controversial, and none were value-free. They all had political implications, and were considered likely to be part of a subversive agenda. Ciphers, of course, always aroused suspicion. Apart from their use in wartime intelligence, the keys to secret systems were by definition the possession of a select group. Universal language systems had precisely the opposite aim. They were intended to make all nationalities intelligible to each other without requiring the acquisition of Latin, thus doing away with the inherent elitism of learned languages.[26]

Yet shorthand systems may have been the most subversive of all. John Wilkins had claimed that, "This short-hand writing is now so ordinary in practice (it being usual for any common Mechanick both to write and invent it) that I shall not need to set down any particular example of it."[27] However, shorthand was not merely a stenographic tool. The ability to record sermons in church was particularly dear to more radical Protestants, and when Comenius visited London in 1641, he was amazed by the numbers of English churchgoers adept in shorthand:

Almost all of them acquire this art of rapid writing, as soon as they have learnt at school to read the Scriptures in the vernacular. It takes them about another year to learn the art of shorthand.[28]

---

[24] Elisabeth to Descartes, October 10, 1646. Translation in *The Correspondence between Princess Elisabeth of Bohemia and René Descartes*, 144–7. Original French in Descartes, *Oeuvres*, IV, 519–24.

[25] The Hartlib Papers include a 1646 pamphlet entitled *A Common Writing, Whereby two, although not understanding the one the others Language, yet by the helpe thereof, may communicate their minds one to another*. Although Thomason ascribes this work to Hartlib, it was probably the work of Francis Lodwick, another member of the Hartlib circle. Thomason Tracts: E. 378 (16). On Lodwick (1619–94), see Vivian Salmon, *The Works of Francis Lodwick: A Study of His Writings in the Intellectual Context of the Seventeenth Century* (London, 1972).

[26] Lois Potter, however, argues that there was almost always a "secret elitism" underlying universal language schemes. Lois Potter, *Secret Rites and Secret Writing: Royalist Literature, 1641–1660* (Cambridge, 1989), 42.

[27] John Wilkins, *Mercury: or the Secret and Swift Messenger. Shewing, How a Man may with Privacy and Speed communicate his Thoughts to a Friend at any distance*, 2nd edn. (London, 1694), 98–9. Wilkins and other members of the Royal Society used shorthand for scientific communication. Potter, *Secret Rites*, 43.

[28] Young, *Comenius in England*, 65.

Hartlib concurred on the importance of this practice for English radical Protestants, and in his *Ephemerides* for 1634, under the heading of "Didactica stenographica," he wrote:

So when Powerful Preaching began in England then Stenography was invented, which may bee yet made farre more compendious and become a great blessing to the Church. for by it the Speeches may bee taken of as they come fall warme from the ministers mouthes.[29]

Hartlib's source for this was a "Mr. Nye," who said:

hee could perfect much stenography, and approves much of Mr Reinolds New Invented Radiography, as coming neerest to his way, which hee Mr Reinolds et Mr Pell might perfect.[30]

"Mr. Reinolds" and "Mr. Pell" refer to Makin's father Henry Reynolds and her brother-in-law John Pell; there is no mention of Bathsua. Thus despite what appears to have been an accepted view – that it was Bathsua, and not her father, who was the true scholar in the family – the "New Invented Radiography" was already being credited to her father by 1634.[31]

The democratic and destabilizing skill of shorthand was especially alarming when practiced by women, since its ease and universality threatened to undermine a number of hierarchical structures – linguistic, episcopal, and gendered. Critics considered these avenues to constitute a combined threat, as expressed by Sir Ralph Verney:

Let not your girle learne Latin, nor Short hand; the difficulty of the first may keepe her from the Vice, for soe I must esteeme it in a woeman; but the easinesse of the other may bee a prejudice to her; for the pride of taking Sermon noates, hath made multitudes of woemen most unfortunate . . . Had St. Paul lived in our Times I am most confident hee would have fixt a *Shame* upon our woemen for writing (as well as for theire speaking) in the Church.[32]

Given this multi-layered uneasiness, it perhaps is not surprising that Radiography would be attributed to Henry Reynolds, rather than to his

---

[29] Hartlib, *Ephemerides*, 1634, HP 29/2/45A.
[30] *Ibid.* "Mr. Nye" might refer to the Independent minister Philip Nye (1595–1672). My thanks to Paul Seaver for this reference.
[31] Some modern scholars, while noting Makin's 1619 *Index Radiographia*, have also assumed that Radiography itself was her father's invention. See, for example, Poole, "*Nuncius Inanimatus*," 53–4; and Malcolm and Stedall, *John Pell*, 37. However, Henry Reynolds did not put forth his Radiography until 1628: H[enry] R[eynolds], "A Concordance of Letters, to reade all the Learned, vulgar or forraign Languages in Europe: with a most usefull Radiographie or short writing of late invention, 1628", BL Add. MSS 4377, f. 39.
[32] Margaret M. Verney, *Memoirs of the Verney Family During the Commonwealth, 1650–1660*, 3 vols. (London, 1894), I, 72–4.

daughter Bathsua. However, since she was not yet twenty years old, the appearance of this second publication was indeed a remarkable and brave achievement – so, like van Schurman, Makin found herself celebrated as a prodigy and likened to a goddess. For instance, King James' physician George Eglisham, who may have been present for Bathsua's presentation to the king, wrote a poem in 1618, "To a Maiden of Exceptional Learning, Bathsua Reynolds." And in this poem, he claimed: "Daphne was transformed into the laurel, but the laurel is transformed/into you, and you yourself are transformed into a celebrated Goddess."[33]

Yet, unlike van Schurman, Bathsua also had other sorts of work to do; and beyond her function as the cornerstone of her father's career, she had domestic duties to perform. D'Ewes' diary reports the following for 1622:

March 4. I was too day invited to my ould schoolemasters daughters wedding, being the greatest scholler, I thinke, of a woman in England. I was not resolved what to doe, though I had a good mind to goe.

March 5. Yet went I too day, where through Gods mercye, besides the great preparation, there was much companye, whence arose that which is the life of a scholler, good discourse; and soe, after I had seen the bride abedd, I went her courtier, I departed to my rest.[34]

The bride was Bathsua Reynolds, and from this point on, her career as a scholar and educator would be complicated by a heavy share of domestic duties.

The groom was Richard Makin (1599–1659), who seems to have served both King James I and King Charles I, although the capacity in which he served is not clear. The only record of his service is a failed petition from "Richard Makin, an old servant of King James," alleging that he had been swindled by one Robert Wood. Wood, the keeper of the royal cormorants, had promised to pass the position on to Richard Makin for the rather enormous sum of £633; but Wood had then sold the position to a "common broker," exacting a further £250 from Richard Makin in the process.[35] But the Makins needed money immediately because, beginning

---

[33] George Eglisham, *Duellum poeticum. Contendentibus, Georgio Eglisemmio medico regio, & Georgio Buchanano regio praeceptore. Pro dignitate paraphraseos Psalmi centisimi quarti . . .* (London, 1618). This poem was part of Eglisham's poetic duel with George Buchanan over their respective translations of Psalm 104.

[34] D'Ewes, *Diary*, 68–9.

[35] Six months later, Makin's petitions were dead, since "his Majesty refused them once when I presented them to him, and he was pleased to refuse them twice to Mr. Secretary." R. Read to Thomas Windebank, 22 January, 1641, *CSPD* 1640, 356; *CSPD* 1640–1, 427. This Robert Wood was not the economist Robert Wood who corresponded with Ranelagh.

in 1623, Bathsua gave birth to at least six children.[36] The first two children died in infancy; we do not know how many survived to adulthood, but at least three of the children were still living with their mother in the 1650s. This emerges in a letter written to Makin by her brother-in-law, John Pell, wherein he appears to be discouraging her plans to rent a house:

> Your letters seeme to say, You hope to have one gone shortly, and the next, you think, will fly out of the nest before the end of this yeare. Ere it be long, your freinds will begin to tell you, that your youngest is too old to tarry under his Mothers Wing; that he will be better abroad with a Father, a Tutor or a Master. For a hen with one chick, a little roome will suffice. Howsoever, the taking of a house, will not be so fit for you as lodgings, in your Husbands absence.[37]

We do not know why Richard Makin was away. However, since money was always an issue for the expanding Makin family, Bathsua continued to teach.

It was Makin's career, in both linguistics and education, that positioned her at the intersection of three quite different networks: Stuart-Palatine court circles, the Hartlib circle, and van Schurman's network of intellectual women. As we have seen, Makin's location in these three overlapping networks was one she shared with Moore and Ranelagh. And, again like Moore and Ranelagh, Makin was extremely committed to a reformation of learning. Yet her circumstances, in terms of her lower social rank, precarious finances, and numerous children, were quite different; moreover, there is no indication that Makin hoped to bring about a new reformation of Protestantism. Instead, Makin's participation in learned circles seems to have been fuelled and directed by her work. Makin's *métier* was education. As a field of discussion and new ideas, education was the basis for her research, her writing, and her network of connections, while in terms of her career, the practical application of these same ideas enabled her to earn her living as a teacher on the cutting edge of seventeenth-century pedagogy.

Makin's Stuart-Palatine connections had begun with her family networks. First, of course, there was her father Henry Reynolds, the schoolteacher, with his ties to the court of James I. Included in these royalist ties

---

[36] According to Frances Teague, the parish records of St Margaret's, Westminster and St Martin's in the Field record the births of seven children with the surname of Makin: Anna (1623–7); Richard (March 6–8, 1627); Anna (b. 1628); Bathsua (b. 1629); Mary (b. 1630); John (b. 1633); and Henry (b. 1642). While some were christened by Richard and Bathsua Makin, the list also includes babies whose parents are not named, so the number is not certain. Teague, *Bathsua Makin*, 49.

[37] Emphasis in the original. No year in the original, but internal evidence places these letters in 1654. BL, Add. MSS 4280, f. 243.

was a devotion to James' daughter Elizabeth, Queen of Bohemia, and to the restoration of the Palatine house. For instance, we learn from D'Ewes' diary that he visited Reynolds in 1623 to discuss events in the Low Countries, and beyond this, he made a personal connection to the exile court in The Hague, corresponding with the Winter Queen for many years. D'Ewes' papers contain two autograph letters from the queen; they acknowledge his kindness and support, and are signed "Your most assured friend, Elizabeth."[38]

Yet the Stuarts had failed, in the minds of many, to adequately support the Palatine cause, thus support of the exile court in The Hague also carried an implicit criticism of James and Charles. This critique, coupled with membership in godly communities, meant that these court networks often overlapped with groups like the Hartlib circle. This overlap was solidified in Makin's life in 1632, when her sister Ithamar married John Pell. Pell (1611–85) was a mathematician, a clergyman, and a Fellow of the Royal Society, and together with John Dury, he was one of Cromwell's agents on the Continent from 1654 to 1658.[39] There is no doubt that Pell was a brilliant mathematician; he is credited with inventing the division sign ($\div$) as well as the "Pell equation."[40] Pell was also, however, a difficult man; he was cranky, fault-finding, and fatally reluctant to publish. As one of his mathematical colleagues noted, "He hath been a man accounted incommunicable."[41]

Yet Pell had his friends. Through the influence of Theodore Haak and Sir William Boswell, Pell was appointed Professor of Mathematics at the Athenaeum of Amsterdam in 1643, and in 1646 he began teaching at the *illustre* academy of Breda with van Schurman's mentor André Rivet. Pell's years on the Continent also introduced him into other learned networks, through a combination of patronage, teaching, and mathematical correspondence in the republic of letters. There was the Cavendish circle, a group of Royalist exiles congregating in Paris around William Cavendish, Duke of Newcastle, and his brother Sir Charles Cavendish. This exile circle continued the discussions begun in England in the 1630s, when

---

[38] Queen Elizabeth of Bohemia to Sir Simonds D'Ewes, April 26, 1638 and August 21, 1645. BL, Harleian MSS. 6988, ff. 105, 186; D'Ewes, *Diary*, 112.

[39] On Pell, see especially Malcolm and Stedall, *John Pell*, which reviews and corrects many of the errors in earlier scholarship.

[40] The Pell equation is ($x^2 - Ay^2 = 1$), where x and y are integers, and A is a non-square integer. Noel Malcolm, "The Publications of John Pell, F.R.S. (1611–85): Some New Light and Some Old Confusions," *Notes and Records of the Royal Society of London* 54, no. 3 (2000), 275.

[41] Collins to Dr. Beale, 20 August, 1672, in Stephen J. Rigaud, *Correspondence of Scientific Men of the Seventeenth Century*, 2 vols. (Hildesheim, 1965), i, 196–7.

Walter Warner and Thomas Hobbes participated in Cavendish's "little academy" at Welbeck. Then, in Paris, the circle expanded to include René Descartes, Marin Mersenne, and Pierre Gassendi.[42] Pell thus became a point of connection between these mathematical circles on the Continent and the Hartlib circle in England, and he introduced Ranelagh's associate Sir William Petty into the Cavendish circle. Petty thanked Pell for the favor in a letter which clearly demonstrates the overlap of correspondence and face-to-face networking in the republic of letters:

> Father Mersen, his desire to convey this inclosed to you, serves me for an happie occasion, to express my thanckfulnes for the good of that acquaintance with Mr. Hobs, which your letters procured mee. For by his meanes, My Lord of Newcastle, and your good freind Sir Charles Candish have beene pleased, to take notice of mee; and by his meanes also I became acquainted with Father Mersen.[43]

While at Breda, Pell was also a mentor to Sir William Brereton, who became a lifelong friend and patron. Brereton, the grandson of George Goring, would later take possession of Hartlib's papers after the latter's death.

Pell had worked as a teacher in Hartlib's short-lived school in Chichester, and while much of the scholarship on Makin has claimed that her father Henry Reynolds also taught at this school, there is no evidence to support this claim. "Reynolds" was a fairly common name, and while Hartlib does mention Henry Reynolds in his *Ephemerides*, he also mentions Edward Reynolds, whose philosophical work was read by Princess Elisabeth. Confusion might have arisen because both are referred to only as "Reynolds," and Hartlib may have been planning to use some of Edward Reynolds' works as texts in his school.[44] Ithamar's marriage to Pell thus initiated another layer of connection between Makin and the Hartlib circle; yet while some of Makin's intellectual contacts may have been made through Pell, it is highly unlikely that he actually helped to facilitate her career. The distance was in part political; Makin was a strong

[42] On the Cavendish circle, see Timothy Raylor, "Newcastle's Ghosts: Robert Payne, Ben Jonson, and the 'Cavendish Circle,'" in *Literary Circles and Cultural Communities in Renaissance England*, ed. Claude J. Summers and Ted-Larry Pebworth (Columbia, MO, 2000), 92–114; and John Jacquot, "Sir Charles Cavendish and His Learned Friends: A Contribution to the History of Scientific Relations between England and the Continent in the Earlier Part of the 17th century," *Annals of Science* 8 (1952): 13–27. The designation of Welbeck as a "little academy" comes from p. 19.

[43] William Petty to John Pell, November 8, 1645. BL, Add. MSS 4279, f. 183. On Petty, see Ted McCormick, *William Petty and the Ambitions of Political Arithmetic* (Oxford, 2009).

[44] See, for instance, letters in HP 46/6/10A; 46/6/29A-B; and the *Ephemerides* for 1634 and 1635.

advocate for Comenius' pedagogical methods, which she would vigorously promote in her printed work, but she gave no evidence of a similar affinity for his world-changing agenda of reform. Instead, during these revolutionary years, Makin pursued a radical reformation of learning within a traditional context – that of tutor to the children of the aristocracy.

However, Makin does appear a number of times in Hartlib's *Ephemerides*, documenting her active presence in a number of learned networks that were of interest to Hartlib. Hartlib first mentions Makin in 1637, in an excerpt transcribed from a report in Pell's *Repraesentationes Rerum*:

> In Mr Gelebrands study amongst other th[ing]s there was a description of Mr Wrights Uranicúm, with the Construction of it, and the measures of every wheele as hee told mee. Another description of it and the use of it fairely written with a Picture of it is I beleeve in my Sister Makins Library, for shee had all her Fathers bookes.[45]

Given Henry Reynolds' long career as an educator, the fact that Makin had inherited "all her father's books" makes it likely that she was the possessor of a fairly impressive library.

We also learn from Hartlib of Makin's participation in medical networks. Notations in Hartlib's *Ephemerides* for 1650 record the following:

Mris Makin *Recepta Medica*	Very well acquainted with Sir W. Raleigh's son a Parliament man now. From the old Lady shee got all Sir W. Raleigh's Receipts.
Mris Makin *Palpitatio Cordis*	Mris Makin cured Mr Holsworth of Palpitation of the heart. So did Dr Gurdain with his spirit of Amber Greece.[46]

Thus Makin, like Ranelagh, was not only collecting medical recipes, but using them to cure others. It is not clear how she became so well acquainted with Sir Carew Raleigh and "the old Lady," his mother; however, Carew's father, Sir Walter Raleigh, had a reputation for his "greate Skill in Chimistry" in addition to his talents as an explorer, courtier, and poet.[47] It is also unclear whether Raleigh's medical recipes

---

[45] The report continues, enlarging on the uranicum itself, which was a type of astrolabe. Henry Gellibrand (1597–1637) was a mathematician whose primary interests were in magnetism and the determination of longitude. September 16, 1637, HP 22/15/1A.

[46] *Ephemerides* 1650, Part I (January–February), HP 28/1/48A-B.

[47] From *Aubrey's Brief Lives*, 253–60.

had been a gift or a purchase, because in 1652, Carew Raleigh was sending his father's medical receipts to Sir Edward Conway, for use by his wife, the philosopher Anne Conway. Raleigh wrote:

My Lord, I send you a parcell of papers which perchance your selfe will scorne, and I am ashamed off, old, rotten, durtie, and torne things and such as a person less intelligent then your selfe would hardly understand, but they are all of this kynd (recepts) which I have, that you have not alreddy seene: they are most of them in my Fathers owne hand, and therefore I thinke approved ones.[48]

Thus if Makin had "all Sir W. Raleigh's Receipts" in 1650, it would seem that her ever-present financial woes had resulted in her having to return the collection to the family two years later.

Given their shared interests in scholarship, science, and pedagogy, one might have expected that Pell and Makin would be colleagues, as well as kin. Certainly, we have seen how supportive brothers were positive participants in the scholarly networks of Ranelagh, van Schurman, and Marie du Moulin. Yet this was far from being the case with Pell and Makin. In fact, Pell appears to have had very little use for his sister-in-law and seems to have done everything possible to distance himself from her. It is not entirely clear why Pell should have disliked Makin. Upon closer inspection, however, some plausible explanations present themselves. The first possibility is financial. During the 1650s, Pell and Dury were away on the Continent; Pell was acting as Cromwell's envoy, and Dury was continuing on his never-ending ecumenical rounds. Pell's letters home continually criticize his wife for her mismanagement of just about everything – a list that included finances, child-rearing, match-making, arithmetic, and letter-writing. Here, a typical excerpt compares Ithamar unfavorably with Dorothy Moore:

Mrs. Dury sent her husbands hundred pounds unnibled. I thought I had reason to looke for 150: you say, you sent 145: the merchant sayes but 140. Out of 200 pounds a yeare, you cannot abate the fees of the Mony-teller, Sollicitor &c but out of my mony you must abate 5. (it may be 10) pounds a quarter. I have reason to thanke-you that you did not keepe it all.[49]

Thus Pell was already quite sure that his wife was short-changing him on the money she was supposed to send. Yet Makin was continually in dire financial straits, and in the absence of both their husbands, Bathsua seems to have often turned to her sister Ithamar for help with rent money and emergency housing. Pell did not approve, and he wrote to his wife:

[48] Carew Raleigh to Edward Conway, June 28, 1652, in *The Conway Letters*, 19–20.
[49] John Pell to Ithamar Pell, October 7, [1654]. BL, Add. MSS. 4280, f. 213.

"I perceive Mrs. Mak. hath found the way to you againe. Her counsel, added to your owne inclinations, will make you altogether unfit to meddle with any mony of mine."[50] However, he was far away and could do nothing to stop it. One can imagine, then, that so far as Pell was concerned, Makin might just have been the last straw in his ongoing frustration with his wife.

Makin, however, managed to make her own way. It appears that she brought herself into contact with van Schurman's circle of learned women along two pathways – through her work as an educator and through her desire to connect with other female scholars. And in order to accomplish such a connection, Makin worked through her old friend Sir Simonds D'Ewes.

THEORY AND PRACTICE IN EDUCATION: BATHSUA MAKIN AND ANNA MARIA VAN SCHURMAN

In 1645, van Schurman received an unexpected and somewhat unwanted letter from Sir Simonds D'Ewes. D'Ewes, always interested in some intellectual social climbing, had apparently obtained her contact information from Frédéric Rivet, who was in London on diplomatic business. So on January 17, D'Ewes sent off three letters. The first went to Frédéric's father André Rivet. In that letter, D'Ewes discussed politics and mutual friends, and then asked Rivet to forward the two enclosed missives – one addressed to Prince William of Nassau, and the other to "the Most Renowned and Learned Maiden Anna Maria van Schurman in Utrecht."

D'Ewes' letter to van Schurman was full of praise and regrets. He had read her *Dissertatio*, and was enormously impressed; and while he had hoped to meet her in person, the grave political situation in England was hindering him.[51] This type of praise was hardly new to van Schurman; however, her work had not yet appeared in English translation.[52] Thus D'Ewes felt the need to explain how he had managed to learn about her so soon. He pointed out that: "the fame of your extraordinary erudition, and of your extremely cultivated Letters, has reached our ears through various informants," and first among these was Frédéric Rivet.[53] But beyond that,

---

[50] John Pell to Ithamar Pell, March 25, [1657]. BL, Add. MSS. 4280, f. 214.
[51] Simonds D'Ewes to Anna Maria van Schurman, January 17, 1645, from a draft copy in the letterbooks of Sir Simonds D'Ewes, BL, Harleian MS. 378, f. 76.
[52] The inventory of Sir Simonds D'Ewes' library shows that he possessed two copies of van Schurman's *Opuscula*: a duodecimo edition of 1648, and a 1650 octavo. Andrew G. Watson, *The Library of Sir Simonds D'Ewes* (London, 1966), 95.
[53] D'Ewes to van Schurman, January 17, 1645. BL, Harleian MS. 378, f. 76.

the information was coming from a different direction, and for a very different reason:

Bathsua Makin, wife of Richard Makin, who I know has cherished learning from a tender age, inasmuch as I was strictly educated at the school of Henry Reynolds, her very own father, for over half a year, has also laid bare the qualities of your character, and your indefatigable diligence in the most elevated studies. Hence I was inflamed with an extraordinary desire to write to you.[54]

This was the beginning of two new correspondences for van Schurman; and while her connection with D'Ewes would remain very limited, she would continue a much more engaged relationship with the English scholar and educator Bathsua Makin.

In D'Ewes' letter of self-introduction to van Schurman, we encounter another aspect of the learned world at work among women in the republic of letters. D'Ewes was apparently responding to the urging he had received from Makin, who was an old friend, a source of information, and rather an expert on the work of van Schurman. While D'Ewes' aims were his own, his letter also documents how Makin worked through several sets of alliances in order to seek out another female scholar and to pursue a learned career. In this case, Makin's goals were twofold, each one pertaining to a different level of association. On the small-network level, Makin was eager to connect with another female scholar, and she was hoping to accomplish this through the intermediary link of D'Ewes. Like other members of van Schurman's circle, Makin was generally celebrated as unique, so her connections to other intellectual women belied and alleviated that unwelcome status. And on the larger-network level, Makin was bringing together her connections to Stuart-Palatine court circles, the Hartlib circle, and a growing community of intellectual women in order to further her own career as a linguist and educator.

When D'Ewes first wrote to van Schurman in January 1645, the Dutch scholar had not been happy to hear from him. She had already begun reducing her circle of correspondents and was especially averse to being contacted by "foreign, and indeed completely unknown persons." Thus, when D'Ewes' letter showed up, van Schurman was not sure how to respond. In a letter to Rivet, wherein she discussed the National Synod, the work of Marie du Moulin, and her own forthcoming publications, she added the following postscript concerning "that English baronet":

[54] *Ibid.*

Prior to sealing this letter, a letter from you was delivered to me, along with one from that English Baronet. I do not see what grounds I can appropriately respond to him ... unless you, having been persuaded by other considerations, perceive this differently from me.[55]

D'Ewes was indeed an importunate correspondent. He really tried to restrain himself at first, but when van Schurman responded with a polite and courteous reply, he apparently felt encouraged. His subsequent letters grew much longer; they were replete with masses of genealogical data, sad information on the progress of the civil war, and requests for advice on how to inculcate a love of learning in his own daughters. In response to these epistles, van Schurman's responses grew shorter and shorter.[56] He asked her to send portraits of herself. He even wrote to André Rivet asking why van Schurman had not yet responded.

Then finally, nearly a year after his original letter, D'Ewes received his answer from van Schurman. It was kind, courteous, and careful. She thanked him for writing and explained her delay in replying. Van Schurman also took the occasion to point out that she might never have answered at all, if D'Ewes had not had two powerful points in his favor: first, his strong support for women's learning; and second, the fact that his original inspiration had come through Bathsua Makin:

As to what you write concerning the most Learned Matron, Madam Bathsua Metkins, that she so highly commended my Industrie in sublimer studies, and that you were upon that account inflamed with an incredible desire of haveing conference with me: All this, I impute both to her undeserved affection toward me, and to your courtesie in giving so easie an Assent.[57]

And on the same day that she sent this letter to D'Ewes, van Schurman also sent a letter to Bathsua Makin.[58] However, this was not their first

---

[55] Van Schurman to Rivet, March 5, 1645, KB, MS. 133 B8, no. 45.

[56] See the following extant letters in the D'Ewes–Van Schurman correspondence: D'Ewes to van Schurman, January 17, 1645, BL, Harleian MS. 378, f. 76; Rivet to D'Ewes, March 19, 1645, BL, Harleian MS.376, f. 147; Van Schurman to D'Ewes, October 31, 1645, BL, Harleian MS. 376, f. 150; D'Ewes to van Schurman, December 13, 1645, BL, Harleian MS. 378, f. 95; Van Schurman to D'Ewes, March 31, 1646, BL, Harleian MS. 376, f. 152; D'Ewes to van Schurman, [April 25?], 1646, BL, Harleian MS. 378, f. 94–94v.

[57] BL, Harleian MS. 376, f. 150. Translation from Clement Barksdale, *The Learned Maid: or, Whether a Maid may be a Scholar? A Logick Exercise written in Latine by that incomparable Virgin Anna Maria à Schurman of Utrecht* (London, 1659), 47–50.

[58] According to Joyce Irwin, the date given is late October or early November, following the Athenian calendar. Since van Schurman would have sent overseas letters all at once with a reliable carrier, the most likely date would then have been the same as the date of her letter to D'Ewes, October 31. Van Schurman, *Whether a Christian Woman*, 67–8.

interaction; Makin and van Schurman had already been corresponding during the intervening months.

Van Schurman's correspondence with Makin is notable on a number of levels.[59] First, it is in Greek rather than Latin; thus in terms of erudition, it documents two learned women with an impressive command of classical learning. Second, these letters explicitly address the tension between domestic duties and scholarly pursuits; thus, in terms of access to scholarship, they suggest how powerfully a female scholar's career was affected by her financial and domestic status. And third, they are also explicit in referring to professional activity; thus, in terms of practical networking, this correspondence is evidence for the ways in which personal connections and learned correspondence were practices that furthered women's careers in the republic of letters.

Van Schurman's letter of October 31, 1645 operated at all three of these levels. First, after the opening greetings, the letter addressed Makin's scholarship:

I was highly pleased with the reading of your letter. From it it is possible to see that you have touched, not merely dipped into the beauty of the language of the Greeks. Now the most wonderful thing is that in spite of your being pursued by many household duties, you have not seldom conversed with Philosophy and in no way whatever have your Muses become voiceless in the midst of the much-resounding weapons. As therefore I very highly value such a disquisition about Beauty, I can praise you especially because your encyclopedic knowledge compelled you to serve Theology, the Science of Sciences.

Then, van Schurman went on to address the issue of pedagogy, and its importance:

For the rest, you should not be worried about anything in order to lend your talent in the education of the royal little girl, that you may continue revealing to us that famous Elizabeth as living again (under whose saintly and just reign your island prospered so much).[60]

Apparently, then, Makin had already taken the initiative in writing to van Schurman. Moreover, Makin's letter had arrived together with an essay, a "disquisition about Beauty," that had also been written in Greek. Thus Makin had introduced herself to van Schurman by means of a scholarly

---

[59] Only two letters from van Schurman's side of this correspondence are extant, and these are printed in *Opuscula*, 164–6. Makin's letters to van Schurman do not appear to have survived.

[60] Van Schurman to Makin, October 31, 1645, in *Opuscula*, 164–5. Translation in Pieta van Beek, "One Tongue Is Enough," 32; also in van Schurman, *Whether a Christian Woman*, 67–8.

offering.[61] And in contrast to her reluctance to engage with D'Ewes, van Schurman had been "highly pleased" with Makin's letter and had asked her to continue the contact.

Makin had also told van Schurman about her domestic situation and the fact that she had many children. While van Schurman had, of course, commiserated with her on the difficulties of life during wartime, she had been even more amazed that Makin could find time to philosophize in Greek while being "pursued by many household duties." In fact, Makin's success completely contradicted one of the principal caveats of van Schurman's *Dissertatio* – that the higher levels of scholarship could only be recommended for "those women who are prepared for the study of Letters in advance of others due to their leisure and other means and resources."[62]

Makin possessed exactly none of these prerequisites. With an absent husband, no family money, and at least five children, Makin would have had no leisure, no means, and no resources other than her own intellectual labor. This suggests, then, that the arguments van Schurman advanced in her *Dissertatio* were general, theoretical, and perhaps even rhetorical; her real-life community of learned women included those whose circumstances were far from the ideal for which she had argued. And in the case of Makin, these deficiencies in terms of ideal circumstances were powerfully offset by her practical qualifications for the learned life: her intelligence, her network of scholarly connections, and her career as an educator to the daughters of the aristocracy. It was this career to which van Schurman was referring when she encouraged Makin to continue lending her talent to the education of the "royal little girl," who was destined to embody all the qualities of her namesake, Queen Elizabeth.

The "royal little girl" was the ten-year-old Princess Elizabeth Stuart, the daughter of Charles I; she died five years later, at the age of fifteen.[63] Elizabeth was never strong, and it was believed that the combination of her lifelong frailty, the exposure resulting from being shuttled from place to place during the Civil War, and grief over her father's execution caused her early death. The pathos of this situation has resulted in her having a powerfully sentimental and near-hagiographic place in Royalist literature.[64] At the same time, however, the praises accorded to her as a young

---

[61] Makin's Greek essay on "Beauty" does not appear to be extant.

[62] *Dissertatio*, 36. Also in van Schurman, *Whether a Christian Woman*, 36–7.

[63] This English princess will be referred to as Princess Elizabeth with a "z." Her cousin, the princess in The Hague, is referred to as Princess Elisabeth with an "s," spelled in the German manner.

[64] See, for example: Susan Cole, *A Flower of Purpose*, Royal Stuart Papers VIII (Ilford, Essex, 1975); and Cecil Deeds, *Royal and Loyal Sufferers*, Russell Press Stuart Series (London, 1903). For a more

scholar appear to have been well deserved. Elizabeth had indeed been a remarkably intelligent young woman and a promising scholar; among the descendants of James I, she and her cousin, Princess Elisabeth of Bohemia, appear to have been the only ones to inherit James' capacity for learning.

It is not clear when Makin's employment began, or how long it continued. In the constantly shifting landscape of the Civil War, the personnel around the youngest of the royal children – James, Henry, and Elizabeth – were often replaced in order to adapt to political needs, and it is difficult to say exactly who was instructing Princess Elizabeth at any given time. But in 1645, at the time of this letter from van Schurman, Makin was Elizabeth's tutor. John Dury had responsibility for Elizabeth's education beginning in 1646; this, combined with Makin's contact with van Schurman, creates a strong likelihood that Makin was associating with both Dury and Dorothy Moore.[65] Thus, in terms of Makin's professional associations, her education of Elizabeth provides an example of how her many networks came together to facilitate her pedagogical career. Yet while the position would have carried a great deal of prestige, it does not appear to have been lucrative. Like Dury, Makin would later petition Parliament for payment of arrears stemming from this employment; and, again like Dury, who complained that "I have not received a penny," she was destined to fail in her attempt.[66]

Yet Makin was very successful as a teacher, and the praises heaped on her royal pupil attest to her abilities as a language instructor. Moreover, Makin might also have taught the princess a more controversial skill – the use of ciphers. We have already seen that cipher was an element of instruction at the school where Makin taught with her father, and that there was an especially strong level of discomfort with women's use of alternative language systems and shorthand. Yet it appears that Princess Elizabeth may have been using both.

Samuel Torshell preached a sermon called *The Womans Glorie* for Princess Elizabeth on her ninth birthday, and when he had it printed

---

informative account, see Mary Anne Everett Green, *Lives of the Princesses of England*, 6 vols. (London, 1855), VI, 335–92.

[65] John Dury "was called to be with the Kings Children" in 1646. Dury lost that position in 1649. Dury, *The Unchanged, Constant and Single-hearted Peace-maker drawn forth into the World* (1650), 13–14.

[66] *Ibid.*, 14. The following was calendared for August 16, 1655: "Bathshua Makins, for payment of the arrears of 40*l.* a year granted her for life, for her attendance on the late King's children; reported as part of the business laid aside by Council. Dismissed." *CSPD* 1655, 290.

some months later, he recalled that she had already recorded much of the sermon when it was first delivered. Thus he encouraged her to, "Reade over again, what you heard, and in part noted with your own Pen."[67] As noted earlier, the use of shorthand for recording sermons in church was a practice of somewhat alarming popularity among devout young women; according to Torshell, then, Elizabeth must have joined their ranks. In addition, there is a record of an intercepted letter in February 1648 from Elizabeth to her imprisoned father – a letter which contained a passage in cipher that the Parliament could not decode. The letter itself was quite forceful. It opened with inquiries after her father's health, a description of her grief at being separated from him, and fears that her letters were being intercepted; it closed with a denunciation of those who had deprived the king of his rights and an anathema against all his cursed enemies. In the middle, however, was "a mysticall lock of numbers." It was reported that Parliament had "endeavoured to open the Cyphers with such Keyes as they had, but could not."[68]

Makin had therefore been justly proud of this pupil and of the work she had accomplished in teaching her an array of learned and alternative languages. Testaments to Elizabeth's abilities as a linguist came from many directions, including those whose sympathies were strongly Parliamentarian, and who had in fact supported the execution of Elizabeth's father. One example in this category was the Independent minister William Greenhill. Greenhill, who was ejected at the Restoration, served as chaplain to the royal children after Charles' death. Yet despite his anti-Royalist sympathies, his *Exposition of the Prophet Ezekiel* was dedicated to the young Princess Elizabeth and included her in the ranks of learned women throughout history:

Your desire to know the original tongues . . . your writing out the Lord's Prayer in Greek, some texts of Scripture in Hebrew, your endeavor after the exact knowledge of those holy tongues . . . do promise great matters from you. If the

---

[67] Samuel Torshell (1605–50) was a Puritan minister who in 1644 was appointed as tutor to Prince Henry and Princess Elizabeth. Torshell, *The Womans Glorie. A treatise, Asserting The due Honour of that Sexe, and Directing wherein that Honour consists. Dedicated to the young Princesse, Elizabeth her Highnesse* (London, 1645), A2r.

[68] Elizabeth's letter was part of an intercepted packet containing letters to the King from Queen Henrietta Maria, James Duke of York, and Princess Elizabeth. R[ichard] C[ollings], ed., *The Kingdomes Weekly Intelligencer, sent abroad to prevent mis-information* no. 248 (February 15–22, 1647/8), 848; Luke Harruney, Cleric, ed., *Perfect Occurrences of Every Daie journall in Parliament; and other Moderate Intelligence* no. 60 (February 18–25, 1647/8), 425; *Gazetteer de France* (February 1648), 661, cited in Green, *Lives of the Princesses*, 6:366–7.

harvest be answerable to the spring, your Highness will be the wonder of the learned, and glory of the godly.[69]

The model Princess Elizabeth was usually seen to follow was that of her namesake and predecessor, Queen Elizabeth I. Queen Elizabeth had been an English princess, strongly Protestant, and adept in the learned languages. However, Princess Elizabeth was also being compared to a contemporary model of virtuous learned womanhood, and that was Anna Maria van Schurman.

In addition to mentioning Elizabeth's abilities in shorthand, Torshell's *The Womans Glorie* celebrated Elizabeth's intellectual gifts, her great promise, and her "more then ordinary Pregnancie and Capableness in so young and tender yeares."[70] It listed her name in the usual roster of virtuous and learned women from the Bible and antiquity, as well as some more contemporary exemplars: Olympia Fulvia Morata, Lady Jane Grey, and finally "that great Ornament of the Netherlands, Anna Maria van Schurman."[71] But then Torshell went one step further. The following thirty-seven pages contained Torshell's translation of the entire correspondence between van Schurman and Rivet that had formed the second half of van Schurman's *Dissertatio*. This may, in fact, have constituted that work's first appearance in English. When Clement Barksdale published his translation of the *Dissertatio* in 1659, he had referred to his book as: "This strange maid, being now the second time drest up in her English Habit."[72] Although the tract's first English appearance has never been identified, Barksdale may have been referring to Torshell's excerpt. This must also have been quite an undertaking for Torshell, who clearly was not familiar with all of van Schurman's references – as evidenced by the fact that he managed to turn Marie de Gournay into a man.[73]

Given these praises for the young Princess Elizabeth, then, one cannot help but conclude that Makin was indeed an excellent teacher. She also

---

[69] William Greenhill, *An Exposition of the Prophet Ezekiel, with Useful Observations Thereupon. Delivered in Several Lectures in London . . . 1650*, ed. J. Sherman (Edinburgh, 1864), iii–iv.

[70] The Folger Shakespeare Library's copy of *The Womans Glorie* originally belonged to an eighteenth-century collector, John Bellingham Inglis (1780–1870). In the margin next to Torshell's comment about nine-year-old Elizabeth's extraordinary "pregnancie," Inglis drily observed: "Very few young women have been complimented on their pregnancy before they were married or even affianced." Torshell, *Womans Glorie*, A2r. Shelfmark 160-707q.

[71] Torshell, *Womans Glorie*, 32–4.   [72] Barksdale, *The Learned Maid*, A4r.

[73] In Torshell's translation, the phrase: "*utj non minus lepide quam erudite ostendit nobilissimum Gornacensium decus in libello quem inscripsit*" became "as that most noble ornament of the Gornaces hath shewed no lesse pleasantly then learnedly in his little booke." Torshell, *Woman's Glorie*, 47.

had other successful students drawn from the ranks of aristocratic women, and could be justly proud of her work with the Huntington women – Lucy Davies Hastings (1613–79), the Countess of Huntington, and her daughter Elizabeth. Her early association with royal circles, and her experience teaching Princess Elizabeth Stuart, had undoubtedly helped her to make these useful connections.

Lucy Hastings came from a controversial family. Her mother was the prophetess Eleanor Davies Douglas, whose impolitic pronouncements landed her in Bedlam and the Tower; Lucy therefore used her linguistic skills to help defend her mother against charges of madness, heresy, and sedition. And Lucy's uncle was Mervin Touchet, the Earl of Castlehaven, whose trial for sodomy and abetting the rape of his wife was one of the great scandals of the 1630s.[74] Nevertheless, Lucy herself was well known for both her piety and her learning.

Makin gave Lucy Hastings and her daughter Elizabeth Langham an unusually rigorous education in languages; both mother and daughter acquired the learned tongues, Latin, Greek, and Hebrew, in addition to French and Italian. This association continued throughout the 1660s, and Hastings account books for 1662 record four payments to Makin for coming out from London to teach the Huntington children in their home; they included a reimbursement for "coach hire," and a payment on October 4, 1662 of five pounds, "to Mrs Makin in consideration of beeing heere to teach my Brother &c."[75] These records also show six payments of wages and transportation expenses made to a "Nan Makin," who may have been Bathsua's daughter, although the work done is not specified.[76]

When Elizabeth Langham died in 1664, Makin wrote to Lucy Hastings, sending an elegy and a letter of condolence. Makin's grief over the death of her former pupil was quite likely real; however, Makin's need for an income was equally real. She therefore used this occasion to remind the Hastings family of her work as a teacher, and to mention in passing that she was now a poor widow. In the elegy itself, Makin had extolled the late Elizabeth's accomplishments in the study of languages:

---

[74] Eleanor Cope, *Handmaid of the Holy Spirit: Dame Eleanor Davies, Never Soe Mad a Ladie* (Ann Arbor, 1992), 10–11, 149; Tania Claire Jeffries, "Hastings, Lucy, Countess of Huntingdon (1613–79)", *ODNB*. On Castlehaven, see Cynthia B. Herrup, *A House in Gross Disorder: Sex, Law, and the 2nd Earl of Castlehaven* (Oxford, 1999).

[75] The brother mentioned was Theophilus Hastings (1650–1701), who became the seventh Earl of Huntington. Huntington Library, Hastings Accounts and Financial Papers (HAF), box 18, folder 32.

[76] The payments were made between December 28, 1661 and July 11, 1662. Huntington Library, HAF box 18, fols. 21, 26.

> Her houres were all precisely kept, and spent
> In her devotions, and her studies meant
> To share some for her Languages, which She
> In Latin, French, Italian happily
> Advanced in with pleasure.[77]

Makin, of course, was the one who had instilled these selfsame linguistic skills.

The accompanying letter then made reference to Makin's state of widowhood and financial hardship, calling her poetic offering only a "widowes mite".

> I could not but pay something to the Lady Elizabeths memory, which though it come short of hir excellencies, and be unworthy your Honors acceptance yet I presume, a widowes mite will not be despised.[78]

Although the children of this household no longer required her services as tutor, Makin apparently continued as a friend and client of the family. A 1667 letter from Makin to the dowager Countess thanks her profusely for her "bounty."[79] And one year later, Makin wrote again concerning some unnamed difficulty with her son, who was "lying very heavy" upon her. We unfortunately do not know whether this meant her son had died, was ill, or had fallen on the wrong side of the law, but the letter concluded with a plea for a meeting.[80]

Several years later, Makin turned her accomplishments in teaching the women of the Hastings family into a selling point in advertising her services as an educator. In her 1673 *Essay*, for instance, the anonymous author laments that he has been "forbidden" to mention the linguistic skills of the women who had been taught by "Mrs. Makin":

> I am forbidden to mention the Countess Dowager of Huntington (instructed sometimes by Mrs. Makin) how well she understands Latin, Greek, Hebrew, French and Spanish; or what a proficient she is in Arts, subservient to Divinity, in which (if I durst I would tell you) she excels.[81]

---

[77] Bathsua Makin to Lucy Hastings, dowager Countess of Huntington, 2 May, 1664. Huntington Library, Huntington MS. HA 8799. I am grateful to Dr. Kathleen Noonan for these references.
[78] *Ibid.*
[79] Bathsua Makin to Lucy, dowager Countess of Huntington, March 16, 1667. Huntington Library, Huntington MS, HA 8800.
[80] Bathsua Makin to Lucy, dowager Countess of Huntington, October 24, 1668. Huntington Library, Huntington MS, HA 8801.
[81] Makin, *Essay*, 10.

We can also read praises for these linguistic skills in elegies and poetry: in Samuel Clark's *The Lives of Sundry Eminent Persons in this Later Age*, Langham was lauded as "a living Bible Polyglot"; and Makin herself wrote a poem to her pupil the Countess, wherein these linguistic skills were characterized as "rare perfections of both sexes joind."[82] These sorts of praise can certainly be affected by the elevated social status of their recipients, or the hope of patronage, and one might wish to take them with a grain of salt. In the case of Lucy Hastings, however, these praises are also bolstered from two unexpected quarters.

Lucy Hastings had apparently acquired an enviable reputation as a translator of French and Latin, and despite her noble status, she was even being approached by strangers requesting her translation services. First, there appears to have been a long-standing and cordial relationship between Lucy Hastings and Marie du Moulin's brother Peter, spanning at least two decades, and letters from du Moulin show that the Countess was translating some of his works into English. In a letter from 1654, du Moulin thanks the Countess for her translation of his Latin poetry, adding:

Our young Ladys reape the benefit of your Ladyship's verses which they write & learne, & more persons that are not for Latin are obliged to your Ladyship's golden veine, for helping them to the way of Christian felicity.[83]

The letter was written from the Cork estate in Youghal, the childhood home of the Boyle clan, where du Moulin was tutoring the sons of Lady Ranelagh's brother Richard. And in 1672, Lucy was apparently working on a translation of du Moulin's *La Politique de France*, but she needed some help with a particular passage. So du Moulin explained it to her:

I say that "the recreational services he (Cardinal du Perron) and Monsieur de la Varenne performed for King Henry the Great merit having posterity erect statues in their honor, crowned with fennel." It is an allusion to the French cookery of mackerels which are always served with fennel. And in French *au maquereau* signifies both that fish & a pimp.[84]

[82] "A Poem by Bathsua Makin." Undated holograph. *Historical Manuscripts Commission*, Report no. 78, *On the Manuscripts of the late Reginald Rawdon Hastings*, iv, 348. On Langham, see "The Life and Death of the Right Honourable, the Lady Elizabeth Langham, who died, Anno Christi, 1664," in Samuel Clark, *The Lives of Sundry Eminent Persons in this Later Age. In Two Parts* (London, 1683), 197–207; also Retha M. Warnicke, "Langham, Lady Elizabeth (1635–64)," *ODNB*.
[83] Peter du Moulin to [Lucy, Countess of Huntington], September 23, 1654. Huntington Library, HA-Correspondence 9465, Box 19.
[84] In the original, the material in quotation marks is in French (*que les services recreatifs que luy (le Cardinal du Perron) & Monsieur de la Varenne ont rendu au Roy Henry le Grand meritent que la*

The Countess of Huntington was widely revered as a model of piety and devotion; moreover, there was an enormous gap between the two in terms of social rank. Yet du Moulin had apparently felt comfortable enough with her to explain a rather off-color joke involving mackerels, fennel, Cardinals, and pimps. This exchange thus serves as further evidence for the close and ongoing collaborative interaction of translators and educators in networks that were both Royalist and godly.

Secondly, the countess received a letter in 1678 wherein a complete stranger, the man-midwife Percival Willughby, begged her to translate a French medical text into English.

Pardon my rashe folly in presuming humbly to begg, that you would be pleased to translate the worke of Madam Louys Bourgeois into English. It would be a worke that would increase your Honors worth and ever advance your most noble name, by shewing more easy waye for the releeving poore suffering women in their extremitys ... I beseech your pardon, the good of woman, moved me to it.[85]

Willughby, the letter-writer, was one of the earliest male-midwives in England, and a passionate advocate for educating female midwives. He was the author of *Observations in Midwifery, as also the country midwife's opusculum or vade medum*, a manuscript treatise which was not published until after his death.[86] The text referred to in this letter was probably *Instruction à ma fille* by Louise Bourgeois, a renowned French midwife who wrote the first treatise in French on the art of midwifery.[87] The role played by female medical practitioners in medical manuscript networks has already been discussed in relation to Ranelagh; however, there is no reference here to any medical expertise on the part of the Countess. One can only assume, then, that apart from her reputation for virtue, and perhaps the hope that she would feel some womanly empathy, she is being approached solely on the basis of her skill as a translator – the skill taught to her by Makin.

---

posterité leur erige des statues couronnees de fenouil). Peter du Moulin to [Lucy, Countess of Huntington], n.d. [1672], Huntington Library, HA-Correspondence 9466, Box 34.

[85] Percivall Willughby to [Lucy, Countess Dowager of Huntington], April 26, 1678. Huntington Library, HA-Correspondence 13403, Box 41.

[86] Willughby (b. 1596) also trained his daughter as a midwife. The best source on the Willughby midwives, père et fille, is James Hobson Aveling, *English Midwives: Their History and Prospects* [1872] (Reprint, London, 1967), 37–40, 54–60. See also Adrian Wilson, "A Memorial of Eleanor Willughby, a Seventeenth-Century Midwife," in Hunter and Hutton, *Women, Science and Medicine,* 138–77.

[87] Bourgeois' *Observations diverses* ... , first published in 1609, was reprinted five times in the seventeenth century. On Louise Bourgeois (1563–1636), see especially Wendy Perkins, *Midwifery and Medicine in Early Modern France: Louise Bourgeois* (Exeter, 1996).

The women in the Hastings family continued to be remarkable for their learning and piety for several generations. First, Makin taught learned languages to Lucy Hastings, and then to Lucy's daughter Elizabeth. Lucy's granddaughter, another Elizabeth Hastings, became the famous "Lady Betty," who was referred to in the *Tatler* as a "female philosopher." And Lady Betty, the daughter of Theophilus Hastings, who had also been taught by Makin, later helped support a school being run by the feminist writer and educator Mary Astell.[88]

Thus the pedagogical career of Bathsua Makin – a practical school-teacher, linguistic reformer, and champion of women's right to study – compels us to reconsider the concept of what constituted a scholarly career in the republic of letters in the middle of the seventeenth century. Despite being unable to assume any official duties in the academy, female scholars were active in a surprisingly wide range of seventeenth-century pedagogical activity. On both a practical and theoretical level, the issue of teaching constituted an important component in their intellectual careers, intersecting with politics, religious reform, philosophy, feminism, science, and medical education. Although their pedagogical goals were very different, each of the seven women in this network used her own considerable learning to teach others about the value of knowledge; and, in so doing, each one was fully engaged in the work of the seventeenth-century republic of letters, furthering the advancement of learning through the advancement of education.

---

[88] On Elizabeth Hastings (1682–1730), see Ruth Perry, *The Celebrated Mary Astell: An Early English Feminist* (Chicago, 1986), 230–64, passim.

CHAPTER 7

Endings: the closing of doors

As for what the World calls Learning . . .
French will now answer all.

John Norris to Elizabeth Thomas, c.1731[1]

In 1680, Bathsua Makin wrote a poem to Lady Ranelagh's brother, Robert Boyle. Makin, at the age of eighty, was using this literary offering to display her still-impressive command of Latin, Greek, and Hebrew. She began with a rather standard set of compliments: Boyle was great among the number of the Heroes, a true descendant of Maecenas, a man whose intellectual and devotional gifts were too many to recount. It was in the following lines, however, that the real purpose of Makin's poem became abundantly clear:

> You are exceedingly generous to the poor, bounteous of your own free will,
>   And your hand is always open to all the learned.
> Whither you set foot, may you proceed well, may you proceed in the best way;
>   So that you may become accustomed to giving aid to pious widows.

Then, just in case Boyle had missed the hint about open hands and needy widows, Makin signed herself: "The widow Bathsua Makin, who is in her eighty-first year."[2] Makin had always liked to get straight to the point, and it is clear that age had not changed that. Throughout her career, she had been considered one of the learned; now, having become a "pious widow" to boot, Makin was merely pointing out that she was doubly entitled to Boyle's Maecenas-like largesse.

---

[1] John Norris to Elizabeth Thomas, n.d., in "Letters from Mr. Norris to Corinna, for the Direction of her Studies," in Richard Gwinnett and Elizabeth Thomas, *Pylades and Corinna. or, memoirs of the lives, amours, and writings of Richard Gwinnett Esq . . . and Mrs. Elizabeth Thomas . . .* , 2 vols. (London, 1731–2), II, 202–5. Norris' correspondence with Mary Astell, *Letters Concerning the Love of God*, was published in 1695.
[2] "For the right honorable Robert Boil," Royal Society, Boyle Letters, vol. 4, f. 6. I am grateful to Michael Hunter for this archival reference. Also published in Boyle, *Correspondence*, v, 282–3.

Makin was an aged female scholar with no other resources; and in her appeal for funding, we see one example of how female scholars were working to navigate an intellectual landscape that had changed quite dramatically within their lifetimes. At the dawn of the Enlightenment, the learned world was a very different place. The mid-seventeenth-century republic of letters had been an enterprise embracing everything from alchemy to agriculture, an open conversation wherein discussions could range in one breath from metaphysics to mining to millenarian theology. Now, however, that scholarly whirlwind had begun to calm down, and was organizing itself along disciplinary lines. Latin, the *lingua franca* of learning, had been replaced by an assortment of vernaculars – literary discussions were conducted in French, while scientific research appeared in the respective languages of state-sponsored academies. The female scholars who had thrived in the diverse, eclectic, and inclusive intellectual environment of the mid-seventeenth-century republic of letters – along with many of their somewhat unclassifiable male colleagues – now found themselves without an intellectual home. Readjustments were necessary, and scholars had to scramble.

The surviving members of this intellectual women's network had spent the previous decades crafting learned careers that answered the question of how to *be* a female scholar. But toward the end of the seventeenth century, the question became: what do we do *now?* For many of their male colleagues, the question was the same. Their answers, however, were different. Male scholars in this changed world of learning could at least count on the possibility of institutional rescue; they might hope to secure positions in churches, courts, or universities, where they would find both an intellectual community and enough material support to keep themselves alive. Female scholars, on the other hand, could count on nothing of the sort. Moreover, since many female scholars remained single throughout their lives, they also could not rely on the traditional system of family support for older women.

Over half the women being followed in this study – four out of seven – never married. Anna Maria van Schurman, Marie du Moulin, Marie de Gournay, and Princess Elisabeth had been consistently clear about their desire to remain single, and they had succeeded in living their entire lives that way. For van Schurman, her status as "the virgin of Utrecht" had made her unmarried state part of her scholarly identity from the beginning. For Marie du Moulin, belonging to such a prominent and prolific Huguenot clan made her celibate status more problematic. However, this was her choice; and in a letter to his brother Jacob, Pierre Bayle recalled "the illustrious Mlle. Marie du Moulin, who never wanted to marry even though her beauty, her fortune, and her merit procured her a considerable number of suitors."[3] Dorothy Moore had been equally clear about wanting to remain single; but finally, confronted by a range of pressures, she had given in and married her friend John Dury. This had been by all accounts a good marriage, and Moore's children could possibly have supported her; however, her husband could never have become a late-life support system for Moore, since he represented a failed revolution, and became a British exile after 1660. Ranelagh, who had been married to a reprobate, was by 1670 a merry widow; for her, the continuing support of the Boyle clan ensured her continued well-being. Makin, the working widow, was scrambling for support to the very end of her life.

For these aging female scholars, then, the question of, "what to do now?" was addressing two sets of urgent needs: first, the basic human need for sustenance and support; and second, the scholar's need for an intellectual community, or at the very least a space in which to study and materials with which to work. And in addressing these needs, our female scholars came up with two very different sets of answers. One set of answers involved making very few changes at all. And four of these seven female scholars – Makin, Gournay, Moore, and Ranelagh – continued throughout their lives to participate in the public worlds of publishing, polemics, pedagogy, and religious activism. But the three remaining women in this network – van Schurman, Elisabeth, and Marie du Moulin – came up with a solution that was both old and new. Like generations of unmarried women before them, they retired to religious communities. However, these retreats were quite far from being the traditional religious cloister. Each one of these three female scholars constructed her own community, shaped around a specific spiritual practice; each community welcomed other learned women, and each left room for the continuation of scholarly research, connection, and correspondence. Rather than having doors closed upon them, they were constructing and closing the doors themselves.

In this chapter, we examine how each of these seven female scholars in turn negotiated the end of that inclusive intellectual moment that had allowed them to become a Republic of Women within the larger republic of letters.

---

[3] Pierre Bayle to Jacob Bayle, November 26, 1678, letter no. 160 in Bayle, *Correspondance*, III, 80–100. See also Marie's remarks regarding marriage in letters XC and XCIV, dated June 17 and July 1, 1640, in *Claude Saumaise & André Rivet*, 207–10 and 217–19.

MARIE DE GOURNAY (1565–1645)

Marie de Gournay, the elder stateswoman of this female intellectual network, was always hard to place. She belonged to an earlier generation, the *mère d'alliance* to van Schurman and her intellectual sisters. As van Schurman repeatedly noted, in letters and publications, Gournay had led the way for other female scholars; however, this also meant that Gournay did not live long enough to enjoy the benefits of a female scholarly community that she had helped to create.

As a result, Gournay was seen as being the only representative of her kind. Her combativeness in the literary forum, coupled with her resolute spinsterhood, meant that the epithet of "old maid" was nearly inevitable. Biographers kept inflating her years, while also denigrating her character; as Bayle noted, "A person of her sex must scrupulously avoid these sorts of quarrels; satirical writers are boors ... who will attack women where they are most sensitive."[4] Yet as Tallemant des Réaux recounts, with grudging admiration, this "*vieille fille de Picardie*" won a pension from Cardinal Richelieu through sheer force of personality. During the course of an interview that had begun quite badly, she was feisty, clever, and fearless; thus she managed to turn nothing whatsoever into a pension of 200 *ecus*, then negotiated even better terms by insisting that Richelieu also consider the needs of her maidservant, her cat, and the possibility of future kittens.[5]

Certainly, there were other women in this study who found themselves characterized by quasi-complimentary epithets like "alone of all her sex". Van Schurman, Makin, Elisabeth, and Ranelagh had all heard this praise from a number of sources. However, their personal intellectual prime had coincided with the heady intellectual climate of the decades from 1630 to 1660 – and in this they were much more fortunate. They had been able to offset the perception of their gendered singularity with their knowledge that they belonged: they belonged to a number of networks within the republic of letters, and they belonged to a network of intellectual women. Gournay, on the other hand, was part of an earlier intellectual generation, whose boundaries had been much more difficult to cross. Yet "difficult" is not the same as "impossible," and Gournay managed to cross many bridges.

---

[4] "Gournai (Marie de Jars, Demoiselle de)," in Bayle, *Dictionnaire historique et critique*, VII, 184–91; and "Gournay (Mary de Jars, lady of)," in *Biographium Foemineum. The Female Worthies: or, Memoirs of the Most Illustrious Ladies, of all Ages and Nations* ... (London, 1746), 225–30.
[5] Tallemant des Réaux, *Les Historiettes de Tallemant des Réaux*, ed. Georges Mongrédien, 8 vols. (Paris, 1932–4), II, 213–6.

It is perhaps ironic, then, that the very process by which Gournay had allied herself to van Schurman, and reinforced the idea of women's scholarly connection – the intellectual inheritance that made them *mère et fille d'alliance* – was interpreted by others as the process through which nature ensured there would be only one brilliant female scholar in each generation. Louis Jacob, in the *Elogium* that introduced Guillaume Colletet's French translation of van Schurman's *Dissertatio*, described a conversation he had had with Gabriel Naudé, the librarian to Cardinal Mazarin. Naudé in turn was reporting on a conversation with Colletet, concerning the learning and virtue of van Schurman:

> I remember a time in his very charming garden, where he discussed with me the admirable providence of nature, which had wanted to place Anna Maria in the place of Marie de Gournay (who is very advanced in age, and in her declining years, and in such great repute for her wit, eloquence, and learning, that she can shut the mouths of even the most learned men), like a new shoot that might serve to sustain the glory of her sex to the envy of all male rivals, with an equal loftiness of wit, and perhaps with an equal amount of glory and renown.[6]

And even Samuel Sorbière might have thought there could only be one female intellectual star in each nation, even though there were a number of them in each age. In a letter to Elisabeth, wherein he had argued for Gassendi's superiority over Descartes, he had also tried to impress the princess by listing a catalogue of scholarly female worthies. However, his analysis reversed what Naudé had said. Instead of van Schurman being the new Gournay, Sorbière touted Marie de Gournay as "the Anna Maria van Schurman of our France."[7]

In the end, however, the contentious Gournay was indeed honored for her contributions to the republic of letters. Etienne Pasquier, writing to a colleague about Michel de Montaigne, deemed Gournay to have been an essential element of the late essayist's intellectual identity. Pasquier first noted that he did not agree with everything Montaigne had said, then went on to praise Gournay and the *famille d'alliance* that she had constructed with the late Montaigne:

> He left two daughters: one, born from his marriage, inherited each and every one of his goods, and married very well; the other, his covenant-daughter, inherited his studies ... This is Mademoiselle de Jars, the descendant of several great and noble families in Paris. She is a woman who has never imagined having any

---

[6] Louis Jacob, *"Elogium eruditissimae"*, 100–2.
[7] Letter xv, dated June 5, 1652, in Sorbière, *Lettres et Discours*, 73.

spouse apart from her honor, enriched by the reading of great books, and above all the *Essays* of Monsieur de Montaigne.[8]

And after the death of Marie de Gournay in 1645, François Ogier wrote the following epitaph:

> Marie de Gournay, whom the celebrated Montaigne
> acknowledged as a daughter, and Justus Lipsius –
> indeed all learned men – acknowledged as a sister.
> She lived 80 years, left this life July 13, 1645.
> Her spirit will prevail forever.[9]

Thus apart from Montaigne, Lipsius, and van Schurman, her *père, frère,* and *fille d'alliance,* Gournay had possessed a multitude of other siblings in her web of intellectual kinship. It was the final acknowledgment of Marie de Gournay's place within the larger *famille d'alliance* that was the republic of letters.

DOROTHY MOORE (C.1612–64)

There are very few traces of Dorothy Moore's intellectual life after 1660. Following the Restoration, Moore was still in touch with her friends Hartlib and Ranelagh; however, she was isolated on the Continent, suffering from financial hardship and ill health. While illness was, of course, beyond anyone's control, her other difficulties were the consequence of her political and religious activism during the previous decades. Moore and Dury had found themselves on the losing side after the Restoration's reassertion of ecclesiastical and monarchical control. Dury made some brief attempts to persuade Charles II that his work with Cromwell's government had not been politically motivated – that it had been merely the byproduct of his irenic ecumenicism, rather than the working of any real reformationist, revolutionary, or anti-monarchical agenda.[10] As one might have predicted, this effort failed to convince. Thus when Dury lost his employment as library-keeper at Saint James, he

---

[8] Lettre 1, "A Monsieur de Pelgé," in Etienne Pasquier, *Les Oeuvres d'Estienne Pasquier* ... 2 vols. (Amsterdam, 1723), II, 515–20.

[9] Latin text in Ilsley, *A Daughter of the Renaissance*, 262.

[10] John Dury, *A Declaration of John Durie ... Wherein he doth make known the Truth of his way and comportment in all these times of trouble, And how he hath endeavoured to follow Peace and Righteousness therein innocently towards all ...* (London, 1660); and idem, *The Plain Way of Peace and Unity in Matters of Religion.* (London, 1660).

concluded that the signs were uniformly ominous; he fled to the Continent, and never returned.

Moore's exiled husband continued circulating among the Protestant courts of Europe, in an endless quest for patronage and support for his rapidly fading dream of church unification. Moore herself remained in the Netherlands with their children. Moore had given birth to a son in 1649, when Dury wrote to tell Hartlib that: "God hath blessed my family with yong boy; at the beginning of this yeare; and that my wife hath had an easie deliverie."[11] While this child died in infancy, Moore then gave birth to a daughter, Doro-Katherina, in May, 1654. Doro-Katherina's name, combining the first name of her mother with that of Lady Ranelagh, honored the lifelong friendship and collaboration of these two scholars. Then by 1658 Moore was seriously ill, and she and Dury were covering expenses "by pawning of some things which are lesse usefull to us".[12]

Still, despite the hardships, Moore continued to make use of her political connections in England. Hartlib's condition was, if anything, even worse than Moore's. He was suffering terribly from cataracts and kidney stones, and his trickle of funds had dried up completely. Hartlib turned for help to Moore, hoping that her goodwill, connections, and political acumen could be of help. Moore commiserated, but could do very little on her own:

> I am sory your condition exposeth you to straights and difficulties, when my estate is not able to releeve them, I assure you were I not in the same condition you speake of and left by mr Dury indepted to all poeple I deale with, you should not want necessarys.[13]

Moore, ever the preacher *manqué*, went on to remind Hartlib of the spiritual solace that would always be there in the coming world, despite the fact that "the day of wanting money brings with it loss of freinds."[14] The implication here is that Dury was on the run, and Moore was trying to keep home and hearth together in his absence. Her birth should have entitled her to the income from a number of properties in Ireland and England; however, entitlement was one thing, and payment was another. In 1649, Parliament had approved six months' worth of weekly payments, in the amount of £3, to a group of "Distressed Irish ladies" that included Moore; but as Dury noted a year later, Moore's properties in Ireland were

[11] Dury to Hartlib, January 26, 1649, HP 1/7/1A-2B.
[12] Dury to Hartlib, October 15, 1658, HP 2/12/3A-4B.
[13] Moore to Hartlib, September 27, [1661], HP 4/4/34A-B. Also in *The Letters of Dorothy Moore*, 97.
[14] *Ibid.*

worth at least £400 a year. Moreover, they had not "enjoyed one penny of that money since the Uprising of 1641."[15]

However, Moore had not given up on her political connections as a source of assistance for Hartlib in this present world. She immediately contacted both Ranelagh and the Earl of Anglesey, relying on her old Anglo-Irish network. Ranelagh continued to wield political influence, and, according to Sir Henry Bennet, the Secretary of State, Anglesey was one of the three most powerful men in Restoration Ireland – the other two being the Duke of Ormond and the Earl of Orrery, Ranelagh's brother Roger.[16] Thus several weeks later, Moore could write to Hartlib to let him know that there was reason to hope:

> Deare freind: I did acquaint Lord Anglesey with your condition ... I spake alsoe to Lady Ranlaugh who told mee shee hoped to have your necessitys supplied a better way. I shall be glad of that, but I did not tell her what had passed between Lord Anglesy and my selfe. I hope between them you will find sume help.[17]

Despite Moore's best efforts, however, the help did not materialize. Hartlib died five months later, on Monday, March 10, 1662. The following Wednesday, John Pell wrote sadly to his son:

> I am now going out to accompany old Mr Hartlibs corps to the grave. He died last Munday morning early. This day your mother hath beene dead just 26 weeks or halfe a yeare.[18]

Ithamar Pell had died on September 11, 1661. Pell kept meticulous accounts of his wife's funeral expenses, and of the attendees – a list that had included Hartlib and his entire family, while the name of Bathsua Makin, his wife's sister, cannot be found.[19] It is at this point, with the passing of Hartlib and his network of correspondence, that we also lose sight of Dorothy Moore. There is no further extant record of her activities.

Moore probably died in June 1664, since it was at that time that John Dury wrote from Lausanne to the elders of the Dutch Congregation in London, asking them for two favors. First, he was hoping they would act as his archivists; his papers were scattered among many countries and courts, but his mission continued, and he himself could not come back to England.[20] His second request tells us that Dorothy Moore had died:

---

[15] *CSPD* 1649–50, 582.   [16] M. Perceval-Maxwell, "Annesley, Arthur," *ODNB*.
[17] Moore to Hartlib, October 13, [1661], HP 4/4/37A-B. Also in *The Letters of Dorothy Moore*, 98.
[18] John Pell to John Pell, Jr, March 12, [1662], BL, Add. MSS. 4280, f. 318.
[19] BL, Add. MSS. 4280, ff. 261–3; and Add. MSS. 4426, ff. 168–72.
[20] John Dury to the Ministers and Elders of the Dutch Congregation, London, June 11/21, 1664, letter no. 3646 in *Ecclesiae Londino-Batavae Archivum* (Cambridge, 1897), III, part 2, 2505–6.

The second is: that whiles I am thus necessitated to bee absent for the service of the Churches, and cannot make it my worke to oversee the education of my Child, and the management of the estate which is setled upon her, that you would bee pleased to ease me of that care.[21]

In their reply of July 25 / August 4, the elders agreed to take Dury's papers, providing they were "packed together and sealed." In the interim, however, it had apparently been decided that young Doro-Katherina, then ten years old, would be taken in by Henry Oldenburg and his wife; but if Mrs. Oldenburg died, then the elders assured Dury they would "take a care of the good education of your Daughter in your absence."[22]

This promise was put to the test within months, since Mrs. Oldenburg was dead by February of the following year. Moore's daughter is next heard from four years later, on August 13, 1668 – the day on which the fourteen-year-old Doro-Katherina was married to Henry Oldenburg. The rumor mill of the republic of letters immediately went into action. John Collins wrote to Pell within the week, with under-inflated estimates of the bride's youth, and over-inflated ideas of the wealth that she was bringing to the union:

Mr Oldenburgh is newly-married to a Gent of 15 yeares of Age, Mr Martin the Bookseller saith shee is related to Mr Boyle and that her fortune is 2000£, others say 1500£.[23]

Pell corrected him on both counts, writing: "I know the Brides age was but 14 years and 3 months. I very well remember that she was born in May anno 1654; when her father and I were travelling together in Germany."[24] Moore's daughter and her husband set up housekeeping; their daughter, Sophia, was born in the summer of 1672, and a son, Rupert was born several years later.[25]

However, tragedy struck when Oldenburg died suddenly on September 5, 1677, and Doro-Katherina died twelve days later. No will was ever found, and Moore's grandchildren became the immediate financial and

[21] *Ibid.*
[22] Caesar Calandrin to John Dury, July 25 /August 4, 1664, letter no. 3650, *Ecclesiae Londino-Batavae Archivum*, III, part 2, 2508.
[23] John Collins to John Pell, August 20, 1668, BL, Add. MSS. 4278, f. 341. On Oldenburg's guardianship of Doro-Katherina, their marriage, and their children, see Marie Boas Hall, *Henry Oldenburg: Shaping the Royal Society* (Oxford, 2002), 277–92, and the Appendix, "The fate of Oldenburg's children," 312–17.
[24] Cited in Hall, *Henry Oldenburg*, 278.
[25] Noel Malcolm also points to a note in the Pell Papers regarding the death in 1670 of the Oldenburgs' first child, a son, aged less than one month. Malcolm and Stedall, *John Pell*, 216.

legal responsibility of Robert Boyle. No documents name Ranelagh as part of this process, but it is reasonable to assume that it was she who assumed responsibility for the day-to-day care of her late friend's grandchildren. The deep friendship with Moore had been hers, and Boyle, a lifelong bachelor, had no experience whatsoever with the needs of young children.

In the end, a woman named Margaret Lowden was appointed "administratrix" of the estate, so that the children's needs would be considered separately from those of the Royal Society; and the appointment of Lowden demonstrates that Moore's blended network of political and scholarly associates from the exile court was still functioning.[26] Lowden had been born in The Hague, where her father, Sir Robert Stone, had been in the service of the Queen of Bohemia. Lowden's family had also been well acquainted with the family of Sir Robert Honywood; and Honywood, in turn, had been one of Oldenburg's pupils. He was a frequent correspondent of van Schurman's friend Constantijn Huygens, and his daughter Elizabeth Honywood eventually married John Moore, one of Dorothy Moore's sons from her first marriage.[27]

Finally, the remaining friends from her various intellectual circles had one last service to perform for Moore's descendants. A 1678 letter from Dury to Pell documents the continuing interaction of the courtly group from The Hague, and of the collaborators who still shared a vision for a new kingdom of God on earth. Nearing the end of his life, it was to Oldenburg, Boyle, Pell, and Ranelagh that Dury would turn, hoping to secure the legacy of ecumenical reform that was perhaps even more important to him than the care of his children and grandchildren by Dorothy Moore.

Dury was living in Cassel, under the protection of Princess Elisabeth's cousin, the Landgravine Hedwig Sophia of Hesse-Cassel. Elisabeth and Dury were still in touch, and from 1663 until his death in 1680, Dury's home was with Hedwig Sophia. She continued making introductions on behalf of Dury's ongoing mission, and gave him franking privileges for his still-extensive correspondence.[28] However, family had never been the focus of Dury's life, nor of Moore's. The animating vision of their lifelong work, both separately and together, had been a complete revolution of the world, the reforming of education, learning, government, and the church in order to align more perfectly with God's providential design.

---

[26] PRO, MS. PROB 6/52 (1677), f. 105. Cited in Hall, *Henry Oldenburg*, 305.
[27] On Honywood, see Gillian Wright, "Honywood, Sir Robert (1601–1686)," *ODNB*; and *De Briefwisseling van Constantijn Huygens, passim.*
[28] Batten, *John Dury*, 186–7.

In 1678, when Dury wrote this letter to Pell, it was with a clear sense of his approaching end. It was likely that he had never met his grandchildren. But Dury did for them what he had done for Doro-Katherina in 1664, and wrote to ensure that they would be educated, "which is now the chief care I can take for them."[29] Then, as Dury's letter continued, he discussed the disposition of his most important legacy – his work for Christian union. Mrs. Lowden and her lawyer could take responsibility for the grandchildren; Dury had someone very different in mind for this other, more crucial inheritance, the legacy of his life's work:

I have let the Lady Ranelagh Dowager know the state of my Religious negotiation, & in what a posture I desir to stand for the further prosecution thereof; that such as love the worke & are willing to helpe & further it, by counsell or otherwise to support it, may bee acquainted with the dore which God hath opened now more largely unto me, then ever heretofore to proceed.[30]

Dury was evidently sure that his plans were finally coming to fruition. He still had a number of active and influential friends in England – but to his mind, the most influential, active, effective and empathetic friend he had left was Moore's kinswoman and collaborator, the incomparable Lady Ranelagh.

KATHERINE JONES, LADY RANELAGH (1615–91)

The renewed conservatism of Europe at the end of the century had a chilling effect on Ranelagh's activities with the Hartlib circle. Hartlib's death in 1661 brought an end to his widespread web of correspondence and large-scale projects, and there is no further trace of Ranelagh's activities along this line in the historical record. In all likelihood, however, this lack of evidence has more to do with the loss of Hartlib's syndicate of scribal publication than it does with the cessation of the activities themselves. The reasons behind this conclusion are twofold. First, without a central point of collection and distribution, letters would inevitably have ended up being lost or scattered in other locations. This would be especially true in the case of Hartlib's female collaborators, who lacked an institutional affiliation, and whose papers would have become the responsibility of their families alone. And second, we find that in fact Ranelagh's other activities, in medical, religious, and political circles, did not slow down at all.

---

[29] John Dury, Cassel, to John Pell, London, May 28 / June 7, 1678, BL, Add. MSS. 4365, f. 7.
[30] *Ibid.*

For the next thirty years, until her death at the age of seventy-six, Ranelagh remained active in her other networks of association. With physicians, healers, and family, she continued circulating medical manuscripts and recipes, and appears to have retained her position as the Boyle clan's primary doctor.[31] She also remained connected to scientific circles; her brother Robert was living in her home in Pall Mall, where members of the Royal Society met regularly, and she was still close with Benjamin Worsley.[32]

Even Robert Hooke lodged with Ranelagh for a period in 1664.[33] However, the relationship between Hooke and Ranelagh was far from easy. One can only imagine how the outspoken and highly devout Ranelagh might have reacted to Hooke, who was having a sexual relationship with his maidservant Nell, and quite possibly with his adolescent niece Grace as well.[34] Among Hooke's numerous diary references to Ranelagh, we find the following entries:

> *20 January, 1674*   Dind at Lady Ranalaghs.
> Never more.

> *25 August, 1677.*   A Scowring seasd me like an ague,
> occasioned by 3 bunches of grapes eat at
> Lady Ranalaughs yesterday.

> *20 June, 1678.*   At Lady Ranalaughs, she scolded &c. I will
> never goe neer her againe nor Boyle.[35]

Yet despite Hooke's vow on June 20 to "never goe neer" Ranelagh again, we find him back there two weeks later:

> *5 July, 1678.*   At Lady Ranalaughs and Mr. Boyles. She
> still finding fault.[36]

---

[31] Documents in the Althorp Papers at the British Library and Orrery Papers in the Petworth House Archives, Sussex, contain numerous references to Ranelagh's medical activities in the years 1660–91.

[32] A 1677 letter of condolence from Ranelagh to her brother Robert laments the consecutive deaths of their friends Worsley and Oldbenburg. Ranelagh to Boyle, September 11, [1677], BL, Add. MSS. 4292, f. 278.

[33] Lisa Jardine, "Hooke the Man: His Diary and His Health," in *London's Leonardo: The Life and Work of Robert Hooke*, ed. Jim Bennet, Michael Hunter and Lisa Jardine (Oxford, 2003), 198.

[34] Lisa Jardine, *The Curious Life of Robert Hooke, The Man Who Measured London* (New York, 2004), 252–6.

[35] Robert Hooke, *The Diary of Robert Hooke, 1672–1680. Transcribed from the Original in the Possession of the Corporation of the City of London (Guildhall Library)*, ed. Henry W. Robinson and Walter Adams (London, 1968), 81, 184, 308, 364.

[36] Ibid., 365.

We do not know whether Ranelagh was finding fault with Hooke as a person, or as the designer of her new house; it is clear, however, that there was no love lost between them.

Yet the greatest portion of Ranelagh's public activities in these years, as in the years before, was not medical or scientific – it was political. She remained devoted to the same issues that had animated her from the beginning: political ethics, God's kingdom on earth, the improvement of Ireland, and the fortunes of the Boyle family. In each of these areas, she retained an absolute certainty that she knew what was right, and she had no hesitation whatsoever in notifying and correcting any courtiers, politicians, bishops, relations, or members of the royal family who might have erred by thinking otherwise.

Given the shifting sands of seventeenth-century politics in England and Ireland, Ranelagh found herself quite busy. When her brother Roger, now Earl of Orrery, was accused in 1663 of encouraging discontent in Ireland, Ranelagh immediately went into action. She contacted one of her oldest and most powerful political connections, the Earl of Clarendon, to insist that the king move immediately to "have him brought to tryall & Exsamination & tryall thereupon."[37] The context was political, since rumor and slander could have finished Orrery's career; but the main thrust of her argument was based on legal procedure. English law had been been a concern of hers since the 1640s, when she had been investigating the legality of the king's actions in parliament.[38] And in 1659, Hartlib had written to Boyle to let him know that he had received some long letters from John Beale, who was helping Boyle's "excellent sister" to construct "an argument concerning the reformation of English laws and lawyers."[39]

This same combination of legal argumentation and high-level politics can been seen in an exchange from 1689, when Ranelagh was in her mid-seventies. This time, she was returning the favor to Clarendon, and writing a letter to Bishop Gilbert Burnet on behalf of Clarendon's son, Henry Hyde, the Earl of Rochester. When Rochester, whose sister Anne had married King James II, found himself in the political hinterlands in 1689, he turned to Ranelagh for help; and Ranelagh, having determined the quickest route to power, turned to Burnet. She thought Burnet should

---

[37] Ranelagh to Clarendon, June 4, [1663]. Bodleian Library, Oxford. Clarendon Papers, vol. 79, ff. 270–1. My thanks to Ruth Connolly for this reference. For a celebratory account of Roger Boyle, see Eustace Budgell, *Memoirs of the Life and Character of the Late Earl of Orrery, and of the Family of the Boyles . . .*, 2nd edn. (London, 1732).

[38] See Ranelagh's exchange with Sir Cheney Culpeper on this subject in 1648, HP 26/13/1A-2B.

[39] Hartlib to Boyle, May 31, 1659, in Boyle, *Correspondence*, I, 357–9. See also John Worthington, *The Diary and Correspondence of Dr. John Worthington*, ed. James Crossley (Manchester, 1847–86), XIII, 107.

remind Queen Mary that helping Rochester's children was in fact a legal obligation, and: "in assisting them hir Majesty wil need onely to concerne hir selfe to preserve a propertie made theirs by the law of England, & which as queene of this kingdome she is obliged to maintaine."[40] Thus Ranelagh's relationship with Clarendon worked both ways, and she was able to give, as well as receive, political assistance.

However, there were also those who voiced concerns over the scope and scale of Ranelagh's involvement in politics. Part of this concern stemmed from basic and unavoidable facts. Ranelagh was not a politician, nor was she even a propertied male; in truth, she had no real base of power from which to be wielding political influence at all. And another part of this concern stemmed from lingering memories of Ranelagh's revolutionary associations with the Hartlib circle during the previous decades. What Ranelagh did have, however, was a very wide and deep circle of contacts, coupled with an enviable reputation. When combined with her unhesitating use of these in the furtherance of her goals, these factors made Ranelagh a political force to be reckoned with.

One imagines, however, that it may have been difficult to express these concerns to Ranelagh directly. It appears that even Clarendon, the Lord Chancellor, was concerned over her politicking. However, rather than confront Ranelagh herself, he had chosen to convey his opinion to her nephew Charles Clifford. Thus in 1667, Ranelagh's brother Richard received the following letter from his son Charles:

> I am told that my Lord Chancellor does not thinke it proper to have my Aunt Ranelaugh consulted with about what relates to the businesse of the country, but I would not upon any account that your Lordship should take notice of this to any boddy; but I thought it fitt (that haveing bin told such a thing) your Lordship may make so much use of this intimation, as to observe hereafter, whether it bee so or no.[41]

Burlington may or may not have chosen to pay more attention to his sister's politicking – but either way, this letter had few, if any, consequences in terms of curtailing Ranelagh's involvement in political affairs.

A 1681 letter from the Duke of Ormond to Henry Bennet, Lord Arlington, makes this clear. Ormond had two issues to address. First, Ormond was concerned that at this late date Ireland still retained some

---

[40] Ranelagh to Bishop Gilbert Burnet, July 13, 1689, Bodleian Library, MS. Add. A.191, f. 113. I am grateful to Dr. Ruth Connolly for this reference.

[41] Charles, Lord Clifford, to Richard Boyle, First Earl of Burlington, 1 June [1667], BL, Althorp Papers, B5.

traces of "projection" – the reforming and improving policies instituted there in the 1650s by the Hartlib circle, under the aegis of Henry Cromwell. He held Ranelagh's brother Orrery responsible for this, but Orrery was only the most visible layer of this problem. Ormond knew that the real engine behind this annoying holdover from the days of Hartlib was Orrery's indomitable sister Ranelagh, who was ensuring that these projects for Irish improvement would not be forgotten:

those tracings are kept as fresh as my Lady Ranelagh his sister can by her correspondence and influence on her family, which is great, even with her brother of Cork; as for the other branches she governs them very absolutely.[42]

Clearly, then, Ranelagh's willingness to make use of her "intimacy and power" with political figures – both family members and public figures like the Lord Chancellor – had not diminished one bit, and she still governed "absolutely".

As Ormond's letter also makes clear, Ranelagh was still devoted to the Hartlib circle's Irish improvement projects of the previous decades, and still active in their promotion. This is supported by material in the Petty Papers, which show Ranelagh's involvement in one of Sir William Petty's last projects. Petty, an old friend from the Hartlib days, was putting a new proposal together, based upon the maps he had produced for the Down Survey in the 1650s. In 1686, Ranelagh had requested that he send her these materials; Petty complied, writing: "Madam, I do in pure obedience, send you the papers, which I think you meane."[43] His letter apologized for the disorganized state of the papers in question, and then went on to say what it was that he hoped Ranelagh might be able to do with them:

Pray Madam, shew them onely to the true friends of the King Church of England & Emprovement of Ireland and if it bee possible, secure mee, against suffering for those 3 Interests.[44]

Petty was clearly aware that finding friends of this particular trio of interests – the King, the Church of England, and improvement of Ireland – was a somewhat tricky proposition. In fact, Ranelagh herself could scarcely have been called a friend to the Church of England. However, Petty was probably right in turning to her for protection; because, if

---

[42] Ormond to the Earl of Arlington, August 24, 1681, *Calendar of the Manuscripts of the Marquess of Ormond*, new series, vol. 6. Historical Manuscripts Commission, 1911, 137–8.
[43] William Petty to Lady Ranelagh, Petty Papers, BL, Add. MSS. 72,884, f. 4, CS. no. 10, *Speculum Hiberniae*. The letter itself is undated, but the materials referenced in the letter date to 1685–6.
[44] *Ibid.*

anyone could both promote and defend him for these interests, then Ranelagh was that person. She wrote back to reassure him of her help.

I have not Sir binn asleep about what you left me to think on & if you please to trust me by sending the paper you did me the favour to read to me by this bearer. I promise you I wil make noe ill use of it & if I can carry it on to a good accoumpt you shal heare it.[45]

Thus the legacy of Samuel Hartlib clearly lived on in the political acumen and activism of Ranelagh, as she continued to support projects for the improvement of Ireland.

Ranelagh died in 1691, followed one week later by her beloved brother Robert. And when Burnet delivered the funeral sermon for Boyle, he at the same time eulogized his incomparable sister Katherine. He began by recounting the touching circumstances of their lifelong devotion to each other:

His Sister and he were pleasant in their Lives, and in their Death they were not divided; for as he lived with her above Fourty years, so he did not outlive her above a Week.[46]

Burnet then proceeded to say what had made Ranelagh such a force on the seventeenth-century scene. He talked about her political acumen, and about her ability to make use of her vast web of connections in helping those whose causes she supported:

She lived the longest on the publickest Scene, she made the greatest Figure in all the Revolutions of these Kingdoms for above fifty Years, of any Woman of our Age ... She was indefatigable as well as dextrous in it: and as her great Understanding, and the vast Esteem she was in, made all Persons in their several turns of Greatness, desire and value her Friendship.

Burnet then concluded by praising the other side of Ranelagh – her intelligence, spirituality, and kindness:

She had with a vast Reach both of Knowledg and Apprehensions, an universal Affability and Easiness of Access, a Humility that descended to the meanest Persons and Concerns ... and with all these and many more excellent Qualities, she had the deepest Sense of Religion, and the most constant turning of her Thoughts and Discourses that way, that has been perhaps in our Age.[47]

This eulogy, rather than being an excuse for undeserved praise, seems to have been a fitting and accurate description of the life and career of the incomparable Lady Ranelagh.

---

[45] Ranelagh to Petty, Petty Papers, BL. Add. MSS. 72,884, ff. 5–6.
[46] *A Sermon Preached at the Funeral of the Honourable Robert Boyle*, 32–4.   [47] *Ibid.*

BATHSUA MAKIN (C.1600–C.1681)

Like Ranelagh, Makin continued living on the public scene to the end of her life. However, Makin did so in a very different way. Makin was first and foremost a scholar and teacher of languages. And although she and Ranelagh had many associates in common, Makin was also a widowed schoolteacher's daughter – thus her focus, in the decades following the Restoration, was always on earning a living. Yet Makin continued to be an ardent proponent of Comenian educational reform; and although she does not appear to have ever expressed an interest in politics *per se*, the political implications of Comenian pedagogy were inescapable. Makin, then, continued to teach with a foot in each world; and in addition to her tutoring for aristocratic patrons, Makin had also stayed in touch with her colleagues at the other end of the political spectrum.

Makin was part of a group of Comenian educational reformers, who were still trying to implement the new teaching methods Comenius had put forth in the 1640s and 1650s. John Pell and John Aubrey were loosely associated with this group, since Pell had been employed at Hartlib's short-lived school in Chichester in 1630; after the Restoration, the active members of the London Comenian group included Mark Lewis, Arthur Brett, Ezeral Tonge, and Bathsua Makin. But without the glue of the Hartlib circle's revolutionary activities as a focus, these Comenian educationalists would appear to have had almost nothing in common save their mutual interest in a reformation of learning. Mark Lewis (1622–81) was first and foremost a teacher and educational writer; although he was the vicar of Polstead, Suffolk, during the Commonwealth, he was ejected at the Restoration, and subsequently taught languages. Tonge, on the other hand, is known to history as a rabid anti-Catholic plotter, one of Titus Oates' co-conspirators in the Popish Plot.[48] And very little is known of the educator Arthur Brett beyond his authorship of two treatises on the reform of learning.[49]

The one thing this group did agree on was the need to promote Comenian educational methods. There were two major components to this approach: the practical and the philosophical. The practicality lay in the systematization of learning, with a focus on things, rather than words.

---

[48] On the machinations of the Popish Plot, see especially J. P. Kenyon, *The Popish Plot* (London, 1972).

[49] Brett the educator was the author of: *A demonstration how the Latine tongue may be learn't with far greater ease and speed then commonly it is* (London, 1669); and *A Model for a School for the better Education of Youth* (London, [1675?]). There was a poet named Arthur Brett, who was described by

As Makin explained: "The great Thing I design is, the Knowledge of things ... My opinion is, in the Educating of Gentlewomen, greater care ought to be had to know things, than to get words."[50] The philosophical component came from the method's a priori tenet that the desire to learn was innate and universal. And this philosophy, of course, must be considered political – because universal education meant educating all children, regardless of sex or social rank: "Not the children of the rich or of the powerful only, but of all alike, boys and girls, both noble and ignoble, rich and poor, in all cities and towns, villages and hamlets, should be sent to school."[51] Comenius had also asserted that no reasons, scriptural or otherwise, could be found for the exclusion of girls from higher learning:

Nor can any sufficient reason be given why the weaker sex ... should be altogether excluded from the pursuit of knowledge (whether in Latin or in their mother-tongue). They also are formed in the image of God, and share in His grace and in the kingdom of the world to come ... Why, therefore, should we admit them to the alphabet, and afterwards drive them away from books?[52]

Unlike van Schurman, however, Comenius was quite utilitarian. He approached the education of women in the same way that he approached the education of boys from the laboring classes. Thus Comenius did not advocate women learning for pure pleasure; instead, women should learn "those things which it becomes a woman to know and to do; that is to say, all that enables her to look after her household and to promote the welfare of her husband and her family."[53] The difficulty lay in finding a practical way to put these plans into action. Without a revolution to provide the political impetus, other reasons would have to be found for justifying this potentially explosive educational agenda.

Into the fray stepped Bathsua Makin. Her colleague van Schurman had paved the way in her *Dissertatio*. Van Schurman's argument had been based on the benefit that would ultimately accrue to the church from a cadre of theologically accomplished women; her mentor André Rivet had not been

---

Wood as "somewhat crazed"; however, this Brett, who died in 1677, may not be identical with the educator. See the old *DNB*, s.v. "Brett, Arthur.".

[50] Makin, *Essay*, 34–5. On the relationship of Makin's proposal to Comenian educational principles, see Jean Caravolas, "Bathsua Makin and Jan Amos Comenius," *Studia Comeniana et Historica* 26, nos. 55–6 (1996): 77–85.

[51] Jan Amos Comenius, *The Great Didactic: Setting forth The whole Art of Teaching all Things to all Men* [Amsterdam, 1657], ed. and trans. M.W. Keating (London, 1923), 66–8.

[52] *Ibid.*   [53] *Ibid.*

convinced, and his counter-arguments had provided the final word. However, Rivet had also left one possible door open for women's education:

But before you persuade me, I should like you to establish for me colleges of learned women, in whose academies the maidens whom you would dedicate to these studies would be refined. For you yourself would not readily admit that all these women might be self-taught or have parents at home who would themselves undertake this responsibility, as happily befell you.[54]

Van Schurman was not an educator; thus she could not and would not found "colleges of learned women," as Rivet had asked. Her argument had been based instead on history, the Bible, and the two most highly learned women she knew at that time – herself, and Marie de Gournay, her feminist role model and *mère d'alliance*. Rivet was well aware of this fact, and had used it as the basis for his counter-argument: Gournay had been the one who was "self-taught," while van Schurman had been the beneficiary of the parents who agreed to "undertake this responsibility." Her friend Makin, however, had spent a lifetime in education, and had a wealth of experience on which to draw. Thus it was Makin who would pick up the gauntlet Rivet had thrown down before van Schurman.

The result was Makin's 1673 treatise, *An Essay to Revive the Antient Education of Gentlewomen, in Religion, Manners, Arts & Tongues*. Makin's feminism was evident throughout, and she was explicit about what she hoped to accomplish for women:

I hope some of these Considerations will at least move some of this abused Sex to set a right value upon themselves; according to the dignity of their Creation, that they might, with an honest pride and magnanimity, scorn to be bowed down and made to stoop to such Follies and Vanities, Trifles and Nothings, so far below them, and unproportionable to their noble Souls, nothing inferior to those of Men.[55]

Clearly, then, Makin's agenda for change encompassed much more than curriculum alone. Comenius had argued for women learning "those things which it becomes a woman to know and to do." Makin, on the other hand, argued for women learning everything:

I cannot tell where to begin to admit Women, nor from what part of Learning to exclude them, in regard of their Capacities. The whole Encyclopedeia of Learning may be useful some way or other to them.[56]

---

[54] Rivet to van Schurman, March 18, 1638, in *Opuscula*, 88. Translation by Joyce Irwin in van Schurman, *Whether a Christian Woman*, 53.
[55] Makin, *Essay*, 41–2.   [56] Makin, *Essay*, 24.

This was precisely what van Schurman had proposed in the *Dissertatio*. But as they acquired this encyclopedic knowledge, Makin's young gentlewomen would still need to acquire the skills to which Comenius had referred, the ones that were necessary for running a household. The voice of the Objector, the anti-feminist interrogator Makin had created for her *Essay*, pointed out that this presented an insurmountable problem:

Boyes go to School ordinarily from seven till sixteen or seventeen ... Gentlewomen will not ordinarily be sent out so soon, nor is it convenient they should continue so long. Further, half their time, it is supposed, must be spent in learning those things that concern them as Women. Twice as many things are proposed to be taught Girls in half the time, as Boyes do learn, which is impossible.[57]

The Objector had a good point. Makin had indeed proposed that the girls in her school would learn twice as much as boys do, in half the time – literally quadrupling the scholarly pace of their brothers. Makin's answer in this case was not gendered, but Comenian:

Let no Body be afrighted, because so many things are to be learnt, when the learning of them will be so pleasant; how profitable I need not tell you. If any doubt how this may be done, or what Authors we shall use ... I Answer, Comenius hath prepared Nomenclatures for this purpose.

This was followed by an explication of Comenius' *Orbis Pictus* and *Janua Linguarum*.[58] But, again like van Schurman, Makin stopped far short of Comenian democracy in education; this proposal was appropriate only for "gentlewomen," and was not for the daughters of the poor.

As a treatise on educating women, Makin's *Essay* had quite a lot of company in the 1670s. Some of these treatises had very similar titles, and would at first glance appear to be making similar arguments. However, they were often written for very different reasons; and despite their purported stances in favor of women's education, some were arguing for reducing, rather than expanding, the curriculum. By the 1670s, in England and on the Continent, the wars and revolutions of the mid-century had for the most part been resolved; Charles II in England and Louis XIV in France sought to centralize national power and reestablish order. Egalitarianism, radical doubt, and reformations of learning were no longer included in the mix at the higher levels of the academy, or even of the republic of letters.

---

[57] Makin, *Essay*, 36.   [58] Makin, *Essay*, 36–7.

Thus in 1673, when the French Cartesian François Poulain de la Barre published *De l'Egalité des deux sexes*, and followed it up in 1675 with a treatise arguing for women's full access to higher education, the moment of possible acceptance for his ideas had already passed.[59] Although he stated that the letters Elisabeth had exchanged with Descartes should be required reading for women interested in philosophy, Poulain took Cartesian philosophy to a place that Descartes himself had never visited. Arguing from a platform of Cartesian dualism, Poulain declared unambiguously that the minds and spirits of women did not differ from those of men; and in what would later become a rallying cry for feminist philosophy, Poulain stated: "The Mind has no sex."[60] Despite the fact that this moment of Cartesian possibility was over, Poulain's treatise was quickly translated into English, appearing in London in 1677 under the title of *The Woman As Good as The Man: or, The equallity of both sexes . . .*[61]

However, the London political and cultural scene was no more welcoming than that of Paris. So when his first two feminist treatises failed to generate a fruitful debate on women's rights, Poulain had followed them up with a third, purporting to argue the opposite position; however, this facetious work, "On the Excellence of Men Against the Equality of the Sexes," also failed to find its audience.[62] Clement Barksdale, whom we have already encountered as the translator of van Schurman's *Dissertatio*, also published his own ideas on women's education in 1675 in a pamphlet entitled *A Letter Touching a Colledge of Maids*.[63] Given Barksdale's evident admiration for van Schurman, one might have thought that his pamphlet would have reflected the influence of the *Dissertatio*, perhaps rendering van Schurman's ideas into an Anglicized context. However, this was not

---

[59] Erica Harth dates the end of this moment to 1666, the founding of the Académie Royale des Sciences, with its policy enforcing the official exclusion of women. Harth, *Cartesian Women*, 139. See François Poulain de la Barre, *De l'Egalité des deux sexes: Discours physique et moral où l'on voit l'importance de se défaire des préjugez* (Paris, 1673); and idem, *De l'Education des dames pour la conduite de l'esprit dans les sciences et dans les moeurs* (Paris, 1674).

[60] "L'Esprit n'a point de sexe." Poulain de la Barre, *De l'Egalité des deux sexes*, 1673, part II. On Poulain and his influence on the development of feminist thought see especially Stuurman, *François Poulain de la Barre*. See also Marie Louise Stock, "Poulain de la Barre: A Seventeenth-Century Feminist" (Ph.D. dissertation, Columbia University, 1961).

[61] François Poulain de la Barre, *The Woman As Good as The Man: or, The equallity of both sexes written originally in French and translated into English by A. L.* (London, 1677).

[62] François Poulain de la Barre, *De l'Excellence des hommes contre l'égalite des sexes* (Paris, 1675).

[63] Clement Barksdale, *A Letter Touching A Colledge of Maids, or, a Virgin-Society. Written Aug. 12, 1675* (London, 1675). Barksdale's translation of van Schurman was published in 1659 as *The Learned Maid or, Whether a Maid may be a Scholar. A Logick Exercise* (London, 1659).

Barksdale's intent. In fifteen itemized paragraphs, he laid out his ideas for this "Colledge," but there was no mention of learning until Item Ten. There he considered books for the library; this was followed by a discussion of the arts of music, dancing, and drawing in Item Eleven, while Item Twelve focused on the availability of philosophical studies and "some of the easier Experiments in Natural things."[64]

The most useful comparison, however, might be between Bathsua Makin's 1673 *Essay* and a 1671 treatise by Edward Chamberlayne, entitled: *An Academy or Colledge: Wherein Young Ladies and Gentlewomen May . . . be duly instructed.*[65] Based on the curricular focus alone, these two treatises could not possibly be more different. Makin's treatise spent forty-three pages arguing that women should have access to the "whole Encyclopedeia of Learning." Chamberlayne, on the other hand, used only one paragraph to sketch out the planned studies:

Moreover, there will come at due times the best and ablest Teachers in London for Singing, Dancing, Musical Instruments, Writing, French Tongue, Fashionable Dresses, all sorts of Needle-Works; for Confectionary, Cookery, Pastery; for Distilling of Waters . . .[66]

It was a list that bore an uncanny similarity to the useless gentlewoman's education that Dorothy Moore had so bitterly deplored in her own educational treatise, written decades earlier. The aim of Chamberlayne's Academy was to prepare young gentlewomen for marriage, and to preserve them in a state of chastity until the occurrence of that event. Thus it would appear that the educational pendulum for women had swung back fifty years, to where it had rested in the decades before the Civil War.

Yet despite the enormous differences between Makin and Chamberlayne in terms of their ideas about women's education, the similarities in these two treatises are actually far more instructive. They tell us a great deal about the Restoration context for these discussions, and about the practical considerations being faced by professional educators. Both Makin and Chamberlayne situated their treatises historically, hearkening back to the sixteenth century. For Chamberlayne, this had been a gentler, more virtuous age, when the English Lady's "taciturnity" had been

---

[64] Barksdale, *A Colledge of Maids*, n.p.
[65] Edward Chamberlayne, *An Academy or Colledge: Wherein Young Ladies and Gentlewomen May at a very moderate Expence be duly instructed in the true Protestant Religion, and in all Vertuous Qualities that may adorn that Sex: also be carefully preserved, and secured, till the day of their Marriage . . .* (London, 1671). Edward Chamberlayne (1616–1703) was made a Fellow of the Royal Society in 1668.
[66] *Ibid.*, 6.

prominent among her assets.[67] But for Makin, as for van Schurman, the gentlewomen of the Tudor age had been eminent for precisely the opposite reason – far from being taciturn and retiring, they had been highly educated and outspoken in defence of their right to be so. In this view of the "Antient Education of Gentlewomen," Makin and van Schurman were joined by the linguist William Wotton, who wrote of that age that: "there are no Accounts in History of so many very great Women in any one Age, as are to be found between the Years 15 and 1600." As Wotton put it:

When Learning first came up . . . It was so very modish, that the fair sex seemed to believe that Greek and Latin added to their Charms; and Plato and Aristotle untranslated, were frequent Ornaments of their Closets.[68]

The strongest link between these two treatises, however, emerges only when we consider what *kind* of publications they were. Because these were not just essays, nor were they merely pamphlets – they were, in fact, advertising brochures.

Chamberlayne's *Academy* is perhaps the more explicit of the two. Out of ten total pages, four are devoted to a detailed explanation of how interested readers could subscribe to the proposed school, have their investments guaranteed, and have their names "registred and recorded in a fair Velome Book."[69] Then there was a list of persons to contact:

If therefore any Honourable and Worthy Persons desire that their Daughters, or any trustees, that their Orphans, should be admitted Commoners or Pensioners of this Colledge . . . let them repair either to Mr. Horn a Stationer at the South-side of the Royal Exchange, to Mr. Martyn a Stationer at the Bell in St. Pauls Churchyard . . . [etc.]

In all, Chamberlayne's list named six stationers who could provide information in various parts of London.[70]

Makin's *Essay*, on the other hand, had been designed to serve more than one purpose, so she took much longer to reach this same businesslike point. For one thing, the *Essay* was also a treatise on the application of Comenian methods, on learning languages through "things, not words." Yet these pedagogical proposals were not new; they had been under discussion in various iterations of Hartlib's and Comenius' networks since

[67] *Ibid.*, 1–2.
[68] William Wotton, *Reflections Upon Ancient and Modern Learning* (London, 1694), 349–50. Wotton (1666–1727) was a fellow of the Royal Society, and Gilbert Burnet became his patron.
[69] Chamberlayne, *An Academy*, 10.   [70] *Ibid.*, 6–7.

the 1630s. And her catalogue of female *exempla* was not new – it was yet another take on the "female worthy" catalogues that had been periodically published since Boccaccio's *Concerning Famous Women* in the fourteenth century. What clearly *was* new was her attachment of these Comenian proposals to a strongly worded argument for women's educational rights. And in a forty-three-page pamphlet, this feminist disquisition took up thirty-six pages – over eighty-three percent of the work. Yet beyond its feminist argument, Makin's *Essay* is important as evidence for what may have been the last gasp of the Hartlib circle, and its practice of corporate authorship.

There are entire passages in the pedagogical portions of Makin's *Essay* which are identical to passages in the work of her fellow London educationalist, Mark Lewis. This does not mean, however, that we are looking at a case of early modern plagiarism; nor, as has recently been alleged, does this indicate that either Lewis or Brett had in fact been the true author of Makin's anonymously-published *Essay*.[71] What we are looking at instead is a series of productions emerging from a small community of Comenian educationalists, all working and publishing collaboratively on different aspects of the same project.

The evidence comes from that portion of Makin's *Essay* wherein she finally reached her more businesslike point. There, in the Postscript, she began to sound very much like Chamberlayne:

> If any enquire where this Education may be performed, such may be informed, That a School is lately erected for Gentlewomen at Tottenham-high-Cross, within four miles of London, in the Road to Ware; where Mris. Makin is Governess, who was sometimes Tutoress to the Princess Elizabeth, Daughter to King Charles the First.

The "Rate certain" for the school was set at £20 per annum. And she had her own set of instructions for those who might be interested:

> Those that think these Things Improbable or Impracticable, may have further account every Tuesday at Mr. Masons Coffe-House in Cornhil, near the Royal Exchange; and Thursdayes at the Bolt and Tun in Fleetstreet, between the hours of three and six in the Afternoons, by some Person whom Mrs. Makin shall appoint.[72]

---

[71] Malcolm and Stedall, *John Pell*, 232. However, Malcolm does not refer to the thirty-six-page feminist argument preceding the incriminating passages, other than to take Makin's statement "I am a Man" at face value.

[72] Makin, *Essay*, 42–3.

The *Essay's* anonymous author did not name the person whom Mrs. Makin would be appointing to act as her agent for this proposed school. However, an earlier reference in the *Essay* tells us who this must have been.

> Those that do not understand these short hints, may peruse a *Grammar* and an *Apology*, to which is added *Rules for Pointing and Reading Grammatically*, Composed by M. Lewis ... Or they may speak with M. Lewis himself any Thursday in the Afternoon, between three and six of the Clock, at the Bolt and Tun in Fleetstreet.[73]

Thus the educationalist Mark Lewis was going to be at the Bolt and Tun every Thursday between three and six – and coincidentally, this was the precise time and place appointed for meeting Mrs. Makin's unnamed agent.

Moreover, if we turn to Mark Lewis, and the final page of his *Plain and Short Rules*, we find the following instructions:

> Those, that desire to see more of this Subject, may consult a *Grammar*, and an *Apology*, composed by M. Lewis ... or they may be further satisfied by the Author, upon any Thursday at three of the Clock in the After-noon, at the Tun and Bolt in Fleet-street.[74]

So apart from the fact that the Bolt and Tun had now become the Tun and Bolt, Lewis' business arrangement at the tavern was precisely the same as Makin's – Thursday afternoons at three o'clock, in the tavern on Fleet Street. Lewis repeats the instructions, albeit in a somewhat more challenging fashion, in his *Essay to Facilitate the Education of Youth*:

> Any that desire it, may find me at the *Tun* and *Bolt* in *Fleetstreet*, any *Thursday* in the Afternoon, from three till six of the Clock. If I cannot give a fair Answer to what shall be alleadged, I promise to recant.[75]

It is clear, then, that Mark Lewis, the author of these grammatical texts, was Makin's partner in a proposed double school for gentlemen and gentlewomen.

---

[73] *Ibid.*, 41. Makin is referring to: Mark Lewis, *Institutio Grammaticæ Puerilis: or the Rudiments of the Latin and Greek Tongues, Fitted to Childrens capacities, as an Introduction to larger Grammars* (London, 1670); *An Apologie for a Grammar Printed about Twenty Years Since, by M. Lewis and Reprinted for the Use of a Private School at Tottenham High Cross* (London, 1671); and *Plain, and short Rules for Pointing Periods, and Reading Sentences Grammatically, with the great Use of them* (London, [1675?]).

[74] Lewis, *Plain, and short Rules*, 8.

[75] Lewis, *An Essay to Facilitate the Education of Youth, by Bringing down the Rudiments of Grammar to the sense of Seeing, which ought to be improv'd by Sincrisis* ... (London, 1674).

Thus Makin's *Essay*, like the proposed school itself, was a hybrid. She wrote the feminist disquisition, while Mark Lewis wrote the grammatical passages. As such, the *Essay* is also a link to the halcyon days of Makin's network of intellectual women – because Makin's unique contribution to this publication, and to her London circle, was the voice of her impatient, insistent feminism, and her repeated references to her colleague van Schurman. Poulain de la Barre was both more rigorous and more systematic; but Makin's was the first work by a woman to argue in English for women's full access to the "whole Encyclopaedia of Learning."

We unfortunately do not know whether Makin's school was ever operational. We do, however, have two final letters from Makin, dated 1675 and 1681, wherein she was displaying her skills in Latin, Greek, and Hebrew, and clearly seeking patronage. Thus if the school had opened, it must have failed by 1675; and as evidenced by Makin's letter to Boyle in 1681, she was still using her scholarly skill to earn her living at the age of eighty.[76] There is no further trace of Bathsua Makin in the historical record.

The following sections discuss Marie du Moulin, Anna Maria van Schurman, and Princess Elisabeth, who in the end chose a different path from Makin, Moore, Ranelagh, and Gournay – and rather than scrambling to remain viable on "the publick scene" after 1660, they constructed protected intellectual communities in which to pursue their scholarship.

MARIE DU MOULIN (C.1613–99)

Unlike Makin, Moore, and Ranelagh, Marie du Moulin never lived in the British Isles. She was an expatriate French Protestant, living in the Netherlands; thus for Marie it was the Revocation of the Edict of Nantes in 1685 that finally led her to establish a protected community for like-minded women.

This is not to say that Marie was unaffected by events in the British Isles. With the Restoration, Marie's brothers Peter du Moulin and Louis du Moulin, who were both living and working in England, found their fortunes reversed. Louis, the intransigent Independent, was out of favor, while Peter, the Royalist, found his star on the ascendant. He succeeded

---

[76] Makin wrote a letter to Baldwin Hamey of the Royal College of Physicians in 1675. Like the poem she addressed to Robert Boyle, this letter was probably intended to secure employment or patronage. Bathsua Makin to Baldwin Hamey, November 22, 1675, Royal College of Physicians, Papers of Baldwin Hamey, MS. 310, article 84, f. 119.

his father Pierre as Prebendary of Canterbury on June 29, 1660, and Marie travelled to Canterbury to enjoy the dual celebration of Peter's promotion and the coronation of Charles II.[77] She had already met Charles once before, when he had been in Breda around 1651. By that time, Peter du Moulin was known to be the author of the anonymous *Regii sanguinis clamor*, as well as two other Royalist works. As Peter would later describe the scene in Breda, a grateful monarch, highly aware of the debt he owed to this loyal apologist, had approached the author's sister:

And it was so well ressented by his majesty, then at Breda, that, being shewed my sister Mary among a great company of ladies, he brake the crowd to salute her, and tell her that he was very sensible of his obligations to her brother, and that if ever God settled him in his kingdom, he would make him know that he was a grateful Prince.[78]

For Peter, Charles was as good as his word; but as evidenced by a letter Marie wrote to the Queen of Bohemia in October of that same year, things were not going to go quite as well for their brother Louis.

The timing of Marie's letter, dated October 16/26, suggests that it had probably been occasioned by Louis' disappointment and concern following the King's declaration of toleration. The Declaration of Breda had been issued in April 1660, while Charles was still abroad, and because of its adroit combination of conciliatory language and hazy details it was known as "Hyde's masterpiece." The declaration of October was actually one of several that eventually led up to what would come to be known as the Clarendon Code – a series of acts, erroneously attributed to Clarendon, that harshly penalized Dissenters from the Church of England. Louis du Moulin must certainly have been hoping for more. Charles had been somewhat conciliatory, in that he promised amnesty to all but the regicides, and he had been somewhat tolerant of those who did not adhere to the Church of England. However, the declaration of October officially established a moderate Anglican church, with an episcopate.

For the fiercely anti-episcopal Louis, this represented no freedom at all. He turned to his sister Marie for help, and she turned to her old network

---

[77] According to Pierre Bayle, Peter du Moulin's "incomparable sister" Marie went to Canterbury again in 1678 for a long visit, staying with her brother for six months. Pierre Bayle to Jacob Bayle, November 26, 1678, letter no. 160 in Bayle, *Correspondance*, III, 80–100.

[78] "Remarkable Paper in Dr. Du Moulin's own Hand-writing, never before printed," in *The Gentleman's Magazine*, v. 43 (August, 1773): 369–70. According to the contributor of this piece, one "J. D.," the account was found inserted in a copy of Peter's *Histoire des Nouveaux Presbyteriens Anglais et Escossois, Seconde Edition* (1660).

from the exile court in The Hague. Marie wrote to Elizabeth of Bohemia, the mother of her friend Princess Elisabeth:

I must thank Your Majesty for two things; the first is for the fact that she deigned to write back to me in her own hand, and the second is for the fact that she did not see fit to write to the Chancellor concerning my brother's affair. For no sooner had I requested this than I began to repent it, because my brother's affairs having undergone an about-face, as it were, he regretted having begged Your Majesty's favor for something that he hopes to have by another means . . . [79]

This letter is certainly intriguing for what it does not say: we do not know the content of Marie's earlier letter to Elizabeth; we do not know the precise nature of Louis' problem; and we do not know what favor was originally requested. What we do learn from this letter, however, is that the intellectual circle from the exile court in The Hague was continuing to function as a network of influence and support, despite enormous changes in the surrounding world.

Further evidence comes from correspondence between Marie du Moulin and Constantijn Huygens. Marie had apparently been trying to use her old connections to find a place at court in The Hague for an unnamed gentleman that Huygens refers to only as her "young Philosopher." While Huygens was unable to help in this instance, the problem was merely one of timing; and in fact he encouraged Marie to continue sending people to him:

After they have passed through your filter, I am well aware of what is owed to their merit, and do not only willingly allow you to furnish me with men of your choice, but even beg you to do so, being well assured that I can only profit and learn from it [but] . . . We can hardly take on the maintenance of your Philosopher, since you see that the Electress is getting ready to leave. Besides, I assure myself that you have found him a good position at her court.[80]

While the identity of this unemployed young philosopher remains a mystery, this letter shows that Marie was still regularly in touch with Huygens, as well as with other former members of the circle at The Hague, trying to help out those in need of positions at court. It was a list that included van Schurman and Utricia Swann-Ogle, in addition to the women of the Palatine house. Moreover, Marie had apparently been

---

[79] Marie du Moulin to Elizabeth, Queen of Bohemia, dated Canterbury, October 16/26, [1660], BL, Add. MSS 18,744, f. 29. Original in French.
[80] Constantijn Huygens to Marie du Moulin, April 14, 1667. From Huygens' French letterbook, 1667–87, KB MS. KA 49–3, ff. 33–4. A minute of this letter, in Dutch, is no. 6604 in *De Briefwisseling van Constantijn Huygens*, VI, 209.

able to negotiate a position for this young man at the Brandenburg court –
and her connection to that court could only have been Princess Elisabeth.
Although Elisabeth, by this date, was no longer at the Brandenburg court
herself, she had presumably put in a good word for Marie's "*jeune
Philosophe*" before leaving for Herford.

Yet in addition to the quality that Huygens praised – Marie's "noble
desire" to help her friends in any way possible – Marie also continued to
work as a writer and a scholar. And throughout the 1670s, she continued
to publish. She issued new editions of her tract on education, and there is
an intriguing reference in the Bayle correspondence to a possible fourth
publication by Marie du Moulin. It is also a reference that gives
us an indication of why Marie might have chosen to keep publishing
anonymously. Bayle wrote to Jacques Basnage in 1675, trying to explain
the delays in dealing with Marie's manuscript. It was circulating through
many hands, as she tried to obtain a *Privilège* to have it published in
France:

> I had thought I would be able to give an answer this very day to Mlle. du Moulin,
> and toward that end I did everything I could to speak with M. Conrart.
> However, I was not able to do so ... All I can tell him on the subject of the
> manuscript was that it remains in my hands, that I had received it from
> M. Boursier, and M. Palloys had asked him to keep it to give to M. du Frene.
> It remains to see Messieurs Charpentier and Mezeray for the approval, which
> M. Gallois discusses in the letter that Mlle. du Moulin sent to me.[81]

The manuscript in question does not appear to be extant. But given the
fact that Bayle needs to discuss the issue with Valentin Conrart, it seems
likely that Marie's new manuscript would have been based on her 1646
correspondence with Conrart and Madeleine de Scudéry regarding van
Schurman and the reputation of Joan of Arc.[82]

What is abundantly clear, however, is the nearly impenetrable maze of
approvals required in order for Huguenot authors to get their works
published in France. In this letter, Bayle names six people who were
involved in trying to obtain the license, in addition to Conrart himself.
But even the aged founding secretary of the *Académie française* was unable
to get the task done, and it appears this work was never published. Thus

---

[81] Pierre Bayle to Jacques Basnage, letter 90 in Bayle, *Correspondance*, II, 159–66.

[82] Elisabeth Labrousse has argued that since Marie du Moulin's educational treatise was published by
the Elseviers in 1679 as *De l'éducation des enfans*, this was the manuscript whose licensing problems
were being discussed in Bayle's letter; however, that treatise had already appeared in 1654.
Labrousse, "Marie du Moulin, Educatrice,", 261–3; and Bayle, *Correspondance*, II, 63–4.

in this case the fact that the author was a woman appears to have had very little bearing on the practicalities of publishing.

In other cases, however, Marie's identity as a woman appears to have had a great deal to do with her work as a writer. In 1679, Marie produced a new edition of her tract on education, with a completely different preface. Unlike the preface of the 1654 edition, in which Marie had apologized for her archaic French and bad memory, this version talked specifically about women, and apologized for nothing:

This little treatise was created for the use of a Great Princess, who wished to have the advice of a person whom she respected on the early education of her son. That person believed she had satisfied this request by addressing those years during which Princes are customarily placed under the care of women. If these remarks might be of service to those women who have, or will have, Princes to raise, then she will have received all the satisfaction from it that she wanted.[83]

Then, as she continued, Marie pointed out why it made sense for a woman to be writing on this subject, rather than a man who might admittedly be much more learned:

In our times, a number of great men have published various treatises on this subject, which have most assuredly been more enriched with learning and eloquence; but I do not know whether you will find among them a single writer who is more seriously focused on studying early childhood, or one who has more experience in that which is practiced among the nobility in educating their children.[84]

Marie was no longer apologizing for her weaknesses. Now she was seizing those same characteristics – her gender, and her lack of formal schooling – and claiming that they constituted her strengths. They were now the qualities that had led to her superior job performance, and her recognition by that "Great Princess" whom she had served.

There was no dedicatee for this 1679 edition. Mary Stuart, who had commissioned the original treatise while awaiting the birth of the future William III, had died of smallpox in 1660. But her cousins, Princess Elisabeth and Princess Sophie, were still active and still part of Marie du Moulin's life; and her daughter-in-law, another Mary, Princess of Orange, became the patron for Marie's Société des Dames françaises de Harlem.

The Société was founded in 1683, as French persecution of the Huguenot population increased in the lead-up to the Revocation. The Marquis de Venours, a refugee from Poitou, saw the need to take care of the

---

[83] [Du Moulin], *De l'éducation des enfans*, n.p.   [84] *Ibid.*

unmarried noblewomen who had been left without homes or resources. The original proposition of January 30, 1683, called for "the establishment of a society for French Protestant women, to enable them to live communally without making any vows or anything else that approaches or feels like papist superstition." The focus was therefore on helping noblewomen who were religious refugees. Madame du Noyer, on the other hand – a Protestant who had converted to Catholicism in the wake of the Revocation – described the foundation somewhat unkindly as a home for "astres sur le couchant."[85]

The first provisional directress of the foundation was Venours' daughter, but she immediately chose to put the Société de Harlem in more capable hands. She prevailed upon Marie du Moulin, who had just taken up residence there, to take over the directorship, and Marie proved to be an inspired choice. The immediate problem, of course, was money. When Marie took over, there were only 8 *livres* and 3 *sous* in their coffers.[86] At that point, Marie immediately went to work. She turned to the Dutch government, pointing out that, although the Société charged a nominal sum to the women who lived there, most had no way of paying it. This appeal was successful; the foundation was granted 2,000 florins a year through 1726, although after that point the subsidy would be reduced incrementally as the ladies died.[87]

In addition to asking for help from the Dutch government, Marie immediately moved to make contact with her old circle from The Hague. By April 1684, her project had a patron in Mary, Princess of Orange, who promised the Société 1,000 *livres* a year for the duration of her life.[88] This Princess Mary was the daughter-in-law of the "great princess" who had first commissioned Marie du Moulin's tract on education. Marie also turned to Princess Elisabeth's sister, the former Princess Sophie (now Duchess of Brunswick and Lüneburg), recalling their days at the exile court, and the time she had spent with the princesses in The Hague:

---

[85] Madame du Noyer, *Memoires*, in *Lettres historiques et galantes* (London, 1757). Cited in Labrousse, "Marie du Moulin, Educatrice," 261. On the foundation, see Allégret, "Société." The institution flourished from 1683 to 1770.

[86] *Ibid.*, 518.

[87] "Résolutions Prises par les États Généraux, les États de Hollande et de West-Frise, la Commission Permanente de ces états, ainsi, que par le Conseil d'État en faveur des réfugiés," *Bulletin de la Commission de l'Histoire des églises wallonnes*, vol. 4 (1890): 317.

[88] The Princess of Orange was also the patron of similar institutions in Schiedam, Rotterdam, and The Hague. Allégret, "Société," 319.

It was with a sense of extraordinary humility that I was admitted to the Royal House of Bohemia, where the Queen gave me liberal access to her Person; as did all Your Highnesses, with such great kindheartedness that the memory of so many favors still gives me the courage to address myself to Your Highness in order to beg from you the help and consolations that we are seeking in every place where power and goodwill are fortuitously joined together.[89]

The letter then went on to describe the destitute condition of widowed and single women in the *réfuge*, Marie's project to help them, and – most importantly – their desperate need for patronage and financial support. These destitute Huguenots were noblewomen, who had never before had to earn a living. According to Marie, this made their situation even more desperate than that of the artisans, who could at least take their skills with them into exile.[90] Again, the network from the exile court appears to have come through, and Sophie joined Princess Mary in supporting their friend Marie du Moulin and her foundation. Sophie's patronage ended only with her death in 1714.[91]

   Bayle tells us that Marie du Moulin died in The Hague in February, 1699, at the age of eighty-six.[92] We do not know where she had been living at the time, or with whom. Yet the extant evidence of Marie's life after 1660 gives us ample evidence of the strength and adaptability of the network of intellectual women that had formed at the exile court in The Hague in the 1630s – a network that continued to be active and supportive for over fifty years. And when the consequences of religious persecution were such that women like Marie du Moulin needed to seek refuge in a cloister-like environment, Marie was able to make her cloister thrive through her old connections to the exile court. That network had included Anna Maria van Schurman, who had also used these connections to establish and direct a cloister-like community at the end of the seventeenth century.

ANNA MARIA VAN SCHURMAN (1607–78)

Van Schurman's directorship of a cloistered community, like that of Marie du Moulin, cannot be characterized merely as a retreat into a protected environment – because like her *sœur d'alliance*, van Schurman

---

[89] Marie du Moulin to the Duchess of Brunswick and Lüneburg, June 29, 1687, BL, King's MSS 140, f. 141b.
[90] *Ibid.*   [91] Allégret, "Société," 560.
[92] Bayle, *Dictionnaire historique et critique*, III, 478.

continued to stay active in her intellectual life and in her connections to the old circle from The Hague. Instead, these communities are more usefully seen as gender-specific adaptations to the vastly narrowed intellectual and spiritual landscape that confronted female scholars at the end of the seventeenth century.

For van Schurman, this was also a function of having made what she called *Eukleria*, or "the right choice." Throughout the preceding decades, van Schurman had been increasingly retreating from the public intellectual scene of the republic of letters, as she moved through her personal spiritual evolution; and in this regard, her choice had very little to do with changes in the surrounding culture of scholarship. In the end, van Schurman's path was the result of a combination of factors, both internal and external, as her spiritual journey interacted with the loss of the larger supportive structure that had been the mid-century republic of letters.

The catalyst that brought these internal and external factors together – a catalyst that also managed to draw the attention of John Dury, Jan Amos Comenius, Robert Boyle, and Princess Elisabeth – was the fiery, controversial, and visionary mystic Jean de Labadie. Throughout his chequered career, the peripatetic mystic Jean de Labadie had remained physically and doctrinally elusive. As he lurched from one religious identity to another – Jesuit, Jansenist, Calvinist, Pietist, Chiliast, and finally "Labadist" – he was constantly on the run from ecclesiastical authorities. Outraged by his serial betrayals of their teachings, church officials chased him out of Guyenne, Paris, Amiens, Port-Royal, Bazas, Montauban, Orange, Geneva, Utrecht, Middelburg, Amsterdam, and Herford, until death finally tracked him down in Altona, Denmark.

Jean de Labadie was born in 1610 in the town of Guyenne in south-west France.[93] He was sent to study with the Jesuits at the age of seven, and he immediately began to draw attention for his intense spirituality and prodigious knowledge of scripture. By his early twenties, however, he began to make his superiors uncomfortable with his visions of going into the wilderness with a band of apostles, "without bag or staff, in absolute nudity, poverty and suffering; preaching, confounding and converting souls."[94] This brought an end to his association with the Jesuits, and by

---

[93] The bulk of this biographical sketch is taken from what is to date the only monograph available on Jean de Labadie – Trevor Saxby's extremely valuable *The Quest for the New Jerusalem: Jean de Labadie and the Labadists, 1610–1744* (Dordrecht, 1987). See also the chapter on Labadie in Michel de Certeau's lyrical examination of mystic discourse, *The Mystic Fable*, trans. Michael B. Smith (Chicago, 1992).

[94] Jean de Labadie, *Relation touchant le P. Jean Labadie*, in Saxby, *New Jerusalem*, 12, 397–8.

1639, Labadie was a Jansenist. It was also in that year that the first accusations arose concerning Labadie's relationships with spiritual women, and he was accused of a dalliance with a Benedictine nun. Then in 1646, his earlier writings, wherein he had expressed the longing for complete spiritual "nudity," resurfaced in an accusation that he was requiring the women of the couvent des Tiercerettes to strip naked in order to attain a state of original innocence. He was suspended from his duties, and began a two-year period of solitude and meditation. During this period, he developed his chiliasm, and cemented his devotion to the first church. When he returned from his solitude in 1650 he abjured, deciding that his quest for reinstating the apostolic church actually fit much more closely with the tenets of Calvinism.

Looking for a new position, Labadie began to write to English Independents, including Moore's husband John Dury. The response from England was quite positive, and when Dury passed Labadie's letters to John Milton, the magisterial Puritan poet wrote back to inform Labadie of a vacancy in the French Independent church at Westminster. Milton had begun his letter to Labadie by blaming the delay of his reply on Dury; however, the delay had proved providential, since now the old minister of the French Independent Church had died, and "the most influential men in that congregation, knowing that you are far from safe where you are, are most anxious to have you chosen to succeed him, and do indeed extend that invitation to you."[95] In the end, however, Labadie decided instead to go to Geneva. There, because of his fiery preaching, he became known as "a second Calvin."[96]

It was in Geneva, in 1662, that the physician Johann Godschalk van Schurman attended a sermon preached by the charismatic Labadie. He was deeply moved, and wrote enthusiastic letters to his sister Anna Maria, telling her of Labadie's eloquence, zeal, and ideas for a second reformation of the church. Responding to the urging of her brother, van Schurman began her own correspondence with Labadie the following year. They continued writing to one another, and when Labadie became the pastor of the Walloon church in Middelburg, van Schurman made a pilgrimage each year from Utrecht to hear him preach. She would stay for several months at a time, bringing with her a company of other women. And

---

[95] John Milton to Jean de Labadie, April 21 or 27, 1659. Latin text in *The Life Records of John Milton*, ed. J. Milton French, 5 vols. (New Brunswick, NJ, 1956), IV, 259–61. Translation in *Milton: Private Correspondence*, 47–8.

[96] Saxby, *New Jerusalem*, 98–101.

from this point on, the record of Jean de Labadie and of Labadism itself is completely entwined with that of Anna Maria van Schurman.

On a practical level, this proved quite fortuitous for the difficult Labadie. Van Schurman had social status, influential friends, and an enviable reputation for learning and piety. It was through van Schurman's influence and connections, as well as through her skill as a writer, that Labadie would be able to establish his various communes over the last ten years of his life. However, this was an arrangement that was put immediately to the test, as Labadie managed to get himself ejected from Middelburg in 1669. This ejection was due, in part, to Labadie's conflict with another of Marie du Moulin's brothers, Henri du Moulin. When Milton had written to Labadie in 1659, he had also conveyed thanks and greetings to "your Du Moulin of Nimes."[97] Henri du Moulin had originally shared the pastoral duties of the Walloon church in Middelburg with Labadie, but the two came into serious conflict. Henri was doctrinally correct, but vastly unpopular; Labadie was doctrinally suspect, but the congregation's favorite. In the end, correctness prevailed. Labadie was forced out, and left with his followers to go to Amsterdam.

Labadie then wrote to van Schurman, pleading with her to be the Paula to his Jerome. The reference was to a famous episode from the fourth century, when the impoverished scholar Jerome, author of the Vulgate bible, joined a learned circle that included the patrician widow Paula, and her daughter Eustochium. He became their Hebrew tutor, and Paula eventually surpassed her teacher as a Hebrew scholar. After allegations of improper conduct, Jerome was expelled from Rome, and he went to Bethlehem, where he and Paula established a monastic institution. Using her family wealth, Paula also founded a female community, which was inherited by her daughter. Given these details, it is unsurprising that the model of the learned aristocratic Paula and her impoverished tutor Saint Jerome would constantly resurface throughout the career of Jean de Labadie, in terms of both his apostolic mission and the attractiveness of his cause to learned women whose wealth and social

---

[97] Milton, *Life Records*, 260. Geoffrey Nuttall interprets this as a reference to Louis du Moulin; however, there is no evidence of any direct link between Labadie and Louis, while Labadie's contentious relationship with Louis' brother Henri has been well documented. See Geoffrey Nuttall, "Milton's Churchmanship in 1659: His Letter to Jean de Labadie," *Milton Quarterly* 35, no. 4 (December, 2001): 227–31. On the Middelburg years, and Labadie's conflict with Henri du Moulin, see J. H. Gerlach, "Jean de Labadie à Middelbourg. D'après du documents inédits," *Bulletin de la commission de l'histoire des églises wallonnes* 4 (1890):1–28; and Saxby, *New Jerusalem*, 135–72.

rank far exceeded his own – women like Anna Maria van Schurman. The appeal worked, however. Van Schurman originally tried to rent her own lodgings near Labadie in Amsterdam; then, when this proved to be impossible, Labadie offered to let van Schurman and her entourage have the ground floor of the house, while he and his disciples lived upstairs. Van Schurman moved in with her young nephew and her maid in September 1669.[98]

The moment van Schurman moved into the Labadist house, alarms sounded in the republic of letters. Labadie was considered dangerous – morally, culturally, and doctrinally. Calvinist theologians, like Voëtius, had originally thought that Labadie might be brought into the fold, and that he might focus his prodigious energies and talents on the improvement of the Reformed church. When it turned out instead that Labadie repudiated that church – claiming that it was irremediably corrupt, and that salvation was available only to the truly regenerate – that hope died. For the Calvinist theologian Voëtius, the worst part of this was the fact that his former protégée, Anna Maria van Schurman, was the co-founder of Labadie's despised community. Voëtius' sense of betrayal was evident in the propositions he prepared for disputation by his students in Utrecht the following month:

1. Nobody ought to leave the Church simply because some unbelievers are in it.
2. Nobody ought to join a semi-monastic group which does little but meditate and hold meetings.
3. Everyone ought to avoid the private gatherings of such a group in order to avoid implication in error.[99]

While van Schurman was not mentioned by name, it would certainly appear that she was the person whose Labadistic errors were being addressed here.

However, van Schurman stayed put in Labadie's house. It is not surprising, then, that, despite van Schurman's reputation for modesty and piety, rumors of bad behavior abounded. For instance, Bishop Pierre-Daniel Huet – a humanist scholar, anti-Cartesian, and colleague of the classicist Anne Dacier – described a journey on which he just managed to miss meeting van Schurman in Utrecht. The reason for this, he wrote, was that van Schurman had left Utrecht in order to join her new husband, Jean de

---

[98] *Ibid.*, 176–7.
[99] Voëtius, *Politicae Ecclesiasticae* IV, 502ff. (Utrecht, 1676). Cited in Saxby, *New Jerusalem*, 177.

Labadie.[100] Even the urbane Constantijn Huygens, one of van Schurman's staunchest long-time supporters, had heard stories regarding her involvement with the mystic preacher, including reports that she and Labadie had married. Huygens was too sophisticated to believe everything he heard, but, like the rest of van Schurman's intellectual circle, he was alarmed at this change in her life, and wanted to know whether any of the wild rumors were really true. So at this point, Huygens turned to van Schurman's friends from The Hague, Marie du Moulin and Utricia Swann-Ogle.

Marie, whose Calvinism was always quite orthodox, had no interest in Labadism herself; however, she could not help being drawn into Labadist controversy through the contentious involvement of her brother Henri, and the devotion of her *sœur d'alliance*. In a letter he wrote to Marie in 1667, Huygens commented on the preaching skills of "your friend Spanheim," and then moved on to Labadie, "who has very fine talents, they say, but putting up with him is hampered by his extravagances." He recounted a tale he had heard about Labadie's outrageous behavior upon encountering a group of people playing cards in Geneva, and then asked if Marie could get any information from van Schurman:

> I don't know whether our illustrious friend, who adores him, would approve of this behavior; as for me, I would be really pleased to learn what people are saying about this in Sedan.[101]

Huygens also turned to Utricia Swann-Ogle for information. In a letter written in 1673, Huygens discussed at length the tragedy of the third Anglo-Dutch war, which had put these two old friends on opposite sides; the postscript, however, concerned their mutual friend van Schurman, her "antient Sibylle," who had just published an apology for Jean de Labadie:

> If it were possible to penetrate the mysteries of your Labadistical crew by the sincere confessions of your antient Sibylle, especially concerning their holy matches and marriages upon tryal, as we are informed here, we would be very glad to have your Ladyship's good obligation.[102]

---

[100] Pierre-Daniel Huet, *Pet. Dan. Huetii, Episcopi Abrincensis, Commentarius De Rebus Ad Evm Pertinentibvs* (Amstelodami, 1718), 218, 121–2. On Huet's view of learned women, see April Shelford, "'Others Laugh, Even the Learned': An Erudit's View of Women and Learning in Seventeenth-Century France," *Proceedings of the Western Society for French History: Selected Papers of the Annual Meeting* 24 (Greeley, CO, 1997), 221–32.

[101] Huygens to Marie du Moulin, April 14, 1667, KB MS. KA 48, ff. 33–4. See also the minute of this letter in *De Briefwisseling van Constantijn Huygens*, 6:209.

[102] Constantijn Huygens to Utricia Swann-Ogle, 10 March, 1673. From Huygens' English letterbook, 1667–87, KB MS. KA 48, ff. 9r–10r. Also no. 6887 in *De Briefwisseling van Constantijn Huygens*, 6:322–3.

While van Schurman's *Eukleria* certainly went into great detail about doctrinal issues, what was missing from the text were the details Huygens really wanted – information on reputed spiritual unions and trial marriages. Thus although van Schurman had vastly reduced her contacts with many from her former intellectual circle, Huygens calculated, correctly, that she was still in touch with some of the women – Princess Elisabeth, Utricia Swann-Ogle, and Marie du Moulin.

Once she joined the Labadist commune in Amsterdam, the issues of gender, personality, social rank, and apostasy became inextricably and negatively intertwined with van Schurman's scholarship. Reports on the last decades of van Schurman's life – from old friends, fellow Labadists, and visitors, both male and female – were all highly colored by the writers' opinions of Labadie and Labadism itself. There were those, like Voëtius, who felt betrayed and threatened by Labadism's frontal attack on the Reformed church; for them, van Schurman's choice was redolent of heresy. There were those, like Huygens, who were appalled by Labadie's lack of appropriate decorum with women; for them, van Schurman's choice put the modest maiden's chastity in peril, and besmirched her spotless reputation. And then there were those, like van Schurman's associates from the exile court, who felt that appropriate observations of social rank were important; for them, Labadism's disparities in terms of class and gender were suspect and disturbing. Many had noted that the Labadist community was composed primarily of aristocratic women with a random assortment of male artisans and tradesmen; and suspicion that these gentlewomen were being exploited ran high. Accusations of this sort never ceased to circulate around Labadie, with the result that the doctrinal disputes of his career are difficult to disentangle from their erotic over-tones. As Michel de Certeau observes, "sex discredits the text."[103]

However, our concern is not with Jean de Labadie. Our focus is on van Schurman, and she herself had now become "the text" being discredited by these allegations. Van Schurman had always had to fight for her chosen position in the republic of letters – that of a collegial participant, rather than a muse – and she had done so very conscientiously and deliberately. She was also well aware that, since she was a woman, this status rested upon a platform of perceived virtue, as well as evident erudition; thus she had taken great pains to ensure that they both remained intact. Through careful management of the issue of "sex," van Schurman had been able to keep the issue of gender – in terms of preconceived limits and exclusions – at bay.

---

[103] Certeau, *Mystic Fable*, 273.

But while the success of this proceeding was due in part to her own efforts, it was also due to the inclusive intellectual climate of the seventeenth-century republic of letters. Now, things were changing; and for van Schurman, the choice to live in the Labadist community – and, more importantly, to shape that community from the very beginning – meant that she could once again assert some form of managerial control over her intellectual and spiritual life. In the Amsterdam commune, she sat at Labadie's right hand: Labadie was known as "Papa," and van Schurman was "Mama."[104] This was van Schurman's community as much as it was Labadie's, a door she could close herself, on her own terms.

Yet it is equally inaccurate to see van Schurman's choice as merely strategic. Working within the Calvinist context of her birth, she had been seeking a satisfactory spiritual path throughout her life. Finally, in the 1660s, van Schurman found Labadism, and she deemed it the purest and most correct way of knowing God that she had ever encountered. More-over, there were a number of other scholars from her former intellectual orbit – men such as John Dury and Jan Amos Comenius – who had also seen the possibilities inherent in Labadism. In some respects, Labadist doctrine was a reaction to the reinvigorated scepticism of the early modern era, and a response to the Cartesian approach that claimed knowledge could be attained by rational means. Van Schurman and Labadie both rejected the rationalist approach. Like many other scholars, van Schurman valued reason as the primary pathway to learning, while also being sure that the truth of her own beliefs could not be "proved" using reason or evidence. For van Schurman, these contradictions seemed finally to be reconciled through Quietism. The practice of Quietism involved an obliteration of the self, a *quieting* of human volition so that the individual might be completely open to God's will.[105] And as a consequence of this mystic, immediate experience of God, the practition-ers of Quietism rejected the church as a body that ultimately interfered in this intimate relationship. The Lutheran expression of this practice was Pietism, and Labadie's sermons in Geneva were attended by Philip Jacob Spener, who later published a German translation of one of Labadie's tracts, and became the founder of German Pietism.[106]

---

[104] From *Motifs qui ont obligé Anthoine de Lamarque de sortir de la Maison du Sieur Jean de Labadie* (Amsterdam, 1670). Cited in Saxby, *New Jerusalem*, 188–9.

[105] Popkin, *The History of Scepticism*, 184–8.

[106] Theodore G. Tappert, introduction to *Pia Desideria* (1675) by Philip Jacob Spener (Philadelphia, 1964), 11; also Joyce Irwin, "Anna Maria van Schurman and Antoinette Bourignon: Contrasting Examples of Seventeenth-Century Pietism," *Church History* 60, no. 3 (September, 1991): 301–15.

Scholars who had spent the previous decades grappling with issues of how to know God, and how to choose among rational knowledge, revealed faith, and ecclesiology, were drawn to this solution. In van Schurman's case, however, her *Eukleria* is evidence that the tensions between her earlier scholastic theology and her unmediated experiential faith were never truly resolved. On the one hand, she went on at length in this text to defend Labadie and Labadism, while decrying the poverty of an intellectual approach to God; but on the other hand, she did so by devoting numerous pages to a painstaking inventory of her accomplishments. She dropped dozens of illustrious learned names, and quoted liberally from her own publications.

Other scholars had been less tortured by this choice. When Labadie visited Jan Amos Comenius in Amsterdam, where the aged educationalist had been living since the 1650s, he had found himself very welcome. The English revolution for which Hartlib, Dury, and Comenius had worked was a failed dream; but Labadie had spoken to Comenius of a new project, a potential partnership in which the Labadist community would "shake Babylon until it collapses," while Comenius would undertake to "educate Zion."[107] In the end, however, Comenius chose to ally himself with another charismatic Quietist leader, Antoinette Bourignon.

Many saw Bourignon as a fanatic, but she also had her scholarly followers. Bourignon, like Labadie, had been raised in the Catholic church, had associated with the Jansenists, and then finally come to the understanding that she needed to establish a purified church dedicated to the Holy Spirit. She had inherited land on the island of Noordstrand, off the coast of Holstein, and was establishing a community of believers on her property.[108] Jan van Swammerdam, the Dutch anatomist and microscopist, appealed to her in a spiritual crisis, and then joined her community on Noordstrand in 1675.[109] And Ranelagh's brother Robert Boyle, who had been introduced to Bourignon's writings by Petrus

---

[107] The visit took place in 1669, shortly before Comenius' death in 1670. Milada Blekastad, *Comenius* (Oslo, 1969), 722, cited in Saxby, *New Jerusalem*, 174–5.

[108] On Bourignon, see Marthe van der Does, "Antoinette Bourignon: Sa vie (1616–1680) – Son œuvre" (Ph.D dissertation, Groningen, 1974); Mirjam de Baar, "Transgressing Gender Codes: Anna Maria van Schurman and Antoinette Bourignon as Contrasting Examples," in *Women of the Golden Age*, ed. Els Kloek, Nicole Tesuwen, and Marijke Huisman (Hilversum, 1994), 143–52; and idem, '*Ik moet spreken*'. *Het spiritueel leiderschap van Antoinette Bourignon (1616–1680)* (Zutphen, 2004).

[109] *The Letters of Jan Swammerdam to Melchisedec Thevenot*, trans. G. A. Lindeboom (Amsterdam, 1975), 16–19. Swammerdam stayed with Bourignon for nine months.

Serrarius, was so impressed that he offered to translate her texts into English, so that they might reach a wider audience.[110] Comenius also became a believer, and according to one report, he called out her name on his deathbed.[111] One would have thought, then, that Bourignon and Labadie would be natural allies. However, they had severe doctrinal differences, and the issue separating them was predestination. The more radical Bourignon saw predestination as an insult to God, and a symptom of the satanic error of the established church.

In March of 1668, van Schurman met with the prophetess Bourignon in Amsterdam. Van Schurman was attempting to reconcile Bourignon to Labadie's view, and perhaps pave the way for a Labadist home on Noordstrand. The meeting was a complete failure, and the unfortunate result was a flurry of mutually censorious pamphleteering by Labadie's disciple Pierre Yvon and Bourignon's acolyte Pierre Poiret. Yet even eight years after the failure of this initial meeting, Poiret was still hoping to convince van Schurman of the correctness of Bourignon's view.[112] But then Labadie and the Labadists were ejected from Amsterdam, the city with the greatest reputation for tolerance in all of Europe. They needed a new place of safety, and van Schurman turned to another member of her circle of learned women from The Hague. She wrote to Princess Elisabeth, who was now the abbess of a Lutheran abbey, and asked if her Labadist community could take up residence on Elisabeth's lands. Elisabeth was amenable, and wrote to her cousin the Great Elector to obtain his permission.

First, Elisabeth emphasized that this arrangement would be mutually beneficial, since the community "would transfer all their assets to this state."[113] Then she presented her own account of the situation:

Without doubt you already know that the learned Miss Schurmann, together with several other women from Holland and from Seeland, had planned to found a

[110] Boyle's letter of December 25, 1670 is "Le Trente-cinquième Témoignage" in Antoinette Bourignon, *Recœuil des quelques'uns des temoignages publics & particuliers, Rendus à la Personne de Madlle. Anthoinette Bourignon . . .* (Amsterdam, 1682), 274–6. Bourignon's lengthy response, dated February 21, 1671, is letter IX in Bourignon, *The Light Risen in Darkness . . . by Antonia Bourignon. Being a collection of letters written to several persons, upon great and important subjects . . .*, 4 vols. (London, 1703), IV, 65–73.

[111] From the account of Edwoud de Lindt, an alleged witness to Comenius' final hours. Cited in Does, *Antoinette Bourignon*, 137.

[112] Two very long letters from Poiret to van Schurman are in the Universiteit Bilbiotheek Amsterdam. Pierre Poiret to Anna Maria van Schurman, November 24, 1676, and March 2, 1677, MS. Ay 247a,b.

[113] Princess Elisabeth to Kurfürst Friedrich Wilhelm von Brandburg, Herford, August 21, 1670, in Hauck, "Die Briefe," 15–6. Original in German.

convent in Amsterdam. However, the Dutch classes find two preachers who are among them highly objectionable. Therefore they were subjected to slander . . . [114]

While any reading of this letter must take into account the purpose for which it was shaped – that of convincing the Elector that Labadie was harmless – it is noteworthy that Elisabeth finds a number of different ways to say that this was essentially a community being led by van Schurman, for which Labadie was serving as preacher. First, the move to Herford would essentially be the relocation of an Amsterdam "convent" being run by van Schurman. Second, even the Elector was expected to acknowledge and respect van Schurman's reputation for learning and sanctity, and then extrapolate from that to an approval of Labadie. Elisabeth's letter continued:

Now they would like to live here with me and built a house under my *freiheit*, like the noble convent up on the hill, and rely on me as their abbess.[115]

Essentially, Elisabeth was characterizing this migration as one learned woman bringing her community of followers into a haven under the authority of another learned woman. In the end, this combination of arguments worked, and the Labadist community moved into Elisabeth's territory at Herford in 1670.

There still were problems, however, since the Labadist community upset the local townspeople. Elisabeth was forced to write to the Elector once again, describing an attack on her old friend:

After I kindly asked Your Highness yesterday evening to send us a garrison, during the night a group of impudent people attacked the elderly, ill Mlle. Schurman in her room. They broke her window, and in the morning the pieces of wood that they had used were found. Therefore, I hope that Your Highness, as my and my convent's kind patron, will restore our peace, since without your help damage might occur.[116]

In the end, the only way to restore peace was to have the Labadists move out. Van Schurman had to leave the protection of her friend Elisabeth, and in 1672 the community relocated to Altona, in Denmark.

Jean de Labadie died in Altona in 1674; the Labadist community then moved to Wieuwerd, where van Schurman died on May 4, 1678. Ambivalent about her role in the republic of letters, and concerned over the

---

[114] *Ibid.* [115] *Ibid.*
[116] Princess Elisabeth to Kurfürst Friedrich Wilhelm von Brandenburg, Herford, 21 November, 1671, in Hauck, "Die Briefe," 227. Original in German.

possibility of posthumous adulation – from scholarly and pietistic communities alike – van Schurman had already burned most of her correspondence.[117] However, the connection between van Schurman and Elisabeth had remained strong throughout their lives; and, despite the enormous changes in the world around them, these two female scholars had continued to honor the friendship that had begun so long ago in the exile court at The Hague.

PRINCESS ELISABETH (1618–80)

Throughout her life, Elisabeth of Bohemia had a sphere of activities that was determined by rank above all; fields of scholarly interest and considerations of gender followed after. Yet her original circle of male and female scholars from The Hague had continued to keep in touch across boundaries of intellectual division; and even more surprising, perhaps, is the fact that this network managed to survive the fallout from political division and personal tragedy.

The Thirty Years' War and the English Civil Wars had dominated the 1640s. During that decade, the radical activists John Dury and Dorothy Moore had formed part of Elisabeth's circle at The Hague; moreover, as we saw, earlier, Moore had been quite close to the Queen of Bohemia and very active in using her influence with Members of Parliament on the Queen's behalf. But as the 1650s began, allegiances had undergone a drastic realignment. In 1648, the Treaty of Westphalia had restored a portion of the Palatine house's holdings, and Elisabeth's brother Karl Ludwig became the Elector Palatine. Then, on January 30, 1649, Parliament executed her uncle, King Charles I. Although Elisabeth's connection to Dury, like her connection to van Schurman, would endure throughout her life, the pressures on that relationship would thereafter become very pointed and specific.

After Charles' execution, the Commonwealth government had asked Dury to write a series of pamphlets examining the debates underlying their actions. Since Dury and Moore were always short of funds, he had agreed to do so. It was a task that had also included translating Milton's *Ikonoklastes* into English.[118] Dury had not, in fact, approved of Charles' execution. He

---

[117] Saxby, *New Jerusalem*, 258–9.
[118] The "Day's Proceedings of the Council of State" for May 20, 1651 includes the following: "Mr. Durie to proceed in translating Mr. Milton's book, written in answer to the late King's book, and Mr. Frost to give him such fit reward for his pains as he shall think fit." *CSPD* 1651, 208.

had even written a brief for the King to use in preparing his defence, and had it given to two very close and capable political operatives – Ranelagh and Moore – so that they might find someone to convey it to Charles. Another copy had gone to Elisabeth's brother Karl Ludwig.[119] However, as far as the Winter Queen was concerned, there was no going back.

Furious over Dury's apparent betrayal, the Queen of Bohemia wrote to her son in a rage. If she ever saw Dury again, she wrote, she "woulde have him soundlie basted." Even her respect for his profession would not save him, "for though he be a minister, he is the basest rascall that ever was of that coat."[120] The following year, things got even worse. The Queen had seen a new pamphlet, wherein Dury had reasoned that the King's execution had in part been Charles' own fault – because if he had set himself above the law, then "he did by that means actually un-King himselfe as to this Nation."[121] The Winter Queen immediately fired off a letter to her son Karl Ludwig, and another to Dorothy Moore; as she reported to her son, "I did write of it to his wife, who coulde not denie it."[122] Apparently, then, Moore had also become involved, and was having to negotiate the troubled political waters that now separated her husband and other colleagues in the Hartlib circle from her friends at the exile court in The Hague. While we do not know how Moore replied, it is clear that the damage was done.

For Elisabeth, however, matters were somewhat different. She and her brother continued to stay in touch with the Hartlib circle, as evidenced by a letter she wrote to Karl Ludwig after Charles' execution. The letter was primarily concerned with the success of Elisabeth's negotiations for the marriage of their younger sister Henriette; for our purposes, however, it is most interesting to note the source of her intelligence:

a man by the name of Figulus, who accompanied Comenius to Hungary (perhaps you saw him in the company of Dury, because he was with him for a long time) has returned to Lisse, and reports that Prince Sigismund and his mother were very pleased with their ambassadors' negotiations.[123]

[119] Dury, *A Declaration*, 11.

[120] Queen Elizabeth of Bohemia to Karl Ludwig, October 16/26, 1654, in "Briefe der Elisabeth Stuart, Köningen von Böhmen, an Ihren Sohn, Der Kurfürsten Carl Ludwiig von der Pfalz, 1650–1662," ed. Anna Wendland, *Bibliothek des Litterarischen Vereins in Stuttgart* 228 (Tübingen, 1902), 51–2.

[121] While Elizabeth does not name the publication, it was most likely Dury's *Considerations Concerning the present Engagement, Whether It may lawfully be entered into; Yea or No?*, 2nd edn. (London, 1650), 2–3.

[122] Elizabeth of Bohemia to Karl Ludwig, September 10/20, 1655, in "Briefe der Elisabeth Stuart," 60–1.

[123] Elisabeth to Karl Ludwig, December 21/31, 1650, in Hauck, "Die Briefe," 50–3.

Figulus was Petr Jablonský (1619–70), who had married Comenius'
daughter Alžběta in 1649. It appears, then, that despite all the political
upheaval, Elisabeth was still in touch with the Hartlib circle through
Comenius, Figulus, and Dury throughout the Commonwealth years.

Elisabeth's intellectual allegiances during these years continued to be
multi-layered, complex, and remarkably inclusive. Most of the scholarship
on both van Schurman and Elisabeth has pointed to two events as the
bookends for a purported decades-long break in the friendship between
these two female scholars. On one end, representing the beginning of this
rupture, was van Schurman's disastrous final meeting with Descartes in
1649; and on the other end, representing reconciliation, was Elisabeth's
granting of asylum to van Schurman and the Labadist community in 1671.
But two sources – Elisabeth's correspondence with her family, and letters
exchanged by both Elisabeth and van Schurman with the Cartesian
preacher and scholar Andreas Colvius – provide evidence instead for
continued contact throughout these decades.

Van Schurman's rupture with Descartes would come in 1649. In this
oft-cited episode, Descartes had stopped in Utrecht to visit van Schurman
on his way to the court of Queen Christina in Sweden. Seeing a Hebrew
bible on van Schurman's desk, he expressed his amazement that she would
waste her precious time and admirable mind on such busy work. Van
Schurman replied that sacred scriptures could never be adequately translated from their original inscription in the holy tongue – to which
Descartes responded that this might very well be true, but he had tried
this route himself and found that it led to more confusion about the
innate ideas, rather than less. So he had abandoned the effort as worthless.
Van Schurman's friend and co-Labadist Pierre Yvon described the episode
at length, with the following conclusion:

This response surprised Mlle. van Schurman very much. And since it wounded
her heart so deeply, it immediately gave her such a distaste for that Philosopher
that she took care ever after to have nothing to do with him.[124]

This could certainly be considered a dramatic rupture. However, a closer
look at the timing puts the event in better perspective – Descartes would
in fact be dead within several months, thus van Schurman would not have
had the opportunity to see him again no matter how she felt. Nor did van
Schurman's rupture with Descartes himself necessitate a rupture between
van Schurman and her Cartesian colleagues.

---

[124] Yvon, "Abregé sincere," 1263–4.

We find evidence for this in a letter from Elisabeth to her cousin Elisabeth Louise, Abbess of the convent at Herford. The Abbess Elisabeth Louise held the position to which Elisabeth herself would be elected in 1667. In the meantime, though, the ever-politic princess, with an eye to the future, kept up a strong and supportive relationship with this extremely useful cousin. In 1654, Elisabeth Louise was having a conflict with her deaconess. Elisabeth gave her cousin some very blunt and practical advice about how to deal with the problem. She then responded to the Abbess' question about a possible visit from an old friend:

> As far as Miss Schurmann is concerned, I have not asked her to come, but I would be delighted if she would, and I know that she was ready to do so. She got to Cologne, but her relatives there sent her back. She is an honorable and intelligent person, whose company would give me great pleasure.[125]

Apparently, van Schurman had been planning to travel to Heidelberg to visit her friend Elisabeth, but pressing family business had dictated a change in plans.[126] It is clear, then, that the supposed Cartesian break in their relationship between 1649 and 1672 never existed.

Moreover, van Schurman was still corresponding with the Cartesian Andreas Colvius in 1651, recalling their long years of friendship, and thanking him for supporting her life choices.[127] Van Schurman and Colvius shared a powerful connection through their faith, as evidenced by letters van Schurman wrote to Colvius in 1637 and 1651.[128] Colvius and van Schurman would also share a publishing history. At the request of Johan van Beverwijck, Colvius and van Schurman had written treatises on the timing of the end of life, which were published in Beverwijck's 1639 *Epistolicae questiones cum doctorum responsis*, and an exchange between van Schurman and Colvius debating the appropriate limitations for the scholarly life was included in her *Dissertatio*.[129] And at the same time, Colvius was also corresponding with Elisabeth. Thus we see in the correspondence of Elisabeth and her colleagues from the exile court in The Hague a series

---

[125] Elisabeth to Elisabeth Louise, Abbess of Herford, January 16/26, 1654, in Hauck, "Die Briefe," 89–91.

[126] In 1653 and 1654, van Schurman, her brother, and their two aunts were in van Schurman's birthplace of Cologne to reclaim some family property that had been confiscated during the Thirty Years' War.

[127] Anna Maria van Schurman to André Colvius, May 26, 1651, Universiteit Bibliotheek Leiden, MS. Pap. 2, no. 2.

[128] Universiteit Bibliotheek Leiden, MS. Pap. 2, nos. 1 and 2.

[129] Colvius to van Schurman, April 7, 1637, and her reply, dated September 9, 1637, in van Schurman, *Dissertatio*, 80–90. Another version of Beverwijck's *Epistolicae questiones* was published in 1644, with contributions from André Rivet, Claude Saumaise, and René Descartes.

of continuities – the ongoing interaction of royals with radicals even after the rupture of Charles' execution in 1649, and the ongoing interactions of Cartesians with anti-Cartesians in spite of quarrels and religious disputes.

Another personal rupture came when Elisabeth was compelled to leave The Hague and return to Germany in the wake of yet another family disaster. In 1646, her nineteen-year-old brother Prince Philip had stabbed a man to death in a public square in The Hague. Apparently, Philip was defending the besmirched honor of the women in his family. The details are somewhat murky, since the most complete description of the event comes from Tallemant des Réaux, who loved nothing better than to recount a scandalous tale. Nevertheless, we know that the victim was a rogue named L'Espinay, who had ingratiated himself into the company at the exile court. He also boasted of having ingratiated himself quite a bit further with both Queen Elizabeth and her daughter Louise. Enraged, Philip challenged L'Espinay to a duel. Friends prevented the duel from taking place, but the next morning Philip waylaid L'Espinay and stabbed him to death in the market square of The Hague.[130] Elisabeth was not involved in the affair; however, her defence of young Philip caused her mother to order that she leave The Hague at once. The banishment was planned to last only six or seven months, but Elisabeth never returned to live in The Netherlands.

Much of the scholarship on Elisabeth has interpreted this displacement as permanent exile.[131] However, Elisabeth's own words, her range of activities in Germany, and the references to her from the Queen of Bohemia's correspondence, suggest that Elisabeth was in fact a highly active agent for her family's interests during this entire time. Thus it is much more likely that once Elisabeth had settled in to her old home in Berlin, she and her family in The Hague came to a mutually agreeable decision concerning where her time could best be spent.

This is not to say, however, that the move to Germany was not initially difficult for Elisabeth. The Hague, situated at the crossroads of learned Europe, was constantly visited by a wide range of scholars, and the exile court sparkled with intellectual life. Berlin, on the other hand, was a cold and distant cultural backwater. Elisabeth remembered it fondly from her childhood, and was happy to be loved and spoiled by her relatives there.[132]

---

[130] Tallemant des Réaux, *Les Historiettes*, II, 287–90.
[131] See, for instance, Nye, *The Princess and the Philosopher*, 100–1.
[132] Elisabeth to Descartes, October 10, [1646], in *The Correspondence between Princess Elisabeth of Bohemia and René Descartes*, 146. Original French text in Descartes, *Oeuvres*, IV, 519–24. Elisabeth's

But with whom could she hold an intelligent conversation? The problem, of course, was not that there were no scholars in Germany – far from it. The problem was that in 1646 there were as yet no Cartesians.

At first Elisabeth thought that it might literally be true, that there was not one single person in Germany who had read any Cartesian philosophy. Then three months later, she was thrilled to find a single person who actually had. She loaned him her copy of the *Principia*, hoping thereby to initiate some discussion. As she wrote to Descartes:

A little while ago I met one single man who has read some of your writings . . . I have just presented him with a copy of your *Principles*, and he promised to tell me his objections to it. If he finds any, and they are worth the trouble, I will send them to you, so that you can judge the capability of the one I find to be the most intelligent of the doctors here, since he has a taste for your reasoning.[133]

She apparently had some success in stirring up intellectual interest at court, since she gained a reputation for having initiated a learned circle in Berlin, where she "engaged in conversations and discussions about the most fanciful subjects in the areas of philosophy and theology with the court's most learned men ... These conversations earned her much admiration by everybody who witnessed them."[134]

Then in 1651, after arranging the marriage between her sister Princess Henriette and the Transylvanian Prince Sigismund Rakoczy (to less than universal approbation), Elisabeth moved to Heidelberg at the request of her sister Sophie. But when Elisabeth showed up, her siblings were shocked at her appearance:

Her stay at the court of our aunt, the Electress of Brandenburg, had done her no good. We thought her much changed, both in mind and person. Looking at her, Prince Edward whispered to me: "Where has her liveliness gone? What has she done with her merry talk?"[135]

Elisabeth's drastically changed demeanor has usually been attributed to her feelings of loss and devastation following the death of Descartes. However, a letter she wrote to Karl Ludwig in 1648 reveals what the problem had actually been:

Aunt Charlotte, the Electress Dowager, was still living at the Brandenbug court, and her cousin, Frederic William, was now the Great Elector.

[133] Elisabeth to Descartes, February 21, 1647. Translation in *The Correspondence between Princess Elisabeth of Bohemia and René Descartes*, 155–6; original French text in Descartes, *Oeuvres*, IV, 617–20.
[134] Original German text in Gottshalf Eduard Guhrauer, "Elisabeth, Pfalzgrafin bei Rhein, Abtissin von Herford," *Historisches Taschenbuch* (1850), vol. I: 95–6. Guhrauer is citing "an anonymous letter from Berlin." There is unfortunately no further information regarding the author of this letter.
[135] *The Memoirs of Sophia, Electress of Hanover 1630–1680*, trans. H. Forester (London, 1888), 41–2.

I have continued to be tormented by this terrible disease, and despite the fact that the fever has gone, and with it the threat to my life, I am still completely covered with it, and I do not have the use of either my hands or my eyes. People feed me like a little child, yet the doctors try to persuade me that I will not be at all disfigured; I leave them to their faith, having no faith of my own on that subject.[136]

Again, the illness is not named – but it was clearly smallpox, and it is no wonder that her siblings had found her changed.

In 1661, Elisabeth moved to the Lutheran abbey at Herford, succeeding to the position of abbess upon her cousin's death in 1667. Throughout her life, she had been royalty with no realm; now, as the abbess of Herford, Elisabeth had her own territory, to rule as she saw fit. However, this eclectic cloister was quite far from being a conventional convent. At Herford, Elisabeth was the Calvinist queen of a Lutheran abbey that sheltered Quakers and Labadists. The abbey, which did not require its Abbess to convert to Lutheranism, was cash-poor and continually under siege – however, it was hers. As William Penn, who visited Elisabeth in 1677, put it: "She had a small Territory, which she govern'd so well, that she shew'd her self fit for a Greater."[137] And to the extent that circumstances of finance, war, and a changed intellectual landscape permitted, she recreated at Herford her own version of the exile court at The Hague.

Under Elisabeth's leadership, the abbey of Herford was a place where ideas could be discussed, and exiles could find refuge – a place where old friends and scholars of every faith would be welcomed. Elisabeth was in touch with the remaining members of seventeenth-century revolutionary circles, men like Hartlib, Dury, Haak, and Pell; she corresponded with the members of a younger generation of philosophers, men like Leibniz and Malebranche; and she visited with the women who had been part of her intellectual circle at the exile court – Anna Maria van Schurman, and Utricia Swann-Ogle. For instance, in a letter to Secretary Coventry in 1673, Elisabeth conveyed reports on the progress of the war, while also reporting on an upcoming visit with a friend: "I am taking a little trip to Hamburg, where I have promised to visit Madame Swan, and where I will be taking

[136] Elisabeth to Karl Ludwig, Berlin, October 19, 1648, in Hauck, "Die Briefe," 34–5.
[137] William Penn, *No Cross, No Crown: A Discourse Shewing the Nature and Discipline of the Holy Cross of Christ*, 6th edn (Dublin, 1700), 151. On Herford, see Benger, *Memoirs of Elizabeth Stuart*, II, 448.

advantage of the beautiful weather."[138] The visit did, in fact, take place, and as Utricia's husband wrote in a letter two days later, "I am goinge to fetch into this Citty tomorow Princesse Elizabeth, who does my wyfe the Honor to give her a visit."[139] Elisabeth also welcomed and sheltered fugitive Labadists and Quakers. As her sister Sophie would later describe her sister's rule, Elisabeth was "the refuge of all the oppressed."[140]

It had not been easy to find a permanent home for the resolutely celibate and scholarly Elisabeth. Based on the reports of family members, she was generally a difficult guest, who could not refrain from trying to manage affairs wherever she happened to be. After 1660, when her mother returned to live in England, there had been speculation that Elisabeth might join her. Hartlib and Henry More were especially excited that the "Cartesian princess" might soon be gracing their shores.[141] Worthington wrote to Hartlib in October 1660, asking when Elisabeth was due to arrive, since More was anxious to see her, and having her there "would make ye world a more desirable place."[142] Then finally, in May 1661, the Queen of Bohemia arrived, but Elisabeth was not with her. Worthington again wrote to Hartlib:

I hear that the Q. of Bohemia is arriv'd in England; and if so, is not that excellent Philosophical and otherwise accomplish'd Lady, her Daughter, the Princess Elizabeth arrived also? If she be, I believe Dr. More would rejoyce at that good News; he having a great Esteem for her from the high Testimony of Des-Cartes and others concerning her; and if there were an Opportunity of his Converse with her, I believe it would be to a greate mutual Satisfaction and Complacency.[143]

Hartlib was equally enthusiastic, and in a rather whimsical moment wished that Elisabeth would marry More's ideas, and that the offspring of this marriage would be a wonderful Cartesian book:

---

[138] Princess Elisabeth, Abbess of Herford, to Henry Coventry, July 7, [1673]. Original in French. Coventry Papers, Archives of the Marquess of Bath, Longleat. Microfilm, Institute for Historical Research, London. Classmark 9697/91, XR. 60, Reel 1, vol. 1, f. 102.

[139] Swann to Williamson, Hamburg, 9 July, 1673. PRO SP 82/12, f. 34.

[140] Sophie to Karl Ludwig, April 27, 1679, letter no. 360 in Eduard Bodemann, *Briefwechsel der Herzogin Sophie von Hannover mit ihrem Bruder, dem Kurfürsten Karl Ludwig von der Pfalz . . .* (Leipzig, 1885), 356–7.

[141] Samuel Hartlib to John Worthington, October 15, 1660, Cambridge University Library, Baker MSS 29, ff. 209–10; also printed in Worthington, *Diary and Correspondence*, XIII, 210–15.

[142] Worthington to Hartlib, October 25, 1660, in Worthington, *Diary and Correspondence*, XIII, 225–6.

[143] Worthington to Hartlib, May 20, 1661, epistle VIII in John Worthington, *Miscellanies . . . Also, A Collection of Epistles, Written to Mr. Hartlib of Pious Memory . . .* (1704), 248–51; also printed in Worthington, *Diary and Correspondence*, XIII, 310–4.

I wish she were in England, that she might marrie Dr. More's Cartesian Notions, which would beget a noble offspring of many excellent and fruitfull truths.[144]

In the end, Elisabeth did not join her mother in England, and Hartlib's hopes for this marriage of true Cartesian minds would come to naught.

Another exchange between Worthington and Hartlib provides us with further information regarding Elisabeth's ongoing control over the publication of her correspondence, and her ongoing intellectual engagement with their former revolutionary network. At the time of Descartes' death in 1650, there were many who had heard about the new Cartesian methods in metaphysics and mathematics. They had read his publications and were eager to learn more. However, Descartes' works alone were not sufficient for clarifying his method; these publications were condensed and difficult, and they assumed a reader who was already quite familiar with current arguments. Even among the learned, these works were difficult to untangle. Descartes was aware of this; as he wrote in a letter prefaced to *Les Passions de l'ame*:

In fact I had composed it only to be read by a princess whose mental powers are so extraordinary that she can easily understand matters which seem very difficult to our learned doctors. So the only points I explained at length in it are those I thought to be novel.[145]

Since the treatise had been crafted in response to Elisabeth's prodding queries, it therefore assumed a reader whose understanding, like hers, was at a very advanced level. Thus scholars agreed that the key to understanding Cartesianism lay in Descartes' correspondence, and only those who had corresponded with Descartes on these subjects had really been able to grasp his method.

But when an eagerly awaited new volume of Descartes' letters was finally published in October 1661, this only led to further disappointment on Worthington's part. He wrote to Hartlib:

I suppose you have seen or heard of Des-Cartes his Second Volume of Letters; wherein many, or most of them, are about Matters betwixt him and Mersennus. They are all in French that are in this 2nd volume: No Letters to the Princess Elizabeth.[146]

---

[144] Hartlib to Worthington, May 28, 1661, Cambridge University Library, Baker MSS 29, ff. 218–19; also printed in Worthington, *Diary and Correspondence*, XIII, 314–18.

[145] Letter dated Egmond, December 4, 1648; prefaced to *The Passions of the Soul*, in Descartes, *Philosophical Writings*, I, 327.

[146] Worthington to Hartlib, October 7, 1661, epistle XVIII in Worthington, *Miscellanies*, 291–5; also printed in Worthington, *Diary and Correspondence*, XXXVI, 47–54.

Apparently, Elisabeth was continuing to withhold her own Cartesian correspondence, thereby retaining control over its circulation.[147] We also learn from this letter that Elisabeth was critiquing the correspondence that had already been published:

I have read in some of your Papers an Extract of a Letter of hers, wherein she mentions some Letters of Des-Cartes to herself, which are not in the First Volume of his Letters, and are more worthy to be printed than several others in that Volume. She also thought, that the Methodizing and placing of the Letters might have been to better Advantage.

And further, we learn about the ongoing circulation of homeless scholars in a post-Restoration world:

I did much rejoice when I heard of Mr. Dury's journey into Germany, for this (among other) reasons, that possibly he might visit that excellent princess.[148]

Hartlib then responded that he would write to Dury about a possible visit to Elisabeth.

Given the current political situation, one might reasonably have assumed that Elisabeth's connections to the old reforming circles would have ended – her cousin Charles II had assumed the English throne, and her brother Karl Ludwig ruled the Palatinate, while it was clear that Hartlib's revolution had failed. Yet Elisabeth had continued to stay in contact with both Hartlib and Dury, confirming the solidity of these scholarly connections, and their continuing mutual interest in the projects that had brought them together in previous decades.

This phenomenon is also borne out by Elisabeth's continuing presence in mathematical networks. Even after she became abbess of Herford, her control over her portion of the Cartesian correspondence meant that those who needed more information would have to come to her. This included Makin's brother-in-law, the cranky and resentful John Pell. Pell was a man who had no use for royalty, and perhaps even less use for learned women; however, he was always impressed with good mathematics and good mathematicians. Pell's two abiding passions were algebra and the calculation of tables; a scholar who did

---

[147] Worthington is referring to the letters published by Clerselier; Elisabeth's side of the correspondence would not appear in print until published by Foucher de Careil in 1879. *Lettres de Monsieur Descartes*, ed. Claude Clerselier, 3 vols. (Paris, 1657–67); and Foucher de Careil, *Descartes, la Princesse Elisabeth, et la Reine Christine, d'après des lettres inédites* (Paris and Amsterdam, 1879).

[148] Worthington to Hartlib, October 7, 1661. Worthington, *Miscellanies*, 291–5; and Worthington, *Diary and Correspondence*, XXXVI, 57.

good mathematical work in either of these areas, whether male or female, would be deemed worthy of his consideration. And when it came to algebra, even Pell acknowledged Elisabeth as an authority on Cartesian mathematics.

In a letter to Hartlib in 1657, Pell complained about some "professed Mathematicians at Heidelberg," for whom he had little respect. Pell was especially appalled when one of them, Joannes Luneschloss, tried to style himself a Cartesian mathematician:

You sent me an extract of Letters from Frankford, which speake of him as if he were a profound Cartesian. I hope he did not professe himselfe such, whilest the Princesse Elizabeth was at Heidelberg. Now shee is gone; he may, perhaps justly, say, that he understands Des Cartes better than any Hee or Shee in that University.[149]

And in Pell's letterbooks in the British Library, there are copies of both letters written by Descartes to Elisabeth on the problem of the three circles. Even more surprising, perhaps, is the fact that Pell made his own translation of the letters into English and wrote them out in his letterbook as well.[150] And as late as 1665, John Pell was trying to decipher some diagrams that Descartes had drawn in his letters to Elisabeth on the problem of the three circles.

However, while Pell had great admiration for Elisabeth as a mathematician and Cartesian, he had never had any contact with her directly; thus he availed himself of Theodore Haak as his intermediary. Haak had the Palatine connections, although Pell coached him throughout on how to approach this particular princess. First, Haak sent Elisabeth a copy of the first issue of the Royal Society's *Philosophical Transactions*; as we saw in Elisabeth's earlier exchange with Colvius, she was keeping up with scientific news from all corners of Europe. Then, in return for the journal, Haak asked the princess if she might provide copies of her correspondence with Descartes on the problem of the three circles. Elisabeth did so, but the diagram in the second letter was hard to decipher. Haak wrote back, hoping she might help him out again, this time with an explanation:

---

[149] Pell to Hartlib, July 9/19, 1657, BL. Add. MSS. 4364, f. 150v (no. 33). Pell's source for this information on Elisabeth's teaching of Cartesianism may have been the polymath Joachim Jungius, since they corresponded on scientific matters. See Stephen Clucas, "The Atomism of the Cavendish Circle: A Reappraisal," *The Seventeenth Century* 9, no. 2 (autumn 1994): 247–73.

[150] French copies in BL, Add. MSS. 4278, ff. 150r–154v. Pell's English translation was a paraphrase of the first letter, followed by a full translation of the second. BL Add. MSS. 4278, ff. 155r–156r.

Though those letters were written 22 yeares agoe, I am willing to hope that her Highness hath them by her & will finde leisure to send me not onely those Diagrams, but also her owne solution of that Probleme.[151]

It is not clear if it had originally been Henry More who asked for this information, or if More was perhaps serving as another link in the chain of connection. However, Elisabeth's reply references him first of all:

I have lately sent you, for that excellent person M. More, two letters by the late Descartes, in which the diagrams are badly drawn, because the person who transcribed them does not understand Geometry in the least, and in the entire territory of Westphalia one cannot find a single person who understands it. You will see here that fault corrected.[152]

Apparently, Elisabeth's low opinion of Cartesian scholarship in Germany had not improved since the 1650s. She then went on to describe the exchange on the problem of the three circles, and repeated the praise she had received from Descartes:

He responded to this by saying that the method I had chosen to solve this problem was better than the one that he had proposed to me himself, and then proceeded to demonstrate how the three unknown quantities could be further reduced.[153]

But when it came to providing the solution to this problem, she left that up to her recipient; she was sure that he was able, and it would be hard for her to locate her papers at this point in time.

Then at the end of Elisabeth's letter, she told Haak what she wanted in return:

I thank you for taking the trouble to send me printed copies of *Philosophical Transactions*, and I would ask you further to send me the Effects of the new microscope, and Mr. Boyle's observations concerning Cold once they are published.[154]

Apparently, then, Elisabeth's interest in scientific interests had not waned, and she was highly interested in the "new microscope." This ongoing interest might also be borne out in an intriguing instrumental reference from the papers of Benjamin Furly, a Quaker who visited Elisabeth in 1676 along with William Penn and Robert Barclay. Apparently, as Furly

---

[151] From Pell's letterbook, BL, Add. MS. 4365, f. 198. The entry is undated. However, as Barnett points out, this sequence is the most logical. Pamela Barnett, *Theodore Haak, F.R.S. (1606–1690): The First German Translator of 'Paradise Lost'* (The Hague, 1962), 133–5.
[152] Elisabeth to Haak, May 9/19, 1665. Original in French. BL, Add. MS. 4365, f. 196.
[153] *Ibid.* [154] *Ibid.*

was leaving Herford, Elisabeth had given him a memento of the visit – "a Microscop of fine silver, gilded," which had been made for her by order of Descartes.[155]

But prior to causing a stir by welcoming persecuted Quakers, Elisabeth had caused a stir by sheltering the persecuted Labadists. The learned world had been aghast that the philosophical princess, with her Cartesian reasoning and scientific understanding, would allow herself to be drawn into the orbit of this fanatic. Thus even before Elisabeth and Leibniz met in person at Sophie's court, Leibniz had been receiving reports about the goings-on at Herford. Spener, the "father of Pietism," wrote to Leibniz in 1671:

Labadie, who is at Herford with the virgin van Schurman and her group, is already putting things into motion, availing himself of the protection of the Most Serene Princess Palatine, who is the abbess. Many people are amazed that she is offering asylum to these people, whom their own country did not want to support: but even now it is said that the friendship contracted between the Princess and van Schurman had in former times been very close.[156]

Again, this community is being characterized as van Schurman's group, being accompanied by Labadie. And apparently another visitor had joined them, in the person of John Dury. We do not know why he was there; however, Spener was clear that he still believed in the centrality of his mission:

I do not know whether many hopes survive for Dury, or if truly in this way the old man is continuing on with the mission that has been so great a cause for so many years, lest he be said to have abandoned the objective which was his former life path.[157]

Spener needn't have worried about Elisabeth, and he needn't have worried about Dury. Both the Labadists and the Quakers had hoped to bring Elisabeth to their side; in the end, however, both she and her old friend Dury were resolutely tolerant, respectful, and spiritually independent to the ends of their lives.

---

[155] William Hull, *Benjamin Furly and Quakerism in Rotterdam*, Swarthmore College Monographs on Quaker History 5 (Swarthmore, 1941), 48–9. Hull cites a note by Joseph Green in *The Journal of the Friends Historical Society* 17, no. 3 (1920), 101–2. However, Green's note itself makes no specific mention of a microscope. Given Descartes' precarious finances, this seems like a rather unlikely gift, and this reference requires further substantiation.

[156] Jacob Spener to Leibniz, January 10, 1671, in Gottfried Wilhelm Leibniz, *Sämtliche Schriften und Briefe*, series 1, vol. 1 (Berlin, 1950), 111. Original in Latin.

[157] *Ibid.*, 112–13.

While van Schurman and the Labadists were resident in Herford, Elisabeth also received a visit from her sister Sophie. Sophie, like Leibniz, had been hearing reports of the goings-on at Herford long before she got there. However, Sophie was also hearing reports from van Schurman, so she was privy to several sides of the story. She frequently reported to their brother Karl Ludwig on what was happening in Elisabeth's convent, and the earthiness of her letters provides us with a useful counterpoint to the ethereality of van Schurman's *Eukleria*.

Van Schurman had prepared Sophie for this meeting by sending her two of Labadie's pamphlets beforehand. Sophie had thanked her, and then lamented the fact that, sadly, she herself had no hope of attaining such spirituality in this world; she would just have to wait for the next one.[158] But on a practical level, Sophie also knew that finances had been an ongoing issue for Elisabeth from the moment she took over at Herford; her philosophical sister had needed "to sell all her precious stones in order to buy dishes and furniture."[159] Thus Sophie could definitely see the benefit in having Labadie as part of the community. Despite the fact that Labadie drew trouble in his train wherever he went, she pointed out that he had one big point in his favor: "He does, however, have this one good quality, that he has enough money to build an abbey for my sister."[160]

After her visit to Herford in 1671, Sophie wrote a long and lively description of Labadie – his physical appearance, his behavior, and his apparently fascinating mouth:

> He is quite witty, with lively eyes, a good nose, and his mouth is nice enough in spite of his teeth, which have completely abandoned it . . . As to his tongue, one might call it a perpetual motion machine; he preaches well, and with great facility.[161]

And while van Schurman had described the Labadist mealtimes as a type of communal worship, Sophie saw the Labadist mealtime as a performance: "My sister and I ate with them; de Labadie was seated between us. You have never seen anything more amusing than this little Kinglet among all his saints."[162]

---

[158] Anna Maria van Schurman, "À S.A. Madame la Duchesse de Brons. et de Luneb," November 16, 1670; and "Réponse de Lad^te A. à Mad^lle Schurman," BL, Kings MSS. 140, fol. 24b. Also printed in Anna Wendland, "Beiträge zur Geschichte der Kurfürstin Sophie," *Zeitschrift des Historischen Vereins für Niedersachsen* (1910): 338–9.

[159] Sophie to Karl Ludwig, June 9/19, 1661, letter no. 46 in Bodemann, *Briefwechsel*, 43.

[160] Sophie to Karl Ludwig, November 5, 1670, letter no. 161 in Bodemann, *Briefwechsel*, 152–3.

[161] Sophie to Karl Ludwig, March 19, 1671, BL, Kings MSS. 140, f. 219. Also printed in Wendland, "Beiträge," 344–7.

[162] *Ibid.*

Sophie also reported to her brother on having encountered van Schurman there:

As to the women, Mlle. van Schurman is foremost because of her age. I told her that I was very happy to see her again, to which she replied, Your Highness does not see in me the same person that she saw in the past, because now I am a Christian, and I was not so before.[163]

Van Schurman had focused on her inner journey, and as she put it in her autobiography, "I wish to be nothing, to own nothing or to do nothing other than that which He always shows through His workings to be His will."[164] Sophie, however, put Labadist doctrine into much more worldly terms:

As for his Religion, it is the Reformed faith, which he has purified a second time, reducing it to an essence so pure, that I believe it would evaporate as soon as one tried to get hold of it. He says that it is necessary to renounce one's faith, even when it is quite perfect, because one must not derive pleasure from anything other than the glory of God ... When one dons or removes a glove, if one does not do it for the glory of God, then it is a sin ... They are all quite gay, because they believe that they are the only Elect. In the end, they are good people who have damned us all.[165]

Thus neither Sophie, nor Elisabeth, would ever be persuaded to join the Labadists.

However, Elisabeth does appear to have come much closer to being converted by the Quakers. The philosopher Anne Conway was already in the Quaker fold, and Elisabeth was kept apprised of Conway's spiritual progress by the Platonist Henry More, as well as by her friends Penn and Barclay.[166] Although Conway did not officially convert to Quakerism until 1677, the Queen of Bohemia had been reporting it as a fact as early as 1655, when she wrote to one of Conway's relatives, Sir John Finch, to report:

---

[163] *Ibid.*
[164] From the 1684 Dutch translation of *Eukleria*, 334. Cited in Mirjam de Baar, "'Now as for the faint rumours of fame attached to my name ...': The Eukleria as Autobiography," in *Choosing the Better Part: Anna Maria van Schurman (1607–1678)*, ed. Mirjam de Baar et al. (Dordrecht, 1996), 87–102, 94. On van Schurman's spiritual self-denial, see Bo Karen Lee, "'I wish to be nothing': The Role of Self-Denial in the Mystical Theology of Anna Maria van Schurman," in *Women, Gender and Radical Religion in Early Modern Europe*, ed. Sylvia Brown (Leiden, 2007), 189–216.
[165] Sophie to Karl Ludwig, March 19, 1671, BL, Kings MSS. 140, f. 219.
[166] See, for instance, More's letter to Lady Conway, dated July 14, 1671, wherein he discusses the possibility of Conway presenting his work to Elisabeth. *The Conway Letters*, 340.

As for the countess I can tell you heavie news of her, for she is turned quaker and preaches everie day in a tubb; your nephue can tell you of her quaking, but her tubb preaching is come sine he went I beleeve, she I beleeve at last will prove an adamite.[167]

There are no further references to sightings of Anne Conway preaching in a tub. However, after Conway's actual conversion to Quakerism, the pressure on Elisabeth increased. She had indeed been a good friend to the Quakers. Beyond welcoming them to Herford, she had been partly responsible for having Robert Barclay's father David released from Edinburgh Castle, where he had been imprisoned since 1665.[168]

William Penn had in fact made several visits to Herford. The first was in 1671, while the Labadists were there, and Penn had hoped to have a meeting of the minds with Labadie; like many before him, Penn had walked away frustrated. Labadists were sometimes referred to pejoratively as Quakers. But as Penn describes it, Labadie's behavior was such that he knew him to be a "false Quaker," and he felt it was his duty to educate Elisabeth and her community about the difference.[169] Then in 1677, Penn had returned with a group of Friends, as part of their tour through Germany and the Low Countries. Elisabeth had seemed receptive. She had been impressed with what Penn said at a meeting, and found herself filled with "that power and presence of God, which was amongst us."[170] Engaged correspondences ensued among Elisabeth, Penn, and Barclay, and the example of Anne Conway was repeatedly put before her. Finally, Elisabeth had to make herself perfectly clear:

I cannot submit unto the oppinion or practise of any others though I grant that they have more light than myself. The Countess of Conoway doth well to go on the way which she thinks best, but I should not do well to follow her, unless I had the same conviction, neither did it ever enter into my thoughts so to do. I love all that love God, & am ready to embrace all that is undoubtibly good.[171]

---

[167] Elizabeth, Queen of Bohemia, to Lord Finch, March 4, 1655, in *The Letters of Elizabeth, Queen of Bohemia*, ed. L.M. Baker (London, 1953), 231–2.

[168] Henry Mill, *Genealogical Account of the Barclays of Urie, for Upwards of Seven Hundred Years . . .* (London, 1812), 63.

[169] William Penn, "An Account of W. Penn's Travails in Germany & Holland," *The Friends' Library* 5 (1841): 72–3.

[170] *Ibid.*, 75. See also Amelia Gummere, "Letter from William Penn to Elisabeth, Princess Palatine, Abbess of the Protestant Convent of Hereford, 1677, with an Introduction," *Bulletin of Friends' Historical Society of Philadelphia* 4, no. 2 (March, 1912): 82–97.

[171] Princess Elisabeth to Robert Barclay, March 1/11, 1677, in *Reliquiae Barclaianae. Correspondence of Colonel David Barclay and Robert Barclay of Urie, and his Son Robert, including Letters from Princess Elizabeth of the Rhine . . . William Penn, George Fox, and others, etc.* Lithograph. (London, 1870), 27–8.

Penn had also pursued Anna Maria van Schurman to the Labadist community in Wieuwerd, where he hoped to obtain from the "ancient maiden" a better understanding of her faith, and perhaps convince her to convert to Quakerism. He had been impressed by the improvement in the community since Labadie had died, and by how closely their practices now resembled those of the Quakers. In the end, van Schurman gave a moving testimonial, but remained resolute in her refusal to convert to Quakerism. Despite this, Barclay wrote to Elisabeth that same year, claiming: "I question not but thy old Friend Anna Maria Shurman would be one [a Quaker] if yet in the body."[172]

Letters written during Elisabeth's final years show that the last stage of her intellectual life was consistent with what had preceded it – her mind was always engaged, open, and interested in everything new. As a woman of faith, the Calvinist abbess of a Lutheran convent, she explored what it might have meant to be a Labadist or a Quaker. As a scholar of science and mathematics, she corresponded with members of the Royal Society about physics, geometry, algebra, and the latest scientific instruments. As a philosopher, she kept pursuing new ideas, and new permutations of Cartesian reason. For instance, Elisabeth was in touch during these years with both Leibniz and Malebranche. Nicolas Malebranche was a Cartesian philosopher and a Catholic priest, and, while Elisabeth was impressed with his *Conversations Chrestiennes*, she had apparently become quite annoyed when he tried to convert her to Catholicism. Nevertheless, on a visit to Sophie's court in 1678, it was Elisabeth who introduced Leibniz to the work of Malebranche, and Leibniz acknowledged that debt in a letter from 1679.[173] Elisabeth was complimented for her learning, and consulted for her algebraic expertise. Samuel Chappuzeau, the playwright who had also known Marie de Gournay in Paris, said that "she was the admiration of this century and the one before."[174]

---

[172] Since van Schurman did not die until the following year, she was still occupying her body at the time. Robert Barclay to Princess Elisabeth, from Aberdeen Prison, March 16, 1677, in Barclay, *Reliquiae Barclaianae*, 18–21.

[173] Leibniz to Malebranche, January 13, 1679, letter no. 103 in André Robinet, *Malebranche et Leibniz: Relations personnelles* (Paris, 1955), 103–5. See also E. J. Aiton, *Leibniz: A Biography* (Bristol, 1985), 90–1. The Cartesian letter from Leibniz to Elisabeth is in *Sämtliche Schriften und Briefe*, series 2, vol. 1, (Berlin, 1987), 433–8. On Elisabeth's correspondence with Malebranche, see *Malebranche: Oeuvres complètes*, ed. André Robinet, 20 vols. (Paris, 1958–78), XVIII, 130–3.

[174] Reported in a letter from Sophie to Karl Ludwig, July 14/24, 1669, letter no. 151 in Bodemann, *Briefwechsel*, 143. On Chappuzeau and Gournay, see Samuel Chappuzeau, *Le Théatre François* [1674], ed. Georges Monval (Paris, 1875), I, 6, 29.

Moreover, the political princess who had always defended the interests of her family continued in this role with her new family in Herford. When enemy troops entered the town in 1679, the villagers had been terrified – but Elisabeth had not been afraid. As Sophie reported, "It was yet another scare for the poor townsfolk, whom Elisabeth harangued in her bathrobe and slippers in order to reassure them."[175] And finally, she continued to honor her friendships with her learned circle from The Hague, writing to Penn about "good old Dury," and welcoming her fugitive former mentor, Anna Maria van Schurman.[176] Elisabeth died at Herford on February 8, 1680.

*

Doors had closed in the republic of letters for these collegial female scholars at the end of the seventeenth century. Yet despite this, the women who had begun forming their intellectual network in the 1630s – Marie de Gournay, Marie du Moulin, Anna Maria van Schurman, Princess Elisabeth, Dorothy Moore, Bathsua Makin, and Lady Ranelagh – continued pursuing active scholarship throughout their lives. Some did so in the public realm, while others constructed cloistered communities, behind whose doors they could continue their intellectual activities. And beyond remembering each other, they were still remembered, consulted, and contacted by those male colleagues with whom they had worked in previous decades. For their contemporaries and fellow scholars, no account of the mid-century republic of letters, and no history of their shared work for the advancement of learning, would have been complete without them.

---

[175] Sophie to Karl Ludwig, June 27, 1679, letter no. 366, in Bodemann, *Briefwechsel*, 363–4.
[176] Penn, "An Account," 93–4.

Conclusions

> in the history of great expanses of time, the memorials to women's names are no more in evidence than the traces left by a ship crossing the ocean.
>
> Anna Maria van Schurman, 1637[1]

In 1637, Anna Maria van Schurman had reflected on her role in the republic of letters. In doing so, she had become acutely aware of two things: first, that she was a full and active participant; and second, that all memory of her participation was destined for obscurity because she was a woman. The problem did not reside in the quality of her scholarship, the attitudes of her contemporary colleagues, or in the seventeenth-century enterprise for the advancement of learning. The problem, she knew, was History.

This study thus concludes by moving forward from the seventeenth century to consider whether van Schurman was right. Would van Schurman and her fellow female scholars in this ephemeral Republic of Women be swallowed by the ocean of History? And if so, what processes were at work?

THE NEXT GENERATION: FEMALE SCHOLARS IN THE EIGHTEENTH CENTURY

By 1742, van Schurman had been dead for over sixty years – and yet, the apparently indestructible scholar had not let this stop her. She was still corresponding with other intellectual women, and at some point in the 1740s van Schurman paused amid the joys of her learned Elysian circle to take a moment to write to Lady Mary Wortley Montagu. Montagu had

---

[1] Anna Maria van Schurman to André Rivet, November 6, 1637, KB MS. 133 B 8, no. 14; also printed in *Opuscula*, 69–70. See also the translation by Joyce Irwin in van Schurman, *Whether a Christian Woman*, 41–8.

then returned the favor. She wrote back to say that she was flattered van Schurman would find her worthy of her time and attention, when the ethereal scholar might so easily have been bantering with Petronius instead. Montagu was also impressed by the improvement in van Schurman's posthumous literary style; she pointed out that van Schurman's writing had been excessively stiff while she was still in the flesh, much like her use of scholastic argumentation:

I believe that you are now sufficiently free of prejudices to allow even criticism of your works without impatience, and you will allow me to say freely that your reasons to prove your thesis "*Feminae christianae convenit studium Litterarum*" appear to me sometimes rather weak, and always recited in a dry and scholastic manner.[2]

Yet Montagu finally excused van Schurman for both these faults, deeming that her disputation, like her writing style, had been unavoidably and inevitably shaped by her era.

However, she had no quibbles whatsoever with the content of van Schurman's work. She agreed that learning was necessary for women; it was only that the new century required feminist arguments to be made instead "from a political point of view," since it was the state that would ultimately benefit. And then, of course, there was another contribution that learned women could make:

Our frailty prevents us from serving in war, but this same frailty gives us great leisure for study. Those who succeed will be able to contribute to the Republic of Letters.[3]

Thus Montagu saw learned women, including herself, as having value as potential contributors to the eighteenth-century republic of letters – an outlook that would surely have pleased van Schurman.

Van Schurman might also have been pleased with the output of Montagu's intellect. Montagu was a writer who produced work in a number of genres – satires, poems, plays, essays, and travel writing – in addition to being active in medical reform. She had spent many years in Constantinople, where she learned about the practice of inoculation using live smallpox virus and then introduced this practice to England. Her letters also document her command of Latin, and an early love of

---

[2] The letter is undated, but the location of Avignon places it sometime between 1742 and 1746. Montagu, *Essays and Poems*, 165–7, 392–3. On Montagu (1689–1762) see also *The Complete Letters of Lady Mary Wortley Montagu*, ed. Robert Halsband, 3 vols. (Oxford, 1965–7).

[3] Montagu, *Essays and Poems*, 166.

learning, which had given way to the exigencies of social and domestic responsibilities. Finally, Montagu concluded her letter to Heaven with a plaintive postscript:

I am so charmed by your coterie that if you promise to admit me immediately I shall throw myself into the Rhône to seek you, half through desire of seeing you, and half from boredom with all those whom I do see.[4]

Van Schurman's "coterie," like van Schurman herself, had ceased to exist. But Montagu clearly wanted more than just inclusion in the republic of letters – what she wanted was to be included in the Republic of Women.

In Montagu's whimsical letter to the long-dead Star of Utrecht, we have a telling example of the legacy of van Schurman's community of female scholars. Their moment of inclusion had definitively died at the end of the seventeenth century – however, this did not mean the end of female scholarship, nor did it mean that this "coterie" had been forgotten. There would always be women who were drawn to a life of the mind, and who would have liked nothing better than to spend their lives in scholarly fellowship and pursuits. What these women would lack, however, was the place in which to do this. Female scholarship was a constant – female scholarly communities were not.

But beyond the constant presence of intellectual women, we can still detect, in eighteenth-century Europe, traces of the scholarly community that had begun in The Hague in 1634. Some of these traces were textual: for instance, van Schurman's *Dissertatio* and *Opuscula*, as printed works, continued to be read by women like Montagu, and the fact that Montagu quotes van Schurman in the original Latin indicates that she must have owned at least one of these texts. And these readers were apparently influenced not only by the content, but by the evidence of female community as well. Other traces show the descent of the *famille d'alliance* – through close intellectual kinship, and sometimes through an intertwining with biological descent. And some of these traces survive in the different types of women's intellectual communities constructed by these later generations of female scholars.

Montagu was not the only one to remember the late van Schurman. For Elizabeth Elstob (1683–1756), an Anglo-Saxon scholar known as "The Saxon Nymph," scholarship was a struggle against inimical influences.[5]

---

[4] *Ibid.*
[5] On Elizabeth Elstob see Mary Elizabeth Green, "Elizabeth Elstob: The Saxon Nymph (English, 1683–1765)," in Jean Brink, ed. *Female Scholars: A Tradition of Learned Women Before 1800* (Montreal, 1980), 137–60; Myra Reynolds, *The Learned Lady in England, 1650–1760* (Vassar, 1920;

While her mother was "a great admirer of learning, especially in her own sex," she had died when Elstob was eight years old; and at that point, Elizabeth had been sent to live with an uncle. As Elstob describes the situation, her uncle "was no friend to women's learning, so that she was not suffered to proceed."[6] Elstob eventually became a linguist, first translating the works of Madeleine de Scudéry, then moving on to master Anglo-Saxon.

In 1709, when she was twenty-six years old, Elstob began compiling her own catalogue of learned women; and in the list of exemplary ancestresses that prefaced her *English-Saxon Homily* we see a familiar name:

The usual Objections that are made by Gentlemen to Womens Learning, are fully answer'd in a Scholastick way, and in very elegant *Latin*, by that Glory of her Sex, Mrs. *Anna Maria a Schurman*, who hath also writ several Latin Epistles, to Andreas Rivetus on the same Subject. See her *Opuscula Hebraea, Graeca, Latina, Gallica, Prosaica & Metrica*.[7]

It appears that Elstob, like Montagu, owned a copy of van Schurman's work, and was conscious of being part of a female intellectual genealogy that included the Dutch scholar of a century before. Yet times had changed, and this was no longer the world of the exile court in The Hague, or of Hartlib's inclusive network of reformers.

After the death of her brother, Elstob's isolation and poverty inspired the linguist George Ballard to celebrate learned women. Ballard was appalled that such deserving scholars could not find the recognition and support they deserved, and the result was his 1752 work, *Memoirs of Several Ladies of Great Britain, Who Have Been Celebrated for their Writings of Skill in the Learned Languages, Arts and Sciences*. However, the accuracy of his observations foretold the failure of his project. And when Ballard's lovingly compiled volume failed to generate any interest whatsoever, he wrote a letter of bitter complaint to Elstob herself. In reply, she sadly reflected on the times, and the current repugnance for learned women:

---

reprint, Gloucester, MA, 1964), 169–85; and George Ballard, *Memoirs of Several Ladies of Great Britain, Who Have Been Celebrated for their Writings of Skill in the Learned Languages, Arts and Sciences* (1752), ed. Ruth Perry (Detroit, 1985).

[6] From a fragment appended to a letter from George Hickes. George Hickes to Dr. Charlett, December 23, 1712, "Recommending Mrs. Elstob to his patronage and that of the University, with a great character of her learning and abilities." Letter XCI in John Walker, *Letters Written by Eminent persons in the Seventeenth and Eighteenth Centuries . . . and Lives of Eminent Men, by John Aubrey, Esq.*, 2 vols. (London, 1813), I, 243.

[7] Elizabeth Elstob, *An English-Saxon homily on the birth-day of St. Gregory . . . Tr. into modern English, with notes, etc., by Eliz. Elstob* (London, 1709), iii.

This is not an Age to hope for any encouragement to Learning of any kind. For your part I am sorry to tell you the choice you have made for the Honour of the Females was the wrongest subject you could pitch upon. For you can come into no company of Ladies or Gentlemen where you shall not hear an open and vehement exclamation against Learned women, and by those women who read much themselves to what purpose they know best.[8]

Ballard aside, there was no longer any intellectual home for female scholars. However, Elstob did become acquainted with other learned women in her world, beyond her mother and the ghosts of earlier centuries. Following this trail of connections allows us to examine examples of women's scholarship, and to detect the fading traces of women's intellectual community into the eighteenth century.

First, we have the comparison that matches Elstob against the French classicist Anne Dacier (1651–1720).[9] The two were not acquainted. However, both were celebrated scholars of classical languages, and this is what formed the basis of comparison. Anne Dacier was the daughter of the humanist and educator Tannegui le Fevre, a professor of Greek and Latin at the Protestant academy of Saumur. Her husband, André Dacier, was also a classicist. However, Anne was considered to be the superior scholar and, according to an epigram by Boileau, "In intellectual productions common to both, she is the father."[10] Like van Schurman, Dacier had benefited from being educated at home by a doting and observant father. In a story reminiscent of the one van Schurman recounted in her autobiography, the beginning of Dacier's education is described as a consequence of the lessons her father was providing to someone else:

He had a son, whom he was educating with great care. Anne le Fèvre, the girl with whom we are concerned, was eleven years old at the time. While he was giving lessons to his son, she was usually present. One day it happened that this young schoolboy gave a wrong answer to one of his father's questions. His sister, while still continuing to work on her embroidery, whispered to him, and suggested the answer he should give to their father. Their father

---

[8] Bodleian Library, Ballard MSS. 43, f. 47. Cited in Florence M. Smith, *Mary Astell* (New York, 1916), 169–70.

[9] On Anne Dacier see especially Fern Farnham, *Madame Dacier: Scholar and Humanist* (Monterey, CA, 1976). See also Emmanuel Bury, "Madame Dacier," in *Femmes savantes, savoirs des femmes: du crépuscule de la Renaissance à l'aube des Lumières* (Geneva, 1999), 209–20; Joseph M. Levine, *The Battle of the Books: History and Literature in the Augustan Age* (Ithaca, 1991), 132–45; and Paul Mazon, *Madame Dacier et les traductions d'Homère en France* (Oxford, 1935). Gilles Ménage dedicated *The History of Women Philosophers* (1690) to Anne Dacier, "*feminarum doctissima*."

[10] Cited by Paul Lejay, *The Catholic Encyclopedia*, vol. IV (1908).

overheard, and delighted by this discovery, he resolved to extend his care to her, and to educate her in letters.[11]

Later, as Dacier gained a reputation throughout Europe as a classicist and professional translator, her father's pedagogical methods would gain credibility through being associated with her success – an example that resonates powerfully with Bathsua Makin as her father's most famous pupil.[12] But apart from the charm of the story itself, this episode is interesting because of its source – the anecdote comes from Queen Christina's first biographer, because the two women had been in touch.

This was not, however, because Dacier and Christina had a relationship as friends and mentors, like van Schurman and Princess Elisabeth, or because they had engaged in an extended intellectual correspondence. Dacier had written a letter in Latin to Queen Christina on March 15, 1678, sending her two books, and hoping Christina would deign to add them to her library. Christina had responded with thanks on May 22 – but then proceeded to harangue Dacier for remaining obstinately Protestant. What good was all that knowledge, when Dacier refused to see the beauty and truth of the Roman faith?[13] These were the only two letters in their correspondence. However, Dacier did, in fact, follow Christina's example and advice. She abjured in 1685, in a move that stunned many in her intellectual orbit. Since she did not discuss her reasons for doing so, many speculated that this was a practical, rather than spiritual choice in the powerfully anti-Huguenot atmosphere of France after the Revocation.[14]

Dacier was clearly a first-rate female scholar of the eighteenth century; however, she had no interest in either the company of other learned women or using her own abilities as the basis for a feminist argument about learning. Unlike van Schurman, Dacier would often refuse to sign the *album amicorum* of a visiting scholar, saying, "Silence is the ornament of women."[15] Yet other connections in the life of Elizabeth Elstob

---

[11] Johan Arckenholtz, *Memoires Concernant Christine Reine de Suede, Pour Servir d'eclaircissement a l'histoire de son regne et principalement de sa vie privee . . .* 4 vols. (Amsterdam and Leipzig, 1751), II, 187–9; and Appendix no. LXXXIII, 154.

[12] For example, Jenkin Thomas Philipps rendered Tannegui le Fevre's treatise on classical education, *Methode courte et facile pour apprendre les humanités Grecque et Latines* (London, 1703), into English as *A Compendious Way of Teaching Ancient and Modern Languages, Formerly practised by the Learned Tanaquil Faber, in the Education of one of his Sons, and of his Daughter the Celebrated Madame Dacier . . .* (London, 1723).

[13] Arckenholtz, *Memoires*, 2:187–9, and Appendix LXXXIII, 154.

[14] Farnham, *Madame Dacier*, chapter 5, "Marriage and Conversion."

[15] Nicolas Trublet, *Mémoires pour l'histoire de la vie et des ouvrages de Fontenelle* (Amsterdam, 1759), 108–9. Cited in Levine, *Battle of the Books*, 135.

show us female scholars who did work communally in this inimical environment, and who certainly did not feel that silence was their ornament.

Elstob's contact with the feminist writer George Ballard had come about through mutual acquaintances in the eighteenth-century literary salon known as the Bluestockings. Many of the most accomplished literary women in eighteenth-century London – Elizabeth Montagu, Hannah More, Frances Burney, Anna Laetitia Barbauld, Sarah Fielding, and Hester Chapone – were regular members of this circle.[16] Hester Chapone's mother-in-law was Sarah Chapone, also a Bluestocking, and a close friend of Ballard. Sarah Chapone introduced them, and through Elstob Ballard learned of many more intellectual women. Elstob had also met and been inspired by the feminist philosopher Mary Astell, and Elstob later became Ballard's source for information on Astell when he was compiling his *Memoirs* of learned women.[17] The relationship between Elstob and Astell never ripened into the community enjoyed by van Schurman and her circle; however, the composition of Astell's inner circle of friends and supporters suggests that perhaps the *famille d'alliance* had not yet ceased to function in the lives of female scholars. There is also a suggestion that biological descent played a part in the continuation of intellectual kinship. Two of Astell's closest friends and supporters were Elizabeth "Lady Betty" Hastings, and Lady Catherine Jones – Lady Betty was the granddaughter of Makin's pupil Lucy Hastings, and Catherine Jones was the granddaughter of Lady Ranelagh.[18]

At the end of the seventeenth century, it was Mary Astell (1666–1731) who assessed these still-present longings for a women's intellectual community, and gave those longings their most concrete form.[19] Astell's voice was powerfully feminist, and she demanded to know, in her *Reflections upon Marriage*, "If all men are born free, how is it that all women are born

[16] On the Bluestockings, see Sylvia Harcstark Myers, *The Bluestocking Circle: Women, Friendship, and the Life of the Mind in Eighteenth-Century England* (Oxford, 1990); and Gary Kelly, ed., *Bluestocking Feminism: Writings of the Bluestocking Circle, 1738–1785* (Brookfield, VT, 1999).

[17] Ballard, *Memoirs*, 25.

[18] On Lady Betty, see Thomas Barnard, *An Historical Character Relating to the Holy and Exemplary Life of the Right Honourable the Lady Elisabeth Hastings* ... (Leeds, 1743); and Charles Edward Medhurst, *Life and Work of Lady Elizabeth Hastings, the Great Yorkshire Benefactress of the XVIIIth Century* (Leeds, 1914). Catherine Jones was the daughter of Lady Ranelagh's son Richard Jones, Lord Ranelagh.

[19] On Mary Astell, see especially Patricia Springborg, *Mary Astell: Theorist of Freedom from Domination* (Cambridge, 2005). See also William Kolbrener and Michal Michelson, eds., *Mary Astell: Reason, Gender, Faith* (Aldershot, 2007); and Perry, *The Celebrated Mary Astell.*

slaves?"[20] She also gave attention to women's education, and in *A Serious Proposal to the Ladies* Astell sought funds to establish an all-female enclave, a women's "Retreat from the World." Although she called her institution a "Seminary," its purpose, she assured her female readers, was academic. As Astell defends the educational curriculum for her institution, her *Serious Proposal* sounds very much like Bathsua Makin's *Essay*:

If any object against a Learned Education, that it will make Women vain and assuming, and instead of correcting, encrease their Pride: I grant, that a smattering in Learning may; for it has this effect on the Men, none so Dogmatical, and so forward to shew their Parts as your little *Pretenders* to Science. But I wou'd not have the Ladies content themselves with the *shew*, my desire is, that they shou'd not rest till they obtain the *Substance*.[21]

And, again like Makin's *Essay*, Astell's *Proposal to the Ladies* was an advertisement, intended to reach potential subscribers to her plan.

What generous Spirit that has a due regard to the good of Mankind, will not be forward to advance and perfect it? Who will think 500 pounds too much to lay out for the purchase of so much Wisdom and Happiness?[22]

Astell was part of a new generation, making her argument on political and philosophical grounds, rather than using *exempla* in the humanist tradition. Nevertheless, Astell could not resist pointing out some useful examples – the accomplishments of contemporaries like the classicist Anne Dacier, and the "fashion" for learned women in sixteenth-century England.[23]

Astell in fact provides a connection to a new generation of learned women, and perhaps the descent of the *famille d'alliance*, through her friendship and association with Montagu. Just as Marie de Gournay had been moved and delighted by having van Schurman as her intellectual daughter, Astell appears to have felt the same way toward the younger Montagu. As Montagu's granddaughter recalled Astell:

She felt for Lady Mary Wortley that fond partiality which old people of ardent tempers sometimes entertain for a rising genius in her own line. Literature had been hers; and she triumphed in Lady Mary's talents as proofs of what it was her first wish to demonstrate, namely, the mental equality of the sexes.[24]

And, if we follow the trail of the intellectual family even further, we will find ourselves in America in 1773, where the poet Phillis Wheatley was

---

[20] Mary Astell, *Reflections upon Marriage, To which is added a Preface in Answer to Some Objections* (London, 1706), xi. Cited in Springborg, *Mary Astell*, 105.
[21] Astell, *A Serious Proposal to the Ladies*, 73–6, 153–4.   [22] *Ibid.*, 157.   [23] *Ibid.*, 10, 78–9.
[24] Cited in Perry, *The Celebrated Mary Astell*, 273.

about to set sail for London. Although she was enslaved, Phillis had been highly educated by the family who owned her, and was familiar with the works of the Greek and Latin poets. However, her poetry could not find a publisher in the United States, since the "attestations" to her authorship of the poems were not convincing enough for an American publisher in 1772. Thus her work – the first book of poetry ever published in English by someone of African descent – was going to be published in England. And her patron in that project was Selina Hastings, the Methodist Countess of Huntingdon, who had married one the descendants of Makin's original patron.[25]

A further indication of a biological descent in the families of intellectual women comes from the example of Sophie-Charlotte, the niece of Princess Elisabeth. Sophie-Charlotte, the daughter of Elisabeth's sister Sophie, had been an engaged correspondent and patron of Leibniz. And on her deathbed, her final words were reportedly about philosophy and the infinite:

I am going now to satisfy my curiosity concerning the basic principles of things, which Leibniz was never able to explain to me, principles of space, of the infinite, of being and nothingness.[26]

One imagines that Elisabeth would have approved of this philosophical niece. Yet this was no longer the intellectual world in which Elisabeth and the other members of her scholarly network had been so active, and so integrated.

Perhaps the most telling indicator of this difference is the way in which women were becoming associated with institutions of learning, and we see this most clearly in the example of eighteenth-century Italy. Italy was the first country in Europe to admit women to university. However, this was not a policy, but rather an exception made in some very few individual cases. In 1678, Elena Cornaro Piscopia became the first woman to be awarded a university degree, when she graduated from the University of Padua with a degree in philosophy. Then, less than a year later, Padua closed its doors to women.[27] Over fifty years later, the Newtonian Laura Bassi became the second woman to be awarded a university degree, graduating in philosophy from the University of

---

[25] Henry Louis Gates Jr., *The Trials of Phillis Wheatley: America's First Black Poet and Her Encounters with the Founding Fathers* (New York, 2003), 28.

[26] Frederick the Great, *Oeuvres Historiques de Frédéric II, Roi de Prusse*, ed. J. D. E. Preuss, 7 vols. (Berlin, 1846–7), I, 112.

[27] Rebecca Messbarger and Paula Findlen, eds. and trans., *The Contest for Knowledge: Debates over Women's Learning in Eighteenth-Century Italy* (Chicago, 2005), 7.

Bologna in 1732.[28] Piscopia subsequently was elected a member of the illustrious Academy of the Ricovrati, one of whose founders was Galileo; Bassi was made an honorary member of the Bolognese Academy of Sciences. And in 1727, the nine-year-old Maria Gaetana Agnesi gave an oration in Milan on the subject of women's education; the three modern female *exempla* she used were Isabelle Roser, a Spanish would-be Jesuit, Elena Cornaro Piscopia, and Anne Dacier.[29]

But what did these elections, admissions, and orations actually mean? Was the intellectual culture of universities in Enlightenment Italy so open that women could indeed participate at the highest levels, and contribute to these institutions? The answer is no, followed immediately by "and yet . . ." On the one hand, the presence of women in these institutions was a rare, wonderful, and largely honorary thing. For the most part, they were *illustri* – above their own sex, and set apart from their male colleagues. Their role in the Italian Enlightenment republic of letters was to serve as examples of how new attitudes, and the new science, could produce real improvement in the human condition, thus these learned women were on a pedestal. And yet – that pedestal was solidly positioned in dignified academies and respected universities. The women were physically present, and could not be denied.[30]

This was a contradiction that Montagu, who had written the letter to van Schurman in Heaven, understood completely. In 1753, while in Italy, she wrote a letter to her daughter, describing some of the differences between Italy and England:

The character of a learned Woman is far from being ridiculous in this Country, the greatest Familys being proud of having produce'd female Writers, and a Milanese Lady being now proffessor of Mathematics in the University of Bologna, invited thither by a most obliging Letter wrote by the present Pope, who desir'd her to accept of the Chair not as a recompense for her merit, but to do Honor to a Town which is under his protection.[31]

According to Montagu, then, the impetus for granting Agnesi this post in the academy was not the desire to welcome an outstanding new colleague; it was rather the desire to promote a town under the Pope's protection. Local boosterism, rather than a shared intellectual enterprise, was the

---

[28] On Laura Bassi (1711–78), see Paula Findlen, "Science as a Career in Enlightenment Italy: The Strategies of Laura Bassi," *Isis* 84, no. 3 (1993): 441–69; and idem, "The Scientist's Body: The Nature of a Woman Philosopher in Enlightenment Italy," in *The Faces of Nature in Enlightenment Europe*, ed. Lorraine Daston and Gianna Pomata (Berlin, 2003), 211–36.

[29] Messbarger and Findlen, *The Contest for Knowledge*, 117–40.   [30] *Ibid.*, ii, 69.

[31] Montagu to Lady Bute, October 10, [1753], in Montagu, *Complete Letters*, iii, 38–41.

engine for this unique promotion of female excellence. And yet, as Montagu describes the nation of her birth, she realizes how much Italy surpasses England in this regard:

To say Truth, there is no part of the World where our Sex is treated with so much contempt as in England . . . We are educated in the grossest ignorance, and no art omitted to stifle our natural reason; if some few get above their Nurses' instructions, our knowledge must rest conceal'd and be as useless to the World as Gold in the Mine.[32]

Montagu realized that at least these Italian female scholars – pedestal or no pedestal – were allowed to work in the academy. And on the whole, Montagu would rather be in Italy.

The eighteenth-century republic of letters was thus a very different world, presenting female scholars with a different set of choices. A century after death had disbanded van Schurman's "coterie," the world that she and her colleagues Princess Elisabeth, Dorothy Moore, Marie du Moulin, Marie de Gournay, Bathsua Makin, and Lady Ranelagh had known was no more. In the place of the transnational seventeenth-century republic of letters, we find nationalized republics of letters, and local academies; and rather than existing in an idealized space, they were the pride of their cities, and of their nations. And yet, learned women were there. Some, like Montagu and Elstob, remembered, honored, and envied the collegial female scholars of a previous century. Some, like Astell, looked forward to promoting female scholarship with a new set of argumentative tools – but their colleagues in this endeavor were the descendants of learned women involved in the network of female scholars that had originated in the exile court at The Hague. For intellectual women of the eighteenth century, the longing for a female scholarly community had not gone away – it was only the model that had disappeared, along with the inclusive intellectual enterprise that had supported it.

RETHINKING THE REPUBLIC OF LETTERS

In a 1637 letter to André Rivet, van Schurman had argued for the right of women to achieve – to become scholars, artists, and theologians. The stakes were high, since she was also arguing for her personal and professional identity, and that of every female scholar with whom she had become acquainted. Certainly, a female scholar might be remembered

---

[32] *Ibid.*

in later ages as someone's daughter, sister, or wife, but this conveyed nothing about the woman herself. Van Schurman thus reflected that if female scholars were barred from those activities that delighted and fulfilled them, it would be as though they had never existed at all:

In vain do we women boast of the nobility we have inherited from our ancestors, since it is soon enveloped by a useless obscurity. Thus we find that in reading the history of great expanses of time, the memorials to women's names are no more in evidence than the traces left by a ship crossing the ocean.[33]

It was a fear borne out a century later by Nicéron's assessment of the legacy of Marie de Gournay, van Schurman's role model and *mère d'alliance*:

Nothing can equal the praise she received during her lifetime: but we can no longer give her such eulogy, and whatever merit she may have had as a person, her works are no longer read by anyone and have slipped into an oblivion from which they will never emerge.[34]

Like Gournay, van Schurman had known from childhood that she would not marry, and would not have children. Who, then, would remember her? And for what achievements would she be remembered?

The answers to van Schurman's implicit questions require a reformulation of the premise. The real question here is not "Who is remembered?" but "Who is doing the remembering?" and "Why?" For Anna Maria van Schurman and the other women who have been the focus of this study, these answers have been difficult to find.

Memories alone, unattached to larger reasons or purposes, are very short-lived. As early as 1752, all knowledge of Lady Ranelagh and Bathsua Makin had nearly vanished from the places in which they had lived and worked and taught. Thus George Ballard, compiling his encyclopedic volume on learned Englishwomen, had found himself frustrated:

Those whose memoirs are here offered to the public I have placed in the order of time in which they lived, omitting none of whom I could collect sufficient materials. For as there may yet be some learned women of those times whose character I am an entire stranger to, so there are others whom I well know to have been persons of distinguished parts and learning, but have been able to collect very little else relating to them.

---

[33] Van Schurman to Rivet, November 6, 1637, KB MS. 133 B 8, no. 14. Also printed in *Opuscula*, 69–70, with a translation by Irwin in *Whether a Christian Woman*, 41–8.
[34] Jean-Pierre Nicéron, *Mémoires pour servir à l'histoire des hommes illustres dans la république des lettres*, 43 vols. (Paris, 1729–45), XVI, 231.

Among those women whose materials were eluding Ballard we find some familiar names:

Such are ... Lady Ranelagh ... Mrs. Makins (who corresponded in the learned languages with Mrs Anna Maria à Schurman) ... together with very many other learned and ingenious women since the year 1700.[35]

And three centuries after van Schurman wrote to Rivet, there was an educated woman who also wanted very much indeed to find these very traces of collegial female scholarship. However, like Ballard, she would fail to turn up the evidences of the intellectual circle that had formed in The Hague in the 1630s. The lament was that of Virginia Woolf, from *A Room of One's Own*:

But by no possible means could middle-class women with nothing but brains and character at their command have taken part in any one of the great movements which, brought together, constitute the historian's view of the past ... what I find deplorable, I continued, looking about the bookshelves again, is that nothing is known about women before the eighteenth century. I have no model in my mind to turn about this way and that.[36]

Thus it is clear that van Schurman's fears had been borne out – the traces of the names of these women had indeed vanished into the ocean of History.

And yet, there is another line of memory, in which these women's names did not disappear. Instead, they were repeatedly invoked, and used as a source of strength and continuity and intellectual modeling for women throughout the early modern era. For the fifteenth-century humanist Laura Cereta, female scholars constituted a "noble lineage." She called them *respublica mulierum*, or the Republic of Women – a women's republic of letters, whose members were accomplished, virtuous, and scholarly:

I am impelled to show what great glory that noble lineage which I carry in my own breast has won for virtue and literature – a lineage that knowledge, the bearer of honors, has exalted in every age. For the possession of this lineage is legitimate and sure, and it has come all the way down to me from the perpetual continuance of a more enduring race ... the republic of women, so worthy of veneration.[37]

Cereta's vision of the Republic of Women was a network of female scholars and teachers bound together through time by common

---

[35] Ballard, *Memoirs*, 54.   [36] Viriginia Woolf, *A Room of One's Own* (New York, 1929), 46–7.
[37] Cereta, *Collected Letters*, 76–80.

intellectual interests – it was her own version of Christine de Pizan's *City of Ladies*, with its own genealogy and history.[38]

This literary ideal of the republic of women had begun in the waning years of the Middle Ages, with Christine de Pizan's *The Book of the City of Ladies* (1405). De Pizan was an educated woman and a widowed single mother who supported her three children, her mother, and herself through her writing. Her *City of Ladies* was a powerful defense of the female sex, and it was de Pizan's entry into the *querelle des femmes*. It recounts how Christine, distraught over misogynist attacks, had been visited in a dream by three noble Ladies named Reason, Rectitude, and Justice. Instructing her to construct a city by and for virtuous women, the Lady Reason also told Christine that she need not be alone, because there were other learned women like her:

> If it were customary to send daughters to school like sons, and if they were then taught the natural sciences, they would learn as thoroughly and as well as sons. And by chance there happen to be such women.[39]

This was followed by Christine de Pizan's catalogue of exemplary women. It was a catalogue that would continue to be remembered, embellished, and invoked by female scholars throughout the early modern era; and in 1673, we find it again, in Bathsua Makin's *Essay*.

What we have here, then, is a historical paradox. On the one hand, there is the truth of van Schurman's prediction – the historical record of this community of female scholars had faded away, leaving barely detectable traces in its wake. And on the other hand, we have the repeatedly iterated rosters of intellectual women whose names were invoked and passed down through the generations by female scholars themselves. Reconciling these contradictions requires rethinking both how and why we have constructed the narrative of early modern intellectual history. And the key to doing so is an understanding that what we have come to know as the history of intellectual change has in many ways been the history of intellectual institutions instead.

Institutions have always been central to the early modern historical landscape. Churches, parliaments, and courts have formed the basis for understanding and investigating the nature of life and thought; and in the case of intellectual history, it is to libraries, universities, and scientific

---

[38] On Christine de Pizan (*c.*1365–1430), see Susan Groag Bell, *The Lost Tapestries of the City of Ladies: Christine de Pizan's Renaissance Legacy* (Berkeley, 2004).
[39] De Pizan, *The Book of the City of Ladies*, 63.

societies that the historian turns for information. Since these institutions are also the repositories of archival records, this makes them sites of documentary memory as well.

However, when we are confronted with evidence of intellectual activity and collegiality from a group not associated with any of these institutions, it is incumbent upon us to start asking new questions. We must begin to interrogate the nature of these institutions themselves, and to question whether these institutions can truly be deemed representative of the intellectual cultures that spawned them. And in particular, we must begin asking ourselves how we understand the formation of institutional memory. Institutions have no historical mandate other than to preserve institutional memory, through the formation of archives and the creation of appropriate documents. These might be intended to support their own creation myths, rules of conduct, and central mission, or to define the relevant internal and external communities.[40] And since these archives are formed with an organizational identity and sensibility at their core, not all records will be kept. Some documents, which might seem irrelevant to the institutional mandate, could find themselves without an archival home.

The Royal Society could certainly be seen as an example of this. In 1678, John Wallis described the founding of the Royal Society as a group with particular guidelines: "we barred all Discourses of Divinity, of State-Affairs, and of News . . . confining our selves to Philosophical Inquiries, and such as related thereunto."[41] This may indeed have been the case. Religious and political differences had been tearing England apart for decades, thus it made perfect sense to bar these topics from this new scientific society. However, Wallis certainly did not mean that the persons involved were not highly partisan in terms of their beliefs – far from it. The agreement was merely a sensible strategy for making their meetings as efficient, productive, and problem-free as possible. In time, however, this strategic solution has come to be seen as the soul of the machine. The foundational myth of the Royal Society is now constructed around a core of secularity that did not exist at the time of its founding. Thus we find Enlightenment ideals being pushed back into an era that should more rightly be seen as the end of a theological age.

---

[40] Anne Goldgar and Robert I. Frost, eds., *Institutional Culture in Early Modern Society* (Leiden, 2004), xiii.
[41] John Wallis, *A Defence of the Royal Society, and the Philosophical Transactions, Particularly those of July, 1670 . . . In a Letter to the Right Honourable, William Lord Viscount Brouncker* (London, 1678), 7–8.

For the seven women who have been the focus of this study, and for the men with whom they associated, this sort of institutional mythmaking was the beginning of the end for their historiographical presence. Theirs was a distinctly non-institutional moment – or rather, it was a moment characterized instead by ephemeral locations like the exile court in The Hague, and immaterial institutions like the Hartlib circle and the republic of letters. These evanescent locations, by their very nature, are historiographically elusive, and this elusiveness has many levels.

First, immaterial institutions did not inhabit a concrete location, thus they had no physical home where their records might be stored. The fate of the Hartlib Papers, which contain the history of a movement as well as a man, are an instructive example of what happens to the archives of an immaterial institution. The papers disappeared almost immediately after Hartlib's death in 1662, and were missing for nearly three centuries, until they surfaced in 1933 in the office of a London solicitor.[42] For Dorothy Moore and Lady Ranelagh – the women who were so vitally involved in the Hartlib circle, and who were published only through Hartlib's syndicate of scribal publication – this network was their primary institutional affiliation. Thus the eccentricities of archival survival sentenced certain members of this immaterial institution, both male and female, to documentary inaccessibility, and left their history untold for many years.

A transitory location, like the ephemeral academy that inhabited the exile court in The Hague, might function temporarily as an intellectual institution. However, the exile court, by its very definition, was characterized by its marginality – thus the only possible futures for it were either extinction or legitimacy, neither of which would give a home to female scholars. Imagining alternative physical locations – such as Christine de Pizan's *City of Ladies*, or the academic cloister of Mary Astell's *Serious Proposal* – was one way in which female scholars tried to mitigate this lack of an institutional home. Another solution was for female scholars to create their own practical institutions in which to pursue their learning: for instance, van Schurman's Labadist community, Marie du Moulin's refuge for Huguenot women, and Princess Elisabeth's abbey in Herford. However, since these institutions did not survive in the same form after these scholars died, their institutional memory was also lost.

---

[42] Turnbull, *Hartlib, Dury and Comenius*; and Mark Greengrass, "Archive Refractions: Hartlib's Papers and the Workings of an Intelligencer," in *Archives of the Scientific Revolution: The Formation and Exchange of Ideas in Seventeenth-Century Europe*, ed. Michael Hunter (Woodbridge, 1998), 35–47.

Second, these immaterial institutions inhabited a transitional moment in early modern intellectual history. It was a moment when humanism was giving way to reason on one side, and empiricism on the other; when millenarian views were being expressed and investigated by scholars at every level of the republic of letters; and when science did not aim merely to investigate nature, but to undertake the reformation of the entire world. Henry Oldenburg explained this in 1667 to Governor John Winthrop of Connecticut, hoping Winthrop would join the Royal Society, and reminding him of their mandate:

Sir, you will please to remember that we have taken to taske the whole Universe, and that we were obliged to doe so by the Nature of our Dessein.[43]

The hopeless optimism and breadth of this "Dessein" plays no part in modern academic culture, nor is there a niche for it in intellectual history.

The women who shared this liminal moment, trying to reform religion, politics, and knowledge all at once, shared the fate of the projects themselves. These projects were eventually split into various epistemological and disciplinary streams, and each staked its claim for the men involved – Boyle the scientist, Dury the ecumenicist, Comenius the educationalist, Rivet the polemicist, and Descartes the rationalist. The women with whom they were involved – Anna Maria van Schurman, Dorothy Moore, Lady Ranelagh, Bathsua Makin, Marie du Moulin, Marie de Gournay, and Princess Elisabeth – have not generally been claimed for the histories of science, faith, education, or philosophy. By rights, they belong to all of these at once; but with the fracturing of this moment, the inclusive immaterial institutionality was dismantled.

And third, these immaterial institutions relied on a particular set of practices and technologies that are no longer used; some are not even fully recognized. Scribal publication, for instance, has not been considered "publication" at all. Thus for those female scholars whose works reached the public primarily through this mode of communication, the record of their authorship has appeared non-existent.

There is perhaps a fourth element to be found in the historiographical veil that has obscured the Republic of Women, and that is the blinding glare of the eighteenth-century Enlightenment. The Enlightenment has been seen as the intellectual phenomenon that articulated, institutionalized, and reified the secular approach to knowledge that is still familiar to

---

[43] Oldenburg to Winthrop, October 13, 1667, in Dorothy Stimson, "Hartlib, Haak and Oldenburg: Intelligencers," *Isis* 31, no. 84 (April 1940), 323.

us today. It is therefore a relatively comfortable historical destination, and, as a result, its chronological territory seems to continually expand backward. The moment we have been considering here – the middle of the seventeenth century – was liminal, and the scholars who inhabited it knew they were dealing with a crucial and agonizing dilemma. They were trying to reconcile the new learning with their understanding of God, and trying to determine the boundaries between reason and faith. They did not know at the time how this story would end, and for several generations there really "was no canon."[44]

Yet the Enlightenment did happen, and although millennial thinking posited a very close event horizon, the efforts to reconcile these irreconcilable goals would eventually prove fruitful.

In the battle of the books, the outcome was a compromise: arts and literature went to the "ancients," while science and philosophy became the province of the "moderns."[45] Literary territory was seen as appropriate for female participation, while the world of science became a place that intellectual women were welcome to visit, but they certainly could not live there. Thus the female scholars who had been operating with a foot in either world were finally impossible to place.

It has been the goal of this study to help remedy that situation – to locate the intellectual place in which these female scholars flourished, and to embark on the history of the inclusive and immaterial institution that Laura Cereta hailed as the Republic of Women.

---

[44] Stuurman, *François Poulain de la Barre*, 298. Stuurman, however, places this moment somewhat later in the seventeenth century.
[45] Levine, *Battle of the Books*.

Bibliography

PRIMARY SOURCES

Manuscripts

The Netherlands
Koninklijke Bibliotheek, The Hague.
    MSS: KA 42a through KA 49–3. Letterbooks of Constantijn Huygens.
    MS. 133 B 8. Letters and poems of Anna Maria van Schurman.
    MS. 135. C.79. Letter from Anna Maria van Schurman to Marie de
        Gournay.

University of Amsterdam.
    Diederichs Collection, MS 16 Ag. Marie du Moulin to Anna Maria van
        Schurman.

University of Leiden.
    MS. PAP 2. Letter from Johan Godschalk van Schurman to Caspar Barlaeus.
    BPL 282, 286, 288, 290. Rivetiana.
    BPL 1923. Letters from Marie de Gournay to Nicolaas Heinsius.
    BPL 2212. Huygens Correspondence.
    BPL 288. Letters from Valentin Conrart to André Rivet.
    HUG 37. Correspondence of Constantijn Huygens.
    LIP 4. Correspondence of Justus Lipsius.

University of Utrecht.
    HS 983, 7.E.7; HS 1655, 5. H. 40. Letterbooks of Buchellius and van
        Engelen.
    HS 8*F.19 ff. 1–3v. Letters and papers of Anna Maria van Schurman.

United Kingdom
Bodleian Library, Oxford University.
    MS. ADD. A.191, f. 113. Lady Ranelagh to Bishop Burnett, 13 July 1689.

British Library.
  Add. MSS. 4278–80; 4364–5; 4394–4404; 4407–31; 18,744; and 72,884.
  Lansdowne MSS. 745–55. Correspondence and papers of Dr. John Pell.
  Harleian MSS 373–88. Papers of Sir Simonds D'Ewes.
  Kings MSS 140. Letters and papers relating principally to the House of
    Hanover.
  Sloane MSS. 417, 649, 654, 1289, 1367, 2764.

Cambridge University Library.
  Baker MSS 29. Letters of Mr. Hartlib to Dr. Worthington.

Chatsworth, Derbyshire.
  Lismore MSS.

London Metropolitan Archives.
  Baptismal Records, St. Dunstan's, Stepney, 1568–1656.

Petworth House, Sussex.
  MS. 13,219, Folder 24. Orrery Papers.

Public Record Office, The National Archives (PRO).
  SP 82/10–12. Diplomatic letters concerning Princess Elisabeth, 1665–73.

Royal College of Physicians.
  MS. 310. Papers of Baldwin Hamey: Correspondence.

Royal Society.
  RSL MS 1. Liber Epistolaris of Henry Oldenburg.
  Boyle Letters, Vols. 1–7.

University of Sheffield.
  Hartlib Papers.

Victoria and Albert Museum. National Art Library.
  Forster Collection: Pressmark 48.g.25.
  Correspondence of Charles Ist and Sister Queen of Bohemia, 1617–58.

United States
Huntington Library, San Marino.
  Hastings MSS., 8799–801. Letters and poems by Bathsua Makin.
  Loudon MSS. (Scottish Collection). Moore family letters.

Whitney Medical Library, Yale University.
  Lady Ranelagh to the Earl of Clarendon, ND.
  Peter du Moulin to Samuel Bochart, 15/25 July, 1657.

PRINTED MATERIALS

Agnesi, Maria Gaetana, *et al. The Contest for Knowledge: Debates over Women's Learning in Eighteenth-Century Italy.* Ed. and trans. Rebecca Messbarger and Paula Findlen. The Other Voice in Early Modern Europe. Chicago, 2005.

Arckenholtz, Johan. *Memoires Concernant Christine Reine de Suede, Pour Servir d'eclaircissement a l'histoire de son regne et principalement de sa vie privee, et aux evenemens de l'histoire de son tems civile et literaire.* 4 vols. Amsterdam and Leipzig, 1751.

Arnold, G. H. *Historia Joannis Dvraei.* Wittenberg, 1716.

Astell, Mary. *A Serious Proposal to the Ladies for the Advancement of their True and Greatest Interest, By a Lover of her Sex.* London, 1694.

[Aubrey, John]. *Aubrey's Brief Lives. Edited from the original manuscripts by Oliver Lawson Dick.* Reprint, Ann Arbor, 1957.

Aveling, James Hobson. *English Midwives: Their History and Prospects* [1872]. Reprint, London, 1967.

Baillet, Adrien. *La Vie de Monsieur Descartes* [1691]. 5th edn. [Paris], 1946.

Baillie, Robert. *The Letters and Journals of Robert Baillie, A.M. Principal of the University of Glasgow, M.DC.XXXVII – M.DC.LXII.* 3 vols. Edited by David Laing. Edinburgh, 1841–2.

Bainbrigge, Christopher. "To His Vertuous Sister." In *Justa Edovardo King* [1638]. Ed. E. C. Mossner. New York, 1939.

Ballard, George. *Memoirs of Several Ladies of Great Britain, Who Have Been Celebrated for their Writings or Skill in the Learned Languages, Arts and Sciences.* London, 1752. Edited by Ruth Perry. Detroit, 1985.

Barclay, Robert. *Reliquiae Barclaianae. Correspondence of Colonel David Barclay and Robert Barclay of Urie, and his Son Robert, including Letters from Princess Elizabeth of the Rhine . . .* (Lithograph). London, 1870.

Barksdale, Clement. *The Learned Maid: or, Whether a Maid may be a Scholar? A Logick Exercise written in Latine by that incomparable Virgin Anna Maria à Schurman of Utrecht.* London, 1659.

A Letter Touching A Colledge of Maids, or, a Virgin-Society. London, 1675.

Barlaeus, Caspar. *Faces Augustae, sive, Poematia: quibus illustriores nuptiae, a nobili et illustri viro, D. Jacobo Catsio . . .* Dordraci, 1643.

Barnard, Thomas. *An Historical Character Relating to the Holy and Exemplary Life of the Right Honourable the Lady Elisabeth Hastings . . .* Leeds, 1743.

Bayle, Pierre. *Correspondance de Pierre Bayle.* Ed. Elisabeth Labrousse, *et al.* Three volumes. Oxford, 1999–2004.

Dictionnaire historique et critique de Pierre Bayle. 16 vols. New edition. Paris, 1820–4.

Benzelius, Carolus Iesper. *Dissertatio Historico-Theologica de Johanne Duraeo, Pacificatore Celeberrimo, maxime de actis eius suecanis.* Helmstad, 1744.

Beverwijck, Johan van. *Epistolica quaestio, de vitae termino fatali, an mobili?: cum doctorum responses.* Leiden, 1639.

Van de Wtnementheyt des Vrouwelicken Geslachts, verciert met kopere platen; ende verssen van Mr. Corn. Boy. Dordrecht, 1643.

Biographium Faemineum. The Female Worthies: or, Memoirs of the Most Illustrious Ladies, of all Ages and Nations, Who Have Been Eminently Distinguished for their Magnanimity, Learning, Genius, Virtue, Piety, and other excellent Endowments . . . London, 1746.

Birch, Thomas. *The History of the Royal Society of London for Improving of Natural Knowledge from its First Rise* [1756–7]. Facsimile, edited by A. Rupert Hall and Marie Boas Hall. New York and London, 1968.

Boccaccio, Giovanni. *De mulieribus claris* [1360–2].

Bodemann, Eduard, ed. *Briefe der Kurfürstin Sophie von Hannover an die Raugräfinnen und Raugrafen zu Pfalz.* Publicationen aus den K. Preusischen Staatsarchiven vol. xxxvii. Leipzig, 1888.

Briefwechsel der Herzogin Sophie von Hannover mit ihrem Bruder, dem Kurfürsten Karl Ludwig von der Pfalz, und des Letzteren mit seiner Schwägerin, der Pfalzgräfen Anna. Leipzig, 1885.

Bourignon, Antoinette. *The Light Risen in Darkness . . . by Antonia Bourignon. Being a collection of letters written to several persons, upon great and important subjects* . . . 4 vols. London, 1703.

Recœuil des quelques'uns des temoignages publics & particuliers, Rendus à la Personne de Madlle. Anthoinette Bourignon . . . Amsterdam, 1682.

Boyle, Robert. *The Correspondence of Robert Boyle.* Edited by Michael Hunter, Antonio Clericuzio and Lawrence M. Principe. 6 vols. London, 2001.

The Works of Robert Boyle. Ed. Michael Hunter and Edward B. Davis. London, 1999.

Brett, Arthur. *A demonstration how the Latine tongue may be learn't with far greater ease and speed then commonly it is.* London, 1669.

[Brett, Arthur]. *A Model for a School for the better Education of Youth.* London, [1675?].

Bromley, Sir George, ed. *A Collection of Original Royal Letters, Written by King Charles the First and Second, King James the Second, and the King and Queen of Bohemia . . . And Several other distinguished Persons; from the Year 1619 to 1665.* London, 1787.

Bruyère, Jean de la. *Les Caractères de Théophraste. Traduits du Grec avec Les Caractères ou Les Moeurs de ce siècle* [Paris: 1687]. Ed. Louis van Delft. Paris, 1998.

Buchell, Arend van. *Notae Quotidianae.* Ed. J. W. C. van Campen. Werken, uitgegeven door het Historisch Genootschap, 3rd Series, no. 70. Utrecht, 1940.

Budgell, Eustace. *Memoirs of the Life and Character of the Late Earl of Orrery, and of the Family of the Boyles, Containing Several Curious Facts, and Pieces of History* . . . 2nd edn. London, 1732.

Burnet, Gilbert. *A Sermon Preached at the Funeral of the Honourable Robert Boyle; at St. Martins in the Fields, January 7, 1691/2. By the Right Reverend Father in God, Gilbert Lord Bishop of Sarum.* London, 1692.

Cats, Jacob. *Virgo Batava, sive Encomia Clarrisimæ doctissimæque ANNÆ MARIÆ SCHURMANS, à Nobilissimo, Amplissimoque viro Dno. JACOBO CATSIO nuper edita . . .* Delphis, 1639.

Cereta, Laura. *Collected Letters of a Renaissance Feminist.* Transcribed, trans., and ed. Diana Robin. The Other Voice in Early Modern Europe. Chicago, 1997.

Chamberlayne, Edward. *An Academy or Colledge: Wherein Young Ladies and Gentlewomen May at a very moderate Expence be duly instructed in the true Protestant Religion, and in all Vertuous Qualities that may adorn that Sex: also be carefully preserved, and secured, till the day of their Marriage, etc.* London, 1671.

Chappuzeau, Samuel. *L'Academie des femmes* [1641]. In *Le Cercles des Femmes et L'Academie des Femmes.* Ed. Joan Crow. Exeter, 1983.

Le Théatre François. [1674]. Ed. Georges Monval. Paris, 1875.

Clark, Samuel. *The Lives of Sundry Eminent Persons in this Later Age. In Two Parts.* London, 1683.

Collet, John. "Commonplace-Book." In *Anecdotes and Traditions, Illustrative of Early English History and Literature, derived from MS. Sources.* Ed. William J. Thoms, Esq. F.S.A. London, 1839.

Comenius, Jan Amos. *The Great Didactic: Setting forth The whole Art of Teaching all Things to all Men, etc.* Amsterdam, 1657. Trans. and ed. M. W. Keating. London, 1923.

Conway, Anne. *The Conway Letters: The Correspondence of Anne, Viscountess Conway, Henry More, and their Friends 1642–1684.* Ed. Marjorie Hope Nicholson. Revised edn. by Sarah Hutton. Oxford, 1992.

Culpeper, Sir Cheney. *The Letters of Sir Cheney Culpeper (1641–1657).* Ed. M. J. Braddick and M. Greengrass. Camden Miscellany xxxiii, 5th Series, vol. 7, *Seventeenth-Century Political and Financial Papers.* Cambridge, 1996.

De Bujanda, J.M. *Index Librorum Prohibitorum 1600–1966. Index des Livres Interdits.* 11 vols. Montreal, 2002.

Descartes, René, *Lettres de Monsieur Descartes.* Ed. Claude Clerselier. 3 vols. Paris, 1657–67.

Oeuvres de Descartes. Ed. Charles Adam, and Paul Tannery. 12 vols. Paris, 1974–89.

Descartes, René, *The Philosophical Writings of Descartes,* trans. John Cottingham, Robert Stoothoff, and Dugald Murdoch. Cambridge, 1985

Descartes, René, and Martin Schook. *La querelle d'Utrecht [Querela apologetica ad amplissimum magistratum Ultrajectinum].* Trans. Theo Verbeek. Paris, 1988.

D'Ewes, Sir Simonds. *The Autobiography and Correspondence of Sir Simonds D'Ewes, Bart., during the Reigns of James I. and Charles I.* 2 vols. Ed. James Orchard Halliwell. London, 1845.

The Diary of Sir Simonds D'Ewes, 1622–1624: Journal d'un étudiant londonien sous le règne de Jacques 1er. Ed. and trans. Elizabeth Bourcier. Paris, 1974.

Journals of all the Parliaments during the Reign of Queen Elizabeth. London, 1682.

Diderot, Denis, ed. *Encyclopédie ou dictionnaire raisonné des sciences, des arts et des métiers.* 17 vols. Paris, 1751–65.

Dupuy, Jacques. *Correspondance de Jacques Dupuy et de Nicolas Heinsius (1646–1656).* Ed. Hans Bots. The Hague, 1971.

Dury, John. *Considerations Concerning the present Engagement, Whether It may lawfully be entered into, YEA or NO?* 2nd edn. London, 1650.

A Declaration of John Durie . . . Wherein he doth make known the Truth of his way and comportment in all these times of trouble, And how he hath endeavoured to follow Peace and Righteousness therein innocently towards all . . . London, 1660.

A Motion Tending to the Publick Good of This Age, and of Posteritie. Or, The Coppies of certain Letters written by Mr. John Dury, to a worthy Knight, at his earnest desire. Published by Samuel Hartlib. [1642].

The Plain Way of Peace and Unity in Matters of Religion. London, 1660.

The Unchanged, Constant and Single-hearted Peace-Maker drawn forth into the World, Or, a Vindication of Mr. John Dury from the aspersions cast upon him in a nameless Pamphlet called The Time-serving Proteus and Amidexter Divine, uncased to the world . . . London, 1650.

Ecclesiae Londino-Batavae Archivum. Epistulae et Tractatus. Cambridge, 1897.

Eglisham, George. *Duellum poeticum. Contendentibus, Georgio Eglisemmio medico regio, & Georgio Buchanano regio praeceptore. Pro dignitate paraphraseos Psalmi centisimi quarti . . .* London, 1618.

Elisabeth, Princess Palatine. *The Correspondence between Princess Elisabeth of Bohemia and René Descartes.* Ed. Lisa Shapiro. The Other Voice in Early Modern Europe. Chicago and London, 2007.

Elizabeth, Queen of Bohemia. *Briefe der Elisabeth Stuart, Köningen von Böhmen, an Ihren Sohn, Der Kurfürsten Carl Ludwiig von der Pfalz, 1650–1662.* Ed. Anna Wendland. Bibliothek des Litterarischen Vereins in Stuttgart CCXXVIII. Tübingen, 1902.

The Letters of Elizabeth, Queen of Bohemia. Ed. L. M. Baker. London, 1953.

Ellis, Sir Henry. *Original Letters of Eminent Literary Men of the Sixteenth, Seventeenth, and Eighteenth Centuries.* London, 1843.

Elstob, Elizabeth. *An English-Saxon homily on the birth-day of St. Gregory . . . Tr. into modern English, with notes, etc., by Eliz. Elstob.* London, 1709.

Englands Thankfulnesse, or An Humble Remembrance Presented to the Committee for Religion in the High Court of Parliament, with Thanksgiving for that happy Pacification betweene the two Kingdomes. By a faithfull Well-wisher to this Church and Nation. London, 1642.

Erasmus, Desiderius. *Opus Epistolarum Des. Erasmi Roterodami.* Ed. P. S. Allen. 12 vols. Oxford, 1906–55.

Foucher de Careil, Le Comte Louis Alexandre. *Descartes, La Princesse Élisabeth, et La Reine Christine, d'après des lettres inédites.* Paris, 1909.

Frederick the Great. *Oeuvres Historiques de Frédéric II, Roi de Prusse.* Ed. J. D. E. 7 vols. Preusss. Berlin, 1846–7.

Gardiner, Samuel Rawson. *Letters Relating to the Mission of Sir Thomas Roe to Gustavus Adolphus, 1629–30*. Camden Miscellany, vol. vii. [Westminster], 1875.

Gigas, Émile, ed. *Lettres Inédites de Divers Savants: de la fin du XVIIme et du commencement du XVIIIme siècle*. 3 vols. Copenhagen, 1890.

Gournay, Marie le Jars de. *Abregé d'institution, pour le Prince Souverain*. In *Les Advis, ou, les Presens de la Demoiselle de Gournay (1641)*. Ed. Jean-Philippe Beaulieu and Hanna Fournier. Amsterdam, 1997.

Apology for the Woman Writing, and Other Works. Ed. and trans. Richard Hillman and Colette Quesnel. The Other Voice in Early Modern Europe. Chicago, 2002.

Égalité des hommes et des femmes. Grief des dames. Suivis du Proumenoir de Monsieur de Montaigne. Ed. Constant Venesoen. Geneva, 1993.

Fragments d'un discours féminin: textes établis, présentés et commentés par Elyane Dezon-Jones. Paris, 1988.

Le Proumenoir de Monsieur de Montaigne. Par sa fille d'alliance. Paris, 1594. Facsimile reproduction, New York, 1985.

Greenhill, William. *An Exposition of the Prophet Ezekiel, with Useful Observations Thereupon. Delivered in Several Lectures in London ... 1650*. Revised by James Sherman. Edinburgh, 1864.

Guhrauer, Gottshalf Eduard. *De Joachimo Jungio. Commentatio Historico-Literaria*. Universitate Literarum Vratislaviensi [Wroclaw], 1846.

Gwinnett, Richard and Elizabeth Thomas. *Pylades and Corinna. or, memoirs of the lives, amours, and writings of Richard Gwinnett Esq ... and Mrs. Elizabeth Thomas ...* 2 vols. London, 1731–2.

Hartlib, Samuel. *A Faithfull and seasonable Advice, or, The necessity of a Correspondencie for the advancement of the Protestant Cause*. [London], 1643.

A further Discoverie of The Office of Publick Addresse for Accommodations. London, 1648.

The Hartlib Papers. A Complete Text and Image Database of the Papers of Samuel Hartlib (c.1600–1662). 2nd edn. Sheffield, 2002.

Hauck, Karl. "Die Briefe der Kinder des Winterkönigs." *Neue Heidelberger Jahrbücher* 15 (1908).

Hooke, Robert. *The Diary of Robert Hooke, 1672–1680. Transcribed from the Original in the Possession of the Corporation of the City of London (Guildhall Library)*. Ed. Henry W. Robinson and Walter Adams. London, 1968.

Huet, Pierre-Daniel. *Pet. Dan. Huetii, Episcopi Abrincensis, Commentarius De Rebus Ad Evm Pertinentibvs*. Amsterdam, 1718.

Huygens, Constantijn. *De Briefwisseling van Constantijn Huygens (1608–1687)*. Ed. J. A. Worp. 6 vols. Rijks Geschiedkundige Publicatiën, nos. 15, 19, 21, 24, 28, and 32. The Hague, 1911–17.

De Gedichten van Constantijn Huygens, naar zijn handschrift uitgegeven. Ed. J. A. Worp. 9 vols. Groningen, 1892–9.

Hyde, Edward, Earl of Clarendon. *The history of the Rebellion and civil wars in England begun in the year 1641*. Ed. William Dunn Macray. 6 vols. Oxford, 1888.

Jacob, Louis. *Elogium eruditissimae virginis Annae Mariae a Schurman, Batavae.* In *Question celebre. S'il est necessaire, ou non, que les Filles soient sçavantes. Agitée de part & d'autre, par Mademoiselle Anne Marie de Schvrman Holandoise, & le Sr. André Rivet Poitevin.* Paris, 1646.

Justa Edovardo King naufrago, ab Amicis moerentibus, amoris, etc. Cambridge, 1638.

Laboureur, Jean le. *Relation du voyage de la Royne de Pologne . . . par la Hongrie, l'Austriche, Styrie, Carinthie, le Frioul, & l'Italie. avec vn discours historique de toutes les Villes & Estats, par où elle a passé . . .* Paris, 1647.

Le Fevre, Tanneguy. *A Compendious Way of Teaching Ancient and Modern Languages, Formerly practised by the Learned Tanaquil Faber, in the Education of one of his Sons, and of his Daughter the Celebrated Madam Dacier . . .* 2nd edn. Ed. J. T. Phillips. London, 1723.

Leibniz, Gottfried Wilhelm. *Sämtliche Schriften und Briefe.* Ed. Deutsche Akademie der Wissenschaften zu Berlin. 7th Series. Berlin, 1950–.

Lewis, Mark. *An Apologie for a Grammar Printed about Twenty Years Since, by M. Lewis and Reprinted for the Use of a Private School at Tottenham High Cross.* London, 1671.

An Essay to Facilitate the Education of Youth, by Bringing down the Rudiments of Grammar to the sense of Seeing, which ought to be improv'd by Sincrisis . . . London, 1674.

Institutio Grammaticæ Puerilis: or the Rudiments of the Latin and Greek Tongues, Fitted to Childrens capacities, as an Introduction to larger Grammars. London, 1670.

Plain, and short Rules for Pointing Periods, and Reading Sentences Grammatically, with the great Use of them. London, [1675].

Lipsius, Justus. *La Correspondance de Juste Lipse conservée au Musée Plantin-Moretus.* Ed. A. Gerlo and H. D. L. Vervliet. Antwerp, 1967.

Epistolarum Centuria Secunda: Nunc primum edita. London, 1590.

Justi Lipsi Epistolarum Selectarum Chilias, In qua: I.II. Centuriae Miscellaneae; III. Singularis ad Italos & Hispanos; IV. Singularis ad Germanos & Gallos; V. Miscellanea tertia; VI.VII. VIII. ad Belgas; IX.&X. Miscellaneae, quarta & quinta Postumae. [Leiden?], 1618.

Lodge, John, Esq. *The Peerage of Ireland: Or, A Genealogical History of the Present Nobility of that Kingdom.* Rev. and ed. Mervyn Archdall. London, 1789.

[Makin, Bathsua]. *An Essay to Revive the Antient Education of Gentlewomen, in Religion, Manners, Arts & Tongues. With an Answer to the Objections against this Way of Education.* London, 1673.

Malebranche, Nicolas. *Malebranche: Oeuvres Complètes.* Ed. André Robinet. 20 vols. Paris, 1958–78.

Marvell, Andrew. *The Character of Holland.* London, 1665.

Ménage, Gilles. *The History of Women Philosophers* [1690]. Translated and Introduced by Beatrice Zedler. Lanham, MD, 1984.

Mersenne, Le Père Marin. *Correspondance du P. Marin Mersenne, Religieux Minime.* Ed. Mme. Paul Tannery and Cornelis de Waard. 17 vols. 2nd edn. [Paris], 1960–88.

Mill, Henry. *Genealogical Account of the Barclays of Urie, for Upwards of Seven Hundred Years ... also Letters that passed between him, the Duke of York, Elizabeth Princess Palatine of the Rhine ...* London, 1812.

Milton, John. *John Milton: A Critical Edition of the Major Works.* Ed. Stephen Orgel and Jonathan Goldberg. Oxford, 1991.

    The Life Records of John Milton. Ed. J. Milton French. 5 vols. New Brunswick, NJ, 1956.

    Milton: Private Correspondence and Academic Exercises. Trans. Phyllis B. Tillyard. Cambridge, 1932.

Montagu, Lady Mary Wortley. *The Complete Letters of Lady Mary Wortley Montagu.* Ed. Robert Halsband. 3 vols. Oxford, 1965–7.

    Essays and Poems, and 'Simplicity, a Comedy'. Ed. Robert Halsband and Isobel Grundy. Oxford, 1993.

Montaigne, Michel. *The Complete Essays of Montaigne.* Ed. and trans. Donald Frame. Stanford, 1965.

Moore, Dorothy. *The Letters of Dorothy Moore, 1612–64: The Friendships, Marriage, and Intellectual Life of a Seventeenth-Century Woman.* Ed. Lynette Hunter. Aldershot, 2004.

[Moulin, Louis du]. *La tyrannie des prejugez ou reflexions sur le fragment d'une lettre de Mademoiselle Marie du Moulin ... pour servir de Response a Monsieur Jurieu.* London, 1678.

[Moulin, Marie du]. *An Account of the Last Hours of Dr. Peter du Moulin, Minister of God's Word, and Professor of Divinity at Sedan ... Translated into English out of the French Copy printed at Sedan.* Oxford, 1658.

    De la premiere education d'un Prince, Depuis sa naissance jusqu'a l'aage de sept ans. Traitté tres-utile non seulement aux grands, mais encor a tous ceux qui desirent de bien élever leurs enfans. Rotterdam, 1654.

    De l'éducation des enfans, et particulierement de celle des princes, où il est montré de quelle importance sont les sept premieres années de la vie. Amsterdam, 1679.

    Les dernieres heures de Monsieur Rivet, vivant. Ministre de la Parole de Dieu, Docteur & Professeur honoraire en Theologie en l'Université de Leyden, & Curateur de l'Eschole Illustre, & College d'Orange à Breda. Fidelement receüillies. Delf, 1651.

    Directions for the Education of a Young Prince. Till Seven Years of Age. Which will serve for the Governing of Children of all Conditions. Trans. Pierre du Moulin. London, 1673.

    The Last Houers of the Right Reverend Father in God Andrew Rivet, in his life time Dr. and Professour Honorable of Divinity, in the University of Leyden ... Faithfully Collected. Trans. "G. L." The Hague, 1652.

    Récit des dernières heures de Monsieur du Moulin. Sedan, 1658.

Moulin, Peter du. Introductory Epistle for *Apologie de la Religion Reformée, et de la Monarchie et de l'Église d'Angleterre, contre les Calumnies de la Ligue rebelle de quelques Anglois et Escossois* [c.1650]. Transcribed by "J. D." *The Gentleman's Magazine and Historical Chronicle* 43 (August 1773): 369–70.

Moulin, Pierre du. "Autobiographie de Pierre du Moulin, d'après une copie manuscrite." *Bulletin de la Société de l'Histoire du Protestantisme français* 7 (1858): 170–82, 332–44, and 465–77.

Nicéron, Le Révérend Père Jean-Pierre Barnabite. *Mémoires pour servir a l'histoire des hommes illustres dans la République des Lettres. Avec un Catalogue Raisonnée de leurs Ouvrages.* 43 vols. Paris, 1729–45.

Oldenburg, Henry. *The Correspondence of Henry Oldenburg.* 13 vols. Ed. A. Rupert Hall and Marie Boas Hall. Madison and London, 1965–86.

Pasquier, Etienne. *Les Oeuvres d'Estienne Pasquier, contenant ses Recherches de la France; son Plaidoyé pour les jesuites de Lorraine; celuy de me Versoris, pour les jesuites . . . Ses lettres; ses oeuvres meslées; et les Lettres de Nicolas Pasquier, fils d'Estienne . . .* 2 vols. Amsterdam, 1723.

Peacham, Henry. *The Compleat Gentleman. Fashioning him absolut, in the most necessary and commendable Qualities . . .* London, 1634.

Penn, William. "An Account of W. Penn's Travails in Germany & Holland." *The Friends' Library* 5 (1841): 64–145.

   No Cross, No Crown: A Discourse Shewing the Nature and Discipline of the Holy Cross of Christ. 6th edn. Dublin, 1700.

Pizan, Christine de. *The Book of the City of Ladies.* Ed. and trans. Earl Jeffrey Richards. New York, 1982.

[Plattes, Gabriel]. *A Description of the Famous Kingdome of Macaria . . . In a dialgoue between a Schollar and a Traveller.* London, 1641.

Poulain de la Barre, François. *De l'Education des dames pour la conduite de l'esprit dans les sciences et dans les mœurs.* Paris, 1674.

   De l'Egalité des deux sexes: Discours physique et moral où l'on voit l'importance de se défaire des préjugez. Paris, 1673.

   De l'Excellence des hommes contre l'égalite des sexes. Paris, 1675.

   Three Cartesian Feminist Treatises. Ed. Marcelle Maistre Welch, trans. Vivien Bosley. The Other Voice in Early Modern Europe. Chicago, 2002.

   The Woman As Good as The Man: or, The equallity of both sexes written originally in French and translated into English by A. L. London, 1677.

[Prynne, William]. *The Time-Serving Proteus, and Ambidexter Divine, Uncased to the World: Containing two Letters of M. John Dury . . .* [London], 1650.

Reynoldes, Edward. *A Treatise of the Passions and Faculties of the Soule of Man With the severall Dignities and Corruptions thereunto belonging.* London, 1640.

Reynolds, Bathsua [Makin]. *Musa Virginea Græco-Latino-Gallica, Bathsuae R. [filiae Henrici reginaldi Gymnasiarchae et philoglotti apud Londonienses]. Anno aetatis suae decimo sexto edita.* London, 1616.

   [Makin]. *Index Radiographia* (c.1619). Reprinted in R. C. Alston, *Treatises on Short-hand.* London, c.1866.

[Reynolds, Henry]. *Mythomystes. Wherein a Short Survay is Taken of the Nature and Value of True Poesy, and Depth of the Ancients Above our Moderne Poets.* London, [1632].

Robertson, William. *A Gate or Door to the Holy Tongue, Opened in English.* London, 1653.

The Second Gate, or The Inner Door to the Holy Tongue. Being a compendious Hebrew Lexicon or Dictionary ... London, 1654.

Salmon, Nathaniel. *The Lives of the English Bishops: From the Restauration to the Revolution. Fit to be Opposed to the Aspersions of some late Writers of Secret History.* London, 1731.

Sauerbrei, M. Johannes. *Diatriben Academicam de Foeminarum Eruditione Posteriorem.* Dissertation presented at the University of Leipzig, September 6, 1671. Leipzig, 1676.

Saumaise, Claude. *Miscellae Defensiones pro Cl. Salmasio, De variis observationibus & emendationibus. ad Ius Atticum et Romanum Pertinentibus.* Leiden, 1645.

Saumaise, Claude, and André Rivet. *Claude Saumaise & André Rivet: Correspondance Echangée entre 1632 et 1648.* Ed. Pierre Leroy and Hans Bots. Amsterdam, 1987.

Schurman, Anna Maria van. *De vitae termino.* Leiden, 1639.

Eukleria seu Melioris Partis Electio. Tractatus Brevem Vitae ejus Delineationem Exhibens. Altona, 1673.

The Learned Maid or, Whether a Maid may be a Scholar. A Logick Exercise. Trans. Clement Barksdale. London, 1659.

Nobiliss. Virginis Annae Mariae a Schurman Dissertatio De Ingenii Muliebris ad Doctrinam, & meliores Litteras aptitudine. Accedunt Quaedam Epistolae eiusdem Argumenti. Leiden, 1641.

Nobiliss. Virginis Annae Mariae à Schurman, Opuscula Hebraea, Graeca, Latina, Gallica: Prosaica & Metrica. Leiden, 1648.

Paelsteen vanden tijt onses levens ... *In Latijn aen d'Heere Johan van Bevervvyck geschreven door de Edele, Deught-en-Konst-rijcke Joffrouvv, Joffr. Anna Maria van Schvrman.* Dordrecht, 1639.

Question celebre. S'il est necessaire, ou non, que les Filles soient sçavantes. Le tout mis en François par le Sr Colletet. Paris, 1646.

Whether a Christian Woman Should Be Educated: and Other Writings from Her Intellectual Circle. Ed. and trans. Joyce L. Irwin. Chicago, 1998.

Shelton, Thomas. *Tachygraphy. The Most exact and compendious methode of short and swift writing that hath ever yet beene published by any.* London, 1641.

Sophie de Hanovre. *Mémoires et Lettres de voyage.* Ed. Dirk van der Cruysse. Mesnil-sur-l'Estreée, 1990.

Sophie of Hanover. *The Memoirs of Sophia, Electress of Hanover 1630–1680.* Trans. H. Forester. London, 1888.

Sorbière, Samuel. *Lettres et Discours de M. de Sorbiere Sur diverses Matieres Curieuses.* Paris, 1660.

Sorberiana: ou Bons mots, rencontres agreables, et pensées judicieuses ... Paris, 1694.

Swammerdam, Jan. *The Letters of Jan Swammerdam to Melchisedec Thevenot.* Trans. G. A. Lindeboom. Amsterdam, 1975.

Tallemant des Réaux. *Les Historiettes de Tallemant des Réaux.* Ed. Georges Mongrédien. 8 vols. Paris, 1932–4.

Thomasius, Jacob. *Diatriben Academicam de Foeminarium Eruditione Priorem.* Leipzig, 1676.

Torshell, Samuel. *The Womans Glorie: A Treatise, Asserting The Due Honour of that Sexe, and Directing wherein that Honour consists. Dedicated to the young Princesse, Elizabeth her Highnesse.* London, 1645.

Vaughan, Robert. *The Protectorate of Oliver Cromwell, and the State of Europe during the Early Part of the Reign of Louis XIV. Illustrated in a Series of Letters between Dr. John Pell ... Mr. Secretary Thurloe, and Other Distinguished Men of the Time.* 2 vols. London, 1839.

Visscher, Anna Roemers. *Gedichten van Anna Roemers Visscher.* Ed. Nicolaas Beets. The Hague, 1925.

Vives, Juan Luis. *The Instruction of a Christen Woman.* Ed. Virginia W. Beauchamp, Elizabeth H. Hageman, and Margaret Mikesell. Urbana, 2002.

Voltaire, François Marie Arouet de. *Letters Concerning the English Nation, by Mr. de Voltaire.* London, 1733.

Le Siècle de Louis XIV [par] Voltaire. Paris, 1966.

Walker, John. *Letters Written by Eminent persons in the Seventeenth and Eighteenth Centuries. To Which Are Added, Hearne's Journeys to Reading, and to Whaddon Hall, the Seat of Browne Willis, Esq., and Lives of Eminent Men, by John Aubrey, Esq.* 2 vol. London, 1813.

Wallis, John. *A Defence of the Royal Society, and the Philosophical Transactions, Particularly those of July, 1670 ... In a Letter to the Right Honourable, William Lord Viscount Brouncker.* London, 1678.

Weston, Elizabeth Jane. *Collected Writings.* Ed. and trans. Donald Cheney and Brenda M. Hosington. Toronto, 2000.

Wilkins, John. *Mercury: or the Secret and Swift Messenger. Shewing, How a Man may with Privacy and Speed communicate his Thoughts to a Friend at any distance ...* 2nd edn. London, 1694.

Wood, Anthony à. *Athenæ Oxonienses: An Exact History of all the Writers and Bishops who have had their Education in The most ancient and famous University of Oxford from the Fifteenth Year of King Henry the Seventh, Dom. 1500, to the End of the Year 1690 ...* 2 vols. London, 1691–2.

Worthington, John. *The Diary and Correspondence of Dr. John Worthington. Remains* Historical & Literary Connected with the Palatine Counties of Lancaster *and Chester.* Ed. James Crossley. Vols. XIII, XXXVI, and CXLII. Manchester, 1847–86.

Miscellanies ... Also, A Collection of Epistles, Written to Mr. Hartlib of Pious Memory ... With the Author's Character, by Arch-Bp. Tillotson. London, 1704.

Wotton, William. *Reflections Upon Ancient and Modern Learning.* London, 1694.

Yvon, Pierre. "Abregé sincere de la vie & de la conduite & des vrais sentimens de feu Mr. De Labadie." In Gottfried Arnold, *Forsetzungen und Erläuterungen, Unpartheyische Kirchen- und Ketzerhistorie*, 1234–70. Frankfurt am Main, 1715.

SECONDARY SOURCES

Aiton, E. J. *Leibniz: A Biography*. Bristol, 1985.

Åkerman, Susanna. *Queen Christina of Sweden and her Circle: The Transformation of a Seventeenth-Century Philosophical Libertine*. Leiden, 1991.

Allégret, D. "Société des dames françaises de harlem." *Bulletin de la Société de l'Histoire du Protestantisme Français* 27 (1878): 315–22; 518–24; 557–63.

Baar, Mirjam de. *'Ik moet spreken': Het spiritueel leiderschap van Antoinette Bourignon (1616–1680)*. Zutphen, 2004.

——— "'Now as for the faint rumours of fame attached to my name …': The Eukleria as Autobiography." In *Choosing the Better Part: Anna Maria van Schurman (1607–1678)*. Ed. Mirjam de Baar *et al.*, 87–102. Dordrecht, 1996.

——— "Transgressing Gender Codes: Anna Maria van Schurman and Antoinette Bourignon as Contrasting Examples." In *Women of the Golden Age: An International Debate on Women in Seventeenth-Century Holland, England and Italy*, edited by Els Kloek, Nicole Tesuwen, and Marijke Huisman, 143–52. Hilversum, 1994.

Baar, Mirjam de, and Brita Rang. "Anna Maria van Schurman: A Historical Survey of Her Reception since the Seventeenth Century." In *Choosing the Better Part: Anna Maria van Schurman (1607–1678)*. Ed. Mirjam de Baar *et al.*, 2–21. Dordrecht, 1996.

Baar, Mirjam de, Machteld Löwensteyn, Marit Monteiro, and A. Agnes Neller, eds. *Choosing the Better Part: Anna Maria van Schurman (1607–1678)*. Dordrecht, 1996.

Bachrach, A. G. H. *Sir Constantine Huygens and Britain: 1596–1687*. Leiden, 1962.

Barbier, A.-A. *Dictionnaire des ouvrages anonymes*. Ed. Olivier Barbier and René and Paul Billard. 3rd edn. 4 vols. Paris, 1882.

Barnard, Toby C. "The Hartlib Circle and the Cult and Culture of Improvement in Ireland." In *Samuel Hartlib and Universal Reformation: Studies in Intellectual Communication*. Ed. Mark Greengrass *et al.*, 281–97. Cambridge, 1994.

——— "The Hartlib Circle and the Origins of the Dublin Philosophical Society." *Irish Historical Studies* 19, no. 73 (March 1974): 56–71.

Barnett, Pamela R. *Theodore Haak, F.R.S. (1605–1690): The First German Translator of "Paradise Lost."* The Hague, 1962.

Barthélemy, Edouard de. *Un Tournoi de trois pucelles en l'honneur de Jeanne d'Arc: Lettres inédites de Conrart, de Mlle. de Scudéry, et de Mlle. du Moulin*. Paris, 1878.

Bartlett, Thomas. "A New History of Ireland." *Past and Present* 116 (1987): 206–19.

Bastiaensen, Michel, ed. *La Femme lettrée à la Renaissance: Actes du Colloque international.* Brussels, 1997.

Batten, J. Minton. *John Dury: Advocate of Christian Reunion.* Chicago, 1944.

Battigelli, Anna. *Margaret Cavendish and the Exiles of the Mind.* Lexington, KY, 1998.

Beardslee, John W. *III. Reformed Dogmatics: J. Wollebius, G. Voëtius, F. Turretin.* New York, 1965.

Becker-Cantarino, Baerbel. *Daniel Heinsius.* Twayne's World Authors Series, no. 477. Boston, 1978.

Beek, Pieta van. "Alpha Virginum: Anna Maria van Schurman (1607–78)." In *Women Writing Latin: From Roman Antiquity to Early Modern Europe.* Ed. Laurie J. Churchill *et al.*, 271–94. New York and London, 2002.

⸻ "Een Vrouwenrepubliek der Letteren? Anna Maria van Schurman (1607–78) en haar netwerk van geleerde vrouwen." *Tydskrif vir Nederlands en Afrikaans*, 3, no. 1 (1996): 36–49.

⸻ "'One Tongue Is Enough for a Woman': The Correspondence in Greek between Anna Maria van Schurman (1607–78) and Bathsua Makin (1600–167?)." *Dutch Crossing* 19, no. 1 (Summer 1995): 24–48.

Bell, Susan Groag. *The Lost Tapestries of the City of Ladies: Christine de Pizan's Renaissance Legacy.* Berkeley, 2004.

Benger, Miss [Elizabeth Ogilvy]. *Memoirs of Elizabeth Stuart, Queen of Bohemia, Daughter of King James the First.* 2 vols. London, 1825.

Bennett, J., Michael Hunter, and Lisa Jardine. *London's Leonardo: The Life and Work of Robert Hooke.* Oxford, 2003.

Bernot, Jacques. *Les Palatins, Princes d'Europe.* Paris, 2000.

Binns, J. W. *Intellectual Culture in Elizabethan and Jacobean England: The Latin Writings of the Age.* Leeds, 1990.

Birch, Una [Constance Pope-Hennessy]. *Anna van Schurman: Artist, Scholar, Saint.* London and New York, 1909.

Blok, Frans F. *Caspar Barlaeus: From the Correspondence of a Melancholic.* Amsterdam, 1976.

Bots, Hans, ed. *Constantijn Huygens: Zijn Plaats in Geleerd Europa.* Amsterdam, 1973.

Bots, Hans, and Françoise Waquet, eds. *Commercium Litterarium: La Communications dans la République des Lettres 1600–1750.* Amsterdam, 1993. *La République des Lettres.* [Paris], 1997.

Bots, J. A. "André Rivet en zijn positie in de Republiek der Letteren." *Tijdschrift voor Geschiedenis* 84, no. 1 (1971): 24–35.

Brink, Jean R. "Bathsua Makin: Educator and Linguist." In *Female Scholars: A Tradition of Learned Women Before 1800.* Ed. J. R. Brink, 86–100. Montreal, 1980.

⸻ "Bathsua Reginald Makin: 'Most Learned Matron.'" *Huntington Library Quarterly* 54, no. 4. (1992): 313–26.

Broad, Jacqueline. *Women Philosophers of the Seventeenth Century.* Cambridge, 2002.

Brown, Harcourt. *Scientific Organizations in Seventeenth Century France (1620–1680).* New York, 1934.

Brown, Peter. *The Body and Society: Men, Women, and Sexual Renunciation in Early Christianity.* New York, 1988.

Bulckaert, Barbara. "L'Education de la femme dans la correspondance d'Anna Maria van Schurman (1607–1678) et André Rivet (1572–1651)." In *La femme lettrée à la Renaissance: Actes du Colloque international.* Ed. Michel Bastiaensen, 197–209. Brusells, 1997.

Burke, Peter. *A Social History of Knowledge: From Gutenberg to Diderot.* Cambridge, 2000.

Bury, Emmanuel. "Madame Dacier." In *Femmes savantes, savoirs des femmes: du crépuscule de la Renaissance à l'aube des Lumières,* 209–20. Geneva, 1999.

Butler, E. H. *The Story of British Shorthand.* London, 1951.

Canny, Nicholas. *The Upstart Earl: A Study of the Social and Mental World of Richard Boyle, first Earl of Cork 1566–1643.* Cambridge, 1982.

Čapková, Dagmar. "Comenius and His Ideals: Escape from the Labyrinth." In *Samuel Hartlib and Universal Reformation: Studies in Intellectual Communication.* Ed. Mark Greengrass, Michael Leslie, and Timothy Raylor, 75–91. Cambridge, 1994.

Caravolas, Jean. "Bathsua Makin and Jan Amos Comenius." *Studia Comeniana et Historica* 26, nos. 55–6 (1996): 77–85.

Careil, Foucher de. *Descartes, la Princesse Elisabeth, et la Reine Christine, d'après des lettres inédites.* Paris and Amsterdam, 1879.

Certeau, Michel de. *The Mystic Fable.* Trans. Michael B. Smith. Chicago, 1992.

Cheney, Donald. "Virgo Angla: The Self-Fashioning of Westonia." In *La femme lettrée à la Renaissance: Actes du Colloque international.* Ed. Michel Bastiaensen, 119–28. Brussels, 1997.

Churchill, Laurie J., Phyllis R. Brown, and Jane E. Jeffrey, eds. *Early Modern Women Writing Latin.* Vol. III of *Women Writing Latin: From Roman Antiquity to Early Modern Europe.* 3 vols. New York and London, 2002.

Clucas, Stephen. "The Atomism of the Cavendish Circle: A Reappraisal." *The Seventeenth Century* 9, no. 2. (autumn 1994): 247–73.

"Samuel Hartlib's Ephemerides, 1635–59, and the Pursuit of Scientific and Philosophical Manuscripts; the Religious Ethos of an Intelligencer." *The Seventeenth Century* 6, no. 1. (spring 1991): 33–55.

Cohen, Gustave. *Écrivains français en Hollande dans la première moitié du XVIIᵉ Siècle.* Paris, 1920.

Cole, Susan. *A Flower of Purpose.* Ilford, Essex, 1975.

Colie, Rosalie L. *"Some Thankfulnesse to Constantine": A Study of English Influence upon the Early Works of Constantijn Huygens.* The Hague, 1956.

Connolly, Ruth. "'A Wise and Godly Sybilla': Viscountess Ranelagh and the Politics of International Protestantism." In *Women, Gender, and Radical Religion in Early Modern Europe.* Ed. Sylvia Brown, 285–306. Leiden, 2007.

Cook, Alan. "Ladies in the Scientific Revolution." *Notes and Records of the Royal Society of London* 51, no. 1 (January 1997): 1–12.

Cope, Eleanor. *Handmaid of the Holy Spirit: Dame Eleanor Davies, Never Soe Mad a Ladie.* Ann Arbor, 1992.

Creese, Anna. "The Letters of Elisabeth, Princess Palatine: A Seventeenth Century Correspondence." Ph.D. dissertation, Princeton University, 1993.

Daston, Lorraine. "The Ideal and Reality of the Republic of Letters in the Enlightenment." *Science in Context* 4, no. 2 (1991): 367–86.

Davies, David W. *The World of the Elseviers, 1580–1712.* The Hague, 1954.

Daybell, James. "'Suche newes as on the Quenes hye wayes we have mett': the News and Intelligence Networks of Elizabeth Talbot, Countess of Shrewsbury (c. 1527–1608)." In *Women and Politics in Early Modern England, 1450–1700.* Ed. James Daybell, 114–31. Aldershot, 2004.

De Boer, Josephine. "Men's Literary Circles in Paris 1610–1660." *Publications of the Modern Language Association of America* 53 (1938): 730–80.

Deeds, Cecil. *Royal and Loyal Sufferers.* London, 1903.

Dibon, Paul. *Inventaire de la Correspondance d'André Rivet (1595–1650).* The Hague, 1971.

Regards sur la Hollande du Siècle d'Or. Naples, 1990.

Dijkshoorn, Johannes Arend. "L'Influence française dans les mœurs et les salons des Provinces-Unies." Ph.D. dissertation, University of Groningen. Paris, 1925.

Does, Marthe van der. "Antoinette Bourignon: Sa vie (1616–1680) – Son œuvre." Ph.D. dissertation, University of Groningen, 1925.

Douma, Anna Margaretha Hendrika. " Anna Maria van Schurman en de Studie der Vrouw." Ph.D. dissertation, University of Amsterdam. 1924.

Evans, R. J. W. *Rudolf II and His World: A Study in Intellectual History 1576–1612.* Oxford, 1973.

Farnham, Fern. *Madame Dacier: Scholar and Humanist.* Monterey, CA, 1976.

Findlen, Paula. "Science as a Career in Enlightenment Italy: The Strategies of Laura Bassi." *Isis* 84, no. 3 (1993): 441–69.

"The Scientist's Body: The Nature of a Woman Philosopher in Enlightenment Italy." In *The Faces of Nature in Enlightenment Europe.* Ed. Lorraine Daston and Gianna Pomata, 211–36. Berlin, 2003.

Fiorenza, Elisabeth Schüssler. "Word, Spirit and Power: Women in Early Christian Communities." In *Women of Spirit: Female Leadership in the Jewish and Christian Traditions.* Ed. Rosemary Ruether and Eleanor McLaughlin, 29–70. New York, 1979.

Fischer, T. A. *The Scots in Germany: Being a Contribution Towards the History of the Scot Abroad.* Edinburgh, [1902].

Fix, Andrew. *Prophecy and Reason: The Dutch Collegiants in the Early Enlightenment.* Princeton, 1991.

Fogel, Michèle, *Marie de Gournay: Itinéraires d'une femme savante.* Paris, 2004.

Foucher de Careil, Le Comte Louis Alexandre. *Leibniz et Les Deux Sophies.* Paris, 1876.

French, J. Milton. *The Life Records of John Milton.* 5 vols. New Brunswick, NJ, 1949–1958.

Fumaroli, Marc, ed. *Les Premiers Siècles de la République européenne des Lettres. Actes du Colloque international: Paris, décembre 2001.* Paris, 2005.

Gardiner, Dorothy. *English Girlhood at School: A Study of Women's Education through Twelve Centuries.* London, 1929.

Gates, Henry Louis Jr. *The Trials of Phillis Wheatley: America's First Black Poet and Her Encounters with the Founding Fathers.* New York, 2003.

Gaukroger, Stephen. *Descartes: An Intellectual Biography.* Oxford, 1995.

Gerlach, J. H. "Jean de Labadie à Middelbourg. D'après du documents inédits." *Bulletin de la Commission de l'Histoire des Églises Wallonnes* 4 (1890): 1–28.

Godfrey, Elizabeth. *A Sister of Prince Rupert: Elizabeth Princess Palatine and Abbess of Herford.* London, 1909.

Goldgar, Anne. *Impolite Learning: Conduct and Community in the Republic of Letters 1680–1750.* New Haven, 1995.

Goldgar, Anne, and Robert Frost, eds. *Institutional Culture in Early Modern Society.* Leiden, 2004.

Goodman, Dena. *The Republic of Letters: A Cultural History of the French Enlightenment.* Ithaca, 1994.

Grafton, Anthony. *Defenders of the Text: The Traditions of Scholarship in an Age of Science, 1450–1800.* Cambridge, MA, 1991.

Green, Mary Anne Everett. *Elizabeth, Electress Palatine and Queen of Bohemia.* Revised by S. C. Lomas. London, 1909.

Green, Mary Anne Everett. *Lives of the Princesses of England.* Six volumes. London, 1849–55.

Green, Mary Elizabeth. "Elizabeth Elstob: The Saxon Nymph (English, 1683–1765)." In *Female Scholars: A Tradition of Learned Women before 1800.* Ed. Jean L. Brink, 137–60. Montreal, 1980.

Greengrass, Mark. "Archive Refractions: Hartlib's Papers and the Workings of an Intelligencer." In *Archives of the Scientific Revolution: The Formation and Exchange of Ideas in Seventeenth-Century Europe.* Ed. Michael Hunter, 35–47. Woodbridge, 1998.

"Samuel Hartlib: 'Intelligenceur' Européen." *Diffusion du savoir et affrontement des idées 1600–1770.* Festival d'histoire de Montbrison, 30 September–4 October 1992, 213–34. Montbrison, 1993.

Greengrass, Mark, Michael Leslie, and Timothy Raylor, eds. *Samuel Hartlib and Universal Reformation: Studies in Intellectual Communication.* Cambridge, 1994.

Guhrauer, Gottshalf Eduard. "Elisabeth, Pfalzgrafin bei Rhein, Abtissin von Herford." *Historisches Taschenbuch* (1850): vol. I, 1–150; vol. II, 417–554.

Gummere, Amelia. "Letter from William Penn to Elisabeth, Princess Palatine, Abbess of the Protestant Convent of Hereford, 1677, with an Introduction." *Bulletin of Friends' Historical Society of Philadelphia* 4, no. 2 (March, 1912): 82–97.

Haag, Eugène and Émile. *La France Protestante.* Paris, 1886.

Haldane, Elizabeth S. *Descartes, His Life and Times.* London, 1905.

Hall, Marie Boas. *Henry Oldenburg: Shaping the Royal Society.* Oxford, 2002.

Harkness, Deborah E. *The Jewel House: Elizabethan London and the Scientific Revolution.* New Haven and London, 2007.

Harth, Erica. *Cartesian Women: Versions and Subversions of Rational Discourse in the Old Regime.* Ithaca, 1992.

Heijden, Marcel van der. *'T Hoge Huis te Muiden: Teksten uit der Muiderkring.* Utrecht, 1972.

Herrup, Cynthia B. *A House in Gross Disorder: Sex, Law, and the 2nd Earl of Caslehaven.* Oxford, 1999.

Hill, Christopher. *Intellectual Origins of the English Revolution Revisited.* Oxford, 1997.

   Milton and the English Revolution. London, 1977.

Hobbs, Mary. "Drayton's 'Most Dearely-Loved Friend Henery Reynolds Esq.' " *The Review of English Studies* n.s. 24, no. 96 (November 1973): 414–28.

Hoppen, K. T. *The Common Scientist in the Seventeenth Century: A Study of the Dublin Philosophical Society 1683–1708.* London, 1970.

Hosington, Brenda M. "Elizabeth Jane Weston and Men's Discourse of Praise." In *La Femme lettrée à la Renaissance: Actes du Colloque international.* Ed. Michel Bastiaensen, 107–18. Brussels, 1997.

Hsia, Ronnie Po-Chia and Henk van Nierop, eds. *Calvinism and Religious Toleration in the Dutch Golden Age.* Cambridge, 2002.

Huizinga, Johan. *Dutch Civilisation in the Seventeenth Century and Other Essays.* Selected by Pieter Geyl and F. W. N. Hugenholtz, trans. Arnold J. Pomerans. New York, 1968.

Hunter, Lynette. "Sisters of the Royal Society: The Circle of Katherine Jones, Lady Ranelagh." In *Women, Science and Medicine 1500–1700: Mothers and Sisters of the Royal Society.* Ed. Lynette Hunter and Sarah Hutton, 178–97. Phoenix Mill, 1997.

Hunter, Michael. *Science and Society in Restoration England.* Cambridge, 1981.

   "Whither Editing?" *Studies in History and Philosophy of Science* 34 (2003): 805–820.

   ed. *Archives of the Scientific Revolution: The Formation and Exchange of Ideas in Seventeenth-Century Europe.* Woodbridge, 1998.

Hutton, Sarah. "Anne Conway, Margaret Cavendish and Seventeenth Century Scientific Thought." In *Women, Science and Medicine 1500–1700,* ed. Lynette Hunter and Sarah Hutton. Phoenix Mill, 1997.

Hyde, Edward, Earl of Clarendon. *The History of the Rebellion and Civil Wars in England, Begun in the Year 1641.* Ed. W. Dunn Macray. 6 vols. Oxford, 1888.

Ilsley, Margaret. *A Daughter of the Renaissance: Marie le Jars de Gournay, Her Life and Works.* The Hague, 1963.

Irwin, Joyce. "Anna Maria van Schurman and Antoinette Bourignon: Contrasting Examples of Seventeenth-Century Pietism." *Church History* 60, no. 3 (1991): 301–15.

"Anna Maria van Schurman: From Feminism to Pietism." *Church History* 46, no.1 (March, 1977): 48–62.

Israel, Jonathan I. *The Dutch Republic: Its Rise, Greatness, and Fall, 1477–1806.* Oxford, 1998.

Jacquot, John. "Sir Charles Cavendish and His Learned Friends: A Contribution to the History of Scientific Relations between England and the Continent in the Earlier Part of the 17th Century." *Annals of Science* 8 (1952): 13–27, 175–91.

Jardine, Lisa. *The Curious Life of Robert Hooke, The Man Who Measured London.* New York, 2004.

Erasmus, Man of Letters: The Construction of Charisma in Print. Princeton, 1993.

"Women Humanists: Education for What?" In *From Humanism to the Humanities*, by Anthony Grafton and Lisa Jardine, 29–57. Cambridge, MA, 1986.

Jones, G. Lloyd. *The Discovery of Hebrew in Tudor England: A Third Language.* Manchester, 1983.

Jones, R. F. *Ancients and Moderns: A Study of the Rise of the Scientific Movement in Seventeenth-Century England.* 2nd edn. St. Louis, MO, 1961.

Joran, Théodore: *La Trouée féministe.* Paris, 1909.

Katchen, Aaron L. *Christian Hebraists and Dutch Rabbis.* Cambridge, MA, 1984.

Keblusek, Marika. "The Bohemian Court at The Hague." In *Princely Display: The Court of Frederik Hendrik of Orange and Amalia van Sohms.* Ed. Marika Keblusek and Jori Zijlmans, 47–57. The Hague, c.1997.

Kelly, Gary, ed., *Bluestocking Feminism: Writings of the Bluestocking Circle, 1738–1785.* Brookfield, VT, 1999.

Kelly, Joan. "Early Feminist Theory and the Querelle des Femmes, 1400–1789." *Signs: Journal of Women in Culture and Society* 8, no. 1 (autumn 1982): 4–28.

Kelso, Ruth. *Doctrine for the Lady of the Renaissance.* Urbana, IL, 1956.

Kempen-Stijgers, Thea van, and Peter Rietbergen. "Constantijn Huygens en Engeland." In *Constantijn Huygens: Zijn Plaats in Geleerd Europa.* Ed. Hans Bots, 77–141. Amsterdam, 1973.

Kenyon, J. P. *The Popish Plot.* London, 1972.

Kerviler, R. and E. de Barthélemy. *Valentin Conrart, premier secrétaire perpétuel de l'Académie Française: Sa vie et sa correspondance.* Paris, 1881. Reprint, Geneva, 1971.

Kessel, Elisja Schulte van. "Virgins and Mothers between Heaven and Earth." In *Renaissance and Enlightenment Paradoxes.* Vol III of *A History of Women in the West.* Ed. Natalie Zemon Davis and Arlette Farge, 132–66. Cambridge, MA, 1993.

King, Margaret L. "Book-Lined Cells: Women and Humanism in the Early Italian Renaissance." *In Beyond Their Sex: Learned Women of the European Past.* Ed. Patricia H. Labalme, 66–90. New York, 1980.

"Thwarted Ambitions: Six Learned Women of the Italian Renaissance." *Soundings* 59 (1976): 280–304.

Kloek, Els, Nicole Tesuwen, and Marijke Huisman, eds. *Women of the Golden Age: An International Debate on Women in Seventeenth-Century Holland, England and Italy.* Hilversum, 1994.

Kolbrener, William, and Michal Michelson, eds., *Mary Astell: Reason, Gender, Faith.* Aldershot, 2007.

Labalme, Patricia H., ed. *Beyond Their Sex: Learned Women of the European Past.* New York, 1980.

Labrousse, Elisabeth. "Marie du Moulin, Educatrice." *Bulletin de la Société de l'Histoire du Protestantisme Français* 139, no. 2 (1993): 255–68.

Larsen, Anne R. "Anne Marie de Schurman, Madeleine de Scudéry et les lettres sur La Pucelle (1646)." In *Lectrices d'Ancien Régime.* Isabelle Brouard-Arends, 269–79. Rennes, 2003.

Lee, Bo Karen. "'I wish to be nothing': The Role of Self-Denial in the Mystical Theology of Anna Maria van Schurman." In *Women, Gender and Radical Religion in Early Modern Europe.* Ed. Sylvia Brown, 189–216. Leiden, 2007.

Lee, Sidney, ed. *Dictionary of National Biography.* London, 1885–1901.

Leng, Thomas. *Benjamin Worsley (1618–1677).* Rochester, NY, 2008.

Leong, Elaine. "Medical Remedy Collections in Seventeenth-Century England: Knowledge, Text and Gender." Ph.D. dissertation, Oxford University, 2005.

Levine, Joseph M. *The Battle of the Books: History and Literature in the Augustan Age.* Ithaca and London, 1991.

Livingstone, David N. *Putting Science in Its Place: Geographies of Scientific Knowledge.* Chicago, 2003.

Lougee, Carolyn C. *Le Paradis des Femmes: Women, Salons, and Social Stratification in Seventeenth-Century France.* Princeton, 1976.

Love, Harold. *Scribal Publication in Seventeenth-Century England.* Oxford, 1993. Reprinted as *The Culture and Commerce of Texts.* Amherst, 1998.

Lynch, Kathleen M. "The Incomparable Lady Ranelagh." In *Of Books and Humankind.* Ed. John Butt, 25–35. London, 1964.

Macewen, Alex R. *Antoinette Bourignon, Quietist.* London, 1910.

Maddison, R. E. W. *The Life of the Honourable Robert Boyle.* London, 1969.

Malcolm, Noel. "The Publications of John Pell, F.R.S. (1611–1685): Some New Light and Some Old Confusions." *Notes and Records of the Royal Society of London* 54, no. 3 (2000): 275–92.

Malcolm, Noel, and Jacqueline Stedall. *John Pell (1611–1686) and His Correspondence with Sir Charles Cavendish: The Mental World of an Early Modern Mathematician.* Oxford, 2005.

Masson, David. *The Life of John Milton: Narrated in Connexion with the Political, Ecclesiastical, and Literary History of His Time.* 7 vols. London, 1873–94.

Mazauric, Simone. *Savoirs et philosophie à Paris dans la première moitié du XVIIe siècle: Les conférences du bureau d'adresse de Théophraste Renaudot (1633–1642).* Paris, 1997.

Mazon, Paul. *Madame Dacier et les traductions d'Homère en France.* Oxford, 1935.

McCormick, Ted. *William Petty and the Ambitions of Political Arithmetic.* Oxford, 2009.

Medhurst, Charles Edward. *Life and Work of Lady Elizabeth Hastings, the Great Yorkshire Benefactress of the XVIIIIth Century.* Leeds, 1914.

Messbarger, Rebecca, and Paula Findlen, eds. and trans., *The Contest for Knowledge: Debates over Women's Learning in Eighteenth-Century Italy.* Chicago, 2005.

Montaigne, Michel de. *The Complete Essays of Montaigne.* Ed. Donald Frame. Stanford, 1965.

[Moore], Anne, Countess of Drogheda. *History of the Moore Family.* Belfast, 1902.

Moore, Cornelia N. "Anna Maria van Schurman." In *Women Writing in Dutch.* Ed. Kristiaan Aercke, 185–230. New York and London, 1994.

Moore, Cornelia Niekus. "'Not by Nature but by Custom': Johan van Beverwijck's Van de wtnementheyt des vrouwelicken Geslachts." *Sixteenth Century Journal* 25, no. 3 (1994): 633–51.

Mout, M. E. H. N., "Limits and Debates: A Comparative View of Dutch Toleration in the Sixteenth and Early Seventeenth Centuries." In *The Emergence of Tolerance in the Dutch Republic.* Ed. C. Berkevens-Stevelinck, J. Israel, and G. H. M. Posthumus Meyjes, 37–48. Leiden and New York, 1997.

Murdock, Kenneth G. *The Sun at Noon: Three Biographical Sketches.* New York, 1939.

Myers, Sylvia Harcstark. *The Bluestocking Circle: Women, Friendship, and the Life of the Mind in Eighteenth-Century England.* Oxford, 1990.

Néel, Margaret. *Descartes et la princesse Elisabeth.* Paris, 1946.

Noonan, Kathleen. "'Martyrs in Flames': Sir John Temple and the Conception of the Irish in English Martyrologies." *Albion* 36, no. 2 (summer 2004): 223–55.

Norbrook, David. "Women, the Republic of Letters, and the Public Sphere in the Mid-Seventeenth Century." *Criticism* 46, no. 2 (spring 2004): 223–40.

North, Marcy L. *The Anonymous Renaissance: Cultures of Discretion in Tudor-Stuart England.* Chicago and London, 2003.

Nummedal, Tara E. "Alchemical Reproduction and the Career of Anna Maria Zieglerin." *Ambix* 48, no. 2 (July 2001): 56–68.

Nuttall, Geoffrey. "John Durie's Sponsors." *Transactions of the Congregational Historical Society* 17 (1954): 91.

"Milton's Churchmanship in 1659: His Letter to Jean de Labadie." *Milton Quarterly* 35, no. 4 (December, 2001): 227–31.

Nye, Andrea. *The Princess and the Philosopher: Letters of Elisabeth of the Palatine to René Descartes.* Lanham, 1999.

Oman, Carola. *Elizabeth of Bohemia.* 1938. Reprint, London, 1964.

Pagels, Elaine. *Adam, Eve, and the Serpent.* New York, 1988.

Pal, Carol. "Republic of Women : Rethinking the Republic of Letters, 1630–1680." Ph.D. dissertation, Stanford University, 2007.

Parente, James A. Jr. "Anna Roemers Visscher and Maria Tesselschade Roemers Visscher." In *Women Writing in Dutch.* Ed. Kristiaan Aercke, 147–84. New York and London, 1994.

Payen, Jean-François. "Recherches sur Michel Montaigne. Correspondance relative à sa mort." *Bulletin du Bibliophile et du Bibliothécaire* 15 (1862): 1291–311.

Perceval-Maxwell, M. *The Outbreak of the Irish Rebellion of 1641.* Montreal, 1994.

Perkins, Wendy. *Midwifery and Medicine in Early Modern France: Louise Bourgeois.* Exeter, 1996.

Perry, Ruth. *The Celebrated Mary Astell: An Early English Feminist.* Chicago, 1986.

Phillips, Patricia. *The Scientific Lady: A Social History of Women's Scientific Interests 1520–1918.* London, 1990.

Pollmann, Judith. "The Bond of Christian Piety: The Individual Practice of Tolerance and Intolerance in the Dutch Republic." In *Calvinism and Religious Toleration in the Dutch Golden Age.* Ed. Ronnie Po-Chia Hsia and Henk van Nierop, 53–71. Cambridge, 2002

Religious Choice in the Dutch Republic: The Reformation of Arnoldus Buchelius (1565–1641). Manchester, 1999.

Poole, William. "Nuncius Inanimatus. Seventeenth-Century Telegraphy: the Schemes of Francis Godwin and Henry Reynolds." *The Seventeenth Century* 21, no. 1 (spring 2006): 45–72.

Popkin, Richard H. *The History of Scepticism: From Savonarola to Bayle.* Revised edn. Oxford and New York, 2003.

"The Third Force in Seventeenth-Century Philosophy: Scepticism, Science and Biblical Prophecy." *Nouvelles de la République des Lettres* I (1983): 37–63.

Postlethwaite, Norman, and Gordon Campbell. "Edward King, Milton's 'Lycidas': Poems and Documents." *Milton Quarterly* 28, no. 4 (December 1994): 77–111.

Potter, Lois. *Secret Rites and Secret Writing: Royalist Literature, 1641–1660.* Cambridge, 1989.

Pursell, Brennan C. *The Winter King: Frederick V of the Palatinate and the Coming of the Thirty Years' War.* Aldershot, 2003.

Rabb, Theodore K. *The Struggle for Stability in Early Modern Europe.* New York, 1975.

Rae, Thomas H. H. *John Dury and the Royal Road to Piety.* Frankfurt am Main, 1998.

Rankin, Alisha. "Medicine for the Uncommon Woman: Experience, Experiment, and Exchange in Early Modern Germany." Ph.D. dissertation, Harvard University, 2006.

Raylor, Timothy. "Newcastle's Ghosts: Robert Payne, Ben Jonson, and the 'Cavendish Circle.'" In *Literary Circles and Cultural Communities in Renaissance England.* Ed. Claude J. Summers and Ted-Larry Pebworth, 92–114. Columbia, MO, 2000.

Reynolds, Myra. *The Learned Lady in England 1650–1760.* Gloucester, MA, 1964.

Ridder-Symoens, Hilde de. *A History of the University in Europe.* Vol. II: *Universities in Early Modern Europe (1500–1800).* Cambridge, 1996.

Rigaud, Stephen J. *Correspondence of Scientific Men of the Seventeenth Century.* 2 vols. Hildesheim, 1965.

Robinet, André. *Malebranche et Leibniz: Relations personnelles.* Bibliothèque des Textes Philosophiques. Paris, 1955.

Ross, Sarah Gwyneth. *The Birth of Feminism: Woman as Intellect in Renaissance Italy and England.* Cambridge, MA, 2009.

Ruether, Rosemary. "Mothers of the Church: Ascetic Women in the Late Patristic Age." In *Women of Spirit: Female Leadership in the Jewish and Christian Traditions.* Ed. Rosemary Ruether and Eleanor McLaughlin, 72–98. New York, 1979.

Ruler, J. A. van. *The Crisis of Causality: Voëtius and Descartes on God, Nature and Change.* Leiden, 1995.

Salmon, Vivian. "Bathsua Makin (1600-*c.*1673): A Pioneer Linguist and Feminist." In *Language and Society in Early Modern England: Selected Essays 1981–1994.* Ed. Vivian Salmon, 239–60. Amsterdam, 1996.

"Henry Reynolds." *Pelliana* 1, no. 3. New series privately printed, 1965: 11–18.

The Works of Francis Lodwick: A Study of His Writings in the Intellectual Context of the Seventeenth Century. London, 1972.

Saunders, Anne Leslie. "Bathsua Reginald Makin (1600–75?)." In *Women Writing Latin: From Roman Antiquity to Early Modern Europe.* Ed. Laurie J. Churchill *et al.*, 247–270. New York and London, 2002.

Savini, Massimiliano. "Sur le contexte de l'Epistola de Cartesii Philosophia de Joachim Jungius et la diffusion du cartésianisme en Allemagne." *Bulletin Cartésien* 34 (2003): 1–4.

Saxby, Trevor. *The Quest for the New Jerusalem: Jean de Labadie and the Labadists, 1610–1744.* Dordrecht, 1987.

Schiff, Mario Lodovico. *La Fille d'alliance de Montaigne, Marie de Gournay: essai suivi de "L'Égalité des hommes et des femmes" et du "Grief des dames" avec des variantes, des notes, des appendices et un portrait.* Paris, 1910.

Schotel, G. D. J. *Anna Maria van Schurman.* 2 vols. in 1. 'S Hertogenbosch, 1853.

Schulz, H., ed., *Der Dreissigjaerige Krieg.* Vol. 1. Leipzig, 1917.

Schwarz, Henry Frederick. *The Imperial Privy Council in the Seventeenth Century.* Cambridge, 1943.

Scott, Joan Wallach. "Gender: A Useful Category of Analysis." In *Gender and the Politics of History,* 28–50. Revised edn. New York, 1999.

Sellin, Paul R. *Daniel Heinsius and Stuart England: With a Short-Title Checklist of the Works of Daniel Heinsius.* Leiden, 1968.

Shapiro, Lisa. "Princess Elizabeth and Descartes: The Union of Soul and Body and the Practice of Philosophy." *British Journal of the History of Philosophy* 7 (1999): 503–20.

Shelford, April. "'Others Laugh, Even the Learned': An Erudit's View of Women and Learning in Seventeenth-Century France." *Proceedings of the Western Society for French History: Selected Papers of the Annual Meeting* 24, 221–32. Greeley, CO, 1997.

Simon, Joan. "The Comenian Educational Reformers 1640–1660 and the Royal Society of London." *Acta Comeniana* 2, no. 26 (1970): 165–78.

Simon, Walter G. *The Restoration Episcopate.* New York, 1965.

Sluijs, Piet van der. "Constantijn Huygens en de Muiderkring." In *Constantijn Huygens: Zijn Plaats in Geleerd Europa.* Ed. Hans Bots, 187–309. Amsterdam, 1973.

Smet, Ingrid A. R. de. "'In the Name of the Father': Feminist Voices in the Republic of Letters (A. Tarabotti, A. M. van Schurman, and M. de Gournay)." In *La femme lettrée à la Renaissance: Actes du Colloque international.* Ed. Michel Bastiaensen, 177–96. Brussels, 1997.

Smith, Florence M. *Mary Astell.* New York, 1916.

Smith, Hilda L. *Reason's Disciples: Seventeenth-Century English Feminists.* Urbana, IL, 1982.

Smits-Veldt, Mieke B. *Maria Tesselschade: Leven met Talent en Vriendschap.* Zutphen 1994.

Sneller, A. Agnes. "'If She Had Been a Man …': Anna Maria van Schurman in the Social and Literary Life of Her Age." In *Choosing the Better Part: Anna Maria van Schurman (1607–1678).* Ed. Mirjam de Baar *et al.*, 133–49. Dordrecht, 1996.

Solomon, Howard M. *Public Welfare, Science, and Propaganda in Seventeenth Century France: The Innovations of Théophraste Renaudot.* Princeton, 1972.

Spinka, Matthew. *John Amos Comenius, That Incomparable Moravian.* 1943. Reprint, New York, 1967.

Springborg, Patricia. *Mary Astell: Theorist of Freedom from Domination.* Cambridge, 2005.

Stevenson, Jane. "Still Kissing the Rod? Whither Next?" *Women's Writing* 14, no. 2 (2007): 290–305.

"Women and Classical Education in the Early Modern Period." In *Pedagogy and Power: Rhetorics of Classical Learning.* Ed. Yun Lee Too and Niall Livingston, 83–109. Cambridge, 1998.

Stighelen, Katlijne van der. "'Et ses artistes mains …': The art of Anna Maria van Schurman." In *Choosing the Better Part: Anna Maria van Schurman (1607–1678).* Ed. Mirjam de Baar *et al.*, 55–68. Dordrecht, 1996

Stimson, Dorothy. "Hartlib, Haak and Oldenburg: Intelligencers." *Isis* 31, no. 84 (April 1940): 309–26.

Stine, Jennifer K. "Opening Closets: The Discovery of Household Medicine in Early Modern England." Ph.D. dissertation, Stanford University, 1996.

Stock, Marie Louise. "Poulain de la Barre: A Seventeenth-Century Feminist." Ph.D. dissertation. Columbia University, 1961.

Strachan, Michael. *Sir Thomas Roe, 1581–1644: A Life.* Salisbury, 1989.

Strengholt, L. *Constanter: Het Leven van Constantijn Huygens.* Amsterdam 1987.

Strien, C. D. van. *British Travellers in Holland during the Stuart Period: Edward Browne and John Locke as Tourists in the United Provinces.* Leiden, 1993.

Stuurman, Siep. *François Poulain de la Barre and the Invention of Modern Equality.* Cambridge, MA, 2004.

"Social Cartesianism: François Poulain de la Barre and the Origins of the Enlightenment." *Journal of the History of Ideas* 58, no. 4 (1997), 617–40.

Taafe, James G. "Mrs. John Dury: A Sister of Lycidas." *Notes and Queries* 207 (1962): 60–1.

Tappert, Theodore G. Introduction to *Pia Desideria* [1675] by Philip Jacob Spener. Philadelphia, 1964.

Teague, Frances. *Bathsua Makin, Woman of Learning.* Lewisburg, 1998.

Thijssen-Schoute, C. Louise. "Een Correspondent van Descartes: Andreas Colvius." *Nederlands Archief voor Kerkgeschiedenis,* n.s., no. 38 (1952): 224–48.

Nederlands Cartesianisme. Amsterdam 1954.

Tiethoff-Spliethoff, Marieke. "Role-play and Representation: Portrait Painting at the Court of Frederik Hendrik and Amalia." Trans. Wendie Shaffer. In *Princely Display: The Court of Frederik Hendrik of Orange and Amalia van Sohms.* Ed. Marika Keblusek and Jori Zijlmans, 161–200. The Hague, *c.*1997.

Tillyard, Phyllis B., trans. *Milton: Private Correspondence and Academic Exercises.* Cambridge, 1932.

Tollefsen, Deborah. "Princess Elisabeth and the Problem of Mind–Body Interaction." *Hypatia* 14, no. 3 (1999): 59–77.

Townshend, Dorothea. *The Life and Letters of the Great Earl of Cork.* London, 1904.

Trevor-Roper, Hugh. *Catholics, Anglicans and Puritans: Seventeenth Century Essays.* London, 1987.

"Three Foreigners: The Philosophers of the Puritan Revolution." In *Religion, the Reformation and Social Change.* 3rd edn. London, 1984.

Turnbull, G. H. *Hartlib, Dury and Comenius: Gleanings from Hartlib's Papers.* London, 1947.

Samuel Hartlib: A Sketch of His Life and His Relations to J. A. Comenius. London, 1920.

"Samuel Hartlib's Influence on the Early History of the Royal Society." *Notes and Records of the Royal Society of London* 10, no. 2 (April 1953): 101–30.

Ultee, Martin. "The Republic of Letters; Learned Correspondence, 1680–1720." *The Seventeenth Century* 2, no. 1 (January 1987): 95–112.

Underdown, David. "Gentlemen, Players, and Media Moguls: Cricket and English Society Since 1600." Plenary address given at the Pacific Coast Conference on British Studies, April 4, 1997, Mills College, Oakland, CA.

Vanderauwera, Ria. "Maria Tesselschade: A Woman of More than Letters." In *Women Writers of the Seventeenth Century.* Ed. Katharina M. Wilson and Frank J. Warnke, 141–63. Athens and London, 1989.

Verbeek, Theo. *Descartes and the Dutch: Early Reactions to Cartesian Philosophy, 1637–1650.* Carbondale, IL, 1992.

Verney, Frances P. and Margaret M. *Memoirs of the Verney Family During the Seventeenth Century: Compiled from the Papers and Illustrated by the Portraits at Claydon House.* 3 vols. London, 1925.

Verney, Margaret M. *Memoirs of the Verney Family During the Commonwealth, 1650–1660.* 3 vols. London, 1894.

Voisine, J. "Un astre éclipsé: Anna Maria van Schurman (1607–1678)." *Études Germaniques* 27, no. 4 (October–December, 1972): 501–31.

Vrooman, Jack Rochford. *René Descartes: A Biography.* New York, 1970.

Waard, Cornelius de. "Un entretien avec Descartes en 1634 ou 1635." *Archives Internationales d'Histoire des Sciences* 32, no. 22 (January–March 1953): 4–16.

Waquet, Françoise. "De la lettre érudite au périodique savant: les faux semblants d'une mutation intellectuelle." *XVIIe Siècle* 140, no. 3 (July–September 1983): 347–59.

"Qu'est-ce que la République des Lettres? Essai de sémantique historique." *Bibliothèque de l'École des chartes* 147 (1989): 473–502.

Watson, Andrew G. *The Library of Sir Simonds D'Ewes.* London, 1966.

Webster, Charles. "The Authorship and Significance of *Macaria.*" In *The Intellectual Revolution of the Seventeenth Century*, 369–85. London and Boston 1974.

"Benjamin Worsley: Engineering for Universal Reform." In *Samuel Hartlib and Universal Reformation: Studies in Intellectual Communication.* Ed. Mark Greengrass *et al.*, 213–35. Cambridge, 1994.

The Great Instauration: Science, Medicine, and Reform 1626–1660. London, 1975.

The Intellectual Revolution of the Seventeenth Century. London and Boston, 1974.

"New Light on the Invisible College: The Social Relations of English Science in the Mid-Seventeenth Century." *Transactions of the Royal Historical Society*, fifth series, 24 (1974): 19–42.

Utopian Planning and the Puritan Revolution: Gabriel Plattes, Samuel Hartlib, and "Macaria." Oxford, 1979.

Wendland, Anna. "Beiträge zur Geschichte der Kurfürstin Sophie." *Zeitschrift des Historischen Vereins für Neidersachsen* (1910): 333–68.

Westby-Gibson, John. *The Bibliography of Shorthand.* London, 1887.

"On Early Shorthand Systems." Part First, Read before the Shorthand Society, December 6, 1881. *Shorthand: A Scientific and Literary Magazine* 1, no. 5 (February, 1882): 73–88.

Westin, Gunnar. *Negotiations About Church Unity 1628–1634: John Durie, Gustavus Adolphus, Axel Oxenstierna.* Uppsala Universitets Ärsskrift, Teologi 3. Uppsala, 1932.

Willems, A. Les Elseviers. In *Annales Typographiques.* Brussels, 1880.

Wilson, Adrian. "A Memorial of Eleanor Willughby, a Seventeenth-Century Midwife." In *Women, Science and Medicine 1500–1700*, ed. Lynette Hunter and Sarah Hutton Phoenix Mill, 1997, 138–77.

Wilson, Katharina M., and Frank J. Warnke, eds. *Women Writers of the Seventeenth Century.* Athens and London, 1989.

Woolf, Virginia. *A Room of One's Own.* New York, 1929.

Worp, J. A. "Nog eens Utricia Ogle en de Muzikale Correspondentie van Huygens." *Tijdschrift der Vereeniging voor Noord-Nederlands Muziekgeschiedenis* 5 (1899): 129–36.

Young, Robert Fitzgibbon. *Comenius in England: The Visit of Jan Amos Komenský (Comenius) the Czech Philosopher and Educationist to London in 1641–1642; Its Bearing on the Origins of the Royal Society, on the Development of the Encyclopaedia, and on Plans for the Higher Education of the Indians of New England and Virginia.* London, 1932.

Zedler, Beatrice H. "The Three Princesses." *Hypatia* 4, no.1 (spring 1989): 28–63.

Index

IDEAS IN CONTEXT

Edited by David Armitage, Jennifer Pitts, Quentin Skinner *and* James Tully

94 JAMES TULLY
Public Philosophy in a New Key
Volume 2: Imperialism and Civic Freedom
hb 978 0 521 44966 3   pb 978 0 521 72880 5

95 DONALD WINCH
Wealth and Life
Essays on the Intellectual History of Political Economy in Britain, 1848–1914
hb 978 0 521 88753 3   pb 978 0 521 71539 3

96 FONNA FORMAN-BARZILAI
Adam Smith and the Circles of Sympathy
Cosmopolitanism and Moral Theory
hb 978 0 521 76112 3

97 GREGORY CLAEYS
Imperial Sceptics
British Critics of Empire 1850–1920
hb 978 0 521 19954 4

98 EDWARD BARING
The Young Derrida and French Philosophy, 1945–1968
hb 978 1 107 00967 7

99 CAROL PAL
The Republic of Women

100 CHRISTOPHER BAYLY
Indian Thought in the Age of Liberalism and Empire
hb 9781 107 01383 4   pb 9781 107 60147 5